ROBIN HOOD
LEGEND AND REALITY

Robin Hood
Legend and Reality

David Crook

THE BOYDELL PRESS

© David Crook 2020

All Rights Reserved. Except as permitted under current legislation no part of this work may be photocopied, stored in a retrieval system, published, performed in public, adapted, broadcast, transmitted, recorded or reproduced in any form or by any means, without the prior permission of the copyright owner

The right of David Crook to be identified as the author of this work has been asserted in accordance with sections 77 and 78 of the Copyright, Designs and Patents Act 1988

First published 2020
The Boydell Press, Woodbridge
Paperback edition 2022

ISBN 978 1 78327 543 4 hardback
ISBN 978 1 83765 010 1 paperback

The Boydell Press is an imprint of Boydell & Brewer Ltd
PO Box 9, Woodbridge, Suffolk IP12 3DF, UK
and of Boydell & Brewer Inc.
668 Mount Hope Ave, Rochester, NY 14620–2731, USA
website: www.boydellandbrewer.com

A catalogue record for this book is available
from the British Library

The publisher has no responsibility for the continued existence or accuracy of URLs for external or third-party internet websites referred to in this book, and does not guarantee that any content on such websites is, or will remain, accurate or appropriate

For Edward, as I promised long ago

In memoriam Aidan Hyland Lawes (1958–2012)
Requiescat in pace

Contents

List of Maps and Illustrations		viii
Preface and Acknowledgements		x
List of Abbreviations		xii
Introduction		1

PART I: THE LEGEND AND ITS INTERPRETERS

Chapter 1	The Medieval Tales of Robin Hood	7
Chapter 2	Chroniclers, Revellers, Playwrights and Antiquarians, c.1420–1765	34
Chapter 3	Editors, the Folklorist and the Archivist, 1765–1889	66
Chapter 4	Folklorists, Literary Scholars and Historians: Robin Hood in the Twentieth Century	98
Chapter 5	The Robin Hood Places	127

PART II: OUTLAW AND EVILDOER OF OUR LAND: THE ORIGINAL ROBIN HOOD

Chapter 6	The Robin Hood Names	163
Chapter 7	Robin Hood and Criminality	185
Chapter 8	Law and Disorder in Yorkshire, 1215–1225	210
Chapter 9	The Sheriff, the Fugitive and the Civil Servant	228
Conclusion		256
Bibliography		260
Index		282

Illustrations

Maps

1: Medieval Barnsdale, showing places linked to the Robin Hood Legend. — 131

2: The distribution of Hood surnames recorded in early Bedfordshire Coroners' Rolls, 1268–76, and the earliest Robin Hood surname, 1295. — 165

3: The distribution of Hood surnames in Northumberland recorded in Legal and Tax Records, 1233–96. — 166

4: Places and routes connected with the Legend: North of Barnsdale. — 208

5: Places and routes connected with the Legend: South of Barnsdale. — 209

All the maps were supplied by Andrew Nicholson.

Figures

1: Eton College MS 213, f. 234r, c. 1460. Reproduced by permission of the Provost and Fellows of Eton College. — 39

2: Glasgow University Library, portrait of John Major 1505. Title page of *In Petri Hyspani Summulas Commentaria* (Lyons, 1505). Reproduced by permission of University of Glasgow Library, Archives & Special Collections. — 41

3: Portrait of the Rev. Joseph Hunter, 1852, by Henry Smith. Reproduced by permission of the Society of Antiquaries of London. — 86

4: Account Book of the Chamber, 17–18 Edward II (TNA, E 101/380/4, f. 20v). Photograph Jonathan Mackman. Reproduced by permission of the Keeper of Public Records. — 87

Illustrations

5: St Mary's church, High Pavement, Nottingham. Photograph Ruth Crook.   145

6: Lincoln Cathedral MS 132, f. 100v. Reproduced with kind permission of the Dean and Chapter of Lincoln Cathedral.   152

7: Lowdham parish church, Nottinghamshire. Photograph Thomas Crook.   233

8: Grant by the prior of Lenton priory, Nottinghamshire, of four acres of land in Sutton (unidentified, Notts) to Alan son of Robert del Wal, c.1233. Reproduced with the permission of the Keeper of Manuscripts and Special Collections, University of Nottingham (UNMASC), Mi D 940.   237

9: Pontefract Castle, Yorkshire, painted by Alexander Keirincx, 1639–40. Reproduced by permission of the Hepworth Gallery, Wakefield.   240

The author and publisher are grateful to all the institutions and individuals listed for permission to reproduce the materials in which they hold copyright. Every effort has been made to trace the copyright holders; apologies are offered for any omission, and the publisher will be pleased to add any necessary acknowledgement in subsequent editions

Preface and Acknowledgements

This book is the work of a retired archivist, one of the last generation of assistant keepers of public records, using knowledge of the surviving early records of national government acquired over several decades (1974 to 2007) while working at what is now known as The National Archives (TNA), but was from 1838 until 2003 called the Public Record Office (PRO). It is the first attempt to make as comprehensive an examination as possible of the surviving evidence for the existence of a real original outlaw, active in the first quarter of the thirteenth century, from whom the legend of Robin Hood may ultimately have derived. Some of the administrative, financial and judicial documents relating to the period from the early thirteenth century to the early fourteenth, on which it is based, remained incompletely identified, listed and publicly available until the early twenty-first century. Even now a little work remains to be done, but an overwhelming proportion of the material is now also available in print or online, especially in the form of images on the Anglo-American Legal Tradition website (AALT), created by Professor Robert Palmer and hosted by the O'Quinn Law Library at the University of Houston, Texas. Most of these endeavours were carried out by the staff of the PRO/TNA itself and others working with or alongside them, including in particular the Pipe Roll Society, the Selden Society, the Universities of Cambridge and York, and King's College London.

In 1981 or 1982 I was systematically searching the memoranda rolls of the Exchequer in the PRO, looking for material for a possible article on the clerks who laboured in that department in the reign of King Henry III, when I made the chance discovery of a reference to a 'William Robehod', a criminal fugitive in Berkshire in 1262. I noted it in square brackets because, even though it was not of relevance to the subject I was researching, I had an instinctive feeling that it might be of some significance, and that I might never search through that document again. A little later James Holt, my former research supervisor, published an important book on the subject of Robin Hood, in which he interpreted the occurrence of the surname 'Robynhod' in a list of Sussex taxpayers written in 1296 as evidence that the outlaw legend was known in some form before the end of the thirteenth century. That prompted me to search for and successfully locate the

Preface And Acknowledgements

original court record mentioning William Robehod's offence, in a Berkshire eyre roll written in 1261, where he appears under a different name. It led to the publication two years later of a short journal article setting out this material and arguing for its importance in the search for an original Robin Hood. The discovery became part of an academic debate about the origins of the legend which had begun in earnest over twenty-five years earlier and still continues at the end of the second decade of the twenty-first century.

Despite the accidental beginning of my involvement, however, it was probably inevitable that I would become interested in the legend of Robin Hood. I was a medieval archivist and historian, brought up in Mansfield, a market town in Sherwood Forest in Nottinghamshire. In the town there once stood an ancient oak, now commemorated by a stone monument incorporated into a building, which had reputedly marked the exact centre of the forest, a traditional haunt of the legendary outlaw. I walked past it every day while returning home from school. The idea of writing a book on the origins of the Robin Hood legend began at about the time of my marriage to Ruth in 1987, our move from London to Lincolnshire and the birth of our first son in the following year. Throughout the three decades since then, I have received support and encouragement in my search for the outlaw not only from her and our sons Edward and Thomas but from numerous friends, colleagues and acquaintances, not all of whom can be mentioned here and many of whom were unaware of the contribution that they were making. They included, in alphabetical order, John Beckett, David Bowler, Paul Brand, Derek Burr, David Carpenter, Duncan Chalmers, Trevor Chalmers, Peter Coss, Barrie Dobson, Gwilym Dodd, Mark Dorrington, Paul Dryburgh, Meryl Foster, Richard Gaunt, Paul Harvey, Sir James Holt, Roy Hunnisett, Michael Jones, Dorothy Johnston, Maureen Jurkowski, Brian Kemp, Aidan Lawes, Jim Lees, Robert Linley, Jonathan Mackman, John Maddicott, Stephen O'Connor, Mark Ormrod, Frank Patmore, David Pilling, Anthony Pollard, John Post, Lloyd Richardson, Peter Seaman, Richard Sharpe, Carrie Smith, Jeffrey Stafford, William Stockting, Henry Summerson and Nicholas Vincent. Any factual errors or flaws in interpretation are mine alone. Above all, I am indebted to Ruth for making her huge range of skills available to me at all times over so many years. Without her, this book would have fallen by the wayside on many occasions.

Finally, I wish to acknowledge the help of the University of Nottingham in providing support in the form of an honorary research fellowship in History and facilitating my use of its library, and of The National Archives for continued access to its records and finding-aids. I am also grateful in particular for access to the libraries of the Society of Antiquaries of London and the Institute of Historical Research in the University of London.

David Crook
Grantham, Lincolnshire, 29 February 2020

List of Abbreviations

AALT	Anglo-American Legal Tradition website
AALT-IMG	Anglo-American Legal Tradition website, image number
AM	*Annales Monastici*
BL	British Library
Carpenter, *Robin Hood*	K. Carpenter, *Robin Hood: The Many Faces of That Celebrated English Outlaw* (Oldenburg, 1995)
CChR	*Calendar of Charter Rolls*
Child (1861)	F. J. Child, ed., *The English and Scottish Popular Ballads*, vol. V (London, 1861)
Child (1889)	F. J. Child, ed., *The English and Scottish Popular Ballads*, vol. III (London, 1889)
CCR	*Calendar of Close Rolls*
CLR	*Calendar of Liberate Rolls*
CPR	*Calendar of Patent Rolls*
CR	*Close Rolls*
CRR	*Curia Regis Rolls*
D&T	R. B. Dobson and J. Taylor, *Rymes of Robyn Hood: An Introduction to the English Outlaw* (3rd edition, Stroud, 1997)
EHR	*English Historical Review*
EPNS	English Place-Name Society
EYC	*Early Yorkshire Charters*
Hahn, *Popular Culture*	*Robin Hood in Popular Culture: Violence, Transgression and Justice*, ed. T. G. Hahn (Cambridge, 2000)
HMC	Historical Manuscripts Commission
Holt, *Robin Hood*	J. C. Holt, *Robin Hood* (2nd edition, London, 1989)

Abbreviations

Hunter, *Robin Hood*	Joseph Hunter, *The Great Hero of the Ancient Minstrelsy of England, 'Robin Hood', His Period, Real Character, etc. Investigated and Perhaps Ascertained, Critical and Historical Tracts IV* (London, 1852).
Keen, *Outlaws*	M. Keen, *The Outlaws of Medieval Legend* (2nd edition, London, 1977)
Knight, *Anthology*	S. Knight, ed., *Robin Hood: An Anthology of Scholarship and Criticism* (Cambridge, 1999)
Knight, *Mythic Biography*	S. Knight, *Robin Hood: A Mythic Biography*, Ithaca, New York, and London, 2003)
Knight, *Complete Study*	S. Knight, *Robin Hood: A Complete Study of the English Outlaw* (Oxford, 1994)
MED	*Middle English Dictionary*
NMS	*Nottingham Medieval Studies*
ODNB	*Oxford Dictionary of National Biography* online
Peasants, Knights and Heretics	*Peasants, Knights and Heretics: Studies in Medieval English Social History*, ed. R. H. Hilton (Cambridge, 1976)
Pollard, *Imagining Robin Hood*	A. J. Pollard, *Imagining Robin Hood: The Late Medieval Stories in Historical Context* (Abingdon, 2007)
PR	*Patent Rolls*
PRS	*Pipe Roll Society*
PRS NS	*Pipe Roll Society New Series*
RBN	*Records of the Borough of Nottingham*
REED	*Records of Early English Drama*
RLC	*Rotuli Litterarum Clausarum*
RLP	*Rotuli Litterarum Patentium*
TNA	*The National Archives, Kew*
TTS	*Transactions of the Thoroton Society*
UNMASC	University of Nottingham Manuscripts and Special Collections
YAS	Yorkshire Archaeological Society
YAS RS	Yorkshire Archaeological Society Record Series

No real original Robin Hood has ever been identified beyond dispute, whereas all other bandit heroes I have been able to check, however mythologized, can be traced back to some identifiable individual in some identifiable locality.

Eric Hobsbawm (1917–2012), *Bandits* (London, 1969)

You know, there's been a heap of legends and tall tales about Robin Hood, all different too ... it's the story of what really happened in Sherwood Forest ... my job is to tell it like it is, or was, or whatever.

Walt Disney cartoon *Robin Hood* (1973)

I wrote many years ago ... that 'every generation gets the Robin Hood that it deserves'. Now though ... I realise that the phrase needs to be modified. Every generation surely creates for itself the Robin Hood that it needs.

Brian Alderson (1995)

Introduction

When my interest in the legend of Robin Hood and its possible historicity was first aroused over thirty years ago, it seemed obvious that the best place to look for evidence of the temporal and geographical context of an infamous criminal was to study whatever contemporary records of criminal law and administration had survived until the present day. That point seemed, surprisingly, to have escaped the notice of historians until relatively recent decades, and is still largely disregarded by literary scholars, concentrating as they do mainly on the surviving tales of the outlaw and their social and cultural context. This is so despite the fact that those tales are generally acknowledged to be very late in date, somewhere between two hundred and three hundred years later than the period where the most recent historical research on the subject places the original outlaw, the early thirteenth century. The approach seems to veer between the view that it is too difficult to try to identify the original Robin and his temporal and geographical context, so that the attempt is not worth making, and a feeling that it does not matter anyway. If one's interests are focused on the literary merits of the fifteenth-century tales and how they relate to what is known about English society in that period, indeed it does not matter. If one's concern is to try to explain how the legend began, and to identify the period and context of its origin, it matters a great deal. My point is that, although it is certainly extremely difficult to identify the original outlaw from surviving evidence, and no attempt can ever be conclusive or sufficient to satisfy the critical enquirer, it is worthwhile to make the search. That is what this book sets out to do.

The context within which the Robin Hood story rightfully belongs has been a matter of dispute between folk-lore enthusiasts, literary scholars and some historians since the nineteenth century. The early proponents of Robin Hood as myth were rebuked in 1889 by the great editor of the Robin Hood tales, Francis Child, who opined that 'I cannot admit that even a shadow of a case has been made out by those who would attach a mythical character to ... Robin Hood'. To him, the outlaw was 'absolutely a creation of the ballad-muse'.[1] Nevertheless, cultural studies scholars have in recent decades become accustomed to classifying Robin Hood as a 'myth', but without defining what that word means in the outlaw context. *The Oxford English Dictionary* defines a myth as 'a purely fictitious narrative usually involving supernatural persons, actions or events, and embodying some popular idea concerning natural or historical phenomena'; or 'a fictitious or imaginary person or object'. A legend, on the other hand, is 'an unauthentic or non-historical story, especially one handed down by tradition from early times and *popularly regarded as historical*' (italics mine).[2] From the fifteenth-century Scottish historians who first tried to place Robin Hood in a thirteenth-century English context, and then from their fellow-countryman John Mair or Major, who a century later set him, without great conviction, in the last decade of the twelfth century, it is clear that Robin Hood was regarded as a person who had really existed but about whom they had no reliable information. The existence of a real original Robin seems much more likely, with the 'green man' myth becoming attached to the outlaw legend by those writing after Robin had become firmly associated in popular imagination with the greenwood. This association, it will be argued, was itself a later addition to the original thirteenth-century legend.

The back-cover summary of a book published by a leading folklore scholar in 1993 asserted that 'we have been looking in the wrong place for Robin Hood by seeking a real person among the dusty records of medieval history. Robin Hood is best sought under the open skies or in the depth of the Greenwood, where he has always been'.[3] The reference to 'dusty records' gives the game away, because users of well-kept early parchment documents know full well that they are rarely dusty; and the further implication that these records are somehow dry and uninteresting is even further from the truth, a fact fully appreciated by those who have taken the trouble to make informed use of them. The reality is that they have not been looked at enough nor in the right way. The two and a half centuries or so before 1450 deserve to be treated in their own right like other periods of English history, and studied by means of the rich supply of contemporary documentation they generated, not seen through the distorting prism of the recently fashionable concept of 'medieval cultural studies'. Thomas Hahn has written persuasively of the importance of Robin Hood in the development of the genre, which has been variously defined as 'the study of what happens to or is done to the middle ages after the middle ages', 'the study of the impact of the middle ages after

---

[1] F. J. Child, ed., *The English and Scottish Popular Ballads*, 5 vols. (Boston, Mass., 1882–98), III, p. 48.
[2] *Oxford English Dictionary*, 2nd edition (Oxford, 1989), vol. VIII, p. 806; vol. X, p. 177.
[3] J. Matthews, *Robin Hood, Green Lord of the Wildwood* (Glastonbury, 1993).

Introduction

the middle ages', and 'the study not of the Middle Ages themselves but of the scholars, artists and writers who ... constructed the idea of the Middle Ages that we inherited'.[4] The approach has resulted in interesting and thought-provoking new interpretations of the outlaw legend during the last quarter of a century, but essentially restricted to the period from the late fifteenth century onwards. It is more profitable, however, to consider medieval England on its own terms, by studying and interpreting what the documents produced by its administrative and legal bureaucracies can tell us about law and order in the countryside, and therefore about the context from which the tales of Robin Hood emerged. When these sources are systematically evaluated, the case for a real original Robin Hood becomes, if not irresistible, then at least very powerful indeed.

---

[4] T. Hahn, 'Robin Hood and the Rise of Cultural Studies', *Medieval Cultural Studies: Essays in Honour of Stephen Knight*, ed. R. Evans, H. Fulton and D. Matthews (Cardiff, 2006), pp. 39–54; D. Matthews, 'What was Medievalism? Medieval Studies, Medievalism and Cultural Studies', *Medieval Cultural Studies*, pp. 9–22, at 9, 13.

Part I

THE LEGEND AND ITS INTERPRETERS

Chapter 1

The Medieval Tales of Robin Hood

The early tales of Robin Hood are the essential starting point for any consideration of the evidence for the origins of the legend, and for any attempt to identify the original outlaw.[1] The first step is to study them; the second to identify the elements of the surviving stories that seem most likely to represent the core of the original legend; and the third to differentiate them from others which are most likely to be later accretions to that core. This process can assist in establishing the chronological context and geographical location of the man from whom the legend derived, if such an individual ever existed. It is therefore necessary to consider in detail the small canon of stories that are now generally agreed to have originated before the early sixteenth century, noting their contents and taking account of the views of recent and contemporary literary scholars and historians about their provenance, their likely dates, how to interpret them, and their late-medieval historical context.[2] The chapter will conclude with a brief review of which elements of the modern Robin Hood legend do *not* appear in the early tales, the origins of which will require explanation. It is convenient to deal with the early stories initially

---

[1] The standard texts of the tales are in F. J. Child, ed., *The English and Scottish Popular Ballads*, 5 vols. (Boston, Mass., 1882–98), vol. III, replacing the earlier edition in F. J. Child, ed., *The English and Scottish Popular Ballads*, 8 vols. (London, 1861), vol. V. The most convenient edition available today is R. B. Dobson and J. Taylor, *Rymes of Robyn Hood: An Introduction to the English Outlaw*, 3rd edition revised (London, 1997), which is normally used here. The most recent and definitive scholarly edition of the early tales is in T. H. Ohlgren and L. M. Matheson, *Early Rymes of Robyn Hood: An Edition of the Texts, ca. 1425 to ca. 1600*, Medieval and Renaissance Texts and Studies 428 (Tempe, Arizona, 2013).
[2] On the latter, see in particular, A. J. Pollard, *Imagining Robin Hood: The Late-Medieval Stories in Historical Context* (London, 2007).

in the chronological order of their recorded appearance, so far as that can be established by the most recent research.

What is known of the medieval legend of Robin Hood as it existed before the early sixteenth century depends mainly on a handful of surviving tales in manuscript and an early printed text in several versions that derives from an original but now lost written source. They comprise five poems or ballads and a fragment of a play, all in the English language, plus a passage in Latin included in a fifteenth-century Scottish monastic chronicle. They represent not the origins of the tales at some earlier indeterminate time, but the stage of development that they had reached by the time the surviving versions were written down. Before then they had taken the form of verses, recited, chanted or sung by professional or amateur entertainers who depended mainly on memory to preserve the details.[3] It cannot be certain that the surviving written tales record all or even the main themes of the oral material that existed earlier, and what we now have is probably only a fragment of what was performed for medieval audiences. In what is known as the B-text of William Langland's *Vision of Piers the Plowman* (most recently considered to have been written in or after 1381), 'rymes of Robyn Hood' are mentioned as being something that Langland's character Sloth, who represented a negligent and half-educated priest, knows better than the Paternoster, so it is clear that by that date, and potentially much earlier, Robin Hood tales were widely known. Sloth also admits a few lines later that 'I am occupied eche day haliday and other with ydel tales atte ale [house] and otherwhile in cherches', so Langland may have intended to portray Piers as an amateur performer himself.[4] This is the earliest known literary reference to the 'rhymes';[5] and clerical criticisms of them were common in the early fifteenth century, further indicating the widespread popularity of the legend for some time before the earliest surviving texts of the tales themselves. It will be argued in this book that tales of the outlaw existed in some form for over a century before Langland's time. The surviving stories derive, as James Holt put it, 'not from the point of origin of the legend, but from different stages in its growth'.[6]

The earliest story is one for which we have no text, simply a summary of it in the *Scotichronicon* of Walter Bower, abbot of Inchcolm, written at

---

[3] On the nature of performance and the genre generally, see in particular D. Gray, 'The Robin Hood Poems', in *Poetica* (Tokyo) 18 (1984), pp. 1–18, reprinted in *Robin Hood: An Anthology of Scholarship and Criticism*, ed. S. Knight (Cambridge, 1999), pp. 3–37, at 9–12. Cf. D&T, pp. 6–7.

[4] *The Vision of William concerning Piers the Plowman in Three Parallel Texts*, ed. W. W. Skeat, 3rd edition revised (Oxford, 1879), I, p. 57 (B-text, passus V, lines 400–03, 409–10); *ODNB*, entry by George Kane.

[5] For a supposed but demonstrably inaccurate earlier reference said to be of about 1304, see J. C. Holt, *Robin Hood*, 2nd edition (London, 1989), p. 200 n. 6.

[6] Holt, *Robin Hood*, p. 16.

some time in the early 1440s.[7] It also differs from all the other texts of early tales, which were in English, by being written in Latin, as the great majority of chronicles were. Bower first describes the popularity of Robin, with Little John and their accomplices: 'these men the stolid commons remember, at times in the gay mood of comedy, at others in the more solemn and tragic vein, and love besides to sing of their deeds in all kinds of romances, mime and snatches'. Chronologically he placed them in 1266, and identified Robin as one of 'the Disinherited' holding out against King Henry III and his son and heir, Lord Edward, after the defeat and death of Simon de Montfort at the battle of Evesham in the previous year. In doing so he assumed that Robin was a real person in a real historical context. He was said to be an outlaw amongst the woodland briars and thorns (*inter fructeta et dumeta silvestria exulabant*). Robin (Robert Hod) was in Barnsdale, sheltering from the fury of the king and prince, hearing mass, as was his normal habit, and unwilling to interrupt the service no matter what occurred. He was tracked down to the secluded woodland place (*in illo secretissimo loco nemorali*) where he was hearing mass, by a certain sheriff and some royal ministers who had often previously been his enemies. Some of his men who anticipated his discovery tried to persuade him to flee, but because of his reverence for the sacrament he refused. While the rest of his men were trembling in fear of death, Robert, having great trust in God, took on these enemies with the few men who were there with him, and easily defeated them. He was much enriched with spoil and by ransom money taken from them, and afterwards chose to hold ministers of the church and masses in even greater veneration. He had paid heed to the common saying, 'God listens to the man who hears mass often'.[8]

This passage in the chronicle may perhaps have been a fragment of a larger story, picked out by Bower because it makes a moral point. The secluded place in Barnsdale where he could hear mass might be an echo of a passage in *A Lytell Gest of Robin Hood*, or one of its sources, where he asks the king's leave to depart from his court for seven days to visit a chapel he had built in Barnsdale, dedicated to St Mary Magdalene.[9] The story is significant also for showing that by the 1440s the legendary outlaw had a reputation for piety and respect for the clergy as well as the mass. This seems to be at odds with his vehement hatred for bishops and abbots, recorded in the *Gest*, but they are princes of the church

---

[7] On Bower and his chronicle, see also Chapter 2.
[8] S. Taylor, D. E. R. Watt, with B. Scott, eds., *Scotichronicon by Walter Bower* V (Aberdeen, 1990), pp. 354–57. A translation of the passage is available in S. Knight, *Robin Hood: A Mythic Biography* (Ithaca, 2003), pp. 5–6; earlier also in his *Robin Hood: A Complete Study of the English Outlaw* (Oxford, 1994), p. 35.
[9] D&T, p. 111, stanzas 439–44.

and therefore perhaps less worthy of respect than ordinary priests who celebrated mass in small rural chapels in Barnsdale and elsewhere.[10]

Robin Hood and the Monk

Robin Hood and the Monk is usually regarded as the earliest surviving Robin Hood poem, and it is longer than any of the others except the *Gest*, which is in any case an amalgam of several tales. It is the story of which we have the earliest written version, included in a manuscript, now in Cambridge University Library, from the collection of John Moore, bishop of Ely (died 1714), and given to the university by George I in 1715.[11] It was first published in Edinburgh in 1806 by Robert Jamieson in his *Popular Ballads and Songs*, and he gave it the title by which it has come generally to be known. It had not been included in Joseph Ritson's edition of the tales published in 1795, because Ritson was unaware of its existence, although he did find another tale, *Robin Hood and the Potter*, among Moore's manuscripts.[12] The relevant section of the manuscript was damaged by water, and Jamieson made matters worse by applying chemicals, so digital scanning had to be used to help produce the most recent and authoritative edition of the text by Thomas Olgren and Lister Matheson; they describe it as 'an unpretentious amateur production', with careless penmanship and spelling.[13] It is a clerical miscellany compiled for a secular cleric, and containing secular stories in verse, such as the comic 'king and subject' story *Tale of King Edward and the Shepherd*, as well as religious matter, including instructions for the parish priest. It was written at some time in the middle or second half of the fifteenth century, but approximately when has been a matter of slightly differing opinions. In the second half of the nineteenth century, Francis Child opined in his first edition of the tales that the story was 'possibly as old as the reign of Edward II', but in his second edition he did not repeat that and simply dated the manuscript in which it appeared to about 1450. More recently, Dobson and Taylor assigned it to the later fifteenth

---

10   D&T, p. 80, stanza 15.
11   Cambridge University Library, Ff.5.48, ff. 128v–135v.
12   D&T, p. 113. On Ritson's work, see Chapter 3.
13   Ohlgren and Matheson, *Early Rymes*, pp. 3–17; a fragment of another copy of the tale from a collection made by John Bagford (1650–1715) is also included, pp. 18–21. Their earlier work is found in T. H. Ohlgren, '"lewed peple loven tales olde"': Robin Hood and the Monk and the Manuscript Context of Cambridge, University Library MS Ff.5.48', in Ohlgren, *Robin Hood: The Early Poems, 1465–1560: Texts, Contexts, and Ideology* (Newark NJ, 2007), pp. 28–67, revised and expanded from 'Robin Hood and the Monk and the Manuscript Context of Cambridge, University Library MS Ff.5.48', *NMS* 48 (2004), pp. 80–115. See also 'From Script to Print: Robin Hood and the Printers', in Ohlgren, *The Early Poems*, pp. 97–134.

century, Holt to about 1450, Stephen Knight to sometime after 1461, and Ohlgren, after detailed contextual study, to after 1465.[14] Such incidental topographical detail about Nottingham as the tale gives does not help to date the story. The town wall and gates mentioned in it were built during the later thirteenth and fourteenth centuries, and St Mary's church, the scene of some of the action, although substantially altered during the fifteenth century, certainly existed centuries earlier.[15] Another possible indication of date, the use of a letter under the king's privy seal, sent to the sheriff of Nottingham, is equally indecisive, since all the English monarchs from King John (1199-1216) onwards used such a seal, and its use became increasingly frequent from the late thirteenth century onwards and into the fifteenth century.[16]

Ohlgren has shown that the manuscript in which the text appears was compiled by and for a Gilbert Pilkington, mentioned in the colophon of one of the texts, and he is probably to be identified as the Gilbert Pilkington who was confirmed in priestly orders in the diocese of Lichfield in three stages between 1463 and 1465, under the sponsorship of the nunnery of Farewell, a short distance from Lichfield itself.[17] Lister Matheson, who made a detailed analysis of the dialect within it, concluded that it was of western Derbyshire provenance, near the Cheshire and Staffordshire borders, from the furthest western reaches of the sheriff of Nottingham's official domain.[18] If this attribution to western Derbyshire is correct, the setting of the story in St Mary's church in Nottingham and the involvement of a monk in the attempt to arrest Robin there is very appropriate. St Mary's belonged, from the time of its foundation by William Peverel in the first decade of the twelfth century until the Dissolution of the Monasteries in the reign of Henry VIII, to the great Cluniac priory of Lenton, west of the town, whose powerful position gave it an important role in the affairs of Nottingham.[19] The presence of a monk in a parish church, not normally to be expected, is therefore readily explicable. Furthermore, Lenton had significant land holdings in the western part

---

[14] Child (1861), p. 1; Child (1889), p. 9; D&T, p. 114; Holt, *Robin Hood*, p.15; Knight, *Complete Study*, pp. 47–48; Ohlgren, 'Manuscript Context', pp. 94–95, and *The Early Poems*, pp. 39–40.

[15] J. Beckett, ed., *A Centenary History of Nottingham* (Manchester, 1997), p. 60.

[16] P. Chaplais, *English Royal Documents, King John–Henry VI, 1199–1461* (Oxford, 1971), pp. 23–32.

[17] This is not undisputed: see M. Truesdale, *The King and the Commoner Tradition: Carnivalesque Politics in Medieval and Early Modern Literature* (New York and Abingdon, 2018), pp. 15, 40.

[18] L. M. Matheson, in Ohlgren, *The Early Poems*, pp. 194–200, and earlier in *NMS* 48 (2004), pp. 109–15.

[19] CCℏR II, p. 79; T. Foulds, 'The Foundation of Lenton Priory and a Reconstruction Lost Cartulary', *TTS* 92 (1988), p. 40; Beckett, *Centenary History*, pp. 69.

of Derbyshire, in the area around Newbold, Tideswell, Bradwell and Bakewell. These were the subject of a long-running dispute between the priory and the dean and chapter of Lichfield that occasionally became violent.[20] As a clergyman from that area, Pilkington would have been aware of the wealth and power of the Nottinghamshire priory, and perhaps of its ownership of St Mary's church. It is possible that the rebuilding of the church and the attention that generated in the wider region was one of the reasons why the story was written, since there is no historical evidence to link Nottingham to the Robin Hood legend until 1485.[21]

The story describes itself as a 'talking', so it was certainly recited, not sung. In it, on an early May morning at Whitsuntide, Robin, not having heard mass for a fortnight, sets off for Nottingham from the greenwood with Little John, acting as his bow-bearer, to attend church. He ignored the advice of Much the Miller's son that he should take twelve armed yeomen with him for protection. On the way Robin quarrels with Little John when Robin refuses to pay him his wager after John won an archery contest between them, and they part. Robin enters St Mary's church in Nottingham, but is recognised by a 'great-headed' monk, who he had earlier robbed of £100. The monk runs out, causes the town gates to be closed and alerts the sheriff. After a fight in which Robin kills twelve of the sheriff's men and breaks his sword on the sheriff's head, he is finally captured, although the description of the moment of his capture and certainly some other material is missing because of an accidental omission by the writer of the manuscript. After this hiatus the story resumes with the reaction of the outlaws in the forest to that event. There is also some damage to the line of the manuscript which mentions that Robin either ran into or out of the church. Dobson and Taylor considered that the sense of the passage means that he must have run *out* of it, but after a re-examination of the manuscript, Ohlgren stated that the correct reading was *in*, as given in Child's edition, and that in running into the church he was claiming sanctuary.[22]

Little John, who had gone to Sherwood after the quarrel, decides together with Much to rescue Robin. In the morning, looking out of a window in Much's uncle's house near the highway, they spy the monk, recognised by virtue of his 'wyde hode', and a page, who they somehow know are on their way with a letter to tell the king of Robin's capture. John talks to the monk, telling him that Robin Hood, who had been captured on the previous day, had robbed him and his fellows of 20 marks; the

---

[20] Ohlgren, *The Early Poems*, pp. 59–60; J. T. Godfrey, *The History of the Parish and Priory of Lenton in the County of Nottingham* (London, 1884), pp. 68–71.
[21] See below, p.144.
[22] D&T, p. 117 n. 11; Ohlgren, *The Early Poems*, p. 62; Ohlgren and Matheson, *Early Rymes*, p. 10.

monk tells him that Robin had earlier robbed him of over £100, and they travel together. Then John and Much take the horses of the monk and page by the head, and John pulls the monk down 'by the golett of the hood', and he falls on his crown. John says that Robin was his master, and that he would not allow the monk to tell the king of his capture, and so he cuts off his head; Much does the same to the page. They bury them both and take the letter to the king themselves, saying that the monk had died on the way. The king makes them yeomen of the crown, with a fee of £20, and sends them back to the sheriff with a letter sealed with the king's privy seal as authority for going to Nottingham and bringing Robin to him. They find the gates of the town barred against them by the porter, who says that John, Much and Will Scathlock are killing men on the town walls, presumably because they are trying to rescue Robin from his 'deep prison'. They tell the sheriff that the king had rewarded the monk by making him abbot of Westminster, so they have come in his place bearing the letter, which Little John opens and gives to him. The sheriff accepts John's story and, after they have dined together, the sheriff falls into a drunken sleep. John and Much kill the gaoler, rescue Robin and escape to Sherwood, where John refuses Robin's offer to make him leader of the band. The sheriff fears being hung by the king for letting Robin escape, but the monarch merely reflects on Little John's loyalty to his master.

In a re-evaluation of this tale, Derek Pearsall has argued that, despite the title, which was imposed by its editors since there is none in the unique manuscript, the most important person in the ballad, and its hero, is Little John. Robin, after originating as a highway robber, in the fifteenth century became the outlaw hero of a 'yeoman culture', which involved loyalty to the king and knighthood but enmity for predatory officials like the sheriff. Little John, on the other hand, in this tale stands rather for a fellowship of those with common interests and goals, somewhat akin to the idea of the equal brotherhood of men preached by the revolutionary preacher John Ball at the time of the Peasants' Revolt. The story does not appear in any of the collections of Robin Hood poems that were later compiled, and 'it seems to belong to another world than the one into which Robin Hood became incorporated, and needs to be understood as an anomaly in the record'.[23]

Robin Hood and the Potter

Like *Robin Hood and the Monk*, the only known text of *Robin Hood and the Potter* is in another of Bishop Moore's manuscripts in Cambridge University Library, where it is untitled.[24] On another page of the manuscript is a

---

23 D. Pearsall, 'Little John and the Ballad of *Robin Hood and the Monk*', in *Robin Hood: Medieval and Post-Medieval*, ed. H. Phillips (Dublin, 2005), pp. 42–50.
24 Cambridge University Library MS Ee.4.35.1.

memorandum giving an itemised list of the meat, fowl and fish served at the wedding of a Queen Margaret, the identification of whom is an important clue to the date of the manuscript as a whole. Joseph Ritson, whose edition of the text was published in 1795, dated it to the reign of Henry VII (1485-1509) on the basis of the appearance of the handwriting, but thought its composition probably took place during an earlier period. Thomas Wright, writing in 1846, believed that it dated from the reign of Henry VI (1422-61, 1470-71), because he identified the 'Queen Margaret' with Margaret of Anjou, wife of that king, and he was followed by J. M. Gutch in his 1847 edition of the tales. Ritson's opinion, however, received general approval for a long period.[25] Child did not suggest a date, but in 1976 Dobson and Taylor thought it 'almost certainly' dated from shortly after 1503. The list of wedding fare was usually considered to relate to the nuptial feast of Margaret, daughter of Henry VII, who married James IV of Scotland in Edinburgh on 8 August that year.[26] However, Ohlgren, who later made a detailed study of the manuscript, has more recently argued that it most likely refers to the marriage of Margaret of York, the youngest sister of Edward IV, to Charles duke of Burgundy, at Damme, near Bruges, on 3 July 1468. He found evidence that the manuscript belonged to Richard Call, a Norfolk man who lived from about 1431 to a date after 1504, possibly 1509, and that it was made for him as a personal miscellany. Call, who seems to have been self-educated, served as bailiff to John Paston I and his two sons, John Paston II and III, in Norfolk during the later fifteenth century, and eventually, to the family's annoyance, married the senior John Paston's youngest daughter, Margery, in 1469. Call makes over a hundred appearances in the 'Paston Letters', which illustrate many aspects of his life, including a period of imprisonment by the sheriff of Norfolk in Norwich prison in connection with the alleged theft of rents from a manor which was the subject of a disputed will.

John Paston II and III both attended the wedding of 1468 as part of the princess's retinue, and it is possible that Call was also present. Ohlgren argues that it is even possible, though less likely, that he supplied some of the livestock for the wedding feast from Paston manors, or at least kept a list of the provisions; he was responsible for keeping accounts, and his father, John Call, had been a grocer as well as a minor landholder

---

[25] J. Ritson, *Robin Hood: A Collection of all the Ancient Poems, Songs and Ballads, now Extant, Relative to that Celebrated Outlaw* (London, 1795), p. 81; T. Wright, 'On the Popular Cycle of the Robin Hood Ballads', in *Essays on Subjects Connected with the Literature, Popular Superstitions and History of England in the Middle Ages* (2 vols., London, 1846), vol. I, pp. 174–184, 201; J. M. Gutch, *A Lytell Geste of Robin Hode, with other Ancient and Modern Ballads and Songs* (2 vols., London, 1847, and second edition 1850), vol. II, p. 21; D&T, p. 123.

[26] D&T, p. 123; their view was followed a few years later by Holt, *Robin Hood*, p. 15.

in Framlingham, Suffolk. There are also, according to Lister Matheson, linguistic grounds for associating the manuscript with Norfolk or Suffolk, most likely southern Norfolk or northern Suffolk.[27] He may also have recorded *Robin Hood and the Potter* because, as a yeoman with mercantile interests, it may have appealed to him. The manuscript also contains two other verse tales, *The King and the Barker* and *The Cheylde and hes Stepdame*, which show tradesmen or merchants in a flattering light, and not intimidated by social superiors. The contents of the manuscript as a whole are 'precisely the types of literary, religious and educational texts that you would expect a young man hoping to rise in the world to possess'. As a result of this evidence, it is possible for the text of the tale to be dated as early as 1468 rather than at least as late as 1503, as previously thought.[28]

It is made clear in the story itself that it was intended to be recited aloud to an audience of yeomen, because the fifth line reads 'herkens, god yemen', and later the two main characters are described as yeomen. The tale ends with a prayer to God to 'saffe all god yemanrey'.[29] It begins with an encounter between Robin and a proud potter. Robin has a wager with Little John, who has already been beaten by the potter in a fight at Wentbridge, that he will be able to make him pay 'pavage' to pass with his cart. He loses the wager because the potter, armed only with a staff against Robin's sword and shield, defeats him. Impressed by his prowess, Robin befriends the potter and they exchange clothes. Robin goes to Nottingham to sell his wares, which he does very successfully because he charges only 3d for pots worth 5d. He gives the last five pots to the sheriff's wife, who invites him to dinner. He meets the sheriff in his hall and is welcomed by him. During the meal two of the sheriff's men talk about a shooting competition for a wager of 40s. Robin asks to see the competition, so after the meal they go to the archery butts. The sheriff's men shoot badly, but Robin, as the potter, joins in after the sheriff sends a yeoman to bring him a good bow. He amazes the sheriff by out-shooting his men using the borrowed bow, and then tells him that he knows Robin Hood, who he has shot with, and that in his cart he has a bow given to him by the outlaw. The sheriff says that he would sooner meet Robin than

[27] L. M. Matheson, in Ohlgren, *The Early Poems*, pp. 189–94; Ohlgren and Matheson, *Early Rymes*, pp. 23–24.

[28] T. H. Ohlgren, 'Richard Call, the Pastons and the Manuscript Context of Robin Hood and the Potter (Cambridge, University Library Ee.4.35.1)', *NMS* 45 (2001), pp. 210–33, esp. 217–18; and '"Pottys, gret chepe!": Marketplace Ideology in *Robin Hood and the Potter* and the Manuscript Context of Cambridge, University Library MS Ee.4.35', in Ohlgren, *The Early Poems*, pp. 68–96, 226–33; Ohlgren and Matheson, *Early Rymes*, pp. 27–38; N. Davis, *Paston Letters and Papers of the Fifteenth Century*, 2 vols. (Oxford, 1971, 1976); Pollard, *Imagining Robin Hood*, pp. 163–64; C. Ross, *Edward IV* (London, 1975), p. 112.

[29] D&T, pp. 123–25 (comments), 125–32 (text); Ohlgren and Matheson, *Early Rymes*, pp. 27, 38.

have £100, and the potter agrees to lead him to the outlaw, the sheriff offering a reward. They both have a supper provided by the sheriff's wife. On the next morning the potter prepares his cart for departure, and before taking his leave of the sheriff's wife he gives her a gold ring. Then he leads the sheriff into the greenwood, where he summons his men by a blast on his horn. Little John asks Robin how he had managed to sell the potter's wares. Robin tells him not to worry, because he has brought the sheriff to serve as merchandise for his men. The sheriff, horrified at his mistake in falling into Robin's power, is sent home, spared further punishment only for the love of his wife, but without his horse and his other possessions. However, Robin sends a white palfrey for the sheriff's wife, who, when she receives it, laughs loudly and says that Robin has now been paid for his pots. Robin pays the potter £10 for his goods, and they part firm friends.

The particular significance of *Robin Hood and the Potter* is, according to Dobson and Taylor, 'to confirm that the farcical elements of the later forest outlaw myth were present within the medieval tradition', although parts of the *Gest* and *Robin Hood and the Monk* also contribute to this.[30] The story is not devoid of deeper meaning, however, and its significance in the context of 'fellowship' as well as yeomanry has been pointed out by Tony Pollard.[31] It is also the only one of the surviving medieval tales to include reference to the commercial activity of a town, with Robin in the guise of the potter selling his wares in Nottingham. Ohlgren has in several papers made a great deal of the use of commercial terminology and economic concepts in the tale.[32] Another unique point is the inclusion of a woman with individual character, the sheriff's wife. It is possible that we are meant to assume that Robin's visit to Nottingham in disguise was intended to enable him to flirt with the sheriff's wife and thus humiliate the sheriff himself. A play directly based upon the tale, with close similarity of language at some points, and 'verye proper to be played in Maye games', was appended to an edition of the *Gest* published about 1560 by William Copland, although it breaks off well before the end of the ballad story, at the point where Robin and the potter are about to fight.[33] The post-medieval tale, *Robin Hood and the Butcher*, first known

---

30 D&T, p. 36.
31 Pollard, *Imagining Robin Hood*, pp. 55, 143–44.
32 T. H. Ohlgren, 'The '"Marchaunt" of Sherwood: Mercantile Ideology in *A Gest of Robyn Hode*', in Hahn, *Popular Culture*, pp. 175–90; T. H. Ohlgren, 'Merchant Adventure in *Robin Hood and the Potter*', in *Robin Hood: Medieval and Post-Medieval*, ed. Phillips, pp. 69–78; '"Pottys, gret chepe!": Marketplace Ideology in *Robin Hood and the Potter* and the Manuscript Context of Cambridge, University Library MS Ee.4.35', in Ohlgren, *The Early Poems*, pp. 68–96; 'The "Marchaunt" of Sherwood: Mercantile Adventure in *A Lytell Geste of Robyin Hode*', in Ohlgren, *The Early Poems*, pp. 135–82.
33 D&T, pp. 215–19.

from a broadside version printed about 1640, largely derives from it, with similarities in the narrative and echoes of the actual language of the *Potter* at several points.[34] The favourable view of the tradesman in each of these versions of what is essentially the same story may have been designed to appeal to the tradesmen in the audience for its performance.

The reference to pavage in the tale provides a potential piece of chronological evidence for the period from which the tale of the potter comes. An urban tax associated with the improvement or repair of a road or street, the earliest known reference to it comes from 1223, in relation to Chepstow, and grants of it for a period of five years were first made in 1255, in respect of Beverley and Grimsby.[35] It is often associated with 'murage', another urban tax for the building of town walls, which first appears in 1305, being granted during royal pleasure to the earl of Warwick.[36] In the tale of the potter, however, it seems to be being levied by Robin and Little John in Barnsdale, hardly an urban setting. In a forest setting the appropriate levy would have been 'cheminage', a levy on the passage of goods through the forest, levied by foresters, under rules prescribed by the Charter of the Forest of 1217 and 1225, but cheminage is nowhere mentioned in the early tales. The origin of pavage about two and a half centuries before it is mentioned in the tale of the potter means that it is of no use as dating evidence for the origin of this tale. Pavage, in the form 'passage', made a further appearance about 1560 in Copland's play of 'Robin Hood and the Potter'.[37]

A Lyttel Gest of Robin Hood

A Lyttel Gest of Robin Hood is the longest Robin Hood tale. No manuscript copy has survived, and it is first known from two printed versions. The first, a partial one known as the Lettersnijder edition, includes only about 43% of the whole text. It was printed in Antwerp between 1510 and 1515, but the single surviving copy only came to light in Scotland in about 1790. The second version, by the English printer Wynken de Worde, originally from the duchy of Lorraine and the apprentice of William Caxton until the latter's death in 1491, was published in London sometime between 1492 and his death in 1534. It provides the only complete text and survives in only one copy, printed in Fleet Street, to where he moved his business in 1500/1501. The book, which is thought to have belonged to various owners at Blechingley, Godstone, Oxted and Titsey in Surrey

---

34 D&T, pp. 150–7.
35 *Medieval Latin Dictionary from British Sources*, British Academy, 3 vols. (London, 1975–2011), I p. 2155; *Monasticon Anglicanum* V, ed. J. Caley, H. Ellis and B. Bandinell (London, 1825), p. 268b; CPR 1247–58, pp. 397, 408.
36 *Rotuli Parliamentorum* I (London, 1767), p. 163.
37 D&T, pp. 215–19.

between about 1546 and 1625, was acquired by Cambridge university library in 1715 after the death of Bishop Moore of Ely, its previous owner, for whom it had been purchased by John Bagford.[38] There were also several later versions of the ballad, including one printed in York, by Hugh Goes, in about 1506-9.[39]

The *Gest* is usually regarded as a compendium of several stories, exactly how many is a matter of dispute, linked together in a long narrative divided into eight sections or 'fyttes', rather than a single simple tale like the ones already described. It has always held pride of place in the body of early Robin Hood literature, and it is now generally agreed that the two early printed versions came from a single original manuscript source that has not survived but which was composed after 1400, probably around the middle of the fifteenth century.[40] Several literary scholars of the last hundred years or so have sought to isolate the particular original stories embodied in the *Gest*, their possible sources and literary analogues, and which passages were supplied by the compiler of the poem to link together the various ballads he already knew. In 1861 the American ballad editor Francis Child described it as an 'heroic poem' formed out of several earlier and previously unconnected ballads which had been skilfully strung together at an unknown date; he also adopted Joseph Hunter's recent division of the *Gest* into six different ballads.[41] In 1889 Child described it as 'a popular epic, composed from several ballads by a poet of a thoroughly congenial spirit'. He then described the story as 'a three-ply web' of the adventures of Robin Hood with a knight, with the sheriff of Nottingham, and with the king', followed by a short epilogue ending with his death. Following a much more detailed analysis than he had made in his earlier edition, he dated it to about 1400 or earlier, although he thought that there were 'no firm grounds on which to base an opinion'.[42] W. H. Clawson, who in 1909 undertook the most detailed investigation made until then of the literary analogues to the *Gest*, considered the author to be 'possessed of admirable artistic skill...his poem is not a mere mechanical stringing together of ballads, but a complete rehandling and fusion of ballads and medieval tales ... into a unified narrative'.

[38] Cambridge University Library, printed book Sel.5.18; Ohlgren, *The Early Poems*, pp. 116-20; Ohlgren and Matheson, *Early Rymes*, pp. 89-90.
[39] On the details of the different versions, see in particular D&T, pp. 71-74; Ohlgren, *The Early Poems*, pp. 97-134; and Ohlgren and Matheson, *Early Rymes*, pp. 57-58, 89-90, 149-50, 157, 169, 239-40, 245-47 (including fragments). The most important later version was by Copland, printed in full in *Early Rymes* at pp. 166-237.
[40] M. Ikegami, 'The Language and Date of "A Gest of Robyn Hode"', *Neuphilologische Mitteilungen* 96 (1995), pp. 271-81.
[41] Child (1861), pp. 43-44.
[42] Child (1889), pp. 39-56.

He made a full analysis of the story structure, tabulated with the probable sources and analogues, and concluded with a table to identify the passages provided by the compiler, and the sources and surviving analogues lying behind the rest of the poem.[43] Historians like Holt, Dobson and Taylor, Coss and Pollard have consistently agreed with the literary scholars that the tale is a compendium of several stories woven together, disregarding the dissonant view of D. C. Fowler in 1968 that the poem was 'the work of a skilled artist' and had 'remarkable unity' and a 'narrative symmetry'.[44] Fowler's view, however, has recently received support from another English historian, Richard Hoyle, who even tentatively pointed to a specific incident that took place in 1357 as a possible inspiration for the composition of what he described as a 'bravura piece of fictional writing'.[45]

Clawson suggested a date before 1400 for the composition of the *Gest*, on the basis of his compilation of a complete list of the instances of final inflexional *e* and *es*, more comprehensive than that earlier attempted by Child, and his assertion that such endings were still then a current feature of spoken English.[46] Some later scholars have not been inclined to agree with him on that issue. Jeffrey Singman has argued that the poetry of the period around 1400 was very conservative and continued to preserve –*e* inflections well into the fifteenth century, one prominent user being John Lydgate (c.1370-1451).[47] A suggestion in 1978 that it originated in the first half of the fourteenth century resulted from detailed work on government records by the Oxford historian John Maddicott, depending partly on his proposed identification of possible originals for some of the characters that appear in the *Gest*. His view was not sustained by subsequent commentators such as Dobson, Taylor and Holt. In 1985, however, John Bellamy, a historian familiar with many of the legal and administrative sources for the period, used the same approach to argue that the story itself derived from court politics in the 1360s.[48] In 1993 Colin Richmond suggested that the first half of the fourteenth century was the most likely date, because it must have fallen between the expulsion of the Jews from England and the introduction of the office of justice of the peace in the English counties, since neither Jews or JPs appear in it.[49]

---

43 W. H. Clawson, *The Gest of Robin Hood* (Toronto, 1909), pp. 125–28.
44 D. C. Fowler, *A Literary History of the Popular Ballad* (Durham, North Carolina, 1968), p. 10, n. 18, pp. 72–79.
45 R. W. Hoyle, 'A Re-Reading of the Gest of Robyn Hode', *NMS* 61 (2017), pp. 67–113.
46 Clawson, *The Gest of Robin Hood*, pp. 3–6, 125–27.
47 J. L. Singman, *Robin Hood: The Shaping of the Legend* (Westport, Conn., 1998), p. 14. See also D. Gray, 'The Robin Hood Poems', note 58. For a valuable discussion of the varying views see also Knight, *Complete Study*, pp. 46–48.
48 See below, pp. 117–18.
49 C. Richmond, 'An Outlaw and Some Peasants: The Possible Significance of

More recently, Hoyle has argued that the evidence suggested that the second quarter of the fourteenth was the context from which the *Gest* derived, partly because of the usage of the term 'broad targe' for either the king's privy or great seal, which pointed to a date before 1350, that usage being anachronistic by 1500.

Despite these ideas, the generally accepted way of dividing up the *Gest* is still into distinguishable narratives, which have been given modern working titles without any specific warrant in the original text. The tale of 'Robin Hood and the Knight' consists of fyttes I, II and IV; 'Little John and the Sheriff' is in fytte III, breaking up that story; 'Robin Hood and the Sheriff', in fyttes V and VI; and 'Robin Hood and the King', in fyttes VII and VIII. The last fytte also incorporates what might be called 'The Death of Robin Hood', and Hunter and Child treated fytte IV as 'Robin Hood and the Monks of St Mary' rather than just part of the story of the knight.[50] Later, in 1974, J.B. Bessinger proposed another alternative episodic analysis, identifying three plots: Robin Hood, Knight and Abbot; Robin Hood, Little John, Sheriff and Knight; Robin Hood, Knight and King; with a short epilogue concerning the 'Morte' of Robin Hood.[51] Pollard divides the *Gest* into 'Robin Hood and the Knight', 'Robin Hood and the Sheriff', 'Little John and the Sheriff', 'Robin Hood and the King', and finally 'The Death of Robin Hood'.[52] Hoyle's very recent view that the tale 'forms an entire and coherent narrative' by 'a single unknown author of genius and unappreciated imagination', whose structure is built around a series of four successive visits to the forest, followed by two short epilogues about 'Robin Hood at court' and 'the death of Robin Hood', dissents from the views of the main commentators and seems unlikely to attract general assent.[53] According to Hoyle, the different elements of the complex tale are connected together by a series of literary devices. The story of the knight is linked with the story about Little John and the sheriff by means of John's service with the knight. These two stories are then linked with that of Robin and the sheriff by identifying the originally nameless knight as the Sir Richard atte Lee who appears in this third story. In it the sheriff promises not to harm the outlaws, but then in the story of Robin and the sheriff he breaks that undertaking. The king is then brought in as a means of resolving

---

Robin Hood', *NMS* 37 (1993), pp. 90–101, at 90, reprinted in Knight, *Anthology*, p. 364.

[50] Child (1861), pp. 43–44; Hunter, p. 21; followed by Singman, *Robin Hood: The Shaping of the Legend*, pp. 14–16.

[51] J. B. Bessinger, '*The Gest of Robin Hood* Revisited', in *The Lered and the Lewed*, ed. L. D. Benson (Cambridge, Mass., 1974), reprinted in Knight, *Anthology*, pp. 39–50, at 48.

[52] Pollard, *Imagining Robin Hood*, pp. 4–5.

[53] Hoyle, 'A Re-Reading of the Gest of Robyn Hode', pp. 69, 75, 109.

the resulting conflict, and finally the outlaw's departure from court and much later death at Kirklees rounds off the complex structure of the whole in a rather peremptory fashion.

Mark Truesdale, in the most recent contribution to the debate about the elements in the story, tries to fit the story of the king and the outlaw into an established tradition, characterised as 'the king incognito', or the 'king and commoner', some elements of which he traces back to classical antiquity. It was represented in medieval England by stories such as that of King Alfred burning the cakes, found in the twelfth century annals of St Neots, and a story about Henry II (1154-89) recorded by Gerald of Wales in the early thirteenth. The story in the *Gest* is only one of six known fifteenth-century examples of the genre. The earliest of these is the tale of *King Edward and the Shepherd*, which Truesdale dates to between about 1400 and 1450, and which is found in the same manuscript that also includes *Robin Hood and the Monk*. The story in the last two fyttes of the *Gest* are identified as the latest of that group, and Truesdale dates it to c.1495. These stories all include unique details and variations but have a standard basic plot, in which a monarch, lost in a forest, is unrecognised by a commoner, who complains to him about unjust laws and oppression by royal officials. They feast together and the king invites the commoner to visit him in return, and, when his true identity is revealed to the by-now frightened commoner, the king rewards him with a position at court.[54] Truesdale asserts that these stories characteristically 'merrily invert norms and twist expectations', 'breaching boundaries ... presenting the commoner as a satiric mock king, and the king as an ignorant ... fool'. In this particular version, however, the king actively disguises himself as an abbot to meet the outlaw, while in most of the others the encounter between the two is accidental, with the king becoming lost and separated from his companions.

The tale begins with at least the implication that Robin was a real historical figure. The second stanza notes that 'Robyn was a prude outlaw, Whyles he walked on grounde'. The main story is that of *Robin Hood and the Knight*, which takes up the first two of the eight fyttes into which the Gest is divided. It concerns Robin's dealings with a poor, indebted knight, and begins at the outlaws' camp in Barnsdale. We are told that Robin, because of his veneration for the Virgin Mary, will not attack any company containing women. He tells his men that they are not to harm husbandmen, yeomen, knights or squires, but that they can severely treat bishops, archbishops and, especially, the high sheriff of Nottingham. Robin will not dine until he has a guest to entertain. He sends Little John, Much the Miller's son and Will Scathlock to a place called 'the Saylis' on Watling Street, to waylay an earl, baron, abbot or

---

54 Truesdale, *The King and the Commoner Tradition*, pp. 98–106, 172–76.

knight. There they in fact meet a knight, who is in a poor and sorry state, with his foot only in one stirrup on his horse and his hood hanging in two parts. In conversation with Little John, he says that he has heard that Robin is a 'good yeoman' and agrees to come to dinner, although he had intended to go on to dine at Blyth or Doncaster, and they bring him to the lodge door. After eating a dinner of bread, wine, deer entrails, swans, pheasants and river fowl, which the knight says was his best meal for three weeks, he explains to Robin that he is unable to pay. He has no more than ten shillings, a fact confirmed by Little John's search of his baggage, and that is through no fault of his own. He explains that, although he is of an ancient knightly family, he has had to mortgage his lands to the abbot of St Mary's at York, in return for a loan of £400. He needed it to help his son, who at the age of twenty had killed 'a knight of Lancaster' and a squire in a joust. He is on his way to York because the debt he owes is due for repayment on the next day. He expects to lose his land and, having been deserted by his friends because of his poverty, and with no-one to borrow from, he intends to travel to the Holy Land. He bursts into tears, but Robin befriends him, lends him £400 repayable in one year, with the Virgin Mary as the only guarantor for repayment. He also provides him with new livery and a horse, a grey courser, plus a palfrey and a pair of gilt spurs, and lends him Little John as a servant. With this the first fytte comes to an end, but the story immediately continues and is concluded in the second fytte.

The knight goes to York to repay the abbot on the following day, because otherwise he will be disinherited and his land lost for ever. The abbot hopes that he will not be able to pay and that the land will therefore fall to him. His subordinate, the prior, expects the knight not to appear in time to redeem his property, because he thinks he must be suffering overseas. He warns the abbot however that it should be against his conscience to take the land. Then the abbey's cellarer arrives, saying that the knight must be dead, and the abbey would be able to spend £400 a year. He and the 'high justice of England', the abbot's legal advisor, resolve to disinherit the knight if he should not appear on that day and settle the debt. They think he will not come, but to their surprise he does, with his following, dressed in their 'simple weeds'. Refusing to let the porter stable their horses, the knight goes into the abbot's hall, where the lords are at dinner. Pretending at first to be unable to pay, he asks for an extension of the loan period, in return for faithful service, until he can pay. The abbot refuses and orders him to leave the hall, and the 'high justice of England' suggests that he should pay a further £200 more for the knight to release the claim on his land. The knight says that he would not do that even for £1000 and, to the consternation of the abbot and his associates, shakes £400 out of a bag, asserting that he will recover his land. He puts his better clothing back on, and returns home to his wife in Wyresdale, where he saves the money needed to repay Robin. He then sets off to do so, accompanied by a hundred men, but is delayed by stopping to help a yeoman, threatened by hostile rivals after winning a wrestling match; he does so because of his regard for Robin. Meanwhile in Barnsdale Robin awaits repayment.

The fourth fytte begins with a brief but inconsequential reference to the sheriff living in Nottingham. Meanwhile, in Barnsdale Robin and his men await the arrival of the knight with the money they are owed, with some impatience. Little John, Much and Scathlock are sent back to the Sayles to bring another guest from the road for dinner in the outlaw camp, this time a black monk. He has an escort of 52 men and seven pack horses, who are driven off when he is detained at bow-point, leaving just a page and a groom, while Robin is able to summon 140 yeomen. At dinner the monk proves to be the high cellarer of St Mary's, and Little John remarks that he must have brought the borrowed money as a messenger for the Virgin Mary, to whom the abbey is dedicated. He says he is carrying only 20 marks, but Little John finds £800 in his trunk, twice what was owed. The monk was on his way to a 'great moot' in London to bring a knight 'that rode so high on horse' into submission. The outlaws keep the money in the belief that it represents payment for the loan to the knight, since it had been pledged by the Virgin Mary, to whom the abbey is dedicated. The monk rues having dinner with the outlaw when it would have cost him less at Blyth or Doncaster. The knight finally arrives just before dusk to repay Robin the £400, explains that the delay was caused by his need to help the yeoman, and to make him a present of bows and arrows. Robin will not however accept payment and gives him £400 from the money taken from the cellarer. Thus, poetic justice is done.

The story of *Little John and the Sheriff of Nottingham* is intercalated between the two parts into which the story of Robin and the knight is divided, and forms the relatively short third fytte, an arrangement presumably made by the compiler of the *Gest*. After what is apparently a new beginning ('Lyth and lystyn gentilmen, all that nowe be here'), Little John, described as someone 'that was the knight's man', but using the name Reynold Greenleaf of Holderness, takes part in an archery contest watched by the sheriff. He is so impressed by John's shooting that he takes him into his service for a year for a fee of 20 marks, with the permission of his master the knight. Little John is already an enemy of the sheriff, and vows to be the worst servant that he has ever had. One Wednesday, while the sheriff is out hunting, John quarrels with his steward, who objects to his helping himself to food and drink in the absence of his master. The butler tries to shut the buttery door, but John strikes him and helps himself to ale and wine. The cook is however made of sterner stuff, and strikes John three times, impressing him with his boldness. They fight with swords over a distance of two miles, without injuries. John is so impressed with the cook's swordsmanship that he recruits him to Robin Hood's band for a fee of £20 and two changes of livery a year. After plundering the sheriff's treasury of £300 and valuable silver tableware, they run off to join Robin in the greenwood. Little John meets the sheriff, still on his hunt, and, promising to show him a fine hart, the leader of a herd of 140 deer, leads him to Robin's camp, where he is made to dine off his own stolen plate. The sheriff then spends a night in the forest in his shirt and breeches, and wrapped in a green mantle, the outlaw garb, which he regards as more uncomfortable than that of a hermit or friar. Rather than spend a year with the outlaws, or even another night in the forest, the sheriff is released after taking an oath not to pursue Robin or his men in future.

Next comes the story of *Robin Hood and the Sheriff of Nottingham*, beginning in the short fifth fytte, in which, after the departure of the knight, the sheriff organises an archery contest for the best archers in the North, the prize being a gold and silver arrow. Taking 140 of his men, Robin goes to Nottingham for the contest, six of them to shoot and the rest for protection in case the sheriff breaks his oath. The others shooting include Gilbert 'with the white hand', Little John, 'good Scathelocke', Much and Reynold (perhaps Reynold Greenleaf), but Robin wins the prize arrow. Then, as Robin is about to return to the greenwood, the outlaws are treacherously attacked by the sheriff's men, blowing loud horns, the sheriff thus breaking his promise made in the forest. They are driven off, but Little John is wounded in the knee by an arrow, and so cannot escape. Not wishing to be captured alive by the sheriff, John asks Robin to decapitate him with his sword. Robin and Much refuse to do so, and Much carries him on his back for many miles until they reach a castle, a little inside the wood, with walls and a double ditch. It belongs to Sir Richard at the Lee, not previously named but who is then identified as the knight that Robin had helped in the earlier story. The gates and drawbridge of the castle are closed, and it is besieged by the sheriff, but Sir Richard refuses to give up the outlaws.

The sixth fytte seems in its first two lines to hint at a new beginning ('Lythe and lysten gentylmen, and herken unto your songe'), then continues with the sheriff setting a siege, accusing the knight of being a traitor for protecting the king's enemies against the law. The knight insists that the sheriff consults the king about what he wishes to be done. The sheriff therefore goes to London to see the king, and tells him that the knight is trying to usurp his royal authority in the north by protecting the outlaws. The king promises to be at Nottingham within a fortnight to capture Robin and the knight, and sends the sheriff to raise more archers. Robin and Little John, the latter now recovered from the arrow in his knee, return to the forest, but Sir Richard is captured by the sheriff while out hawking on the riverside. He is led, bound hand and foot, towards imprisonment in Nottingham. His wife rushes to the forest to tell Robin, and asks him to prevent the death of her husband. Robin, taking over 140 archers with him, quickly rescues the knight in a Nottingham street. Robin shoots the sheriff with an arrow and then cuts off his head, while his men attack the sheriff's men with swords. The outlaw leader takes Sir Richard to the greenwood for safety, leaving his horse behind, until they can secure a pardon from 'Edward, our comely king', now named for the first time.

This leads on to the seventh fytte and the story of *Robin Hood and King Edward*, in which the king comes to Nottingham to capture the knight and Robin Hood, seizing all Sir Richard's lands. He then travels on to Lancashire, reaching Plumpton Park and finding his deer herds there very depleted, leaving scarcely one deer with 'any good horn'. He is full of rage against Robin, and also promises that if anyone can bring him Sir Richard's head he will give that man his lands for ever by issuing a royal charter. However, a 'fayre olde knyght' tells the king that no-one could obtain those lands while Robin Hood can carry a bow, so that he would be well-advised not to make a grant of the lands to anyone whom he wished well. Edward then spends over six months at Nottingham but cannot find and capture Robin, who meanwhile kills as many of the royal deer as he wishes. On the advice of a 'proud forester', the king goes into the greenwood, guided by the forester, with five of his knights, disguised as an abbot with some of his monks, to encounter the outlaw. When they do so, they are of course apprehended by Robin, who points out that his men are yeomen of the forest, by necessity having to live on the king's deer, whereas the supposed abbot has churches, rents and gold. The outlaw demands money from them, but the disguised king claims that he has only £40, because of the expenses he has just incurred by spending two weeks at the king's court in Nottingham. He gives the £40 to Robin, who distributes half of it to his men and gives the rest back to the supposed abbot. The latter then produces a letter sealed with the king's seal, and says he has been ordered by the king to give it to Robin to summon him to Nottingham to enjoy royal hospitality. Expressing his love for the king, Robin takes the abbot hunting deer so that they can dine together 'under my trystell tre'.55 He then summons 140 of his men by blowing his horn. Their loyalty to their leader greatly impresses the monarch, since they are so completely at his bidding, more so than his own men are to him. The outlaws entertain the monks to a dinner of the king's deer, good white bread, red wine and ale, and Robin says that he wants the abbot to tell the king about the life he and his men lead. Afterwards Robin organises an archery contest in which those missing a difficult target, including Little

---

55 The expression 'trystel' tree, in its variant spellings, has more than one meaning in the *Gest*. For the fullest account, see Pollard, *Imagining Robin Hood*, pp. 51–53, 230.

John and Scathlock, suffer a clout on the head. One of Robin's arrows misses, so he allows the supposed abbot to buffet him. He does it so hard that Robin and Sir Richard look closely at him, then recognising him as the king. Now on their knees, Robin and Sir Richard ask for mercy. All are pardoned, and the king asks Robin and his men to come and serve him at court. Robin agrees, and takes 143 of his men with him, although he says that if he does not like being in the king's service he will return and shoot the king's deer as he has been accustomed to do.

In the eighth and final fytte, the tale continues with the king and his followers, all being clothed in Lincoln green cloth provided by Robin, casting away their grey clothing. They and the outlaws all go to Nottingham, shooting arrows and giving and receiving buffets as before. They momentarily alarm the inhabitants, who fear that the king has been killed by the outlaws. The king then restores Sir Richard at the Lee's land to him. The story then proceeds at a much faster pace to its conclusion. Robin stays at the royal court for only fifteen months, spending £100 on his men's pay, as well as other money on both knights and squires, to gain him 'great renown'. In the end he has only two men left, Little John and Scathlock, all his wealth having been spent. He recalls that he had earlier been the best archer in England, and begins to feel that he will die of sorrow if he remains with the king. He obtains royal permission to spend a week visiting a chapel he had established in Barnsdale. When in the greenwood he cannot resist the temptation to shoot a large hart. He then blows his horn, and 140 young men assemble and acknowledge him as their master. He stays in the greenwood for 22 years, fearing to go again to King Edward after leaving his court and failing to return. In the end Robin is betrayed by a wicked woman, the prioress of Kirklees, who is related to him but who plots with her lover, Sir Roger of Doncaster (or Donkesley) to kill him, for a reason which is not explicitly stated. Robin decides to go to Kirklees to be bled, but is betrayed by the wicked pair. The story ends with a lament for Robin, 'for he was a good outlaw and did poor men much good'.

Robin Hood's Death

Robin Hood's Death is one of two items about the outlaw known from the famous and partly damaged manuscript now known as the 'Percy Folio', found by Thomas Percy, bishop of Dromore (1729-1811), probably in 1753, in a country house at Shifnal in Shropshire owned by his friend Humphrey Pitt.[56] After Pitt had given the book to him, and when he was planning to lend it to Dr Samuel Johnson, he had it bound in half-calf by a binder who pared off the top and bottom lines of text in various places.

---

[56] For the story of the manuscript and its publication, see p. 68.

The manuscript was written in the middle of the seventeenth century, perhaps in the 1640s, since events from that decade, like the siege of Newark, are mentioned in it.[57] Many of the texts in it were used by Percy in his *Reliques of English Poetry*, first published in London in 1765 and reprinted many times, but he did not include *Robin Hood's Death* in that printed collection.[58] It is clear that this story, and also *Robin Hood and Guy of Gisborne*, were composed much earlier than the others included in the manuscript. *Robin Hood's Death* gives a much fuller account of the outlaw's demise than is found in the briefer details given at the end of the *Gest*, but it is quite consistent with the former in what it does provide. However, because only half of each page of this part of the Percy Folio has survived, about half of the story, which probably consisted of more than fifty stanzas, is missing; what remains has long been designated as the 'A' version. An eighteenth-century edition of the story, often referred to as the 'B' or Garland version, and which is complete, suggests what some of the missing material might have been, but it cannot be relied upon since in some respects it differs in content as well as style from the earlier version. The 'B' version did however enter public consciousness before the 'A', because it was first published in York in about 1767.[59]

The 'A' version begins with Robin going to Kirklees to be bled. Will Scathlock advises him to take fifty of his best bowmen with him for protection, as there is a 'good yeoman' who will be sure to try and molest him. However, he insists on travelling with Little John alone. When they reach a stream and lay a plank over it in order to cross, an old woman kneels on it and curses Robin. Half a page is missing at this point, so we do not know what the curse was, and this part of the story is not included in the 'B' version. After the gap the story resumes with Robin saying that the prioress of Kirklees is his cousin and that he can be certain that she will not harm him, and so they travel to the priory. The prioress lets Robin in, he gives her £20 in gold, and she begins to bleed him with lancing knives; his blood is at first thick, but then it becomes thin and Robin begins to suspect treachery. At that point another missing half-page breaks the narrative again. When it resumes, Robin is being attacked by Red Roger, presumably the equivalent of the Sir Roger of Donkesly or Doncaster who appears in the *Gest*, who wounds him in the side with a sword. Robin wounds his adversary between the head and the shoulders and leaves him to die, because he wants to receive the last rites himself. Little John asks Robin to allow him to burn down

---

[57] BL, Add MS 27879, f. 97v.
[58] *Bishop Percy's Folio Manuscript: Ballads and Romances*, ed. J. W. Hales and F. J. Furnivall, 3 vols. (London, 1867–68), vol. I, pp. xii–xiii, 53–58. See also Chapter 3.
[59] On these texts, see in particular D&T, pp. 133–39, and the references cited there.

the priory, but he will not agree because he fears what God will do if he harms a widow just before his own death. Instead, he asks John to carry him out into the road, and to make him a grave of gravel and grit, placing his sword at his head, his arrows at his feet and his bow by his side. From that point the remainder of the poem is missing.

The 'B' version, written in much more modern English and clearly of much later date than 'A', possibly as late as the first half of the eighteenth century, gives more attention to the details of what happened at Kirklees, but makes no reference to any equivalent of Red Roger. It does mention a story that Robin shot an arrow to determine where the site of his grave should be, and also the existence of an eight-line epitaph alleged to be upon the grave, which is recited. Although the date of the origin of the story of the arrow is unknown, it is certain that it was at too late a date to allow this version of the tale to be regarded as part of the medieval outlaw legend.[60]

Robin Hood and Guy of Gisborne

Robin Hood and Guy of Gisborne is known only from the 'Percy Folio'. It is fortunately to be found in an undamaged section of the manuscript. It apparently lacks only a few lines omitted by a scribe's copying error, although some confusion in parts of the story implies that the text is somewhat corrupt.[61] Robin tells of a dream in which he is beaten by two strong yeomen and his bow taken. Telling his men to make ready, he sets off for the greenwood with Little John to seek the yeomen. They see one leaning against a tree, clothed in horse-hide and bearing a sword and dagger. Little John offers to check on him for Robin, but Robin wants to do so himself and roughly rebukes him. Little John angrily sets off for Barnsdale, where he finds two of the band dead and Scarlock trying to escape from 140 of the sheriff's men, who are chasing him. John shoots one of the sheriff's men, William a Trent, but the bow is weak and breaks. He is captured and tied to a tree. The sheriff tells him that he will be hung, but he remains defiant. Meanwhile Robin meets the yeoman, referred to as Guy, who says he is lost, so Robin offers to show him the way. Guy says he is seeking an outlaw called Robin Hood. They agree to compete with each other at archery in the woods, in the hope that they will come across Robin there. Robin impresses Guy with his shooting, and is asked who he is. He will not reveal his own identity until Guy has done so. Guy says he is Guy of Gisborne, and Robin replies: 'My name is Robin Hood of Barnsdale, a fellow thou hast long sought'. They fight with swords for two hours. Robin stumbles and is wounded in the side, but, after calling

---

[60] For the site at Kirklees, see pp. 141–44.
[61] BL, Add. MS 27879, ff. 129r–130v; *Bishop Percy's Folio Manuscript*, I, pp. 102–16; D&T, pp. 140–41.

on the Virgin Mary, leaps up and kills Guy. He sticks his severed head at the end of his bow, slashing it with an Irish knife to make it unrecognisable. He dons Guy's clothing, takes his bow, arrows and horn, and sets off to Barnsdale to see how his men are faring. He blows the horn, and the sheriff of Nottingham takes it as a signal that Guy has killed Robin. Robin comes to him, still disguised as Guy, and says that rather than take the sheriff's gold the only reward he wants to be allowed is to strike Robin Hood's servant Little John. The puzzled sheriff agrees, and Robin cuts Little John loose, again with an Irish knife, and hands him Guy's bow. Seeing him draw it, the sheriff flees towards his house in Nottingham and his men scatter, but he cannot run fast enough and Little John cuts his heart in two with an arrow.

The appearance of an Irish knife in this tale has been the subject of some interest, and it can be interpreted in very different ways by historians and literary scholars. It provides an excellent example of the contrast between different assumptions and approaches to the legend. With the knife, Robin both nicks and disfigures Guy's severed head, and later cuts the ropes binding Little John (stanzas 42 and 55). The historian would take this simply to mean a knife of a type known to have been of Irish origin, and perhaps quote a description of one used on 8 September 1303 by a Norfolk woman to kill a man in a house at Attleborough, 'with an Irish knife ... of which the handle was of ash and the blade of iron and steel'.[62] Additionally, they might point out that the term may also have referred to what was subsequently known as an Irish skein or skene, and marshal evidence tracing its development. This relatively large weapon is illustrated in a slightly smaller form in the drawing of Chaucer inserted into some copies of Hoccleve's *De Regimine Principis*, hanging from a button on his breast.[63] The will of John Baddesworth, rector of Laxton in Nottinghamshire, dated 2 February 1472/3, indicates that he left a 'baselard vocatum Iresch skene ornatum cum auro et argento [a baselard [sc. of the type] called Irish skene, decorated with gold and silver]'.[64] This suggests that, by the time of the widespread currency of the established Robin Hood stories, an Irish knife, whether or not it had been used earlier by common criminals, also had an ornamental function which justified its encrustation with gold and silver and its possession by the leading

---

[62] TNA, KB 27/178, rot. 63: 'cum uno cultello hibernie ... unde mannbrum fuit de fraxino et cindula de ferre et assero'; AALT-IMG 5995.
[63] BL Harleian MS. 4866; Cotton Otho A 18; Sloane 5141; H. Todd, *Illustrations of Gower and Chaucer* (London, 1810), glossary, citing T. Ewing and others, *Collectanea de Rebus Hibernicis* (4 vols., Dublin, 1770–84), IV (1784), no. 13, plates 3–4.
[64] H. L. Blackmore, *Hunting Weapons from the Middle Ages to the Twentieth Century* (1971), pp. 53–54; *Testamenta Eboracensium* III, ed. J. Raine, Surtees Society XLV (1865), p. 202, no. lix.

clergyman of an important Nottinghamshire village. However, it was still also a military weapon, for the Irish men fighting in the rebel army against Henry VII at East Stoke in 1487 were, according to Sir Francis Bacon, armed mainly with 'skaynes'.[65] So, by the time of the earliest surviving tales, the Irish knife was a well-known implement in England, but no written evidence of a weapon known by that name before 1300 has yet been found.[66] Literary scholars who have written about the story eschewed any temporal context. George Swan has contended that the word 'Irish' used in this tale is not an attribution of that form of knife to a Hibernian cultural background, but is rather a pun on Old French *irais*, meaning bad-tempered or wrathful, thus being a reference to the wrath the two protagonists in the tale feel towards each other. It incorporates demonstrable literary turns far removed from any objective record of fact, and the Irish knife brandished by Robin is probably an ironic pun.[67] Stuart Kane, on the other hand, regards the tale as one which 'peculiarly embodies the anticipation, deferral, and finally the performance of violence across the ambiguously coded bodies of its protagonists', and which is characterised by 'the excessive focus of the narrator on the poem's bodies'. The knife is merely the implement which happens to be used.[68]

The Play of Robin Hood and the Sheriff

The final item of the body of medieval Robin Hood literature is a 21-line fragment of a play, *Robin Hood and the Sheriff*, which has survived among the archives of Trinity College, Cambridge.[69] Each line is in effect two, since the first part rhymes with the second. There is no title to the piece in the manuscript, and the one usually applied derives from the probable reference to it made in one of the letters of the Paston family of fifteenth-century Norfolk. Ohlgren has characterised it as 'the schematic text' for a play, while David Wiles sees it as little more than 'a scenario or mnemonic providing a framework for improvisation'.[70] The content of the fragment

---

[65] *Bacon's History of the Reign of King Henry VII*, ed. J. R. Lumby (Cambridge, 1885), p. 37. For skeens as an Irish infantry weapon see also C. Falls, *Elizabeth's Irish Wars* (1950), p. 69. *Oxford English Dictionary* XV, p. 591 has no reference to the name earlier than a will of 1527.

[66] For a late-thirteenth century reference to a Welsh knife (*un cutel galays*), see the legal treatise *Placita Corone*, ed. J. M. Kaye, Selden Society Supplementary Series IV (1966), p. 3.

[67] G. Swan, "Robin Hood's 'Irish Knife'", *University of Mississippi Studies in English*, N. S. 11–12 (1993–95), pp. 51–80.

[68] S. Kane, 'Horseplay: Robin Hood, Guy of Gisborne, and the Neg(oti)ation of the Bestial', in Hahn, *Popular Culture*, pp. 101–10, at 101–02.

[69] Cambridge, Trinity College, MS. R.2.64. On the history of the manuscript, see D&T, pp. 203–04.

[70] D. Wiles, *The Early Plays of Robin Hood* (Cambridge, 1981), p. 37.

is clearly closely related to *Robin Hood and Guy of Gisborne*, of which it seems to be a dramatic version, and so is useful in confirming beyond doubt that the story of Guy is of medieval origin. It is written on a single piece of paper, on the other side of which is a short account of six receipts recording payments, made by Richard Wytway to John Sterndalle, for the rent of a named property. The third payment is dated to 1475/6, and so the play fragment was probably written down at about that date.[71] It is therefore apparently the third-oldest Robin Hood manuscript, following those of the *Monk* and the *Potter*, and is noteworthy for being the earliest text to include Friar Tuck, who does not appear in *Robin Hood and Guy of Gisborne*.

The play lacks the clear narrative of the ballads and is at some points difficult to make sense of. It begins with an unnamed knight agreeing with a sheriff to capture Robin Hood for him for a reward. He meets Robin under a linden tree in the greenwood, and they compete at shooting, throwing a stone and wrestling, Robin winning all three contests. The knight then recognises his opponent. They fight, Robin kills him, puts on his clothing and carries his severed head in his hood. Robin's men have meanwhile been captured by the sheriff; mention is made of Friar Tuck shooting his bow, presumably at the sheriff's men. The fragment ends with them contemplating captivity, and the assumption may perhaps be that in the missing part of the story Robin, probably through his disguise, contrives to rescue them.

One of the letters of the Paston family, written by John Paston II to his brother John Paston III, and dated 16 April 1473, mentions a servant called W. Woode, a horsekeeper, one of whose functions in the Paston household was to perform a play about Robin Hood and the sheriff of Nottingham. He had 'kepyd hym thys iij yere to pleye Seynt Jorge and Robynhod and the shryff off Notyngham, and now when I wolde have good horse he is goone in-to Bernysdale, and I wyth-owt a keper'.[72] Clearly he had left Paston's service unexpectedly, after earlier having been employed in 1469 to defend Caister castle against the duke of Norfolk, a very important task.[73] The manuscript of the play and many of the family's letters once belonged to Peter le Neve (1661-1729), a keeper of government records in the Chapter House of Westminster abbey, so it is probable that the play was once part of the Paston collection and is the one the performance of which is referred to in the letter. If so, it is probably the only Robin Hood

---

71 Ohlgren and Matheson, *Early Rymes*, p. 39. This item was first noticed by Child, when it was in the possession of William Aldis Wright of Trinity College: Child (1889), p. 90.
72 N. Davis, *Paston Letters and Papers of the Fifteenth Century*, 2 vols. (Oxford, 1971), I, no. 275; see also J. Marshall, '"goon in Berynsdale": The Trail of the Paston Robin Hood Play', *Leeds Studies in English* 29 (1998), pp. 185-217.
73 J. H. Harvey, ed., *William Worcestre Itineraries* (Oxford, 1969), p. 190.

item now surviving that was used for a Robin Hood performance before 1500. Nevertheless, it was certainly not the first Robin Hood play, because there is evidence that one was performed in 1427. The Exeter receivers' rolls for 1426-7 record that some unnamed players were given 20d for playing the play of Robin Hood (*dato lusoribus ludentibus lusum Robyn Hood*) before the mayor.[74] Nothing, however, is known of the nature of their performance, nor whether it had any relationship to the Robin Hood 'riots' held by the young men of a parish in the city in 1510, subject to punishment by the mayor since it was not held on a holy day.[75]

Wiles has disputed the interpretation which makes the play an adaptation of *Robin Hood and Guy of Gisborne*, pointing out what he considers significant differences from the ballad, and denies that it is unfinished.[76] According to his alternative reading, it consists of two playlets. The first, up to the point at which Robin puts Guy's head in his hood, is based on at least the same source as Guy's tale, although he points out a few significant differences. The second, which he thinks has no apparent connection with the ballad, is not cut short but is complete, because it ends with the sheriff and his men, not Robin and his, being pushed into a prison after the latter turns the tables in a fight. Wiles emphasises the shortness of the text, which he sees as providing only a framework for improvised physical activities, including archery and fights, and provides a version of the text with appropriate stage directions added. He sees those activities as taking place on the village green, not in the Paston household, and as part of the May Games.[77] More recently, John Marshall has argued that that it is improbable that the play inspired the ballad because the latter was more elaborate, and the former takes from the ballad only the characters, narrative outline and fragments of dialogue needed to make the action, to which text is subordinated, comprehensible to the intended audience. Sometimes the identity of speakers is not given but rather deduced from a preceding or following speaker who is named. Marshall thinks that, rather than looking at the play as a crude adaptation of the ballad, or the ballad as a sophisticated embellishment of the play, it is better to view the ballad 'as providing the literary framework that contextualises a series of physical contests'. After a detailed chronological comparison of the relationship between the two texts, highlighting their similarities and differences and their possible significance, he concludes that 'the play strips the ballad to a skeletal plot sufficient to explain the heroic action with which it is primarily concerned'.[78]

---

[74] *REED Devon*, ed. J. M. Wasson (Toronto, 1986), p. 89.
[75] *REED Devon*, pp. xvii, 119.
[76] Wiles, *The Early Plays of Robin Hood*, pp. 33-36.
[77] On the May Games, see Chapter 2.
[78] J. Marshall, 'Playing the Game: Reconstructing *Robin Hood and the Sheriff of Nottingham*', in Hahn, *Popular Culture*, pp. 161-74.

The early tales: what they do *not* contain

These acknowledged medieval tales of Robin Hood lack many, perhaps most, of the elements and themes that in the early twenty-first century are popularly taken for granted as being parts of the outlaw legend. The *Gest* is set in the time of a King Edward, and there is no mention of King Richard I or his successor, King John. The early tales are set in Barnsdale as well as Sherwood Forest, and in fact Barnsdale is the more prominent of the two locations. They contain no suggestion that Robin Hood is a dispossessed nobleman, the earl of Huntingdon, and he is explicitly stated to be a yeoman. He does not rob the rich in order to give to the poor, although he does help an impoverished and deserving knight. There is no hint that he was a Saxon hero fighting against the oppressive Norman conquerors, like Hereward the Wake. He is not a social rebel, taking the part of downtrodden peasants against landlords, or opposing taxation, in the style of modern revolutionaries. The only tax mentioned in any of the early tales is an urban one, pavage. Although Robin feeds himself illegally on the king's deer, there is nothing in the tales explicitly condemning the forest laws or the officials who administered them. The forest setting of the outlaw may itself be a later accretion to the earliest form of the legend. The stories have no supernatural element. They contain no Maid Marian, no Allen a Dale, and no Friar Tuck, although the latter does appear in the play *Robin Hood and the Sheriff*. The only regular characters are Robin himself, Little John, Will Scathlock (variously spelt), Much the miller's son and the sheriff of Nottingham. Robin has no connection with a place called Locksley or Loxley, wherever situated, and he fights with the sword, not the quarter staff. Such details have become either central or peripheral parts of the legend as a result of developments since the fifteenth century. The origins of some of them can be fairly precisely dated and explained, while others are not so readily accounted for. The next three chapters will go on to consider the development of the legend from the fifteenth to the nineteenth centuries, and the variety of views about its significance that have emerged from intensive academic debate during the later twentieth century and the first two decades of the twenty-first.

Chapter 2

Chroniclers, Revellers, Playwrights and Antiquarians, c.1420–1765

Chroniclers and historians: early attempts to date Robin Hood

The *Vision of Piers the Plowman* from the late 1370s or early 1380s makes the earliest dated reference to the existence of tales of Robin Hood.[1] Other references or allusions to the outlaw occur in England in the late fourteenth and early fifteenth centuries, from the time of Geoffrey Chaucer (d. 1400) onwards.[2] Chaucer's yeoman, who appears in the prologue of the *Canterbury Tales*, closely resembles Robin: both are of yeoman social status, skilled archers and carry bows and horns, and wear hoods. The Lettersnijder edition of the *Gest*, printed in 1508, even illustrates Robin by reusing the image of Chaucer's yeoman from the beginning of Pynson's printed edition of the *Canterbury Tales*, of c.1491, something first noticed by Frank Isaac in 1930.[3] Prominent among explicit references to the outlaw are criticisms by clergy. The treatise *Dives et Pauper* (c.1405-10) attacked those who preferred to visit the tavern to hear 'a songe of Robynhode' rather than attend Mass or Matins. Two sermons also referred to the legend with disgust: one the

---

[1] See p. 8.
[2] For details of these references, see T. H. Olgren and L. M. Matheson, *Early Rymes of Robyn Hood: An Edition of the Texts, ca. 1425 to ca. 1600*, Medieval and Renaissance Texts and Studies 428 (Tempe, Arizona, 2013), pp. xiii–xvi. For fifteenth-century variants of the saying that 'many speak of Robin Hood that never bent his bow', meaning that they comment on matters of which they have no personal experience, see D&T, p. 289.
[3] D&T, p. 35; Holt, *Robin Hood*, pp. 121–22; J. Marshall, 'Picturing Robin Hood in Early Print and Performance: 1500–1590', in *Images of Robin Hood: Medieval to Modern*, ed. L. Potter and J. Calhoun (Newark, Delaware, 2008), pp. 60–81, at 62–65.

undated context of which is a manuscript of an Oxfordshire parish priest, the other preached before king and parliament by the chancellor John Stafford, bishop of Bath and Wells, in 1433. The first complained that many men preferred fables to the Gospel, and a 'romaunce of Robyn Hode' to St. Paul's Epistles; the second thought that the tales threatened social harmony and respect for the clergy, and the people paid more heed to 'wanton prophets' like Robin Hood than to the prophets of God'.[4] Other references, however, are not overtly or even implicitly critical. A scribbled note, made in the early fifteenth century on a spare page of a fourteenth-century liturgical manuscript which survives in Lincoln cathedral library, perhaps by someone practising cursive handwriting and translation from English into Latin, merely describes the outlaw, said to be standing in Sherwood, his clothing, and his possession of 24 arrows.[5] In 1429 occurs the first example of the use of the phrase 'Robin Hood in Barnsdale stood' in verbal pleading by a serjeant at law in a case heard in one of the central courts of common law at Westminster. It was used as a way of insinuating that the pleading of the opposing serjeant in a case was irrelevant nonsense.[6] This was two years later than the first known reference to a performance of a Robin Hood play, in Exeter, and three years before a reference to the outlaw and several of his men included in a playful acrostic which used fictitious names for the pledges in a parliamentary election return for Wiltshire.[7] None of these references gives any indication as to when it was thought that he had lived, or even if he was thought to have been a real person at all. The first recorded thoughts on these issues came from Scotland, and they placed Robin in two different contexts in the second half of the thirteenth century.

Scottish chroniclers of the fifteenth century: Wyntoun and Bower

The legend of Robin Hood was well developed, popular and widely known in both England and Scotland by the fifteenth century. According to an Aberdeen burgh council register, a ship called alternately 'Robyne Hode'

[4] T. H. Ohlgren, *Robin Hood: The Early Poems, 1465-1560: Texts, Contexts, and Ideology* (Newark NJ, 2007), pp. 50–51.
[5] Lincoln Cathedral Library, MS. 132, f. 100v, first noticed by G. E. Morris, 'A Ryme of Robyn Hode', *Modern Language Review* 43 (1948), pp. 507–8. It is illustrated in Figure 6. For its importance, see also pp. 151–53.
[6] Ohlgren, *Robin Hood: The Early Poems*, p. 19. For the full list of known uses of the saying, with minor variants, in the Courts of Common Pleas and King's Bench, compiled by David Seipp, see ibid., p. 212. The latest example is from 1751. See also Singman, *Robin Hood*, pp. 148–49. The phrase was described in Nicholas Udall's translation of the *Apophthegmes of Erasmus* (ed. R. Roberts, Boston, 1877), pp. 83–84 as a 'another foolish song'.
[7] *REED Devon*, ed. J. M. Wasson (Toronto, 1986), p. 89; TNA, C 219/14/3, part 2, no. 101; Holt, *Robin Hood*, pp. 69–70.

or 'ly Robert Hude' lay at Aberdeen in 1438, and it has been suggested that the legend may have been transmitted there by Scottish monarchs and nobles (or perhaps their entourages) returning from exile or imprisonment in England.[8] However that may be, it was certain that at some point those who set out to give accounts of the histories of those countries would have to fit him into their chronological framework, however much they might disdain the 'foolish people' (*stolidum vulgus*) whose entertainments celebrated the famous outlaw. In Scotland historians attempted to place Robin in context several decades before any English writer is known to have done so. Andrew Wyntoun's *Metrical Chronicle* of about 1420 set Robin and Little John in Inglewood and Barnsdale in 1283-85:

> Than Litill Johne and Robyne rude
> Waichmen were commendit gud,
> In Yngilwod and Bernysdale,
> And usit þis tyme þar trawale.[9]

Wyntoun (*c.* 1350–*c.* 1422), became prior of St Serf's, Lochleven, in 1393, remaining in office until 1421.[10] In his chronicle he complained of old age and ill health, and it is his reference to these afflictions that has supplied the commonly accepted dates for his life. His work is a vernacular account of the history of the world and Scotland's place within it, and 1420 has long been accepted as the date of his final revision of the chronicle. In the prologue, the author tells us that he wrote it at the behest of Sir John Wemyss, a Fife landowner, who was constable of St Andrews Castle between 1383 and 1400. Although the exact nature of Wemyss's status as literary patron remains unclear, his interest in Wyntoun's work provides important evidence for the growing literary sophistication of the fifteenth-century laity in Scotland, and it was this secular audience that Wyntoun explicitly addressed in his chronicle. To judge by the number of surviving manuscript copies, it became very popular in fifteenth and sixteenth-century Scotland, although it was not published in print until 1795. His reference to Inglewood, the great Cumberland Forest between Carlisle and Penrith, has been generally assumed to have arisen from associating Robin Hood with Adam Bell, another yeoman outlaw who, with his companions Clim of the Clough and William of Cloudesley, according to legend hid there from their enemies, the justice, sheriff and mayor of Carlisle.[11]

---

[8] A. J. Mill, *Medieval Plays in Scotland* (Edinburgh, 1927), p. 23, note 1; D&T, p. 40 and note 2. Aberdeen burgh court registers are online at https://scotlandsplaces.gov.uk/digital-volumes/burgh-records/aberdeen-burgh-registers/.
[9] *The Original Chronicle of Andrew of Wyntoun*, ed. F. J. Amours, Scottish Text Society (5 vols., 1903–14), V (1907), pp. 136–37.
[10] ODNB, article on Wyntoun by C. Edington, accessed 5 May 2018.
[11] D&T, pp. 4, 260 n. 2.

Chroniclers, Revellers, Playwrights and Antiquarians

Walter Bower (1385-1449), the abbot of the monastery of Inchcolm in Fife from 1418, was a man of affairs and involved in the political life of Scotland. In the 1440s, at the request of a neighbouring laird, Sir David Stewart of Rosyth, he became engaged in continuing the chronicle of John of Fordun, the *Scotichronicon*, to his own time. John had written the *Scotichronicon* about 80 years earlier, ending his narrative in 1153. Bower's working copy of the chronicle still exists.[12] In two passages he placed Robin, Little John and their accomplices among the dispossessed followers of Simon de Montfort in 1266, the year after Simon's defeat and death at the battle of Evesham, a time 'of no peace, no security'.

> 'At this time there arose from among the disinherited and outlaws and raised his head that most famous armed robber Robert Hood, along with Little John and their accomplices. The foolish common folk eagerly celebrate the deeds of these men with gawping enthusiasm in comedies and tragedies, and take pleasure in hearing jesters and bards singing [of them] more than in other romances'.

In the second reference he mentioned Robin among the different groups resisting the king, but without the specific geographical information given about the others: 'amongst them Roger de Mortimer occupied the Welsh Marches and John Dayville occupied the Ile of Ely', but by contrast 'Robert Hood was an outlaw among the woodland briars and thorns'.[13] This strongly suggests that Bower was guessing where to place the outlaw chronologically as well as geographically, but at least assumed that he was a real individual. The reasons for Bower and Wyntoun's assignations of the outlaw to those two different dates are unknown: they cite no evidence for doing so, and their views do not carry any great conviction. Their knowledge may have derived solely from Scotland, since Bower at least is not known to have ventured outside his native land. Indeed, as Holt suggested, they may simply provide variants of a single tradition which made its way across the border from England in the fifteenth century.[14] They had no influence on the way matters developed in England, perhaps because they wrote before the invention of printing and too long before the English took an interest in the date of Robin's career.

---

12 Corpus Christi College, Cambridge, MS. 171.
13 S. Taylor, D. E. R. Watt, with B. Scott, eds., *Scotichronicon by Walter Bower* V (Aberdeen, 1990), pp. 354–57, 470; *ODNB*, entry by Watt, accessed 7 April 2018. See also Chapter 1.
14 Holt, *Robin Hood*, p. 52.

An English historical reference to Robin Hood, c.1460

The earliest known historical reference to Robin Hood in an English document occurs in a marginal annotation to a manuscript of Ranulf Higden's *Polychronicon*, which was written probably about 1420, when its chronological coverage ends. It was identified by Julian Luxford, who suggested in 2009 that the annotation was made in the 1460s. Luxford based this dating on the fact that a reference to the senior pro-Lancastrian justice Sir John Fortescue, very active in that decade but not before about 1461, was, like most of the annotations, written in the same hand.[15] The annotation places the outlaw in the reign of Edward I between 1294 and 1299. It is added to a page that begins in the middle of an account of English military activities in north Wales, going on to describe the accession of Pope Boniface VIII in 1294, and ends with Edward I's marriage to Margaret of France in 1299. The anonymous annotator included material relating to the diocese of Bath and Wells, and Luxford suggested that he was a member or associate of a Charterhouse in Somerset. He seems to have been as uncertain about the exact period during which the outlaw was active as Wyntoun and Bower had been, but like them assumed that he was a real person. Luxford also contends that the importance of this item of independent information may be further confirmed by the fact that, uniquely, he expressed a wholly negative opinion about Robin. That the author of the reference was clerical, and probably monastic, helps to explain his hostility.

The short inscription reads as follows: 'Circa hec tempora vulgus opinatur quemdam exlegatum dictum Robyn Hode cum suis complicibus assiduis latrocinijs apud Shirwode et alibi regios fideles Anglie infestasse.' Luxford translated this as 'Around this time, according to popular opinion, a certain outlaw named Robin Hood, with his accomplices, infested Sherwood and other law-abiding areas of England with continuous robberies'. However, in 2013 his translation was criticised by members of the Ranulph Higden Society, and their comments were posted on-line by Paul Booth.[16]

---

[15] J. M. Luxford, 'An English Chronicle Entry on Robin Hood', *Journal of Medieval History* XXXV (2009), pp. 70–76. It is found in Eton College MS 213, f. 234r, and is illustrated in Figure 1.

[16] 'A comment on Julian Luxford's discovery of an 'unpopular' Robin Hood', posted online in 2013: http://www.academia.edu/5456965/A_comment_on_Julian_Luxfords_discovery_of_an_unpopular_Robin_Hood; accessed 1 May 2018. Luxford read 'regios fideles' in the Latin text as 'law-abiding areas of England', while Booth argued that it should be translated as that he 'constantly attacked and stole from the faithful (servants) of the king of England'. 'For Luxford to be right, the Latin word has to be 'regiones', while 'regios', which is clearly written in the manuscript, is an adjective meaning 'belonging to, or associated with the king'. The idea that the note 'revealed resentment towards

FIGURE 1. Eton College MS 213, f. 234r, c. 1460. Fifteenth-century historians in England and Scotland assumed that Robin Hood had been a real individual, but did not know when he had lived. They therefore made reference to him at what seemed a suitable chronological point in their narratives. In this version of Ranulph Higden's *Polychronicon*, thought to have been written in Somerset, he is assumed to have been active in the 1290s, with the passage added about him being inserted, in a later and very different hand, and using the words 'at about this time', at the foot of the folio below the main narrative.

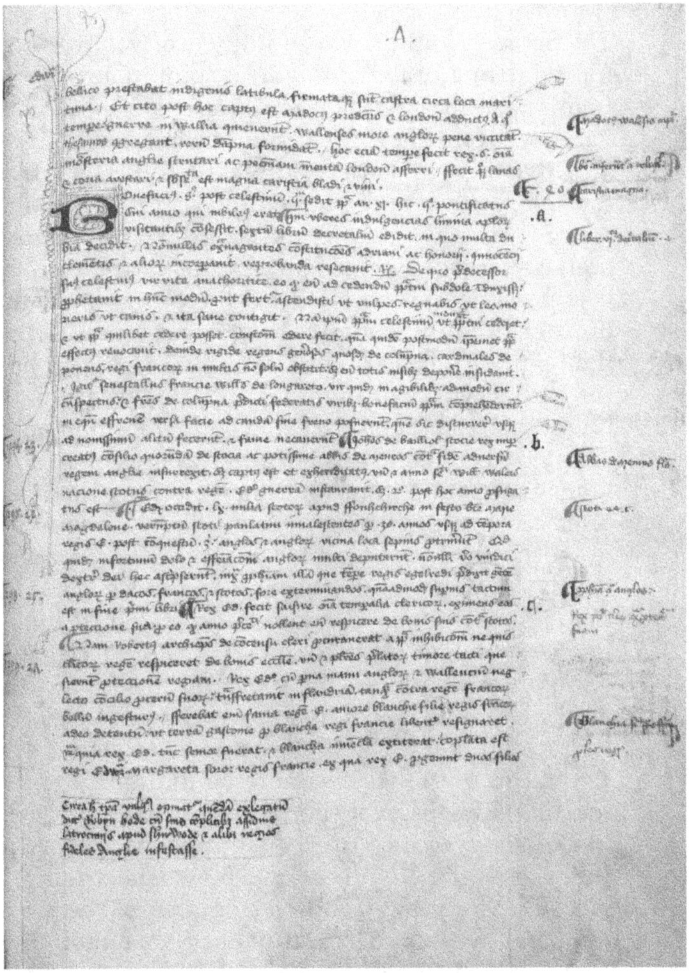

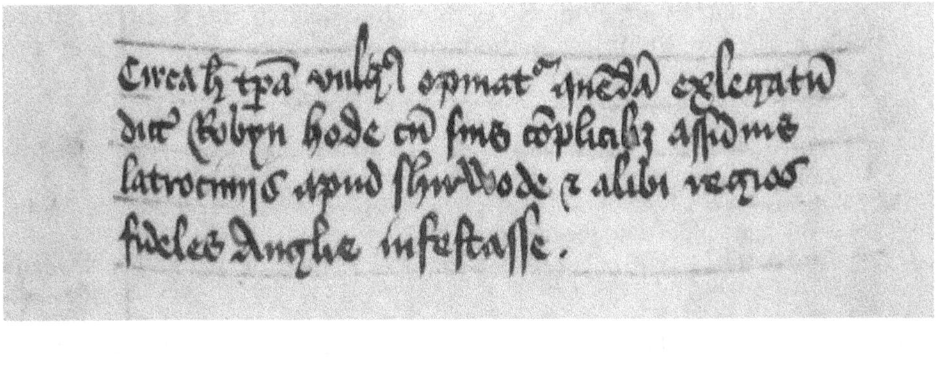

A Scottish academic, John Major

The Scottish author whose influence was from the beginning decisive for the dating of the outlaw was John Major, or Mair, of Haddington in Lothian (c.1469-1550) whose *Historia Majoris Britanniae* was published in Paris in 1521.[17] He was a distinguished university teacher of philosophy and theology in Paris until 1518, and again from 1525-31, spending the intervening and succeeding years in the universities at Glasgow and St Andrews. His book was the only history he wrote during a lifetime largely devoted to writing on philosophy and theology, and it is possible that he intended thereby to promote the idea of a union of England and Scotland. In it he assigned Robin for the first time to the reign of Richard I, but with the same lack of conviction evident in the earlier works of Wyntoun and Bower; nevertheless, there seems no doubt that, like them, he believed that Robin had been a real person. He inserted his reference to the outlaw between a moralising passage about kings who failed to produce heirs, with which he was rounding off his brief account of Richard's reign, before beginning to describe that of his successor King John. He began his paragraph about Robin with the words 'it was about this time, as I suppose' (*circa haec tempore ut auguror*) that there flourished those most famous robbers Robin Hood, an Englishman and Little John (...).'[18] More explicitly than his two predecessors, he was guessing about the historical context in which Robin was to be found. What his source of information was, or the reason why he guessed that Richard's reign was the right period, is one of the most significant mysteries encountered in the study of the legend, because it remains a widespread notion about Robin in the twenty-first century. Its decisive variance from the thirteenth-century dates in the 1260s and 1280s given by Wyntoun and Bower is striking, and suggests that he picked up a variant tradition from theirs. The source of such knowledge as he had was not necessarily Scottish, although Robin Hood was very well-known in Scotland; a Robin Hood and Little John game took place in Haddington, where he attended grammar school, in 1589, although there is no surviving evidence to show that such games were held there in Major's own lifetime.[19] As he remarked, 'the feats of this Robert are told in song all over Britain'.

Robin Hood among the general population and the clergy', is not therefore really borne out by the evidence.

[17] Reference has been made to the article in *ODNB* by Alexander Broadie. For his only known portrait, see Figure 2.

[18] J. Major, *Historia Majoris Britanniae*, ed. R. Fairbairn (Edinburgh, 1840), p. 128; A. Constable, ed., *A History of Greater Britain* (Scottish History Society X, 1892), pp. 156–57.

[19] J. L. Singman, *Robin Hood: The Shaping of the Legend* (Westport, Connecticut, 1998), p. 189.

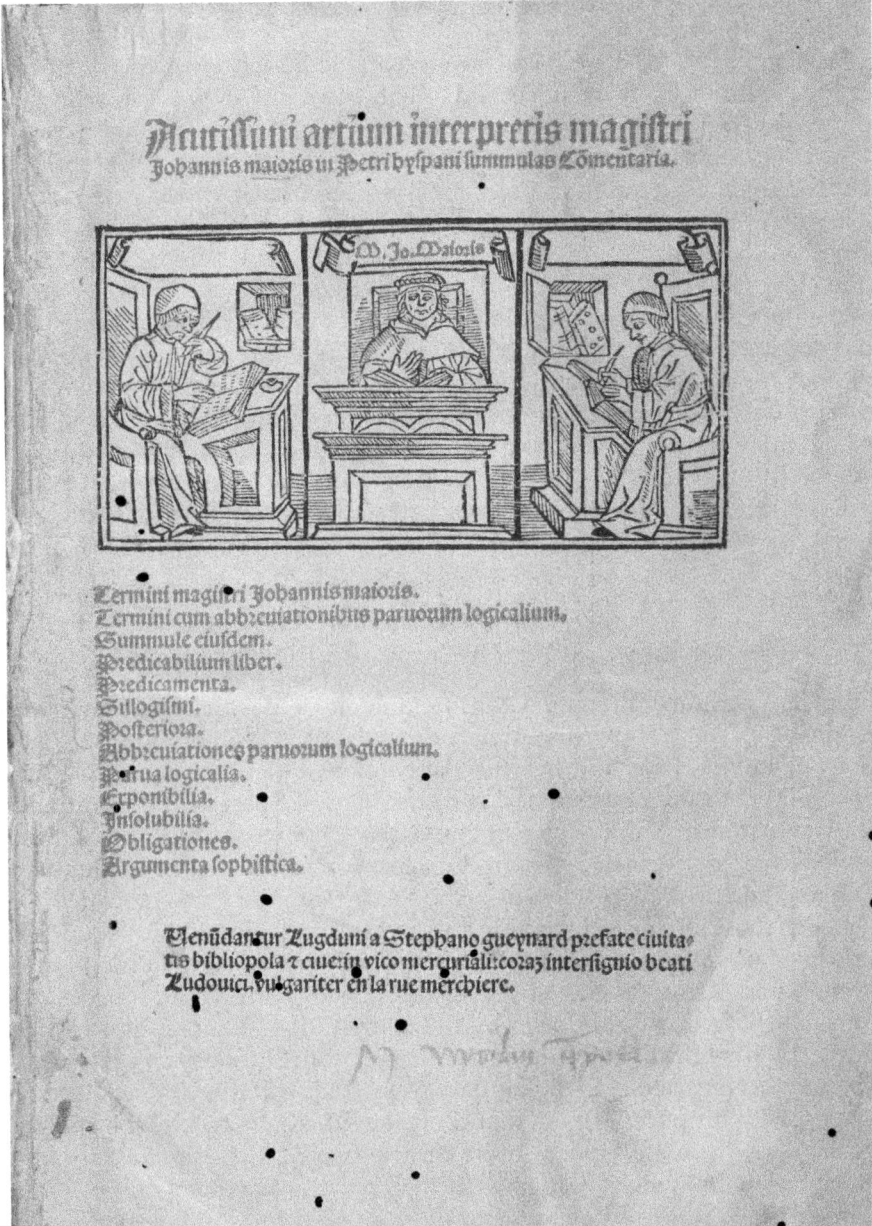

FIGURE 2. Title page to John Major's *In Petri Hyspani Summulas Commentaria* (Lyons, 1505). Peter of Spain was an obscure thirteenth-century logician. This is the only known portrait of Major, or Mair, an important Scottish academic, whose apparently casual attribution of Robin Hood to the reign of Richard I (1189-99) in 1521 has influenced the dating of the outlaw legend for 500 years.

Major tells us that he had 'seven years' experience' of the northern English, although it is uncertain what precisely it was or who the particular northern English were. Furthermore, as a young man in about 1491-2, on his way to study in Paris, he spent a year at Cambridge University and attended lectures for three months at what later became Christ's College. He may therefore have picked up knowledge of Robin Hood from English fellow students at Cambridge, where he noted that 'the students are all adults, and carry swords and bows'. He certainly picked up from somewhere the notion of Robin as a thief benevolent to the poor. 'He permitted no woman to be oppressed, nor stole the goods of poor men, indeed he enriched them with goods taken from abbots. I disapprove of his robbery, but he was the most humane and the prince of all thieves'. Major's dating of Robin and his comments about his character have had a profound influence on the legend down to the present day, although his characterisation of the outlaw as a 'prince of thieves' was not unprecedented.[20]

Robin Hood and the May Games: 'robbing the rich to give to the poor?'

From the later fifteenth century considerable and widespread documentary evidence exists to show that more peaceful and law-abiding impersonations of Robin Hood and his men, often alongside other characters like St George and the Dragon, had become a regular part of the traditional festivals of dances, sports, pageants and plays, known as the 'May Games', which were performed in some villages, towns and cities throughout England and Scotland in the spring and early summer.[21] No evidence has yet been found to indicate that they took place in Wales. Robin Hood was not an essential participant in the games, and was indeed not mentioned in the famous invective against them and against church ales, occasions for the selling of ale produced by the church to raise money for church funds, by the Elizabeth Puritan polemicist Phillip Stubbes (c. 1555-c.1610) in 1583.[22] Nevertheless, the outlaw was frequently included in such events, with his popularity in that context evidentially reaching its height in the early Tudor period. It even attracted royal interest, since in 1515 an elaborate 'maying' of Henry VIII took place at Shooter's Hill in Kent, while in 1503 James IV of Scotland gave a present to the Robin Hood of Perth.[23] Although for convenience the games are collectively related to

---

[20] See p. 197.
[21] R. Hutton, *The Rise and Fall of Merry England: The Ritual Year, 1400–1700* (Oxford, 1996), pp. 31–33, 60, 66–67, 100, 114.
[22] *Phillip Stubbes' Anatomy of the Abuses in England in Shakspere's Youth*, part 1, ed. F. J. Furnivall (London, 1877), pp. 147–53.
[23] Singman, *Robin Hood*, pp. 68–69.

May, some of them certainly took place in June, and Robin Hood's main activities normally took place around Whitsuntide. At Kingston upon Thames in Surrey, 'Robin Hood's gatherings', which are first recorded in 1506 and continued until 1539, are sometimes specifically said to have been made at Whitsuntide.[24] Such impersonations are known to have taken place in many counties in England at various dates between 1475 and 1652. Much of the evidence relates to the receipt of the income, payments for clothing or equipment for the use of those taking the parts of Robin Hood and his companions, or the provision of food and drink; and comes from the accounts of churchwardens, who normally organised these events in England, as well as from municipal records.[25]

The best surviving material comes from the southwest and the south, but there are examples from elsewhere. Robin Hood was associated with a church ale at Thame in Oxfordshire in 1475, and there are further references to him there in 1497 and 1502.[26] At Wells in Somerset in 1498 a 'time of Robin Hood', including exhibitions of dancing girls and church ales, was paid for by the corporation, while in 1513 11s. was received from 'Robin Hoods ale' at Tintinhull in the same county.[27] The gathering of money for the benefit of the church other than by church ales also took place. By 1477 and on until 1512, and again briefly in 1527, Robin was raising money for the church at Croscombe, near Wells, since payments, Robin Hood's 'recones' (reckonings), were brought in by the men, some of whose names are known, who were chosen to perform his role. In 1501, at the very least, Robin was assisted by a Little John. Money raised in Croscombe was first put towards the building of a new church house and then for a chapel at the east end of the north aisle of the church.[28] At Glastonbury in 1500, 40s. was received for Robin Hood

---

24 Singman, *Robin Hood*, pp. 179, 181–83.
25 Records of these events are being collected, along with other dramatic material, by the *Records of Early English Drama (REED)* project, based in Toronto, and many of the volumes have now been published, although not the important one for Surrey, and recent publications have been online. For a general account, see A. F. Johnson, 'The Robin Hood of the Records', in *Playing Robin Hood: The Legend as Performance in Five Centuries*, ed. L. Potter (Newark, New Jersey, 1998), pp. 27–44. For a useful summary of the known evidence, the chronology and geographical locations of these references, and maps, see Singman, *Robin Hood*, pp. 62–76.
26 Singman, *Robin Hood*, p. 181. The *REED* volume for Oxfordshire has not yet been published.
27 *REED Somerset, including Bath*, ed. J. Stokes and R. J. Alexander (2 vols., Toronto, 1996), pp. 231, 841.
28 *REED Somerset*, pp. 86–90, 126, 483–84, 532; Pollard, *Imagining Robin Hood*, pp. 169–70. Some of the men of Croscombe involved in the fundraising took part in the western rising against Henry VII in 1497, part of 'a tradition of protest against a corrupt government in defence of social order': Pollard, pp. 180–82, 249; and Pollard, 'Political Ideology in the Early Stories of Robin Hood', in J.

and the parishioners.²⁹ In St Lawrence's parish, Reading, Berkshire, the churchwardens were collecting 'the gatherings of Robin Hood' from 1498 to 1510,³⁰ while a 'Robin Hood's Bower' was erected at Abingdon in the same county in 1567.³¹

The extensive material for the four south-western counties is worth mentioning in detail. In Devon, at Ashburton, Robin appears in 1527 and then again in 1542; in Exeter in 1554 (with Little John); in Woodbury from 1541 to 1577 (with Little John), and in 1575 a house made of canvas was built for Robin there.³² In 1555 Robin Hood was introduced at Chagford, perhaps for the first time, and continued there until at least 1564.³³ His only recorded appearance at Chudleigh was in 1561 (with Little John), while in Braunton (again with Little John) he appears from 1561 to 1564.³⁴ In 1572 the Robin Hood of Colyton in Devon seems to have visited Honiton.³⁵ In Somerset Robin appears at Yeovil from 1517 to 1579, and in many years the names of those who played him there are recorded, but Little John occurs only once, in 1569, when his horn is mentioned.³⁶ In Dorset Robin is found at Bridport (1555-8), Netherbury (1566-8, with Little John) and Poole (1509-11). In Cornwall he is recorded at Antony (1554-9), Bodmin (1506), St Breock (1574-92), St Ives (1584-88) and Stratton

---

C. Appleby and P. Dalton, eds., *Outlaws in Medieval and Early Modern England: Crime, Government and Society* (Farnham, 2009), pp. 119–20, giving more detail.

29 *REED Somerset*, p. 126.
30 Berkshire Record Office, D/P 97/5/2, pp. 1, 84; https://ereed.library.utoronto.ca/records/berks-ridm253724448/; https://ereed.library.utoronto.ca/records/berks-ridm253220672/.
31 Abingdon, St. Helen's Churchwarden's Accounts (A), p. 16; https://ereed.library.utoronto.ca/records/berks-ridm243021552/; Singman, *Robin Hood*, p. 179. Even monks, traditionally enemies of Robin Hood, supported the gatherings. William More, prior of Worcester cathedral priory, made several contributions, recorded in his journal, from paying Robin and his men for 'a gathering to Tewksbury bridge' in 1519 to a small payment to the Robin Hood and Little John of Ombersley in 1535: *REED Herefordshire, Worcestershire*, ed. D. N. Klausner (Toronto, 1990), pp. 462, 503, 507, 513, 529. There is other evidence of visits by Robin Hood companies to neighbouring parishes to collect money. For example, Reading was visited from Henley (1504) and Finchampstead (1505), while the Kingston Robin Hood visited Croydon in 1515: Berkshire Record Office, Reading St Lawrence Churchwardens Accounts, D/P 97/5/2. pp. 21, 25; https://ereed.library.utoronto.ca/records/berks-ridm253562880/; https://ereed.library.utoronto.ca/records/berks-ridm253495632/; Kingston History Centre, Kingston Borough Archives, KG2/2/1, p. 74; Singman, *Robin Hood*, pp. 94, 180, 182. Henley's own Robin Hood's gatherings are mentioned in 1499 and 1520: Singman, *Robin Hood*, p. 181.
32 *REED Devon*, pp. xxv, 21, 25, 145, 284–85.
33 *REED Devon*, pp. 54–56.
34 *REED Devon*, pp. xxxv, 52, 57, 310.
35 *REED Devon*, p. 207; Singman, *Robin Hood*, p. 174.
36 *REED Somerset*, pp. 405–11.

(1536-44), where money was received in 1544 for the sale of Robin Hood's house.[37] St Breock hosted Robin Hoods from St Columb Minor in 1591 and Mawgan in 1592, and St Ives one from St Columb Major in 1588. Robin and Little John are also found together in 1526 in St Nicholas parish in Bristol.[38]

References in the south-east are rare, but in the City of London on 24 June 1559 there was a May Game involving Maid Marian and Friar Tuck as well as Robin and Little John, noted by a diarist.[39] In east Kent they were banned by the constable of Dover castle in 1528 but nevertheless evidently took place in New Romney in 1532.[40] Further north, a visitation of the hospital of St Mary at the Newarke in Leicester in 1525 reveals that the parishioners of St Margaret's brought their May Games, including representations of Robin Hood and St George, to entertain the canons and the poor folk in the alms house, for the profit of the church. In the following year the parish of St Leonard was owed 40s. by John Laverock for a Robin Hood play put on for the benefit of the church, while in 1534 the registrar of the archdeaconry court of Leicester claimed expenses incurred in participating in a Robin Hood game, including 16d. for 1½ yards of Kendal cloth, 4d. for a coat hired for two days, and 8d. for the loan of a sword and buckler.[41] At Melton Mowbray in the same county, 'Robin Hood's Money' was collected in 1555-56 and 1567.[42] In neighbouring Nottinghamshire, the county most often associated with the outlaw in popular imagination from the seventeenth century onwards, no examples have yet come to light, but in Shropshire Robin is found at Shrewsbury (1553), Ludlow (1567) and Bridgnorth (1588).[43] In the north of England, there was a Robin Hood and May Games at Burnley in Lancashire in 1579, and a possible reference in Manchester c.1555, but

---

[37] *REED Dorset, Cornwall*, ed. R. C. Hays and C. E. McGee, S. L. Joyce and E. S. Newlyn (Toronto, 1999), pp. 13, 32–33, 138, 230, 238, 332, 351, 397–400, 407, 439–40, 468–69, 471, 506–09, 516–17, 521–22, 594, 602, 605, 608.

[38] *REED Bristol*, ed. M. C. Pilkinton (Toronto, 1997), p. 37.

[39] *The Diary of Henry Machyn*, ed., J. G. Nichols, Camden Society XLII (London, 1847), p. 201. For earlier but not so clear London references in 1502, c.1531–45 and 1552, see Singman, *Robin Hood*, p. 180.

[40] *REED Kent, Diocese of Canterbury*, ed. J. M. Gibson (3 vols., Toronto, 2002), pp. 427, 770; *Records of Plays and Players in Kent, 1450–1642*, ed. G. E. Dawson, Collections Volume VII (Malone Society, Oxford, 1965), p. 133; Singman, *Robin Hood*, p. 184.

[41] *Visitations in the Diocese of Lincoln, 1517–31*, ed. A. H. Thompson, Lincoln Record Society XXXVII (1947), p. 145; A. P. Moore, 'Proceedings of the Ecclesiastical Courts in the Archdeaconry of Leicester, 1516–1535', *Associated Architectural Societies' Reports and Papers* 28:1 (1905), p. 202; W. Kelly, *Notices Illustrative of the Drama* (London, 1865), p. 61.

[42] Singman, *Robin Hood*, p. 67.

[43] *REED Shropshire*, ed. J. A. B. Somerset (2 vols., Toronto, 1994), pp. 19, 83, 203, 404, 632–33, 658.

none has been identified in Yorkshire, the traditional location of Robin Hood, before 1600, the earliest recorded being at Brandsby in 1616.[44] In Scotland Robin Hood games were important in Edinburgh throughout the sixteenth century, even after the Scottish parliament abolished them by statute in 1555, on pain of five years' imprisonment in burghs, a fine of £10 elsewhere, and, in the case of women, being put in a cookstool:

> it is statute and ordanit that in all tymes cumming na maner of persoun be chosin Robert Hude nor Lytill Johne, Abbot of Unressoun, quenis of Maii nor utherwyse, nouther in burgh nor to landwart, in ony tyme tocum, and gif ony provest, baillies, counsall and communitie chesis sic ane personage as Robert Hude, Lytill Johne, Abbottis of Unressoun or quenis of Maii within burgh, the chesaris of sic sall tyne thair fredome for the space of fyve yeiris and utherwyse salbe punist at the quenis grace will, and the acceptar of siclyke office salbe banist furth of the realme; and gif ony sic persounis sic as Robert Hude, Lytill Johne, Abbottis of Unressoun, quenis of Maii beis chosin outwith burgh and uthers landwart townis, the chesaris sall pay to our soverane lady x pundis and thair persounis put in waird thair to remane during the quenis grace plesoure; and gif ony wemen or uthers about simmer treis singand, makis perturbatioun to the quenis liegis in the passage throw burrowis and uthers landwart townis, the wemen perturbatouris, for skafrie of money or utherwyse, salbe takin, handellit and put upone the cukstulis of everie burgh or towne.[45]

They were also prominent in rural Lothian, the North Sea coast (Aberdeen, Perth, Dundee and St Andrews) and the southern lowlands (Dumfries and Ayr).[46]

Painted paper delivery badges, the equivalent of flags sold on a flag day, were, in those few places from which detailed evidence survives, pinned to those contributing, thus symbolically making their recipients members of Robin Hood's band. They were probably the 'small liveries' mentioned in the most detailed accounts. At Kingston upon Thames in 1506 2300 liveries and 2500 pins were prepared, although the numbers were usually much smaller, for example only 200 at Reading in 1502.[47]

---

44 *REED Lancashire*, ed. D. George (Toronto, 1991), pp. 6, 283; Singman, *Robin Hood*, pp. 185–86.
45 The actis and conventiounis of the Realme of Scotland maid in Parliamentis … anno domini 1566, f. clxviii v; National Archives of Scotland, PA7/1/14, ff.17r–v; online at http://www.rps.ac.uk/trans/A1555/6/33
46 Singman, *Robin Hood*, pp. 67–70, 187–92, gives the details.
47 Berkshire Record Office, D/P 97/5/2, p. 7; https://ereed.library.utoronto.ca/records/berks-ridm253690544/; D. Wiles, *The Early Plays of Robin Hood* (Cambridge, 1981), pp. 68–70; Holt, *Robin Hood*, p. 212. The 'great liveries' were the brightly-coloured uniforms prepared for Robin's immediate attendants, who at Kingston usually numbered about twenty. It was suggested by Holt that such 'Robin Hood's gatherings' were a possible origin of the

Maid Marian and Friar Tuck: Robin's companions in the May Games

The expenses for the games at Kingston include not only Robin and Little John but a friar (not actually called Tuck) and Maid Marian, who first appears in Kingston in 1510, receiving some Kendal cloth for her coat, a pair of gloves, and money for her work for two years.[48] She is found there again in 1537, receiving a costume, but does not appear elsewhere except at Crowle in Worcestershire, with Robin, in 1531, as recorded in Prior More's account book, and in London in 1559.[49] The infrequent occurrence of her name in these records is probably due mainly to the brevity of the entries in most of the relevant sources; it is in the most detailed accounts available from Kingston that she actually appears. There seems no reason to doubt that she was widely known in the early sixteenth century. Marian is not mentioned in the earliest surviving tales and became connected with Robin only through the May Games: she is not found in a ballad until the seventeenth century, but appears in stage-plays at the very end of the sixteenth. She originated in the French May Games, where she was associated with a shepherd called Robin in a pastoral play called 'Robin et Marion', which was written as early as about 1283 by Adam de la Halle (also known as Adam le Bossu and Adam de Arras) of Arras in Artois.[50] As Adam le Bossu he is found in England in a list of entertainers at the Pentecost feast at Westminster in 1306.[51] Robin and Marion are first mentioned in England in John Gower's

---

characteristic now universally attributed to him, that he robbed from the rich to give to the poor, something that is not mentioned in any of the early tales: Holt, *Robin Hood*, pp. 195–96. The idea was first made explicit in John Major's *Historia* in 1521, where he remarked that Robin did not seize the goods of the poor but helped them generously with what he took from abbots. However, no evidence has yet been found that the poor benefited directly, since the profits seem normally to have been used for church expenses, but that does not in itself rule the idea out, since churchwardens may have encouraged the idea that the money helped the poor. Major's notion that Robin helped the poor had become well established by the end of the sixteenth century. John Stow asserted in his annals in 1592 that 'poore mens goods hee spared, aboundantlie relieuing them with that which by thefte hee gotte from Abbeies [and] the houses of riche Earles: whome Maior blaimeth for his rapine and theft: but of all theeues hee affirmeth him to be the Prince, and the most gentle Thiefe': J. Stow, *Annals of England* (London, 1603 edition), p. 234.

48 Kingston History Centre, Kingston Borough Archives, KG2/2/1, p. 66, Kingston Churchwardens Accounts, costs of Robin Hood, 1509. The related *REED* volume has not yet been published, but see Singman, *Robin Hood*, p. 182.
49 *REED Herefordshire, Worcestershire*, ed. D. N. Klausner (Toronto, 1990), p. 513; above, n. 31; Singman, *Robin Hood*, pp. 66, 180.
50 *Le Jeu de Robin et Marion par Adam le Bossu*, ed. E. Langlois (Paris, 1896).
51 J. Southworth, *The English Medieval Minstrel* (Woodbridge, 1989), p. 72.

Mirour de l'omme of 1376-79, at the time of Langland's first reference to tales of Robin Hood, participating in popular festivals, but the earliest Robin Hood tales do not include Marian or anyone like her. Once the two traditions coalesced Marian became an essential element in Robin Hood's legend, belatedly providing the love interest which is entirely lacking in the early tales, but it is impossible to establish precisely how her story became associated with that of Robin Hood. Robin himself seems to have replaced the King of May as 'summer lord', although sometimes, as at Kingston, he appears alongside him. Sometimes he replaced a local 'lord of misrule', most clearly at Aberdeen, where in 1508 he replaced the 'abbot of Bon Accord', and in Edinburgh, where by 1518 he supplanted the 'abbot of Narent'.[52]

The May Games also included a jolly friar, who was associated with the Queen of May in the Morris dances. Since he is almost always found alongside Marian, it has been suggested that they joined the outlaw band and so the legend as a whole at about the same time.[53] The friar, who is later invariably Friar Tuck, probably became more firmly incorporated in the legend because of his involvement in the May games. However, he had already been mentioned in the 'Play of Robin Hood's Death', dated 1475/6, and a Sussex outlaw of c.1417 to 1429 had either already used his name or was the original of the character. Furthermore, the tale of *Robin Hood and the Curtal Friar*, which includes what became the famous fight between Robin and the friar at the crossing of a stream, first appears in the mid-seventeenth century 'Percy Folio' (where it is called *Robin Hood and Friar Tuck*), but may be based on a tale which was current in the later fifteenth century. It therefore seems likely that the character, later brilliantly portrayed (as the Clerk of Copmanhurst) by Sir Walter Scott in *Ivanhoe* (1819), resulted from an amalgamation of the two friars, the anonymous one of the May Games and the outlaw.

Robin Hood as a rioter: Willenhall Fair, 1498

Despite the benevolent motives that Major associated with Robin Hood, his name continued to be associated with violence and social disorder, even when he was engaged in raising money for the church. One well-documented incident that took place in Staffordshire at the end of the fifteenth century illustrates this. In 1498 Roger Dyngley, the mayor of

---

52 Singman, *Robin Hood*, p. 68; Knight, *Complete Study*, p. 108. The texts of the relevant documents are conveniently available at https://www.irhb.org/wiki/index.php/Aberdeen_festivals, accessed 21 May 2018. Maid Marian replaced the Queen of May, and together they presided over the 'king game' at Whitsuntide.
53 W. E. Simone, 'The Games and the Robin Hood Legend', *Journal of American Folklore* 64 (1951), pp. 265–74, at 269.

Walsall, Thomas Rice and other townsmen brought an allegation of riot against a group of men from other towns in the Court of Star Chamber, whose jurisdiction covered mainly offences against public order. The procedure of the court was for the person bringing the case to file a written bill of complaint. Dyngley's bill stated that on Wednesday 6 June that year Rice was beaten by John Cradeley of Wednesbury and Thomas Murres of Dudley, and so Cradeley was arrested by the mayor. As a result, John Beaumonde, a squire who lived at Wednesbury, Walter Leveson and Richard Foxe, a priest, both of Wolverhampton, and Roger Marshall of Wednesbury, assembled a force of 200 armed men, equipped with bows, arrows, bills and glaives, saying that they intended to rescue Cradeley, who was a servant of Beaumonde, and destroy Walsall. Two local justices of the peace then ordered them to keep the peace, which prevented an immediate attack. As a precaution against further trouble, the justices ordered that the inhabitants of Walsall, Wednesbury and other places should not go to Willenhall fair on the following Sunday, Trinity Sunday. The men of Walsall obeyed, but about 80 men from Wolverhampton, led by Leveson and William Milner, who called himself the abbot of Marham, did go armed to the fair. It was also attended by Marshall, calling himself Robin Hood, and Foxe and over 100 more armed men. They stayed all day, the leaders commanding their men to strike down any Walsall man who might appear.[54]

On 1 July the court ordered Leveson, Foxe and Marshall to appear in Michaelmas term, when Beamonde, Leveson and Marshall all produced written answers to the bill, denying guilt. Beaumonde's response was restricted to the initial events at Walsall,[55] but Leveson's and Marshall's, although mentioning a peaceable consultation with Beaumonde at Wednesbury over the events at Walsall, were directed towards explaining what they were doing at Willenhall fair. Neither of them admitted to the existence of the magistrates' prohibition which they had been accused of breaking. There was, they said, a long-established custom for the inhabitants of Wolverhampton, Wednesbury and Walsall to come to Willenhall fair under captains disguised as the abbot of Marham or Robin Hood to collect money while making their 'disport' (entertainment, display) for the profits of the churches in their own towns. On Trinity Sunday they had come peacefully as they normally did, and there they had met John Walker and other inhabitants of Walsall in an atmosphere of good neighbourliness.[56]

54 TNA, STAC 1/2/95; REED ONLINE: https://ereed.library.utoronto.ca/records/staff-ridm51915856.
55 TNA, STAC 2/19/101; REED ONLINE: https://ereed.library.utoronto.ca/records/staff-ridm51801568.
56 TNA, STAC 2/13, f. 247; REED ONLINE: https://ereed.library.utoronto.ca/records/staff-ridm51753488; and STAC 1/2/95; REED ONLINE: https://ereed.

The council registers which contained the decrees of the court have not survived, so nothing is known of the outcome of the case. What Dyngley chose to present as a riot may not have been so, since it was customary to allege riot in order to be able to bring cases before the Star Chamber. The court was well used to dealing with cases in which disputes were really about the possession of land but which were brought into it through a fictitious allegation of riot. Nevertheless, there seems to have been no hidden purpose behind this particular bill since the answers do not indicate one, and it was clearly easy to connect Robin Hood with an alleged riot. However, it was equally easy for the defendants to associate their appearance at Willenhall fair with a charitable purpose and expect that their explanation would be taken seriously. There might be genuine confusion between the two, and it cannot readily be determined which view was nearer to the truth.

Puritan opposition to the May Games: Robin Hood as an encouragement to ungodliness

In the late fifteenth century, therefore, it was possible to see Robin in a benevolent light, but his earlier long-standing connection with violence also fitted well with the possibility of disorder at the festive occasions with which he was now associated. That disorder might be seen as a serious threat to law and order, as Sir Richard Morison, an English humanist scholar and an associate of Thomas Cromwell, pointed out to Henry VIII in 1536:

> In somer comenly upon the holy daies in most places of your realm ther be plays of Robin hoode, mayde Marian, freer Tuck; wherin besides the lewdenes and rebawdry that ther is opened to the people, disobedience also to your officers is tought whilest these good bloodes go about to take from the shiref of Notyngham one that for offendyng the lawes shulde have suffered execution.[57]

Morison suggested to the king that the popular Robin Hood plays should be suppressed in favour of some anti-papal propaganda:

> Howmoche better is it that those [Romish] plaies shulde be forbodden and deleted and others dyvysed to set forthe and declare lyvely before the peoples eies the abhomynation and wickedness of the bishop of Rome, monks, friers, nuns, and suche like ... Into the commen people

---

library.utoronto.ca/records/staff-ridm51825312. See also Dyngley's and Rice's replication to Beamonde's answer, STAC 2/28/109; *REED ONLINE*: https://ereed.library.utoronto.ca/records/staff-ridm51692304.

[57] S. Anglo, 'An Early Tudor Programme for Plays and Other Demonstrations Against the Pope', *Journal of the Warburg and Courtauld Institutes* 20 (1957), pp. 176–79 at 179.

thynges sooner enter by the eies, then by the eares: remembryng more better that they see then that they here.[58]

By 1545, in the *King's Primer*, whose authorship Henry VIII claimed, prayers for the dead were mocked by means of a comparison with the stories of the legendary outlaw: 'There is nothing in the Dirge taken out of Scripture that maketh any mention of the souls departed than doth the tale of Robin Hood'.[59]

The old folk revels had long been attacked by reforming clergymen, and following the advance of the Reformation in England in the 1530s they came under a sustained and increasing attack from the growing number of Puritan protestants, who associated them with popery and heathen superstition, drunkenness and sexual licentiousness, neglect of the Sabbath, idleness and social indiscipline. In 1549 Hugh Latimer, one of the most prominent of the early protestants and former bishop of Worcester (1535 to 1539), at the height of the power of the reformers at court during the reign of the Protestant King Edward VI preached a sermon to the king, during which he described an attempt to preach in a town church.

> 'I sent word overnight into the town that I would preach there in the morning because it was a holiday ... and when I came there, the church door was fast locked. I tarried there half an hour and more. At last the key was found, and one of the parish comes to me and says, 'Sir, this is a busy day with us, we cannot hear you. It is Robin Hood's day. The parish are gone to gather for Robin Hood. I pray you, let them not'. ... It is no laughing matter, my friends, it is a weeping matter, a heavy matter ... under the pretence of gathering for Robin Hood, a traitor and a thief, to put out a preacher, to have his office less esteemed – to prefer Robin Hood before the ministration of God's word'.[60]

The decline of the spring festivities under such pressure was a slow one, and was probably even reversed during the Catholic resurgence under Queen Mary, during which Latimer was burned at the stake in Oxford in 1555 for heresy. The process recommenced after the accession of Elizabeth I in 1558, and took place more quickly in areas where Puritans were more numerous, as in eastern England. It was well advanced by the middle of Elizabeth's reign. Ronald Hutton has proposed that the decline of seasonal ceremonies and pastimes in general commenced in the mid-1560s, and that the 1570s were crucial

---

[58] BL, Cotton Faustina C 11, ff. 15v–18v; G. Walker, *Plays of Persuasion: Drama and Politics at the Court of Henry VIII* (Cambridge, 1991), pp. 11 n 9, 31 n 59.
[59] A. Jacobs, *The Book of Common Prayer: A Biography* (Princeton and Oxford, 2013), pp. 11–12. I am indebted to Lloyd Richardson for this reference.
[60] *Seven Sermons before Edward VI*, ed. E. Arber (London, 1869), pp. 173–74.

in the process.[61] In 1579 a prominent Puritan, Laurence Tomson, at that time secretary to Sir Francis Walsingham as well as a translator of John Calvin's sermons, complained that 'God will not have us occupied like little children in puppets or hobbie-horses, as Players and Robin Hoods'.[62] The most systematic published attack on them was, as already noted, made by the Puritan pamphleteer Phillip Stubbes in 1583, who called for 'reformation of maners and amendement of lyfe'; and there are many other disparaging references to Robin Hood activities and tales by clerics. There was also opposition from secular reformers, as for example in 1567 when Sir William Pelham proposed the suppression of Robin Hood plays in favour of military drill as a more useful form of public entertainment.[63] Local church sponsorship of the May Games and support for them by prominent local laymen declined, and the games themselves declined as a result, although they remained well into the seventeenth century in some conservative areas. At the time of the Restoration of Charles II, in 1660-61, before he was enthroned, the Earl of Newcastle, the king's former tutor, advised him to support the May Games because they were helpful to social order. While he did not specifically mention Robin Hood, the 'whitson Lorde and Ladye' who do appear were perhaps the successors of Robin and Marian. The duke thought that 'the devirtismentes will amuse the peoples thaughts, & keep them In harmles action, which will free your Majestie frome faction & Rebellion'.[64] Church ales were gradually replaced by church rates, and in any case Robin Hood never again played such an important part in the games as he did in the early Tudor period. He is rarely mentioned in connection with them after 1600, although a Robin Hood play was performed at Stratford upon Avon in 1622; money was collected by Robin and Little John in Woodstock, Oxfordshire, in 1628; and Robin Hood games were observed at Enstone, also in Oxfordshire, by some foreign visitors, probably from Denmark, as late as 1652.[65] Further north, the latest known were at Brandsby in Yorkshire in 1616, and at Linton in Roxburghshire in 1610.[66] In Scotland, where extreme Protestants were in the ascendant in parliament, official sponsorship of the games by the burghs ceased after a repressive statute of 1555, but efforts to supress them in Edinburgh caused riots there in 1561. In 1577-8 the General Assembly of the Kirk requested the king's council to forbid 'all kind of insolent playis,

[61] Hutton, *The Rise and Fall of Merry England*, chapter 4.
[62] L. Thomson, *Calvin's Sermons on the Epistles to Timothy and Titus* (London, 1579), p. 23a; Singman, *Robin Hood*, pp. 116, 138.
[63] Singman, *Robin Hood*, pp. 115–19.
[64] *A Catalogue of Letters and Other Historical Documents Exhibited in the Library at Welbeck*, ed. S. A. Strong (London, 1903), p. 227.
[65] D. Underdown, *Revel, Riot and Rebellion: Popular Politics and Culture in England, 1603–1660* (Oxford, 1985), p. 262; Singman, *Robin Hood*, p. 181; Oxfordshire Archives, MS DD Par Woodstock c.12, p. 17.
[66] Singman, *Robin Hood*, pp. 186, 192.

as King of May, Robin Hood, and sick others in the moneth of May', and in 1580 the Privy Council issued a decree against them, but the General Assembly was still complaining about Robin Hood games in 1591, and they continued as late as 1610 in Linton.[67]

Puritanism versus tradition: conflicts in Somerset in 1607

Three well-documented disputes in Somerset during the same year illustrate the growth of opposition by puritans to the May Games and the whole range of communal revels in the early seventeenth century. At the cathedral city of Wells, where the Robin Hood tradition stretched back at least as far as 1498, records of proceedings in the Court of Star Chamber provide the details.[68] In 1607 St Cuthbert's parish church in Wells needed repairs to its bells and steeple. The church wardens, after failing to obtain exemption from the prohibition of such events on Sundays but receiving the approval of the dean of Wells and the mayor and corporation, organised a church ale, together with a municipal dinner, to take place in mid-June. Traditional processions, including Robin Hood and morris dancers, were organised for the period leading up to it, on Sundays and other holidays from May Day onwards. On 3 May the town constable, John Hole, a wealthy local clothier and a strict Sabbatarian, halted a procession, aided by three other like-minded constables, and sent the revellers home or to church, for it was a Sunday; and some 'minstrels' were briefly imprisoned. On the following Sunday, 10 May, a full traditional procession was held. One item in the parade, a picture of a spotted calf carried by a satyr, was intended to lampoon a local Puritan woman, Mrs Yard. She had recently denounced the town maypole, sited in the market place, as a 'painted calf', Old Testament imagery for an idol, and would not go past it from her house on the market place to attend church. Furthermore, Hole had earlier been accused before the bishop of adultery with Mrs Yard. Other processions at Whitsun and later on Sundays and other holidays continued to taunt Hole and his associates. At one of these on 31 May, Robin Hood was played by Robert Prinne of Wells, a yeoman, who had a 'Robin Hood's man', Stephen Millard, a tailor aged 43, to carry a bow and arrows. Millard was, and had for six years been, one of the sergeants of the mayor, and on 3 May he had been punished by Hole for playing card games with the minstrels at his house at the time of divine service. In July, 'Robin Hood' was again 'seen with all his gallants arrayed in green, their arrows being a cloth yard long'. Some of the performers were examined by the bishop, and

---

[67] Singman, *Robin Hood*, pp. 160–61, 187–92.
[68] TNA, STAC 8/161/1. The whole of the texts of this case, including additional material from local records, are now printed in *REED Somerset*, pp. 261–367; see particularly pp. 267, 320–21.

they were then brought before the lord chief justice at Taunton assizes, who criticised them severely and bound them over. Hole later brought them before the Star Chamber in London on charges of libel, breaking the J.P.s' orders prohibiting church ales and related offences, because he could there allege that the disturbances were a threat to public order. This well-known case has been characterised by David Underdown as 'a classic case-study of the Puritan individual at odds with the unreformed community'.[69]

At Weston Zoyland in the same year the vicar, Robert Wolfall, was presented at quarter sessions for participating in Robin Hood games, held to raise funds for the parish. He was accused by John Cornish, a carpenter, who reported that on 17 May, Sunday after Ascension, he 'at Morninge prayer presentlye after the second lesson put of his Surplusse and willed his parishioners to departe and followe Robin hoode according to their aunciente Custome to the Alle and to breakfast with him and gave them libertye soe to doe the most parte of An howre and then Came to the Churche and began the service at the tenn Comandementes'. This shows the outlaw as part of a parish ale, which involved travelling from the church to a breakfast venue, and returning to it afterwards, with the approval of the vicar; in that year Robin was played by the vicar's son. The vicar and others were escorted to a room which was probably in the church house, where their 'fyne and Ransome' was to drink two pots of strong ale while holding one leg in the stocks. The vicar, 'being Chiefe Actor of that Comedye', was the first to drink.[70] In Yeovil too in that year Robin Hood was probably used to raise money for the church, although he was not mentioned by name on that occasion. 'It was an usual thinge upon the sabothe daye to have minstrelsie and dauncing and carrying men upon a covell stafe'. A procession made its way through the streets, led by a drummer, 'to gather the liberality of the Inhabitantes', presumably stopping people to ask for contributions. Those refusing to contribute would be 'arrested' and taken to the celebrations at the church house, where they would presumably be ransomed by drinking ale and making a contribution. One opponent, Thomas Jarvis, claimed that the troupe chased him into a house and accused him of being a puritan because he would not take part in what they considered to be a 'good and godly' game.[71]

---

[69] Underdown, *Revel, Riot and Rebellion*, p. 55.
[70] Somerset Heritage Centre, Quarter Sessions Roll 2, f. 7v; *REED Somerset*, pp. 388–89.
[71] *REED Somerset*, pp. 411–13.

Elizabethan and Early Stuart Plays: Robin Hood takes the stage

Robin Hood was represented in plays by the fifteenth century, but the nature of their performance is unclear as the sources do not give any real hints. Some of the plays written in the later sixteenth century were connected with the May Games and based on the early tales. The most well-known are *Robin Hood and the Friar*, based on a version of the tale *Robin Hood and the Curtal Friar*, and *Robin Hood and the Potter*, based on the tale of the same name. They were appended by William Copland to his edition of the *Gest*, published about 1560, and were specifically said to be 'verye proper to be played in Maye games'. During the time of William Shakespeare and Ben Jonson, from about 1590 to 1640, the golden age of English theatre, Robin was frequently alluded to in drama, including a number of references in Shakespeare's own plays. Plays about him are known to have been written, but most have not survived and are known only by their titles. Jonson's own Robin Hood play, a pastoral drama called *The Sad Shepherd*, was left unfinished on his death in 1637. It consisted of two completed acts and the beginning of a third, and was first printed in 1641. The action takes place in the forest of Sherwood, near Belvoir castle in the Vale of Belvoir, home of the earl and countess of Rutland; it also includes a drowning in the River Trent (the real southern boundary of the forest) nearby, and a witch of Papplewick, a real village in Nottinghamshire lying within it. Like the others, it had little influence on the development of the legend, although it was revived, and completed with a continuation and conclusion, by F. G. Waldron in Drury Lane in the 1780s.[72] Two plays which have survived, however, did have a very fundamental effect upon the popular legend.

Anthony Munday: Robin Hood as a dispossessed aristocrat

In the last years of the reign of Elizabeth I, Robin Hood for the first time clearly appears in a professional play performed on the London stage, in the anonymous *George a Greene*, acted in 1588-89 and published in 1599.[73] It was one of seven Robin Hood plays in all, written between 1588 and 1601, five of which survive. Most of them used his traditional characteristics, but supplied no new elements to the legend, and initially portrayed him as a minor figure.[74] However, a significant departure from the old traditions was made by Anthony Munday (c.1560-1633) in *The Downfall of*

---

[72] D&T, pp. 231–36; Knight, *Complete Study*, pp. 139–42.
[73] For a fuller account of the London theatre in the 1590s and the involvement of Robin Hood in it, see Knight, *Complete Study*, pp. 115–34.
[74] E. Davenport, 'The Representation of Robin Hood in Elizabethan Drama: *George a Greene* and *Edward I*', in *Playing Robin Hood*, pp. 45–62.

Robert Earl of Huntington and *The Death of Robert Earl of Huntington*, both apparently written in 1598 and published in 1601.[75] For the first time, he identified Robin not as a yeoman but as a dispossessed nobleman, Robert or Robin earl of Huntington, a perhaps deliberate corruption of Huntingdon, who loses his lands during the absence of King Richard on crusade. By contrast, the sheriff, one of those involved in Robin's loss of land, is an upstart, a cottager's son who becomes a clerk, then Robin's steward and a justice of the peace, gaining his wealth by racking rents. Antecedents for the idea were the description of Robin Hood as 'noble' by the antiquary John Leland in the reign of Henry VIII, and more particularly the assertion by the printer and historian Richard Grafton (1506/7-1573) in his *Chronicle*, published in 1569, that "in an olde and aunciant Pamphlet I finde this written of the sayde Robert Hood' that he 'discended of a noble parentage' and 'was for his manhood and chiualry advanced to the noble dignity of an Erle' before falling into debt and subsequently being outlawed".[76] Adopting the dating of Robin Hood by John Major, who placed the outlaw in 1193-94, Munday brought the then king, Richard I, and his brother and successor King John, into the story. He also incorporated Matilda, daughter of Robert fitz Walter, leader of the baronial army who rebelled against King John in 1215, as Maid Marian, and then created a dramatic tale in which Robin the yeoman is transformed into an aristocrat. He probably did so to cater for the tastes of the patrons of the theatres in which his plays were performed, who would have found a more violent outlaw such as Robin Hood an unsuitable hero for a play, and less acceptable politically in a period of high international and domestic tension. Putting him into the social hierarchy made him less of a threat to the social order.

Munday's inclusion of Marian and Friar Tuck in the plays probably resulted from the widespread popularity of the May Games. The plays seem to be the clearest case of a deliberately manufactured addition to the legend, made simply to fulfil the requirements of an imaginative storyteller. Making Robin an aristocrat made him respectable: as David Wiles put it, 'there was interest in seeing a potentially dangerous and divisive myth reworked in the defence of nationalism and aristocracy'.[77] Also, the choice of the reign of Richard I as the outlaw's time was, as Jeffrey Singman has pointed out, 'particularly felicitous from the point of view of official culture since Robin Hood could now resist royal officials without implicitly challenging the king, whose absence on a crusade explains the

---

[75] D&T, pp. 220–25; J. L. Singman, 'Munday's Unruly Earl', *Playing Robin Hood*, pp. 63–76.
[76] R. Grafton, *A Chronicle at Large* (2 vols., London, 1809), I, p. 221. The full text of Grafton's account of the outlaw is given in Singman, *Robin Hood*, pp. 107–08.
[77] Wiles, *The Early Plays of Robin Hood*, p. 54.

corruption of society in England'.[78] The idea of Robin as a dispossessed nobleman living in the 1190s which Munday purveyed was taken up by eighteenth-century antiquarians and eventually took root; it became an almost constant feature of Robin Hood films and television series of the twentieth century. Nevertheless, it was at odds with the mainstream development of the legend during the late sixteenth and early seventeenth centuries, which took place in the broadsides and garlands cheaply printed for a mass lower class audience who must in many cases been familiar with Robin because of his participation in the May Games. Munday's use of the legend did not end with the plays; for when he wrote a pageant honouring the Drapers' Company in 1615, Robin Hood and his men unexpectedly appear, 'fitted with Bowes and Arrowes'. It ends with a song by Robin Hood and Friar Tuck:

> What life is there like to *Robin Hood*?
> It is so pleasant a thing a:
> In merry *Shirwood* he spends his dayes,
> As pleasantly as a King a.[79]

Robin Hood plays for the upper classes in the later sixteenth century were not entirely limited to the theatre. In 1562 payments to performers in the Wiltshire home of Sir John Thynne at Longleat, and at that of the young Robert Sydney at Penshurst in Kent in 1574, are recorded.[80]

The 'Sloane Life': Robin of Loxley

The 'Sloane Life' of Robin Hood is so called because it is found in a manuscript from the collection of the notable physician and antiquary Sir Hans Sloane (1660-1753), which became one of the foundational collections of the British Museum in 1753. Now in the British Library, the manuscript contains, among other miscellaneous items including a treatise on the astrolabe, the earliest known attempt at a biography of the outlaw in prose.[81] It is written in a secretary hand of the late sixteenth century, and may have been composed before the dissemination of the additions to the legend found in the plays of Munday and the other Elizabethan playwrights, no traces of which appear in it. It states that Robin was born at 'Lockesley' in Nottinghamshire or, 'according to others', Yorkshire, in about 1160, and lived until the later part of the reign of Richard I. He lost or sold his patrimony because he was in debt and became an outlaw, and with others, including Little John. hunted in

---

78 Singman, *Robin Hood*, p. 131.
79 D. M. Bergeron, in *ODNB*, accessed 18 June 2018.
80 Singman, *Robin Hood*, pp. 63, 67, 69, 177.
81 BL, Sloane 780, ff. 46r–48v. See in particular D&T, pp. 286–87, and Singman, *Robin Hood*, pp. 125–26.

'Barnsdale forrest' and 'Clompton parke'. He recruited, among others, the Pinder of Wakefield (already the subject of a well-known tale perhaps as old as the mid-sixteenth century), a friar called Muchel, and Scarloke, whose marriage he facilitated when his fiancée was in danger of being appropriated by a richer suitor. He also mentions Major's commendation of Robin as the prince of thieves and robbers. Much of the 'biography' clearly derives directly from the *Gest*, and often echoes its language. The author deals with the story of the Lancashire knight, Sir Richard Lee, his debt to the abbot of St Mary's, and Robin's loan to him; the archery contest in Nottingham; Little John's period of service to the sheriff in the guise of Reynold Greenleaf of Holderness, and his robbery from him while departing; the sheriff's capture of the knight, Robin's rescue of him and his beheading of the sheriff; the king's visits to Nottingham and Plumpton park; Robin's meeting with the king; his subsequent service in, and departure from, the king's court; and his eventual death at Kirklees at the hands of the prioress, his aunt, and Sir Roger of Doncaster.

The most significant addition to the legend made by the biography is the reference to the place-name 'Lockesley', which consequently appeared in many Robin Hood stories written subsequently. It was even picked up by the great seventeenth century Yorkshire antiquary Roger Dodsworth (d.1654), who noted the existence of a 'Robert Locksley', born in Bradfield parish in Hallamshire, apparently a Robin Hood candidate, who knew Little John.[82] There has never been a Nottinghamshire place called Locksley or Loxley, but there is one in Yorkshire near Sheffield, now a linear village beside a river of the same name. When it first appears in record in the 1330s it was a wooded chase, and its existence as a village does not seem to go back very far. In 1819 Joseph Hunter, as the historian of Hallamshire, noted that Loxley Chase 'in the memory of man was wholly un-enclosed and uncultivated'. He considered that it was 'a district which seems to have the fairest pretensions to be the Loxley of our old ballads where was born our own Robin Hood. The remains of a house in which he was pretended to be born was formerly pointed out in a small wood in Loxley called Bar-Wood'.[83] The association of the name of the place with Robin Hood has no basis in fact and was presumably invented by the unknown writer of the 'Sloane Life' or his unknown source. It is nevertheless still associated with the outlaw in popular folklore, reinforced by the use of the name for the fictional Robin Hood character portrayed in Sir Walter Scott's *Ivanhoe*,

---

[82] Bodleian Library, Oxford, Dodsworth MS. 160, f. 64b; quoted by Holt, *Robin Hood*, pp. 44, 192.

[83] A. H. Smith, *The Place-Names of the West Riding of Yorkshire* I, EPNS XXX (Cambridge, 1961), p. 225; J. Hunter, *Hallamshire: The History and Topography of the Parish of Sheffield* (London, 1819), p. 3.

published in 1819. The later suggested identification of a Warwickshire Loxley, near Stratford on Avon, as Robin Hood's birthplace, made by J. R. Planché in 1864, has never been taken seriously.[84]

Printed Ballads: Robin Hood as popular literature

The *Gest* remained the only printed version of the legend during the sixteenth century, but the most influential means of spreading the Robin Hood legend to a wider audience, after the May Games declined and the great Elizabethan and Jacobean age of drama came to an end, was by means of cheap popular printed ballads sung to the accompaniment of popular tunes.[85] This development was based on the remarkable increase in the literacy of both urban craftsmen and tradesmen and rural yeomen from the later sixteenth century. It has been estimated that by 1640 about 30% of males were literate, three times as many as in 1500.[86] Broadsides were single ballads printed on two sides of a single sheet and sold cheaply in streets and market places.[87] Their golden age was the first half of the seventeenth century, after which they suffered something of a decline when ballad singing was prohibited during the Commonwealth period of the 1650s. They had already achieved a significant growth by the time of the publication by Martin Parker (*fl.*1624-47) of *A True Tale of Robin Hood* in London in 1632, a work which includes within it the main elements of the legend current before the Puritan victory in the civil war which began a decade later.[88] One of the later stanzas (117) claimed veracity: 'I know there's many fained tales Of Robbin Hood and 's crew; But chronicles, which seldome fayles, Reports this to be true'. In reality the only chronicle he used was that of Richard Grafton, and his real sources are easy to identify. While retaining much material from the *Gest*, including the abbot of St Mary's, it incorporated Munday's identification of Robin with the earl of Huntington and placed him in the time of Richard I. It gave greater stress to Robin's generosity to the poor ('That he would give and lende to them, To help them at their neede') but did not mention Maid Marian and Friar Tuck, despite their known earlier popularity in the May Games. The ballad also does not include the comic and plebeian elements which were then coming to dominate the popular legend and which avoided the aristocratic theme. It did, however, provide at the end the earliest version of and reference to the supposed epitaph of the outlaw at

---

[84] D&T, p. 305.
[85] For the main stories of this period, see Singman, *Robin Hood*, pp. 122–26; D&T, pp. 46–49.
[86] D. Cressy, *Literacy and the Social Order* (Cambridge, 1980), p. 176.
[87] M. Plant, *The English Book Trade* (London, 1939), pp. 220, 241.
[88] Child (1861), pp. 353–71; Child (1889), pp. 227–33; D&T, pp. 187–90.

Kirklees, which he said had existed for a hundred years, and which dated Robin's death to the year 1198.[89]

In the later seventeenth, eighteenth and nineteenth centuries broadsides were replaced by anthologies of the standard ballads printed as chapbooks called Robin Hood Garlands, anthologies larger than other kinds of chapbook and rather more expensive, which effectively revived the legend after the setbacks of the 1650s.[90] The first two were published in 1663 and 1670, and along with the original broadsides, they became collectors' items; the diarist Samuel Pepys was an early collector of chapbooks. They did not include new stories, but perpetuated the life of those earlier printed as broadsides in the first half of the seventeenth century. That core of popular tales came to be known as the 'traditional' Robin Hood ballads, and they supplanted the early tales. The language and style of the latter were by then too archaic for all but the scholarly, so newer versions were needed for the popular market, most to be sung to one of a small number of popular tunes, of which 'Robin Hood and the Stranger' was the most often used.[91] The period of the broadsides produced tales most of which were adaptations of the early stories, especially the *Gest*, or made use of themes within it, such as disguise, combat, archery and anti-clericalism. Various modifications of the combat between Robin and the potter from *Robin Hood and the Potter*, for example *Robin Hood and the Butcher*, brought Robin into conflict with and often to defeat by a variety of figures representing the lower classes, including one or more tinkers, beggars, tanners, shepherds, forest rangers and pinders (pound keepers), as well as the butcher. The fighting often took place with a staff, the characteristic plebeian weapon. Robin's doughty opponents in such tales were often invited to join his band. Such tales pandered to the vanity of the increasingly literate tradesmen already mentioned, who bought copies of them in large quantities. Some stories, such as *Robin Hood's Golden Prize* (1656), written by Laurence Price (c.1628-80, credited with at least 62 broadside ballads), were new ones, but using existing themes, in this case Robin's anti-clericalism. A few were written for local purposes, such as *Robin Hood's Birth, Breeding and Valor* for the annual bull-running at Tutbury in Staffordshire, and possibly others. *The Noble Fisherman* provided the outlaw with a short career as a fisherman and attacker of French shipping off Scarborough, perhaps inspired by the existence of nearby Robin Hood's Bay, so called by the second half of the fourteenth century.[92] *Robin Hood and Allen a Dale* brought in a new character who became a permanent addition to the legend, a young man whose lover was rescued by Robin from a forced marriage to an elderly

[89] See p. 144.
[90] D&T, pp. 50–53.
[91] Singman, *Robin Hood*, pp. 122–26.
[92] See pp. 138–41.

knight. Other characters mentioned were imported from other legends, such as those of Gamelyn and Adam Bell, but unlike Allen they did not become permanent additions to the Robin Hood legend. One important character from the *Gest*, the abbot of St Mary's, on the other hand, disappeared from it, the abbeys having been destroyed by Henry VIII. The broadsheet ballads as a whole are more light-hearted than the tales which had been current in the fifteenth century, which by the eighteenth century had been thoroughly mangled and adulterated in order to cater for popular taste.

Biographers and collectors of tales: Robin Hood antiquarianism in the eighteenth century

Antiquarians and historians felt an increasing need to place Robin Hood in an identifiable historical context, as the Scottish chroniclers of the fifteenth century had. The problem is that no medieval English historian had mentioned him, still less had any said that Robin had lived in his own or recent times. They were left essentially with what John Major and the author of the 'Sloane life' had written in the sixteenth century, and the obituaries of Parker and Gale from the seventeenth, both of which called him the earl of Huntington, together with the legends associated with the graves at Kirklees and Hathersage, Little John's alleged burial place. In his *Complete History of the Lives and Robberies of the Most Notorious Highwaymen*, published in 1714, Alexander Smith dismissed as fiction the idea of his descent from the earls of Huntingdon, but on the grounds that he was a butcher, born in a village near Sherwood Forest in the reign of Henry II. During the first half of the eighteenth century two antiquarians from Lincolnshire added to the conflicting mass of material in circulation.

Francis Peck: Robin Hood as a hermit

Francis Peck (1692–1743) was born in Stamford in 1692, the younger son of a merchant, and was educated at St John's College, Cambridge. In 1723 he purchased the living of Goadby Marwood in Leicestershire, and lived at the rectory there for the rest of his life, dedicating himself to his pastoral duties and his antiquarian and literary studies. His principal interests were in the history and antiquities of Lincolnshire, Leicestershire, and Rutland. Peck became a member of the Society of Antiquaries of London in 1732, and he corresponded with some of the leading antiquaries of his day. In that same year he published the first section of his illustrated *Desiderata Curiosa, or, A Collection of Divers Scarce and Curious Pieces, Relating Chiefly to Matters of English History*, the work for which he became best known; the second volume followed three years later. He was also a collector of ballads, and in that second volume included an otherwise unknown story called *Robin Whood Turned Hermit*, which he claimed was 'altogether founded on fact'.[93] It is in reality based on Parker's *A True Tale of Robin Hood*, but Peck's story incorporates into Parker's tale an episode in which, before he goes to his death at Kirklees, Robin becomes a hermit after having a strange dream. He does so at 'Lyndric', a hill near Dale abbey, said to be in Lancashire, but which is a real abbey in Derbyshire to the north-east of Derby, in Deepdale. 'Lyndric' can be identified as a hill a short distance to the west of it. The episode is plainly taken from the story of an anonymous outlaw who lived in the mid-twelfth century and whose existence is recorded in the history of the abbey's foundation written by Thomas of Muskham, one of its canons, in the time of Abbot John Grauncourt (1233-53). Peck has Robin taking refuge in a 'lonely rocky cell', which still exists on the hillside, but Muskham associates the place with another hermit, a former baker of Derby. Muskham was not certain that the outlaw had actually become a hermit at all, although he noted that some people thought that he had. Peck had just published an edition of Muskham's chronicle, in which he also placed Dale in Lancashire. As Holt pointed out, this probably indicated that Peck, despite his protestations concerning its factual nature, compiled the ballad himself.[94] Peck's attitude to historical veracity appears from an anecdote related by a fellow antiquary, George Vertue (1684-1756), to have been of a cavalier nature. Vertue informed him that a print of Milton that Peck wished to use as the frontispiece to his book on the poet was very probably spurious, and later recollected Peck's reply: 'I'll have a scraping from it however, and let posterity settle the matter'.[95] The spuriousness of his biography of Robin is thus relatively easy to detect, compared with other cases where the source of what is apparently new material cannot be traced. It was not influential, however, and did not enter the mainstream of the Robin Hood legend.

Peck had met the antiquary William Stukeley in 1723, and when Stukeley moved to Stamford from Grantham in 1730 they became friends, establishing a couple of 'literary clubs' together. In 1744 Stukeley recalled that Peck 'had a good deal of pride, and after many attempts at London, finding he was not rewarded as he thought he ought to have been, he became a recluse and angry with the world'. Peck died in 1743, and Stukeley informed Roger Gale that 'poor Peck is dead, and made a sad exit, being not quite *compos mentis*'. He was buried in Goadby Marwood church, leaving numerous unfinished manuscripts

---

[93] F. Peck, *Desiderata Curiosa* II (London, 1735), Liber XV, Chapter 6, p. 4; BL Additional MS 28638, f. 16; see also *The Cartulary of Dale Abbey*, ed. A. Saltman, Derbyshire Archaeological Society Record Series II (London, 1967), pp. 1-2.
[94] Holt, *Robin Hood*, pp. 180–81. See also Chapter 7.
[95] F. Blackburne, *Appendix to the Memoirs of Thomas Hollis* (London, 1780), p. 513.

including material on the history and antiquities of Rutland and of Grantham. A few years after his death his friend Stukeley made a further contribution to the search for an historical Robin Hood.

William Stukeley: Earl Robert gains a pedigree

Stukeley's main interest lay in prehistoric monuments, of which he made drawings for publication. He also dabbled in genealogy and heraldry, in which his scholarly methods left much to be desired. A contemporary, William Warburton, bishop of Gloucester, described him as a mixture of 'simplicity, drollery, absurdity, ingenuity, superstition and antiquarianism'. In 1746 he published, in his *Palaeographia Britannica*, a fictitious pedigree linking the earls of Huntingdon with the descendants of a man called Ralph fitz Ooth, who he claimed became lords of Kyme.[96] This was his undoing, since advances in methods of historical source criticism in subsequent centuries have enabled his whole theory to be comprehensively disproved, confirming the suspicion in which he was held by well-informed contemporaries. Stukeley was, as his fellow antiquary Thomas Hearne noted, 'very fanciful'; and the marriage of his great-aunt Hester or Esther Stukeley into the family of Kyme of Rochford near Boston may have brought him into contact with a Kyme family legend claiming descent from Robin Hood.[97] Also, his second wife Elizabeth, whom he married in 1739, was the daughter of Thomas Gale, dean of York (d. 1702). Gale was a reputable classical scholar as well as a senior clergyman, and had been Regius Professor of Greek at Cambridge earlier in his career. Stukeley was also a very close friend of Gale's two sons, Roger and Samuel, with whom he undertook some of his journeys visiting the ancient sites of England. Stukeley's ideas about the outlaw still retained some influence long after his death. The identification of Robin as a member of the Kyme family was elaborated by J. R. Planché in 1864, and had a champion in the late twentieth century in the person of Jim Lees.[98] The earls of Huntingdon still claim to be descended from Robin Hood, the current (17th) earl being named William Edward Robin Hood Hastings-Bass.

---

[96] An 'even more preposterous version' exists in Washington in the Folger Shakespeare Library, PR 2125: D&T, p. 59 note 1. For the fullest treatment, see Holt, *Robin Hood*, pp. 42–43, 201.

[97] *The Family Memoirs of the Rev. William Stukeley*, Surtees Society LXXIII (1882), p. 5. He noted the existence of a Lincolnshire 'Robin Hood's cross' on Aunby heath, not far from his home in Stamford: Corpus Christi College Cambridge MS. 618, p. 28.

[98] D&T, p. 305; J. Lees, *The Quest for Robin Hood* (Nottingham, 1987), pp. 132–43.

The Parker and Gale epitaphs

The study of the Robin Hood legend has since the seventeenth century been bedevilled by the appearance of the two verse epitaphs, very similar in content but giving different purported dates for the outlaw's death, both making him earl of Huntington and both at some point connected with his supposed grave at Kirklees.[99] The first concludes Martin Parker's *A True Tale of Robin Hood*, published in 1632, and gives the date of his death as 4 December 1198, in the ninth year of Richard I.[100] The information was said to be 'carefully collected out of the truest writers of our English chronicles, and published for the satisfaction of those who desire truth from falshood'. The date he gave is in fact impossible, the last day of Richard's ninth year being 2 September 1198. Parker asserted that the prioress of Kirklees had set it up over Robin's tomb, and that 'it was to be read within these hundred years, though in old broken English, much to the same sense and meaning.' The text he gave was in the English of his own time:

> Robert Earle of Huntington
> Lies under this little stone.
> No archer was like him so good:
> His wildnesse named him Robbin Hood.
> Full thirteene years, and something more,
> These northerne parts he vexed sore.
> Such out-laws as he and his men
> May England never know agen.

Where Parker obtained it is unknown, and there is no independent evidence that there was an inscription at Kirklees between the sixteenth and eighteenth centuries. It does reveal the influence already exercised by Anthony Munday's play in assigning Robin to Richard's reign and giving him an earldom, and it is difficult to believe that it was of any great antiquity in 1632, even if it was not entirely invented by Parker himself. The second epitaph was found among Gale's papers after his death in 1702. Unlike Parker's, it is not in contemporary English but in a pseudo-antique form of the language which never existed in reality but which necessitates a translation:

> Here underneath this little stone
> Lies Robert earl of Huntington
> No archer was as he so good
> And people called him Robin Hood
> Such outlaws as he and his men
> Will England never see again.

---

[99] See pp. 141–44.
[100] D&T, pp. 187–90; D. Hepworth, 'Appendix: Written Epitaphs of Robin Hood', *Robin Hood: Medieval and Post-Medieval*, ed. Phillips, pp. 188–89.

Chroniclers, Revellers, Playwrights and Antiquarians

It was followed by the date of Robin's death, given as the 24th kalends of December 1247, another impossible date; the highest kalends of any month in the Roman (Julian) calendar is the 19th. Gale must have known that the date was impossible, and it seems unlikely that he intended the epitaph to be taken seriously. It may be suggested that he knew of Parker's version and amused himself in an idle moment by taking it upon himself to provide suitable 'old broken English' in place of Parker's seventeenth-century variety, although that would not explain his omission of the fifth and sixth lines of the earlier version or the change of date. If, alternatively, Parker and Gale drew on a common source, no other trace of it is known to have survived.[101]

In 1765 William Stukeley died in London, symbolically bringing to an end the period of brilliant but unreliable antiquarian scholarship which he had come to epitomise. It was in that very year that the first truly scholarly edition of the texts of English ballad poems was published there, initiating a process of continual examination and re-evaluation of the texts of the early Robin Hood tales which still continues in the early twenty-first century.

---

[101] For a full account of the supposed graves at Kirklees, see pp. 143–44.

Chapter 3

Editors, the Folklorist and the Archivist, 1765–1889

The Enlightenment of the eighteenth century regarded the medieval period as a time of Gothic uncouthness and barbarity. The chivalry and ritual associated with it, which had survived until the first half of the seventeenth century, hung on only in antiquarian corners of a culture dominated by admiration for classical Greece and Rome, and the Italian Renaissance. However, beginning in the 1760s and 1770s, interest in medieval England underwent a significant revival. This was at least partly derived from an intellectual concern to discover, through the study of historical evidence of various kinds, the true character of past events. Serious attempts were first made, albeit in the context of the much wider search for all old traditional English songs and poems, to collect together the texts of the known Robin Hood stories, and to publish them. The impetus was created not only by a growing interest in medieval and early modern English culture and literature, but by the chance discovery in a country house of an important manuscript, already damaged but fortunately not completely destroyed. The work of publication and interpretation was carried out by several important scholars, not always on the best of terms with each other when their lives and work overlapped. It ultimately culminated in the meticulous edition of the most important poems by Francis Child, initially in America in 1857 and then in 1861 in London, and subsequently, after several more editions in the intervening period, on a more comprehensive basis in 1889. His work became the basis of all subsequent study. Another result of this process was a growing interest in the cultural milieu of the main stories. Did they have a supernatural element and a background in folklore? Did they include any historical truth, or were they, as Child opined in 1889, 'absolutely the creation of the ballad muse'? Were they a suitable subject for academic study and interpretation, or simply, as described by one critic in 1792, 'the refuse of a stall'? These developments really began with the activities of an English Anglican clergyman and scholar, who in his youth and maturity gained academic fame, and some notoriety, before in later life becoming the bishop of a northern Irish diocese.[1]

Thomas Percy and the Reliques of Ancient English Poetry

Thomas Percy (1729-1811) was educated in classics at Christ Church in Oxford, ordained in 1753, and became rector of two parishes in Northamptonshire, as well as chaplain to the earl of Sussex, in 1756. In 1765 he entered a similar position with the Duke of Northumberland, head of the historic Percy family.[2] His *Reliques of Ancient English Poetry* was published in London in 1765, in three volumes, after work over a period of four or five years.[3] Percy offered the dedication to Elizabeth Percy, countess (later duchess) of Northumberland. When she accepted, what was planned as the third volume was brought forward to be volume 1, so giving particular prominence to ballads involving the Northumberland family. In the preface he pointed out that 'the greater part of them are extracted from an ancient folio manuscript, in the Editor's possession, which contains near 200 poems, songs and metrical romances. This MS was written about the middle of the last century, but contains compositions of all times and dates'. He characterised them as 'the rude songs of ancient minstrels' and 'the barbarous productions of unpublished ages', not 'labours of art' but 'effusions of nature', and as the editor, he had 'endeavoured to be as faithful, as the imperfect state of his materials would admit', but 'a scrupulous adherence to their wretched readings would only have exhibited unintelligible nonsense'. The first volume includes the previously unknown tale of *Robin Hood and Guy of Gisborne*, preceded by a lengthy editorial introduction, in which he remarked that it 'carries marks of much greater antiquity than any of the common popular songs on this subject'. He also reviewed such matters as the outlaw's social status, not an earl but a yeoman, as well as making sceptical remarks about the alleged Robin Hood gravestone at Kirklees. The only other poem of relevance to the Robin Hood legend to be included in his book was *Adam Bell, Clim of the Clough, and William of Cloudesley*, which had already been known since 1536.[4]

---

1 For ballad collections before Percy, see A. B. Friedman, *The Ballad Revival: Studies in the Influence of Popular on Sophisticated Poetry* (Chicago, 1961), chapter 5.
2 Some of the following information is taken from the *ODNB* entry on Percy by Roy Palmer, accessed 2 February 2018.
3 On the developments in the period during which the *Reliques* was being prepared, see Friedman, *Ballad Revival*, pp. 187–200.
4 T. Percy, *Reliques of Ancient English Poetry, consisting of Old Heroic Ballads, Songs*

The story of the manuscript which became known as the 'Percy Folio' is therefore important for the study of the Robin Hood legend. While visiting Humphrey Pitt at Shifnal, near Bridgnorth in Shropshire, probably in 1753, Percy noticed a battered volume 'lying dirty on the floor, under a bureau in the parlour ... being used by the maids to light the fire'.[5] It proved to be a seventeenth-century collection of texts, purchased in a library of old books which may have belonged to Thomas Blount, a mid-seventeenth century legal writer of the Inner Temple. Percy persuaded Pitt to reprieve it from the flames, and in due course it provided the basis for Percy's anthology, and for his enduring fame. If Percy did in fact rescue the original folio manuscript in 1753 it was probably kept by Pitt for several years before he was able to obtain it for himself. He may have been reminded of it by his Shropshire friend William Shenstone, whom he visited in the summer of 1757. It was only in November that year that he wrote to Shenstone that he had 'a very curious old MS. Collection of ancient Ballads' which [Samuel] Johnson had seen and urged him to publish. On publication he mentioned the names of others who had encouraged him, and remarked that it had 'been the amusement of now and then a vacant hour amid the leisure and retirement of rural life ... as a relaxation from graver studies. It has been taken up at different times, and often thrown aside for many months, during an interval of four or five years'. He decided not to publish the whole manuscript but to supplement it from other sources. The contents of the Percy Folio in fact provided only about a quarter of the material published in the *Reliques*, much of the rest coming from Magdalene College, Cambridge; the Ashmolean and Bodleian libraries in Oxford; and the Society of Antiquaries library and British Museum in London. He did not, however, publish the ballads in the exact form in which he found them, but radically edited them to make them more acceptable to his potential audience, not only in language but also in matters of substance, detail and meaning. He deliberately omitted two Robin Hood ballads which it might have been expected that he would include, *Robin Hood and the Pinder of Wakefield* and *Robin Hood and Allen a Dale*.[6] When the book was published, the *Gentleman's Magazine* reviewer commended it, and within five months 1100 sets of the three volumes had been sold. Percy's editorial policy seemed to be vindicated, and most of his contemporaries welcomed the *Reliques*. Further editions followed, in 1767, 1775 and 1794; the latter was nominally edited by his nephew and namesake, a fellow of St John's College Cambridge, with some amendments. However, during

---

    and Other Pieces of our Earlier Poets (Chiefly of the Lyric Kind) together with some few of later Date I (London, 1765), pp. 74–86, 129–47.

[5]   J. W. Hales and F. J. Furnivall, *Bishop Percy's Folio Manuscript: Ballads and Romances*, 3 vols. (London, 1867–68), I, p. lxiv.

[6]   Freedman, *Ballad Revival*, p. 221.

his own long lifetime he received fierce criticism from a writer who himself became the first editor of the whole known corpus of major Robin Hood ballads. Meanwhile, another editor had published a collection of popular ballads for a perhaps wider audience.

Thomas Evans and Old Ballads, Historical and Narrative

Thomas Evans (1742–1784), whose background is obscure, was apprenticed to a bookseller in London in 1757, later setting up his own shop at 50 Strand in 1774.[7] Evans was a 'literary' bookseller, a businessman rather than a scholar. Careless about copyright restrictions, he published editions of complete collections of the works of important poets. His own two-volume collection of *Old Ballads, Historical and Narrative, and Some of Modern Date* (1777), included 27 Robin Hood poems in the first volume, many of them from the Garlands of the post-Restoration years, none of them being from what is now the generally acknowledged medieval canon.[8] It did not, however, include any new Robin Hood material. Evans was well aware of the significance of Percy's publication of a dozen years previously, and in his preface he referred the reader to Percy's 'very ingenious essay on the ancient English minstrels, which precludes any attempts of ours to illustrate that subject'. He therefore saw his work as supplementing that of Percy, who by then had become a literary celebrity, and he exploited the new market that Percy had created. Evans regarded the ballad as 'the native species of the poetry of this country', and felt that the surviving material 'should no longer be left subject to accident and chance, to perish in oblivion. A polished age will make allowance for the rude productions of their ancestors, who, if they do not dazzle the imagination, commonly interest the heart'. His preface did not give any indication as to the source of the texts he printed, or provide any critical apparatus to contextualise them, as Percy had attempted, and they mostly consisted of run-of-the-mill material. Nevertheless, Evans's collection proved popular, and a new extended edition of four volumes, padded out by extra material of poor quality, dedicated to the Duke of Northumberland, followed in 1784, the year of his death.

---

7   Some of this biographical information is derived from the *ODNB* entry by J. E. Tierney, accessed 15 February 2018.
8   T. Evans, *Old Ballads, Historical and Narrative, with some of Modern Date; now first Collected, and Reprinted from Rare Copies* (London, 1777), I, pp. 86–236. On Evans, see also E. D. Gregory, *Victorian Songhunters: The Recovering and Editing of English Vernacular Ballads and Folk Lyrics, 1820–1883* (Lanham, Maryland, Toronto and Oxford, 2006), pp. 38–39.

The Robin Hood Society and English Radicalism

The name of the outlaw was used as the title for one of the main radical societies of the third quarter of the eighteenth century. The Robin Hood Society, founded before 1750 and disappearing from view in 1779, preceded the 'ultra' radicalism that followed the French Revolution.[9] Its meetings, and those of similar societies in London and a number of provincial cities, gave opportunities for working men (women were excluded) of limited formal education to express their views on religion, politics and society through debates held under strict procedures and usually in public houses. It was in its day the most famous debating society in England, so well-known that its name became the generic term for debating societies generally. In the American colonies, views regarded as disloyal to established institutions were ridiculed as coming from the Robin Hood Society of New York. The Society met on Mondays in a room at the Robin Hood public house, in Butcher Row, designated by Dobson and Taylor as 'the most famous of all Robin Hood inns', from 1750 to 1779;[10] earlier it had met in the Essex Head public house in Essex Street nearby, being then known as the Essex Head Club. Its new name therefore derived from that of the public house rather than any specific implication of its social and political stance, and its official name was 'The Society for Free and Candid Enquiry'. The more popular name however fitted well enough in terms of its political and social attitudes, with its membership drawn from the middling or lower ranks of London society.[11] Another London radical, a lawyer, himself well aware of the existence of the Society, became the next individual to make a major contribution to the study of the medieval outlaw.

Joseph Ritson and the Tales of Robin Hood

Joseph Ritson (1752-1803) was born and brought up in Stockton on Tees, where at a young age he developed antiquarian and local historical interests relating to the palatinate of Durham. He spent his adult life in London, after he moved there in 1775 to pursue a legal career in conveyancing at Gray's Inn. In 1784 he secured the position of Bailiff of the Savoy, a Duchy of Lancaster office, which provided a useful income, and decided to become a barrister. After the prescribed five years at Gray's Inn he was called to the bar in 1789, but he only practised briefly on the Northern assize circuit. His main academic interest came to be the ballad

---

9   M. Thale, 'The Robin Hood Society: Debating in Eighteenth-Century London', *London Journal* 22 (1) (1997), pp. 33–50.
10 D&T, p. 46 n. 2.
11 S. L. Barczewski, *Myth and National Identity in Nineteenth-Century Britain: The Legends of King Arthur and Robin Hood* (Oxford, 2000), pp. 31–32.

poetry of the Middle Ages, and he carried out some of his research in the British Museum and the libraries of Oxford and Cambridge. In 1782 he became involved in the first of a series of literary controversies when he published a pamphlet, *Observations on the Three First Volumes of the 'History of English Poetry'*, viciously attacking the work of Thomas Warton, a respected literary scholar and antiquary. Ritson accused Warton of ignorance and plagiarism, and the controversy he aroused at that time followed him for the remainder of his scholarly career. He made critical attacks on the textual accuracy of the works of scholars of lyrical English poetry, the narrative ones being defined by him as 'Ballads', as distinct from 'Songs', whose characteristics he considered were 'sentiment, expression, or even description'.

His principal attack was to be on Percy's *Reliques*, and the resulting dispute between them went on until his own death in 1803. While Ritson admitted that Percy's work had its merits, he also accused him of having included forged or garbled versions of many ballads: he had inserted 'his own fabrication for the sake of providing more refine'd entertainment for readers of taste and genius'. His view was that 'a strict adherence to ancient orthography ... is the test of an editors fidelity'.[12] In 1783 Ritson advocated the need for careful reference to the exact sources in manuscript or print, and meticulous attention to the accuracy of the text: 'To correct the obvious errors of an illiterate transcriber, to supply irremediable defects, and to make sense of nonsense, are certainly the essential dutys of an editour of ancient poetry; provided he act with integrity and publicity, but secretly to suppress the original text, and insert his own fabrications for the sake of providing more refine'd entertainment for readers of taste and genius, is no proof of either judgement, candour, or integrity'.[13] He also threw doubt on the existence of the manuscript from which Percy claimed to have derived his ballads, since the latter refused to allow it to be inspected by him or anyone else. In 1792, in a letter to a friend, Percy wrote that 'he shall be disappointed: the manuscript shall never be exposed to his sight in my life-time'.[14] Nevertheless, although in his fourth edition of the *Reliques* in 1794 he did make a few alterations by way of acknowledgement of some of his inaccuracies, in particular by amending the text of *Robin Hood and Guy of Gisborne*, Ritson was obliged in 1795 to reprint Percy's text of that ballad, and so he specifically disclaimed responsibility for it.[15] The eventual publication of the 'Percy Folio' in 1867, shortly before it became Additional Manuscript 27879 in the British Museum,[16] amply confirmed more generally the

12   B. H. Bronson, *Joseph Ritson: Scholar at Arms* (2 vols., Berkeley, 1938), II, p. 548.
13   J. Ritson, *A Select Collection of English Songs* (London, 1783), I, p. x.
14   Bronson, *Ritson* II, p. 550.
15   Bronson, *Ritson* II, pp. 571–72.
16   According to British Library Records, it was acquired from E. Mead on 9 May 1868.

accuracy of many of Ritson's comments on Percy's editorial methods. The final line of the final stanza (58) of *Gisborne* provides a particularly stark example, not corrected in 1794. The sheriff runs away towards his house in Nottingham, and Little John shoots him with a broad arrow. Percy's version of the last line reads:

> He shott him into the 'backe'-syde, -

The manuscript itself has, by comparison:

> Did cleave his head in twinn.

Frederick Furnivall's editorial footnote reads: 'Too bad, Bishop! And to put your inverted commas too, as if you'd only altered the one word 'backe' – F.'[17]

A religious sceptic and a vegetarian, Ritson was a liberal supporter of Charles James Fox and parliamentary reform, greatly disliked George III, and favoured the American colonists in their fight for independence. He acclaimed the early stages of the French Revolution, spending two months near Paris in 1790. He returned filled with enthusiasm for the republican form of government, and remained an advocate of the principles of republicanism until his death. He began, for a time, to address his friends as 'Citizen', and use the French revolutionary calendar, but in 1792, as conservative anti-Revolutionary forces in England grew, he became more circumspect, recommending a friend to 'lay your politics and philosophy upon the shelf, for a few years at least' and attend to normal business. In 1794 some of his acquaintances were arrested or retained as witnesses, and his personal liberty may have been in danger for a time.[18] His views fed into the work upon which his future reputation has most depended, his *Robin Hood: A Collection of all the Ancient Poems, Songs, and Ballads now extant Related to that Celebrated English Outlaw* (2 vols., 1795). For many years he had attempted to collect all the 'historical or poetical remains' concerning Robin Hood, and his book was the result of his labours. Much of his interest in the outlaw hero stemmed from his own political opinions.

In the remaining eight years of his life after the publication of his great work, Ritson's mental and physical health declined, although he continued to take on other projects, publishing a work on medieval English poets in 1802, as well as a book on abstinence from consuming animal food.[19] His circle of friends continued to expand, and came to include Walter Scott, with whom he exchanged visits in 1801 and 1803,

---

[17] Bronson, *Ritson* II, p. 572; Hales and Furnivall II, p. 237; D&T, p. 145.
[18] Bronson, *Ritson*, I, pp. 150–60.
[19] His vegetarianism was lampooned in the year of his death in a famous etching by James Sayers: National Portrait Gallery, D9263.

and they corresponded about Robin Hood in the intervening year. Ritson assisted Scott in collecting Scottish materials, although he managed to offend Mrs Scott by his reaction when she offered him meat at table. He died in 1803, having to be removed from his office in Gray's Inn for burning papers, which threatened to set the building ablaze, and he was sent to a private lunatic asylum, where he died not long afterwards. Bishop Percy heard of his death with apparent satisfaction, confirming how personal the controversy between them had been: 'the wretched man's turbulent and ferocious spirit had ended in insanity … if you look into his edition of the metrical romances, you will see it filled with the grossest scurrility and most illiberal abuse of your humble'. Thomas Park, another literary associate, commented that his 'melancholy and pitiable end' had 'formed the only apology that could be suggested for a life passed in self-created enmity with all mankind'. Scott struck a more positive note in the *Edinburgh Review* in 1806, opining that 'the late Mr Ritson united acute abilities and an intimate acquaintance with every collateral source from which light could be thrown upon his subject', but vitriol from Percy and others continued until the latter's death in 1811, and for some years beyond.[20]

Ritson's book about Robin Hood was a work of great importance in the history of the outlaw legend, not least because of its superior editorial standards, honed by the long controversy with Percy. It provided the standard edition of the texts of the tales, and was reprinted fifteen times between 1820 and 1887, two years before it was superseded by the final edition of the work of Francis Child in 1889.[21] The texts are divided into two parts, the first part including four of what have become the five recognised medieval Robin Hood stories; the exception was *Robin Hood and the Beggar*, not known until the second half of the seventeenth century, which he also included among them. Ritson was the first scholar to establish the *Gest* as the centrepiece of the early tales, a view accepted by all subsequent scholars of the outlaw legend. He was also the first to identify and publish the tale that has become known as *Robin Hood and the Potter*, 'this curious, and hitherto unpublished, and even un-heard-of old piece', coining what has come to be its established title. He had found it 'among bishop More's collections' in Cambridge university library, and dated it by the handwriting to about 1500. He noted that the surviving text, simply entitled 'Robyn Hode' at the end, was corrupted and was probably composed by the original author at an earlier period.[22] The

20 Bronson, *Ritson*, I, pp. 252, 293–94, 302–11. For an assessment of Ritson's achievement, see also E. D. Gregory, *Victorian Songhunters: The Recovering and Editing of English Vernacular Ballads and Folk Lyrics, 1820–1883* (Lanham, Maryland, Toronto and Oxford, 2006), pp. 39–42.
21 D&T, p. 54 n. 2.
22 Ritson, *Robin Hood*, I, p. 81; D&T, p. 113 with an illustration of the opening

single manuscript copy of *Robin Hood and the Monk*, a fifteenth century tale, was in another Cambridge manuscript but was not found by Ritson; it was first published (in Edinburgh) three years after Ritson's death. It was not included in successive editions of his book until it was added in that of 1832, which was the point at which the title of the tale was first coined.[23] Ritson had been well aware that they were not, in every instance, 'so important, so ancient, or, perhaps, so authentic as the subject seems to demand', stating that he was 'desirous to omit nothing that he could find upon the subject' and had 'everywhere faithfully vouched and exhibited his authorities, such as they are'. The second part includes 28 of what he knew to be later tales.

Another remarkable aspect of Ritson's work is the unprecedented attempt at a biography of the outlaw, followed by a much longer supplementary section entitled 'Notes and illustrations referred to in the foregoing life'.[24] This gives a wealth of information of different kinds and of varying importance and accuracy, mentioning for the first time many references to the outlaw legend which have been used and re-interpreted by subsequent writers on the subject. Ritson's opening remarks show how well he understood the limitations of what he could hope to say about the outlaw's life. 'The times in which he lived, the mode of life he adopted, and the silence or loss of contemporary writers, are circumstances sufficiently favourable, indeed, to romance, but altogether inimical to historical truth'; his biography, 'though it may fail to satisfy, may possibly serve to amuse'. Holt regarded this as an excuse for, rather than a warning of, what was to follow, because he then gives an account based largely on the anonymous 'Sloane Life', failing to appreciate that the 'Life' was simply a rehash of the tradition originally stemming from John Major.[25] Nevertheless, Ritson did attempt to make an evaluation of the sources he was aware of, using the critical faculties of his profession. The alleged evidence that the outlaw flourished in the reign of Richard I would not 'be sufficient to decide the point in a court of justice; but neither judge nor counsel will dispute the authority of that oracle of the law sir Edward Coke', who had pronounced in favour of that view. He made disparaging reference to previous attempted 'biographies', including one by 'an ingenious antiquary' who, about 1680, stated that the outlaw had been banished by Henry VIII. He supposed that no mention of him was made by Matthew Paris or other early English historians probably because of 'his avowed enmity to churchmen', but Fordun and Major,

---

lines opposite p. 124. John Moore was bishop of Ely and died in 1714: his collection of manuscripts was given to the university by George I in 1715.

[23] D&T, pp. 113–14.
[24] Ritson, *Robin Hood*, I, pp. xiv–cxviii.
[25] Holt, *Robin Hood*, pp. 40–41, 44–45. On the 'Sloane Life', see, in particular, D&T, pp. 286–87.

'being foreigners, have not been deterred by this professional spirit from rendering homage to his virtues'.

Ritson wrote that Robin was born at Locksley in Nottinghamshire in about 1160; although he could find no such place in gazetteers, he did not regard that as conclusive proof that it never existed. He was, according to authorities such as Richard Grafton and William Stukeley, of noble extraction, perhaps with a claim to the earldom of Huntingdon; his true name was Robert Fitzooth, a descendant of one of William II's barons, according to Stukeley's (fictitious) pedigree of 1746, which he reproduced. The details of his subsequent supposed life are culled from a variety of writers, including textual criticism and comparison of their accounts, and with occasional scepticism: 'as to the credibility of the story [about the distance flown by an arrow], every reader may judge thereof as he thinks proper'. After an extravagant youth, Robin's fortune was lost and, by necessity or choice, he took refuge in the woods, as stated by Major. Other writers had identified these as being in northern forests, Barnsdale in Yorkshire, Sherwood in Nottinghamshire and perhaps also Plumpton park in Cumberland. He was joined by a band, of whom the leading members were Little John (surnamed Nailor), William Scadlock, Scathelock or Scarlet, George A Green, the pinder of Wakefield, Much the miller's son, and a monk or friar called Tuck. His female companion and lover was Marian, and his company consisted of a hundred archers. For many years he reigned like an independent sovereign in the forest, living on the deer and taking fuel from the woods. He was at war with the king's subjects, especially the clergy, monastic and secular, except for the poor and needy, and the oppressed, who he protected. In old age and infirmity, he retired to Kirklees priory, the prioress being a kinswoman, who treacherously bled him to death on 18 November 1247, a date he took from Thomas Gale's epitaph. The equivalent of that date in the Julian calendar is the 14th kalends of December, so he seems to have assumed that Gale's 24th kalends was an error for the 14th kalends and to have silently corrected it.[26] He was buried under some trees nearby, a stone with a memorial inscription being placed over his grave. His account of the inscription gave Ritson the opportunity for sarcastic remarks about Dr Percy, that 'ingenious writer, whose knowledge and judgment of ancient poetry are so conspicuous and eminent'.

Ritson follows his account with a paean of praise for his hero, who he saw as having been a real person who embodied many of his own beliefs and aspirations: 'a man who, in a barbarous age, and under a complicated tyranny, displayed a spirit of freedom and independence which has endeared him to the common people, whose cause he maintained, (for all opposition to tyranny is the cause of the people,) and, in spite of the

---

[26] Holt, *Robin Hood*, pp. 41–42.

malicious endeavours of pitiful monks, by whom history was consecrated to the crimes and follies of titled ruffians and sainted idiots, to supress all record of his patriotic exertions and virtuous acts, will render his name immortal'. 'With respect to his personal character, it is sufficiently evident that he was active, brave, prudent, patient; possessed of uncommon bodily strength, and considerable military skill; just, generous, benevolent, faithful, and beloved or revered by his followers or adherents for his excellent and amiable qualities'.[27] For the first time, Robin became a revolutionary hero, an advocate of popular liberty, in the fashion of the times in which the editor lived. He had become, in the words of Eric Hobsbawm,'the archetype of the social rebel'.[28]

The Legend in Popular Culture: Scott, Peacock and Egan

The events which followed the French Revolution, especially the execution of Louis XVI and Marie Antoinette in 1793, led in England to a strong reaction against revolutionary change, and a corresponding reverence for traditional values and institutions, such as the monarchy, the church and parliament. The centuries before the Reformation seemed to the upper classes in England to have been characterised by a stable, hierarchical social structure and a simple religious faith, contrasting with the turbulent and dangerous forces released by the events in France. Conservatives used the medieval past to demonstrate the continuity and stability of British institutions, while radicals advocated the recovery of the supposed freedom of Anglo-Saxon times extinguished by the 'Norman yoke'.[29] The revival of interest took a number of forms, artistic, chivalric, architectural, and literary, which flourished with vigour following the end of the Napoleonic Wars in 1815. There was a pronounced shift in the nature of popular material about the outlaw legend, outside the realm of the scholarly work carried out during the time of Ritson and his contemporaries.[30] The plays of the period from the 1590s to the 1630s, plus the few comic operas of the late eighteenth century, the commercial productions of printed ballads during the reigns of James I and Charles I, and the garlands bringing them together following the Restoration and continuing thereafter, derived from the outlines of the legend as established by the mid-seventeenth century. They ran in parallel with, but were mostly unrelated to, the scholarly work of Percy and Ritson.[31] With

---

[27] Ritson, *Robin Hood* I, pp. xi–xii.
[28] E. Hobsbawm, *Primitive Rebels: Studies in Archaic Forms of Social Movement in the 19th and 20th Centuries* (New York, 1963), p. 4.
[29] Barczewski, *Myth and National Identity*, pp. 33–34.
[30] The chronological list of Robin Hood literature in D&T, pp. 315–18, is a very useful background guide to this material.
[31] On these developments, see Chapter 2, and D&T, pp. 46–53. For a stimulating

the latter's great work providing the essential source-book, the legend took its place in the Romantic movement in literature. In 1818 John Keats wrote a short poem, published in 1820, entitled *Robin Hood: To A Friend*, so called because it was quickly penned in reply to J. H. Reynolds, who had just sent him two sonnets about the outlaw.[32] Its tone was a nostalgic evocation of 'olde England', a lost past, a golden age of a merry life in the summer greenwood, and a lament for its passing. The outlaw also attracted the attention of novelists like Walter Scott (*Ivanhoe*, 1819) and Thomas Love Peacock (*Maid Marian*, 1822), while Robert Southey wrote a poem of which only a fragment survives.[33]

Peacock's novel was intended to be 'a comic romance of the twelfth century ... the vehicle of much oblique satire on all the oppressions that are done under the sun', to attack what he considered to be evils in his own age; but he succeeded only in romanticising the medieval greenwood. 'So Robin and Marian dwelt in and reigned in the forest, ranging the glades and the greenwoods ... and administering natural justice according to Robin's ideas of rectifying the inequalities of human condition; raising genial dews from the bags of the rich and idle, and returning them in fertilising showers on the poor and industrious'. For the first time, Marian was depicted by Peacock as a sensual, vigorous and assertive figure, in accordance with his broader views of the importance of women in society.[34] *Maid Marian* was immediately adapted as a Christmas comic opera, *Maid Marian; or The Huntress of Arlingford*, performed at Covent Garden and later in New York, but it did not have the long-term influence of *Ivanhoe* on the popular legend. In that novel, which had chivalry as its main theme, Robin appears as a relatively minor character, referred to as 'Locksley' until revealed as Robin Hood, and Friar Tuck as a splendidly rumbustious cleric, the hermit of Copmanhurst. Robin appears as a yeoman, nothing being said about any claim to an earldom. The story was set in the by now conventional period of King Richard's return from captivity, following his crusade, in 1193-4, and included an episode in which Richard pardoned Robin after having dealt with him in the disguise of an ordinary, but disinherited, crusader knight. In *Ivanhoe* Scott further popularised the mainstream legend of Robin Hood as it had developed from the time of John Major, and gave it a new boost just as

---

sociocultural account of Robin Hood in nineteenth-century popular culture, see Knight, *Mythic Biography*, Chapter 3.

32 See J. Barnard. 'Keats's 'Robin Hood', John Hamilton Reynolds, and the 'Old Poets', *Proceedings of the British Academy* 75 (1989), pp. 181-200, reprinted in Knight. *Anthology*, pp. 123-40. Reynolds's sonnets are printed there, pp. 125-26.
33 *Robin Hood, A Fragment, By the Late Robert Southey and Caroline Southey* (Edinburgh and London, 1847), pp. 1-37.
34 Barczewski, *Myth and National Identity*, pp. 190-92.

the long period of garland literature, which had kept it in the popular consciousness for so long, was finally ending.

Scott and Peacock were widely read by the more literate of the working classes, in rural villages as well as towns, in the 1820s and 1830s. This led, for example, at Edwinstowe, in Nottinghamshire in Sherwood Forest, to 'Sherwood Gatherings' in 1841 and 1842, where the outlaw was toasted, and where even the local aristocracy subsequently took an interest in the legend.[35] One element in what he wrote was quite new, however, that is, the notion that Robin Hood was an Anglo-Saxon leader of the oppressed English against the Norman conqueror. Scott admitted that he had taken the idea of the persistence of racial enmity between Saxons and Normans from a play called *Runnamede*, about King John and his rebel barons, which had been written by a Scots Presbyterian minister from Leith, John Logan (1748-88). He had probably seen it performed in Edinburgh as a boy in 1783. The theme was immediately taken up by the French historian Augustin Thierry in his *Histoire de la Conquete de l'Angleterre par les Normands*, published in 1825. He mentioned Robin in his account of Richard's reign, treating the stories about him as real historical evidence. Even though it was in French, Thierry's history became popular in England, and with it his treatment of Robin Hood as the 'hero of the ... Anglo-Saxon race'. By 1856 there had been three editions of his work in English, and in 1860 a London opera, *Robin Hood*, also used the context of the conflict between Saxons and Normans, as did novels and children's stories.[36] Thierry's influence and that of Scott was ultimately responsible for later portrayals of the outlaw in that entirely fictional context.

Pierce Egan and popular fiction

In 1840 Pierce Egan produced a version of the legend in novel format aimed at working-class readers, full of 'violent deaths, amorous encounters, attempted rapes, melodramatic confrontations, abductions and incarcerations'.[37] Egan (1814-1880) was one of the most popular writers of 'penny dreadfuls' in the Victorian period. His novels were first issued in weekly numbers, and some of them contained woodcuts and etchings by the author, who had been to the art school of the Royal Academy as a young man and was a skilled illustrator.[38]

---

[35] D. Crook, 'The Novelist, the Heiress, the Artisan and the Banker: The Emergence of the Robin Hood Legend at Edwinstowe, c.1819 to 1849', *TTS* 119 (2015), pp. 1–13; see also Barczewski, *Myth and National Identity*, pp. 77–80.
[36] Barczewski, *Myth and National Identity*, pp. 129–34.
[37] Carpenter, *Robin Hood*, pp. 197–98.
[38] A useful biography of Egan by Stephen Basdeo (2016), fuller than the entry in *ODNB*, is available online at https://gesteofrobinhood.com/2016/08/06/pierce-egan-the-younger-1814-1880-biography-of-a-penny-dreadful-author/;

Egan made no claims to historical accuracy concerning the outlaw, as he explicitly stated in his preface:

> 'Although his fame is universal, the existing details of his life are but few, and so surrounded by the mists and obscurity of age, but that little certain can be gathered … in the following pages the Author had no material for the earlier portion of Robin Hood's life but such as his imagination supplied him with'.

Some chapters are headed with quotations of passages from some of the tales, especially the *Gest*, and most of the traditional characters appear, with the addition of new ones. Set initially in 1161 in the reign of Henry II, with the birth of a child called 'Robyn Head', 'or as in after times it became corrupted, Robin Hood', the early chapters include a character called 'Roland Ritson of Mansfield', linking the renowned editor of the tales with one of the real places in Sherwood Forest that feature in the story. Later the hero fights against King John, before dying early in the reign of Henry III at the hands of the treacherous prioress of Kirklees and a knight said to be the brother of Sir Guy of Gisborne. Encouraged by the success of his book, Egan rapidly returned to the outlaw theme, publishing *Adam Bell, Clim of the Clough, and William of Cloudeslie* in 1842, before turning to a variety of other subjects. His books started a trend that has been called 'a whole Robin Hood industry in popular fiction'.[39] In the 1860s, by which time he was comfortably off, he was said by one critic to be more popular than Tennyson or Dickens. His work and that of other popular authors like him was unconnected with continuing scholarly work on the texts of the early tales and the possible origins of the legend, which was being undertaken by relatively unknown academic and antiquarian writers. These led to very significant further developments during the following two decades.

Egan's work was quickly followed in 1841 by a version of the legend suitable for children, *Robin Hood and his Merry Foresters*, with coloured illustrations, by Joseph Cundall (1818–95, pseudonym Stephen Percy), a publisher and early photographer. It was published in the United States in the following year, and there seem to have been more editions there than in Britain. It was not the first Robin Hood book aimed at children, because the second edition of Ritson's collection, minus

---

accessed 22 February 2018. *Robin Hood and Little John, or, The Merry Men of Sherwood Forest*, was his second novel, which had been serialised between 1838 and 1840 in 41 penny parts. It was hugely popular and was reprinted many times, including five times before 1850. Its illustrations were not on this occasion by Egan himself, but were by W. H. Thwaites and engraved by John Wall.

39 J. Sutherland, *The Longman Companion to Victorian Fiction* (London, 1988), pp. 208–9.

most of his scholarly notes, had been published in London in 1820; this edition, it was said 'could with propriety be put into the hands of young persons'.[40] The genre continued and developed in both countries during the second half of the nineteenth century and the twentieth and, through the American author Howard Pyle's romanticisation of the legend for American children in his *The Merry Adventures of Robin Hood* (1883), eventually had a significant influence on American cinema. On the stage the nineteenth century ended with Alfred Tennyson's play *The Foresters*, first performed in New York in 1892 after being rejected in England a decade earlier. The history of these developments now has an extensive literature,[41] but they were far removed from the continuing scholarly discourse about the legend which turned in new directions in the second half of the nineteenth century.

Thomas Wright: Robin Hood and Folklore

Thomas Wright (1810–1877) was an historian and antiquary, born at Tenbury, Worcestershire, and educated at grammar school in Ludlow.[42] His early literary promise encouraged a local benefactor to pay for him to attend Trinity College, Cambridge, where he graduated in 1837. The leading Anglo-Saxon scholar J. M. Kemble introduced him to Old English, and his life-long interest in vernacular sources began. From about 1837 until his death Wright lived in London, and was involved in the formation of new antiquarian and literary societies. He was secretary of the Camden Society at its formation in 1838, and secretary and treasurer of the Percy Society (1840-52), named after Bishop Percy. That society had higher editorial standards than its mentor, printing texts in their publications exactly as given in the sources. Wright was elected to the Society of Antiquaries in 1837. His subsequent published work covered a variety of subjects in his areas of interest, principally Old English, Middle English, and Anglo-Norman texts, and perhaps his main and longest lasting contribution to scholarship was to demonstrate the value of this vernacular literature in understanding the everyday lives and beliefs of people in the middle ages. He connected the two in a very important piece he wrote about the Robin Hood legend in 1846, in a book of essays partly about the history of popular superstitions and the written sources which recorded them.[43] He took it as an article of faith that 'the fables and legend now current among the peasantry

---

[40] Carpenter, *Robin Hood*, pp. 184, 220; D&T, p. 59.
[41] See, in particular, D. Petzold, 'Der Rebell im Kinderzimmer: Robin Hood in der Kinderliteratur', in Carpenter, *Robin Hood*, pp. 65–86; D&T, pp. 59–62. On Tennyson, see D&T, pp. 243–50, and Knight, *Complete Study*, pp. 197–201.
[42] ODNB entry by M. W. Thomson, accessed 15 February 2018.
[43] T. Wright, 'On the Popular Cycle of the Robin Hood Ballads', *Essays on Subjects*

are the fictions of the middle ages', and that 'much of history itself is nothing more than legend and romance', although he accepted that the official records of royal government, the publication of which had in recent decades greatly accelerated, could in some cases clarify the truth behind events recorded by legend. He occasionally referred to those sources himself, on such matters as the fate of one of the killers of Edward II, evidence for the English lands of Eustace the Monk (d. 1217) and a pardon by King John to Fulk fitz Warin (d. 1258).[44]

Wright was well aware of the earliest reference to the Robin Hood stories in Langland's *Piers Ploughman,* of which his own edition was first published in two volumes in 1832.[45] In his essay of 1846 he quoted the famous passage about the rhymes of Robin Hood and 'Randolf' earl of Chester, and said that this and other passages 'describe a cycle of poetry essentially popular, which originated with the people and rested with the people'. He went on to consider the text of the tale now known as *Robin Hood and the Monk,* which he thought was a ballad of fourteenth-century date, 'one of those which was sung by the contemporaries of … the author of *Piers Plowman's Visions'*, and might even date from the reign of Edward II. In true scholarly style, he based this partly on attempts to date other poems found in the same manuscript. There follows a long account of the tale, followed by remarks about similarities to that particular story found in *Adam Bell, Clym of the Clough and William of Cloudesley.*[46] He had already noted that the three essays in his volume which preceded his interpretation of Robin Hood were about real historical characters who took on a legendary aspect after their own deaths, Hereward the Saxon (Hereward the Wake, fl. 1070-71), Eustace the Monk and Fulk fitz Warin, the latter described by Wright as 'a true Robin Hood'. Here he pointed them out as being 'the kind of stories which formed the material of our Robin Hood ballads'. He goes on to summarise *Robin Hood and the Potter,* the story we now know as *Robyn and Gandeleyn,* and finally the *Gest.* This entire excursus led him to conclude that 'the character and popular history of Robin Hood was formed upon the ballads, and not the ballads upon the person'.[47]

He continued by savagely attacking the attempts of Ritson to construct a biography of the outlaw, condemning it, 'and the pedantic notes which illustrate it', as the 'barren production of a poor mind'. 'The accurate *mister* Ritson, who condemned with such asperity the slightest

---

Connected with the Literature, Popular Superstitions and History of England in the Middle Ages (2 vols., London, 1846), II, pp. 164–211; Essay XVII.
44 Wright, *Essays,* pp. 81–83, 141–42, 162–63.
45 T. Wright, *'The Vision and the Creed of Piers Ploughman': With Notes and a Glossary* (London, 1844). A revised edition was published in 1856.
46 Wright, *Essays,* pp. 173–84. See also D&T, p. 260.
47 Wright, *Essays,* pp. 90, 186, 200.

wanderings of the imagination of others, has therein illustrated some truly pleasant vagaries of his own. He gives us an essay upon the *private character* of the outlaw!'[48] He also dismissed the suggestion by C. E. A. E. Barry, the French author of *Thèse de Littérature sur les Vicissitudes et les Transformacions du Cycle Populaire de Robin Hood*, published in Paris in 1832, that Robin was a Saxon rebel against the conquering Normans. He associated the outlaw rather with the May games, an early form of which he suggested could be found in practices held at Barnwell in Cambridgeshire in late June, as recorded in an entry in the Barnwell priory cartulary, which he found in the British Museum.[49] He was attracted by the idea that Robin Hood was a corruption of 'Robin of the Wood', which had analogies in other languages, and linked with the notion of hiding from danger in the woods. One of the strongest proofs of the outlaw's mythical character was, he contended, the frequent connection of his name with mounds, stones, hills, wells and other features in the landscape, which 'our peasantry always attributed to the fairies of their popular superstition'. He even listed examples he knew, including Robin Hood's But in Shropshire, near Ludlow where he had been schooled.[50] He concluded that 'the legends of the peasantry are the shadows of a remote antiquity, and ... they enable us to place our Robin Hood with tolerable certainty among the personages of the early mythology of the Teutonic peoples'.[51]

The range and extent of Wright's publications was formidable, despite the fact that he had no inherited wealth or salaried positions, as many other antiquaries did; and much of his enormous output is attributable to his need to earn a livelihood. Later in life, however, his contribution to scholarship was recognised. In 1865 he was granted a pension of £65 from the civil list 'as an author who has contributed much to English literary and political history', increased by £35 in 1872. According a friend, he often had to work almost continuously throughout the day and much of the night to fulfil his tasks, and contemporaries attributed his mental collapse in later life to overwork. It is likely that he developed dementia before he died in London in 1877. By then his views about the origins and nature of the Robin Hood legend had attracted other adherents.

---

[48] Wright, *Essays*, p. 201.
[49] Wright, *Essays*, p. 206; BL, Harley 3601.
[50] Clearly not what is now Robin Hood's Butts, near Church Stretton and too far from Ludlow to fit: cf. D&T, p. 303.
[51] Wright, 'Robin Hood ballads', p. 211.

John Mathew Gutch and 'A Lytell Geste of Robin Hode'

John Mathew Gutch (1776–1861), a journalist and author, was born in Gloucestershire, and educated at Christ's Hospital.[52] He entered business as a law stationer in London, but in 1803 moved to Bristol to become owner and printer of *Felix Farley's Bristol Journal,* and became much involved in local politics. After his second marriage in 1823, to the daughter of a banker from Worcester, he moved there to join his father-in-law in business, although he still supervised the publication of *Felix Farley* and wrote for the Bristol *Country Constitutional Guardian* (1822–4). He helped found the London *Morning Journal* in 1828, but a conviction for libel caused the paper to be suppressed in 1830. Gutch was also a scholar and patron of literature. He wrote several pamphlets on the history of Bristol and Warwickshire, following his father's antiquarian interests, and he was a fellow of the Society of Antiquaries. While in Bristol he was active in the Philosophical and Literary Society, in 1827 publishing a collection of papers he had read there; and he was a collector and seller of antiquarian books.

In 1847 Gutch published, in two volumes, *A Lytell Geste of Robin Hode,* which, despite its claim to be 'grounded on other documents than those made use of by his former biographer "Mister Ritson"', largely consisted of an attack on Ritson's 'biography' of the original outlaw. Although he included the 'Sloane Life' among his texts, which Ritson had not, he used it for the biography of the outlaw.[53] In his preface he announces that his intention was 'to place the life and character of Robin Hood in a more favourable light', and especially in 'an attempt to controvert the noble lineage which Mr Ritson ... has ascribed to him'. After a rambling introduction, he embarks on his own Life of the outlaw 'abridged from that of Mr Ritson', based on his own 'Notes and Ilustrations', criticising Ritson's accounts of a variety of detailed matters, such as the location of Loxley, the outlaw's claim to the earldom of Huntingdon, and many others. He then begins his alternative account, based on material from Thierry's *Histoire* and from an unknown writer (G. F.) in the *Westminster Review* in 1840.[54]

---

52 ODNB entry by Elizabeth Baigent, accessed 19 February 2018.
53 J. M. Gutch, *A Lytell Geste of Robin Hode* (2 vols., London, 1847), I, pp. 379–89.
54 *Westminster Review,* volume 33, no. 65 (1840), pp. 231–63, available on https://babel.hathitrust.org/cgi/pt?id=mdp.39015005912319;view=1up;seq=241 and the following images. It is possible that 'G. F.' was George Finlay (1799–1875), a lawyer trained in Glasgow who campaigned for Greek independence from the Ottoman empire and later became an historian of Byzantium. He held both those authors in high regard, and quotes long extracts from their writings, supplemented by his own 'cursory comments'. His own main criticism of Ritson is that in compiling his Life he made no use of the *Gest,* which 'contained occurrences of much higher and truer import,

Gutch's book was much less commercially successful than Ritson's, although it was initially well received; a second edition was published in 1850, so it was important and influential. In 1848 his father-in-law's bank failed, and in 1858 Gutch's library had to be sold, for over £1800, so when he died in 1861 he was in relative poverty.[55] Meanwhile, other works about the outlaw, catering for a wider reading public unwilling to read long and repetitive medieval texts, using abridgement and adaptation, and emphasising the more interesting parts of the narrative, were also published. For example, *The Life and Exploits of Robin Hood*, published in Halifax in 1862, was 'not intended for the critic or the antiquary, but for that large proportion of the reading public who have no leisure, and but little inclination, for recondite discussions'; they were 'clothed in modern language' and supplemented by a glossary.[56] A decade before that publication, however, the search for the original outlaw had taken a new direction, as he was sought for the first time in the archives of the British state.

The beginning of historical research on the outlaw: The Reverend Joseph Hunter

Joseph Hunter, a distinguished antiquary and record scholar, was born at Sheffield in 1783, the son of a cutler.[57] His mother died in 1787, and he, the only surviving child, was left in the guardianship of the Reverend Joseph Evans, a local dissenting Presbyterian minister. He received a basic classical education at a school in Attercliffe and served a full apprenticeship as a cutler, but he also had access to a subscription library; by the age of fifteen he was developing an interest in the history and antiquities of the area. From about 1800 he was corresponding with local antiquaries and collecting historical and genealogical materials. After deciding against a career as a cutler, Hunter went in 1805 to New College, York, a Presbyterian college under strong Unitarian influence,

---

than the fictions of a mere historical romance. Mr Ritson neither particularizes, compares or unites Robin Hood with the many well authenticated public personages who are mentioned in it'.

[55] For a fuller appraisal of Gutch's contribution, see also E. D. Gregory, *Victorian Songhunters: The Recovering and Editing of English Vernacular Ballads and Folk Lyrics, 1820–1883* (Lanham, Maryland, Toronto and Oxford, 2006), pp. 143–45.

[56] Barczewski, *Myth and National Identity*, p. 89.

[57] On his life, see *ODNB*; D. Crook, 'The Reverend Joseph Hunter and the Public Records', *Transactions of the Hunter Archaeological Society* 12 (1983), pp. 1–15; J. D. Cantwell, *The Public Record Office 1838–1958* (London, 1991); D. Evans, 'Joseph Hunter, Assistant Keeper of the Records, 1838–1861', *Transactions of the Hunter Archaeological Society* 8 (1960–63), pp. 263–71; Silvester Joseph Hunter, *A Brief Memoir of the late Joseph Hunter, F.S.A.*, privately printed (London, 1861).

to study for the ministry. On completing his studies in 1809 he became minister of a congregation in Bath, where he remained for twenty-three years. In 1815 he married Mary Hayward, with whom he had six children. He became a leading member of the Bath Literary and Scientific Institution, and also of the 'Stourhead circle' of Sir Richard Colt Hoare (1758-1838), a baronet, antiquarian and historian of Wiltshire, who held annual meetings of gentlemen scholars from Somerset and Wiltshire in his house at Stourhead. Despite living in Somerset, Hunter continued work on southern Yorkshire, visiting the area when he could and sometimes borrowing Yorkshire manuscripts from their owners. During his holidays he also visited the British Museum in London and the Bodleian Library in Oxford, where the collections of Roger Dodsworth, the seventeenth-century Yorkshire antiquary, were housed. This work culminated in the publication in 1819 of his history of the Sheffield area, *Hallamshire: The History and Topography of the Parish of Sheffield*, and in 1828 and 1831 of his two-volume work on the deanery of Doncaster, *South Yorkshire*, which served to establish his reputation. They included important research on the Yorkshire places connected with the legend of Robin Hood.[58] The publication of the first volume was probably the reason why he was elected a fellow of the Society of Antiquaries of London in 1819 and admitted in 1822. He remained a fellow for the rest of his life, serving as a member of its council five times between 1843 and 1855 and as vice-president from 1855 to 1859.[59]

Until the 1830s Hunter had made no first-hand use of the records of government departments and courts held at various repositories in London because, like many other scholars, he found access to them difficult to obtain. In 1833, however, he was appointed as a sub-commissioner of the public records, under the sixth and last of the Record Commissions (1831–37), and moved to London. There Hunter continued his antiquarian pursuits as a prominent fellow of the Society of Antiquaries and read many papers to the society. He was in favour of the full publication of the texts of government records as a means of making the information they contained more accessible to scholars such as himself, and he was responsible for various editions of records, in some of which he found himself revising unsatisfactory work originally undertaken by others. He also catalogued various collections of private manuscripts for the commissioners, although he regarded such work as of lesser importance. The Commission attracted

---

[58] For this material, see Chapter 5.
[59] Society of Antiquaries of London, Minutes XXXIV, 455, 514. For his contributions to the Society's publications on a variety of subjects, see www.cambridge.org/core/search?q=Joseph+Hunter. His portrait, by Henry Smith (1852), is on view at the home of the Antiquaries, Burlington House: see Figure 3.

FIGURE 3. Society of Antiquaries of London, Portrait of the Reverend Joseph Hunter, by Henry Smith (1852). Painted in the same year during which Hunter's controversial attempt to identify the original Robin Hood through the use of government records was published.

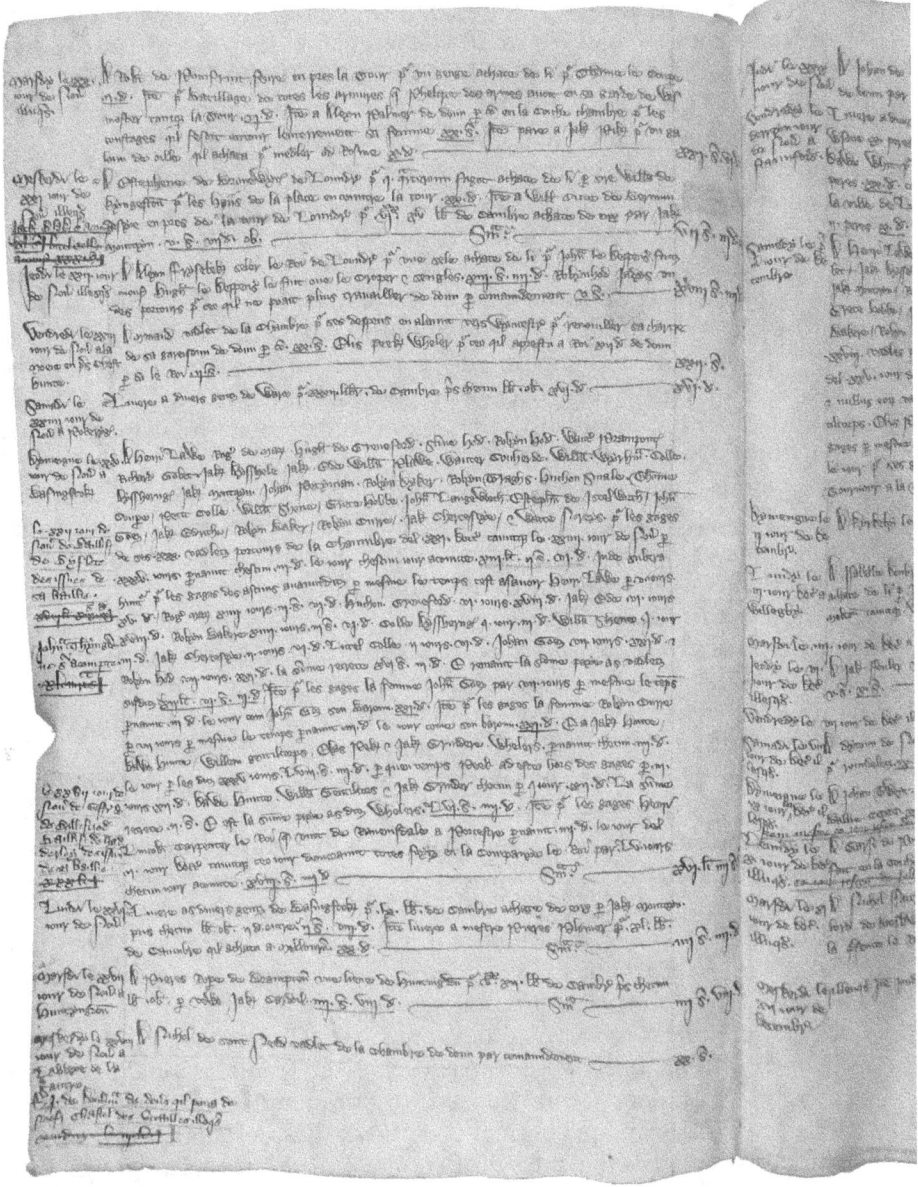

FIGURE 4. Page of a royal wardrobe account of 17-18 Edward II (1324-5), including a record of the retirement of the porter Robin Hood because he was no longer able to work. The last entry in the third paragraph from the top, relating to Thursday 22 November [1324] reads (lines 11-12) 'Robynhod jadys un des portours pur ceo qil ne poait plus travailler de don per comaundement v s.' The sixth paragraph consists of a typical list of payments to the porters, made at Basingstoke on Sunday 25 November [1324], to him and his colleagues: the first line lists 'Henri Lawe, Roger de Mar', Hugh de Greeneford, Simon Hod, Robyn Hod …'.

criticism for extravagance, leading to the appointment of a parliamentary select committee of inquiry in 1836. He gave evidence to it in defence of the Commission, and in 1837 his work moved away from the editing of records for publication to the sorting and cataloguing of the records of the Exchequer, which had effectively been abolished in 1833. At the Augmentation Office, he began work on sorting and listing the 'ancient miscellanea' of the King's/Queen's Remembrancer's department, 751 sacks-full of detailed financial accounts, a task which remained his principal activity for the rest of his life.

In 1840, after a period of great uncertainty about his future, he was confirmed as one of the first generation of assistant keepers of the new Public Record Office, established by an act of parliament in 1838 to preserve the records of government departments and central courts, and make them more readily available to researchers. In 1843 his office moved to the branch record office at Carlton Ride, the former stables of Carlton House, where he remained, with a team of clerks and workmen, for over fifteen years, creating an ordered arrangement and brief descriptions for the previously disordered and often damaged documents. His superior, the Deputy Keeper of the Public Records, Sir Francis Palgrave, had faith in his ability to carry out this work: 'altogether this task is one which requires, besides heavy labour, great critical knowledge and that stimulus of earnest antiquarian zeal and energy, with which Mr. Hunter is so peculiarly endowed'. 'Antiquarian zeal' was an appropriate phrase, for it is clear that Hunter's personal interest in these documents was more in the topographical and genealogical material they contained than what they revealed about the revenue of the medieval state.

During his official work on the archives of the Queen's Remembrancer, Hunter identified documents which, he suggested, indicated that the original Robin Hood might have been a porter working in the household of Edward II in 1323-4, a case he put forward in a long essay, *The Great Hero of the Ancient Minstrelsy of England, 'Robin Hood'*, published in London in 1852.[60] He was the first scholar to try to identify the outlaw through references in early official records. Hunter began his paper by asserting that, despite contrary views, the 'remains of the ancient minstrelsy of England' were very worthy of attentive examination, and that he had 'made an approach at least towards ascertaining the true era of the person who is the subject of so many of these ancient songs, and the class of persons to which he belonged' by study of 'the matter laid up in the obscurest treasuries of history', treating it as 'a subject properly *historical*'. He rejected the view that Robin Hood was a Saxon rebel, defying the authority of the Norman conquerors, and asserted that he did

---

[60] J. Hunter, *The Great Hero of the Ancient Minstrelsy of England, 'Robin Hood', His Period, Real Character, etc. Investigated and Perhaps Ascertained, Critical and Historical Tracts IV* (London, 1852).

not live until long after that animosity had ceased. The outlaw also postdated the resistance of some of 'the Disinherited', who lost their lands under the Dictum of Kenilworth after the defeat of the army of Simon de Montfort at Evesham in 1265, which it had been suggested in 1840 was the time when the legend began. In support of his rejection of the possibility, he was able to refer to his own edition of the Chancery rolls containing information about proceedings under the Dictum, which he had edited and published under the auspices of the Record Commission in 1834.[61]

He went on to criticise Wright and his adherents, those writers who, 'acting in the wild humour of the present age', 'turn the men of former days into myths' and

> would represent this outlaw living in the woods as a mere creature of the imagination of men living in the depth of antiquity, so far back that we know neither when nor where, Hudkin, because his name was Hood, and Robin Goodfellow, because his name was Robert,

or more generally, in Wright's own words, was 'one among the personages of the early mythology of the Teutonic people.' He also rejected the 'much more reasonable conjecture' that the outlaw was 'a mere creation of some poetical mind'. The stories portrayed him as an outlaw living in the woods, an expert bowman with a band of followers, in a period when public roads were 'infested with bodies of discharged soldiers'. 'The whole system of the Robin Hood cycle rests upon a basis of fact and reality, some part of it capable of being brought into light as *proved facts*', despite their being no mention of him in contemporary historical writings. His character could therefore be known on the basis of the earliest tales, there being, he thought, three, which were found 'in manuscript that cannot be later than the fourteenth century', namely *Robin Hood and the Monk*, *Robin Hood and the Potter*, and *Robin and Gandelyn*, as shown by Wright and Gutch, plus the *Lytel Gest*, printed in about 1495 and more important than the other three. They must have existed by the reign of Edward III, and the reference to 'rymes of Robyn Hod' in *Piers Plowman* proved that he was regarded as a real person. He concluded this introduction by criticising those who proposed that the surname 'Hood' was nothing but 'of the Wood': 'as if the surname Hood had not made itself sufficiently famous in England; as if it were not as ancient and as frequently occurring as most in the vocabulary'. He pointed out the use of the surname in the court rolls of the manor of

---

61 *Rotuli Selecti ad Res Anglicas et Hibernicas Spectantes, ex Archivis et Hibernicas Spectantes, ex Archivis in Domo Capitulari Westmonasteriensi*, ed. J. Hunter (Record Commission, 1834), pp. 105–265.

Wakefield under Edward II, and gave a London example from a royal household roll of 1300.⁶²

Hunter then embarked on a detailed account of the *Lyttel Gest*, story by story, bringing in topographical and historical illustrations based on his research among the records in his charge, as well as references already mentioned earlier in his two published works on southern Yorkshire. Much of the material related to the district known as Barnsdale, sometimes called a forest but which had never in fact been one, and within it the location known as 'the Sayles'.⁶³ That it was a dangerous place, and arrangements for transporting royal and clerical treasure safely along the road to York were carefully made by the king's servants in the late thirteenth and early fourteenth centuries, as illustrated in detail from examples taken from royal accounts.⁶⁴ He fully accepted that most of the events in the ballad did not 'admit of any historic elucidation', and that the whole was probably a 'poetic invention', but noted that the appearance of 'Edward our comely king' in later parts of the work gives the first indication of date, and he felt confident about which of the Edwards was referred to. The king is mentioned as visiting Lancashire, and royal itineraries based on government records showed that Edward I never visited Lancashire as king, while Edward III did not do so in the early years of his reign and probably never; and that the epithet 'comely' could be more appropriately attached to Edward II than either his father or his son. Furthermore, the latter made a single progress in the county, for about three weeks in October 1323, following a visit to Yorkshire, shown by the dating clauses of various royal writs. While there he was much concerned with the state of his forests in both counties. Afterwards he travelled through Cheshire, Staffordshire and Derbyshire to Nottingham, near Sherwood Forest, which he had often visited during his reign; he arrived there on 9 November and remained until 23 November. Hunter felt that 'there is a correspondence in all this, between the ballad and the authentic record, which I venture to think is not quite accidental'.⁶⁵

The *Gest* includes a story in which the king, having met Robin incognito, finds him a place in his household, and Hunter mentions a record of the expenses of the king's household during that period, in which a man called 'Robyn Hode', along with 28 others, was paid 3d a day as a porter of the king's Chamber between April and July 1324.⁶⁶ He regarded this as 'a remarkable coincidence between the ballad and the record, hardly to be accounted for by the chance occurrence of two persons of the same name'. The name was not to be found in the preceding account, for July

---

⁶² Hunter, *Robin Hood*, pp. 1–10.
⁶³ For the topographical details, see pp. 129ff.
⁶⁴ Hunter, *Robin Hood*, pp. 14, 22.
⁶⁵ Hunter, *Robin Hood*, pp. 27–35.
⁶⁶ Now TNA, E 101/379/17, f. 4v.

1323 to April 1324, but in it the payments were recorded in gross sums, without specifying individuals, and so Hunter argued that he might already at that time have served in the household in 1323, including during the period when the king had been in Nottingham. As to the Chamber journal for the period following the one in which the name was first found, in August 1324, Robyn continued to serve, but then was first denied payment for eight days for non-attendance. On 21 October he received no pay because of continuing absence, and further deductions followed; according to Hunter this indicates that 'he was growing weary of his new mode of life'.[67] Finally, under 22 November, his name appears for the last time, when it is said that he could not work any longer, and so was given a parting gift of 5s.[68]

Hunter then moved on to elaborate his contention that these entries had 'perhaps as much correspondency as we can reasonably expect between the record and the ballad'. In the *Gest* Robin, after serving the king for 15 months, with his money depleted ('he had not at court the means of replenishing his exchequer which a lonely highway through a forest afforded him') and his men all departed, he became melancholy. After a chance observation he made up his mind to return to the greenwood, explaining to the king that he wished to return to the chapel, dedicated to Mary Magdalene, that he had founded in Barnsdale. While accepting that no such chapel was known, Hunter noted that the parish church of Campsall, just south of Barnsdale, and nearby Monk Bretton priory, were dedicated to that saint, and that there was also a free chapel at Norton, 'which sounds as if there were some lines of historical truth here'. By these means he was 'again installed head of the outlaws of Barnsdale and Sherwood'. He then, according to the *Gest*, lived in the greenwood for another 22 years, before being, according to later popular tradition, treacherously bled to death by his kinswoman, the prioress of Kirklees, at the instigation of his enemy Sir Roger of Doncaster.[69]

Hunter then noted the existence of the alleged Robin Hood's grave, and used his expertise on the sources for genealogy of Yorkshire families in a long attempt to identify the prioress mentioned in the *Gest* as Elizabeth de Stainton, who entered the priory sometime after 1307 and whose gravestone had been discovered in 1706. He went on to mention the existence of a Robert Hood, living in the reign of Edward II, who had been identified in the court rolls of the manor of Wakefield, not far from Barnsdale, at the time of the rebellion and death of Thomas earl of Lancaster in 1322; after which, he suggested, some of his erstwhile

[67] TNA, E 101/380/4, ff. 8v, 16r, 17v, 18v.
[68] TNA, E 101/380/4, f. 20v: 'Robyn Hod jadys un des portours pour ceo qil ne poiat pluis travailler, de donn par comaundement –v s.' (some readings corrected from those given by Hunter). See Figure 4.
[69] Hunter, *Robin Hood*, pp. 35–42.

followers 'secreted themselves in woods and fastnesses with which they were well acquainted' to avoid punishment. He concluded that Robin Hood was neither 'a mere poetic conception, a beautiful abstraction of the life of a jovial freebooter living in the woods', nor a Teutonic myth as suggested by Wright, 'but a person who had a veritable existence quite within historic time'. He must have been born between 1285 and 1295, and been an adult in the reign of Edward II and the early part of that of Edward III, a man of some status in Wakefield or nearby, who supported Lancaster in his rebellion. After the failure of the rising, he fled to the woods of Barnsdale or Sherwood Forest with a band, supporting himself by highway robbery but giving to the poor some of what he had taken from the rich, a sort of 'leveller'.[70] This he did for about 20 months, from April 1322 to December 1323, when he fell into royal hands. For some unknown reason the king pardoned him and made him a porter in the royal household, leaving after a year to return to the greenwood, before eventually dying at the hands of the prioress of Kirklees. Hunter concluded that 'it appears to me to be, *in all likelihood*, the outline of his life; some parts of it, however, having a stronger claim upon our belief than other parts'. He did not think that 'there can be so many correspondences between the ballad and the record without something of identity'. Such an 'advocate of popular rights', and an adherent of such a popular earl, naturally became a favourite of the common people, a hero 'selected as a subject for their art by the minstrels and song-writers of the time'.[71]

Hunter's paper was immediately approved by his fellow Antiquary, Mark Antony Lower, of Lewes (1813-76, elected in 1852), who wrote to him in November 1852, pointing out some further Robin Hood names in fourteenth-century sources.[72] Lower, one of the founders of the Sussex Archaeological Society, subsequently published a dictionary of family names, in which he asserted under 'Robynhod' that 'the Rev. Jos. Hunter has triumphantly asserted his existence, in real flesh and blood'.[73] Hunter continued to work on sorting and listing the public records, and the new Public Record Office building on the Rolls Estate in Chancery Lane was at length completed. He moved into it at the end of 1858, but he had already reached the age of 75, and in the event he spent little time working there, frequently being absent because he was severely afflicted with gallstones. He died in 1861 and, despite his nonconformity, he was buried in the grounds of the parish church at Ecclesfield, near Sheffield. In that very year the validity of his discoveries concerning

[70] Hunter, *Robin Hood*, pp. 43–51.
[71] Hunter, *Robin Hood*, pp. 51–54.
[72] Brotherton Library, Leeds, Special Collections, YAS/MS 166, pp. 9–12.
[73] M. A. Lower, *Patronymica Britannica: A Dictionary of the Family Names of the United Kingdom* (London, 1860), p. 291.

the outlaw was severely criticised in a new edition of the Robin Hood stories, published in London by a talented American literary scholar. It is not known whether Hunter knew about the contents of that publication before he died, although it had first been published in America several years previously. His work on the identity of the outlaw did not catch the public imagination, nor was it taken up by writers of Robin Hood fiction. It only again became a factor in the debate about the outlaw in the second half of the twentieth century.

Francis Child, American Scholar and Publisher of the Robin Hood Ballads

Francis James Child (1825–1896), a philologist and ballad scholar, was born in Boston, Massachusetts.[74] In maturity, he was short-sighted, frequently suffering from gout and rheumatism, and noted for his impeccable scholarship and high principles, his ardent patriotism and religious convictions (like Hunter, he was a Unitarian). He attended school in Boston before studying at Harvard University from 1842 to 1846. He then commenced his lifelong service to the university in various posts, although in 1849 he was granted leave of absence and went to Europe for two years, studying German and Germanic philology at the University of Göttingen. Returning to Harvard in 1851, Child took up a professorship, and it must have been during the following years that he undertook his first edition of the Robin Hood ballads. He established himself as a leading authority on early English ballads, and his first collection, *English and Scottish Ballads*, was published in Boston in 1857-8, followed by a second edition in 1860, which was also published in London shortly afterwards.[75] In the brief preface at the beginning of the first volume he lamented that the Percy Folio was still unavailable:

> We have not even the Percy Manuscript at our command, and must be content to take the ballads as they are printed in the *Reliques*, with all the editor's changes. This manuscript is understood to be in the hands of a dealer who is keeping it from the public in order to enhance its value. The greatest service that can now be done to English Ballad-literature is to publish this precious document.

---

74 ODNB, Sigrid Rieuwerts, accessed 28 February 2018.
75 Many English scholars seem to have been unaware of Child's earlier editions of *English and Scottish Ballads*. F. J. Child, ed., *The English and Scottish Popular Ballads*, 8 vols. (London, Sampson Low, 1861), vol. V, is the version that is used here. The most detailed account of the sequence of Child's publications, and his changing views on the best ways of editing early texts, is in Gregory, *Victorian Songhunters*, chapter 11. There were further editions in 1864 and 1871.

In the edition published in London in 1861, volume 5 was the one which included the ballads of the outlaw, and it does indeed include the altered last line of *Robin Hood and Guy of Gisborn*. Out of this grew Child's later, and better known, exhaustive critical edition of the authentic ballads of the English-speaking people, which included revised treatments of those relating to the outlaw legend.

His introduction to the volume savagely criticised the theories of both Hunter and Wright concerning Robin Hood. He began by briefly reviewing the early evidence as to the period during which the outlaw was thought to have flourished, given by the early Scottish writers up to the time of John Major in the early sixteenth century, ranging from the reign of Richard I to that of Edward II.[76] Tales certainly existed by the time of the writing of *Piers Plowman* (then thought to date to about 1362), but were at that time not new. He therefore concluded that the chroniclers 'had no other authority for their statements than traditional tales similar to those that have come down to our own day', and criticised Thierry and Barry for their conjecture of the outlaw as an Anglo-Saxon hero.[77] His most vehement criticism, however, was reserved for Hunter. The views defended by Hunter were claimed to be confirmed 'by documents of unimpeachable validity', and accorded a considerable degree of credibility to the ballads, and in particular the last two fyttes of the *Gest*, as giving a generally accurate account of real events. Hunter had sought to show that real events had been celebrated in popular song, for example in the case of Hereward the Wake; however, Child pointed out, it was remarkable that the outlaw had been 'passed over without one word of notice from any authoritative historian'. On the other hand, the activities of Adam Gurdon, who in 1267, after the defeat and death of Simon de Montfort led to the loss of his lands, had defied the king in a wooded area of western Surrey, were reported in a number of chronicles. An even stronger argument, Child thought, was that there was no sign of political animosity in the spirit of the ballads, and Robin 'loved no man in the world so well as his king'. He is 'neither patriot under ban, nor proscribed rebel', but an outlawed deer hunter, and 'one who superadds to deer-stealing the irregularity of a genteel highway robber'.

Child then turned to Hunter's detailed evidence, and the appearance of Robyn Hod among the household servants of Edward II in 1324. He regarded it as a coincidence depending on the rarity of the name, and pointed out that by that time the surname 'Hood' was a well-established hereditary surname among the less exalted members of society, frequently found in published government records, while Robert was a common Christian name. The two were often combined, and Child supplied six known examples from the years between 1300 and 1337, at

---

[76] For these sources, see Chapter 2.
[77] Child (1861), pp. vii–xiii.

the same time mocking Hunter's credulity. 'That Robert was an ordinary Christian name requires no proof, and if it was, the combination of Robert Hood must have been frequent also. We have taken no extra-ordinary pains to hunt up this confirmation, for really the matter is altogether too trivial to justify the expense of time.' In a note he joked that

> with a little more rummaging of old account–books we shall be able to "comprehend all vagrom men". It is a pity that the Sheriff of Nottingham could not have availed himself of the services of our 'detective'. The sagacity that has identified the Porter might easily, we imagine, have unmasked the Potter.

He went on to criticise what he regarded as the absurdities that derived from this supposition: that the king should pardon such a long-term offender and receive him into his court; and that such a daring criminal should consent 'to be enrolled among royal flunkies for three pence a day'. The archer, who was said to have gone on to spend a further 22 years in the forest after leaving the court, could not have been the porter who was worn out in less than two years, and discharged as a 'superannuated lackey'.[78]

Moving on, Child argued that the story of King Edward and the outlaw in the *Gest* was not historical, just one form of a multiform legend of a royal personage incognito meeting a lesser person such as, in other known tales, a shepherd or a hermit, 'the personages being varied for the sake of novelty'. The name of a recent or reigning monarch was then substituted as it took the fancy of the story-teller. Having thus denied the historicity of the outlaw, he considered the idea that his name was a corruption of 'Robin of the Wood' (a notion that was 'not merely an idle fancy') or even identical with the god Woden, as suggested by a German scholar. Wright's view that Robin Hood was a product of early Teutonic mythology Child thought 'worthy of respectful consideration'. Child gives a lengthy account of the May Games and the role of Robin Hood in them, drawing on German as well as English material, paticularly the work of Franz Kuhn, a distinguished Prussian folklorist. Like Wright, he also referred to the landscape features of England whose names alluded to the outlaw, but disputed Wright's interpretation of their significance. 'Nothing is more deceptive than popular legends' which 'have no claim to antiquity at all. They do not go beyond the ballads. They are palpably of subsequent and comparatively recent origin. It was absolutely impossible that they should arise while Robin Hood was a living reality to the people'. 'This trick of naming must have begun in the decline of his fame ... and his existence was just not doubted; not elabourately maintained by

---

[78] Child (1861), pp. xiv–xxiii.

learned historians, and antiquarians deeply read in the Public Records'.[79] He could not resist this final jibe against Hunter, although he did make good use of his topographical and more general factual material in some of his notes to his editions of the *Gest* and in a few other places.[80]

As a recognition of Child's edition, F. J. Furnivall founded the Ballad Society in England in 1868; it continued issuing publications until 1899.[81] Child's continuation of his work, however, was delayed for more than a decade by the outbreak of the American Civil War. Although poor health prevented him from enlisting in the Union army, he wrote political articles and pamphlets, and prepared collections of patriotic war songs and religious poems. In 1876 he became Harvard's first professor of English, and was able to pursue his particular interests more fully in research and teaching. When he began to prepare the final version of his monumental ballad collection, his intention was 'to include every obtainable version of every extant English or Scottish ballad, with the fullest possible discussion of related songs or stories in the popular literature of all nations'. Before publication began in 1882, he established a solid textual foundation by thorough investigation of the available material from oral tradition and manuscript sources, with assistance from scholars in other countries. Systematic collation of texts and manuscripts was undertaken, and 305 individual ballads were eventually printed as *The English and Scottish Popular Ballads* (5 volumes, issued in ten parts between 1882 and 1898), with introductory historical and critical notes.[82]

The Robin Hood ballads were included in volume III, published in 1889. Instead of a general introduction, he wrote individual introductions to each ballad, giving either additional comments or material revisions of those of the 1861 version. The amount of editorial and historical apparatus was considerably increased, with more expansive footnotes. This time he was able to include *Robin Hood and Guy of Gisborne*, because the Percy Folio which contained it had been released by the bishop's estate in 1867. His view of Robin Hood had clarified significantly since 1861, and is found in a much-quoted passage in the lengthy and detailed introduction to the *Gest*:

> Robin Hood is absolutely a creation of the ballad muse. The earliest mention we have of him is as the subject of ballads. The only two early historians who speak of him as a ballad-hero, pretend to have no information about him except what they derive from ballads.

---

[79] Child (1861), pp. xxvi–xxxvi.
[80] Child (1861), pp. 44–45, 47, 52, 106, 117, 122.
[81] Some of its archives are in King's College London Archives, Furnivall 6/1–3.
[82] F. J. Child, ed., *The English and Scottish Popular Ballads*, 5 vols. (Boston, Mass., and New York, Houghton, Mifflin and Co., 1882–98), vol. III (1889).

Socially speaking, he is a yeoman, and is courteous, religious, respectful of women, a friend of poor men generally, hates the senior clergy, and loves the king, even though he poaches his deer. He has 'a kind of royal dignity, of princely grace', although this is significantly debased in the later ballads. Child gave far more information about the May Games and the geographical features associated with the outlaw than he had in 1861, but firmly concluded that 'I cannot admit that even a shadow of a case has been made out by those who would attach a mythical character either to Robin Hood or the outlaws of Inglewood'. He therefore gave far less credence to Wright's ideas than he had earlier, describing him as somewhat naïve, and pointed out that no-one had yet undertaken to prove that the ballads were later than the names.[83] He also took the opportunity to make a few additional jibes at Hunter's attempt to identify the outlaw, writing that 'Hunter … could have identified Pigrogromitus and Quinapalus [two enigmatic characters mentioned in Shakespeare's *Twelfth Night*], if he had given his mind to it'; and remarked that

> to detect "a remarkable coincidence between the ballad and the record" requires not only a theoretical prepossession, but an uncommon insensibility to the ludicrous. But taking things with entire seriousness, there is no correspondence between the ballad and the record other than this: that Robin Hood, who is in the king's service, leaves it; in the one instance deserting, and in the other being displaced.[84]

Thanks to his industry, judgement and accuracy, Child's edition of 1889 became the standard reference point for all subsequent work on traditional ballads, although, as Dobson and Taylor pointed out in 1976, his texts in general cannot be held to be absolutely definitive because they included a variety of minor 'improvements' resulting from the difficulties in dealing with several variant texts of the same tale taken from different sources.[85] Child's death, in Boston in 1896, brought to an end the period of little more than a century during which a series of remarkable scholars eventually codified the texts which have come to form the established canon of surviving Robin Hood tales from the origins of the legend, whenever that was, to the seventeenth century.

---

83   Child (1889), pp. 42–48. The volume is now conveniently available online at (https://archive.org/stream/englishandscottio3chiluoft#page/n11/mode/2up), accessed February 2018.
84   Child (1889), pp. 55–56.
85   D&T, p. 65.

Chapter 4

Folklorists, Literary Scholars and Historians: Robin Hood in the Twentieth Century

By the end of the nineteenth century the battle lines of the debate about the origins of the Robin Hood legend had been drawn, and no previously unidentified early tales were found subsequently. Child, as editor of the texts of the tales, assigned them to literary creativity alone, the 'ballad muse', and his conclusion became the orthodox view of Robin Hood among literary scholars. Hunter's historical approach, searching for evidence indicating the existence of an original individual bearing the name of the outlaw in the records of medieval government and administration, receded in the wake of Child's criticisms. Perhaps as a result, professional historians paid very little attention to Robin Hood scholarship for many years, as they concentrated on political and constitutional history at a national level, largely ignoring the local and regional sources used by Hunter and his antiquarian predecessors, from William Dugdale (d. 1686) and Robert Thoroton (d. 1678) onwards, in compiling county histories. In the earlier twentieth century, some progress was made in the interpretation and understanding of the tales, but this was entirely within the province of the literary scholars. The most notable contribution was the detailed examination of the *Gest* published in 1909 by the Canadian scholar W. H. Clawson, which included no historical material.[1] He analysed the *Gest* to determine how many different stories it contained, and to identify links to analogue tales. It was the only one of the early Robin Hood ballads to have received further detailed literary analysis between the time of Child and the late twentieth century. E. K. Chambers took a literary historical approach to the outlaw in an influential volume of the *Oxford History of English Literature* published in 1945, in a chapter covering 'Popular Narrative Poetry and the Ballad'.

---

[1] W. H. Clawson, *The Gest of Robin Hood* (Toronto, 1909).

He was aware of the discovery of a reference to a 'Gilbert Robynhod' in Sussex in 1296, but thought it 'very likely' that the story of the outlaw 'took its start' from the Robin Hood imprisoned in Rockingham castle in 1354 while awaiting trial for breaking the forest law.[2] A few years later another literary scholar, R. M. Wilson, gave a shorter account in which, by accepting the incorrect date given to a charter supposedly of 1322 (but in fact of 1422) in the cartulary of Monk Bretton priory, he assumed an earlier date than most for the widespread fame of the outlaw. He also suggested that what he curiously described as a 'long unhistorical story' recorded by Dugdale and involving Randolf earl of Chester might be one of the lost tales about the earl mentioned by Langland when he referred to the Robin Hood tales in *Piers Plowman*. In fact, the story was one of several historical accounts of the real battle against the French and baronial army at Lincoln on 20 May 1217 in which the earl was a major participant.[3]

Developments did take place in the interpretation of the legend as folklore put forward by Thomas Wright. In 1891 a biography of the outlaw by Sidney Lee (1859-1926), a writer and literary critic, was published in the *Dictionary of National Biography*, of which Lee was the second editor and for which he personally wrote 820 articles.[4] He began by noting that although the outlaw 'has been represented as an historical personage ... there can be little doubt, however, that ... the name belonged to a mythical forest elf", whose name 'was afterwards applied by English ballad-writers... to any robber-leader who made his home in forests or moors, excelled in archery, defied the oppressive forest laws, and thus attracted popular sympathy'. He also considered that 'the word Hood may have been applied to the elf because such creatures, according to popular belief, wore hoods', and that his companions in the May Games, Friar Tuck and Little John, 'doubtless owed their origin to mythological processes, similar to those which produced the hero himself'. Quoting Grimm's *Deutsche Mythologie*, he suggested that 'in its origin the name was probably a variant of 'Hodeken', the title of a sprite or elf in Teutonic folklore'. Lee produced no proof that the name belonged to a woodland elf; the idea derived from a cultural predisposition on his part. The theory's inclusion in the *Dictionary* nevertheless helped enable these ideas to reach the mainstream, as represented by the influential 1910 edition of the *Encyclopedia Britannica*, by J. W. Hales and F. J. Snell. The encyclopaedia repeated Lee's main arguments and opined that 'it

---

2   E. K. Chambers, *English Literature at the Close of the Middle Ages* (Oxford, 1945), pp. 129–37.
3   R. M. Wilson, *The Lost Literature of Medieval England* (London, 1952), pp. 128–29, 138–40. See also M. J. C. Hodgart, *The Ballads* (London, 1950), pp. 67–69. For the charter, see p. 136.
4   *Dictionary of National Biography* 26 (London, 1891), pp. 421–24; reprinted in Knight, *Anthology*, pp. 379–84.

is certain that many mythical elements' appear in the outlaw story, and the entry reflected the growing contemporary interest in an 'anthropological' approach to literature and folklore.[5] Then in 1931 Margaret Murray (1863-1963), a prominent academic archaeologist, anthropologist and folklorist at University College London, and later president of the Folklore Society, argued that Robin was 'the God of the Old Religion', the pagan European witch cult which she believed had once existed and had not been destroyed by the spread of Christianity. She thought that his followers were dressed in green, like fairies, and asserted that Robin [Goodfellow, who she thought to be connected to Robin Hood] was 'so common a term for the 'Devil' as to be almost a generic name for him'. He was always accompanied by twelve companions, 'very suggestive of a Grandmaster and his coven', and his animosity to the church was invariably emphasised in the ballads about him; he was even bled to death by a nun. Murray also drew attention to 'the importance of the head-covering among the fairy folk', and pointed out that in many of the records of witch-trials the Devil was described as wearing a hood. Her views attracted strong criticism, especially after her death. In 1971 Keith Thomas pointed out that there was in fact 'very little evidence to suggest that the accused witches were either devil-worshippers or members of a pagan fertility cult', and that her conclusions were almost totally groundless because she ignored the systematic study of the records of witchcraft trials, which showed that those accused were not practitioners of a surviving pre-Christian religion.[6]

In 1936 further comment on the supposed folklore aspects of the legend was made by Lord Raglan (1885-1964), a former army officer and an anthropologist, who from 1945 to 1947 was himself president of the Folklore Society. His main assumption was that none of the well-known traditional figures had an historical existence, and that no previous writer had surveyed the field as a whole. Instead, each writer on a particular tradition assumed the historicity of those he had not studied. In his book *The Hero*, Raglan proposed to make a simultaneous attack on all the heroes of tradition, and would therefore expose himself to 'the scorn of the pedants, who ... will regard the detection of some minor inaccuracy as a triumphant refutation of my case'. After surveying the alleged evidence for an historical Robin Hood and finding it wanting, he characterised Robin as a traditional hero, a mythical pagan deity associated with Spring and vegetation, who became the hero of a ritual drama as the King of May, with Maid Marian as his Queen. 'The stories are suggestive of an ancient system by which the king reigned from one May-day till the next, when he had to fight for his title, if not for his life, and in which the queen became the wife of the successful combatant.' Raglan also suggested that

---

[5] Knight, *Complete Study*, p. 13.
[6] K. Thomas, *Religion and the Decline of Magic* (London, 1971), pp. 514–15.

the outlaw had been imported from France as an English version of the figure known there as 'Robin du Bois', becoming 'Robin of the Wood'.[7] However, his views were criticised in the *Journal of American Folklore* by W. E. Simone of Southern Illinois University, on the grounds that Robin Hood had already been a ballad hero, and his role as a dramatic hero in the May Games was simply a fifteenth-century development of the legend.[8] Raglan's wife, Lady Julia, also an anthropologist, contributed briefly but even more significantly to the debate. In an article in the journal *Folklore* in 1939 she is said to have been the first to use the term 'Green Man' to describe a sculpture or other artistic representation of a face surrounded by or made from leaves, often with branches sprouting from the mouth, nostrils, or other parts of the face, found in churches and previously simply known as 'foliate heads'.[9] Her interest was aroused by her identification of such sculptures in the church of Llangwm, a village near the family home in Monmouthshire. The article was Lady Raglan's only contribution to the study of folklore, and in it she concluded that:

> This figure I am convinced, is neither a figment of the imagination nor a symbol, but is taken from real life, and the question is whether there was any figure in real life from which it could have been taken. The answer, I think, is that there is but one of sufficient importance, the figure variously known as the Green Man, Jack-in-the-Green, Robin Hood, the King of May and the Garland King, who is the central figure in the May Day celebrations throughout Northern and Central Europe.

Her theory is still much disputed, but it established the name 'Green Man' as the preferred label for a figure sometimes alternatively referred to as 'Robin Hood'. It may nevertheless be significant for the dating of the origin of the term 'Green Man' that a public house in Hockley, a street in Nottingham, which in 1761 was named in borough licencing records as the 'Robin Hood', was in both 1759 and 1762 called the 'Green Man'.[10]

The most recent exposition and the most developed account of these ideas, by John Matthews, was first published in 1993; a second, lengthier treatment, giving more extended coverage of texts, followed in 2016.[11]

---

7   Lord Raglan, *The Hero: A Study in Tradition, Myth and Drama* (London, 1936), chapter 4, pp. 45–53; an extract was reprinted in Knight, *Anthology*, pp. 385–91.
8   W. E. Simone, 'The Games and the Robin Hood Legend', *Journal of American Folklore* 64 (1951), pp. 265–74, at 265; discussion in *ibid.*, 65 (1952), pp. 304–05, 418–20 then followed, in which criticisms of Simone's views in favour of those of Lord Raglan were made by Jay Williams and then refuted by Simone.
9   Lady Raglan, 'The Green Man in Church Architecture', *Folklore* 50 (March, 1939), pp. 45–57.
10 *RBN* VII, ed. E. L. Guilford (Nottingham, 1947), p. 21 and note 3.
11 J. Matthews, *Robin Hood, Green Lord of the Wildwood* (Glastonbury, 1993); and *Robin Hood* (Stroud, 2016). A chapter of the first, 'The Games of Robin Hood', is reprinted in Knight, *Anthology*, pp. 393–410.

Matthews criticised his predecessors in the 'mythological school', whose conclusions were 'summary in nature, briefly stated, and lacking the detailed study of folk-lore, tradition, and myth required'. He gave no indication of when he thought the myth might have emerged, but suggested links with other cultural phenomena: dancing green fairies, the seventeenth-century figure Robin Goodfellow, alias Puck, alias Hob; the Germanic wood-sprite Hudekin; Herne, the ghostly huntsman, first mentioned by Shakespeare and associated with Windsor forest; and the 'Green Man', said to be depicted by the carvings of foliate men's heads peering through leaves, found in some medieval churches. He was a mythical figure who was 'a personification of the power of the natural world', but who later came to be associated with more than one historical personage. Matthews did propose that one or more real people called Robin Hood had existed, but that they assumed the mantle of the 'Green Man'. The Robin Hood plays and Morris Dances grew out of folk-memory of old ritual acts, preserved in those forms against the more recent dominance of Christianity, and Robin became a Spring aspect of the Green Man. 'He originated in the character and tradition of the Green Man, and ... only gradually developed into the Outlaw of Sherwood, shedding certain characteristics and gaining others, until he is ... a far cry from his origins'. 'In the May Day Games and the Robin Hood plays of the 16th and 17th centuries, traces remain which hark back ... to another time and another culture, in which the Green Man was honoured as the most powerful force in the cosmos, the spirit of Nature itself'.[12]

As Matthews realised, one of the main difficulties was the uncertain origin and date of the Morris Dance, in which Robin and his companions participated, and the lack of medieval references to it.[13] He gave no indication of when he thought the myth might have emerged, and the lack of evidence had led literary scholars and historians, following Joseph Hunter and his own contemporary critic Francis Child, to dismiss or ignore all the folklore traditions relating to Robin Hood originally suggested by Thomas Wright.[14] Many literary scholars continue to maintain Child's view of 1889 that not 'even a shadow of a case has been made out by those who would attach a mythical character ... to Robin Hood'. The first historical critique of the whole mythological approach

---

[12] Matthews, *Robin Hood, Green Lord of the Wildwood*, pp. 2, 7–26, 167.

[13] The earliest known written reference to the dance in England yet identified has however now been published, dating to 1448, when the Goldsmiths' Company of London paid 7s. to a group of Morris dancers: M. Heaney, 'The Earliest Reference to the Morris Dance?', *Folk Music Journal* 8, no. 4 (2004), pp. 513–15.

[14] See Chapter 3.

was made by an Oxford historian, Maurice Keen, in 1961.[15] He argued that 'Robin Hood is not only definitely mortal, but also ... the supernatural is markedly absent from his story', and that his activities had ample historical parallels. The natural features named after the outlaw went back no further than the fourteenth century, and there were none from the Dark Ages. The story of the outlaw had no obvious mythological implications, but clear connections with the history of later medieval England. Subsequently, in 1976 Dobson and Taylor concluded that the evidence showed that Robin Hood was based on a memory of a real outlaw or outlaws; that his association with place-names and natural features, researched in detail for an appendix in their book, developed long after the first literary development of the legend; and that the outlaw's appearance in the May Games came after, and probably resulted from, the popularity of the tales.[16] In 1982 James Holt argued that Wright had failed to prove that the legend derived from Teutonic mythology, and based his arguments on mythological elements in the May Games and Robin Hood place-names, which 'were concerned with the outer growth rather than the inner core of the legend'; the links with the Games only developed long after the legend had taken root. Wright did not try to show that the earliest Robin Hood tales were myth, but only that, as the legend developed, it mixed with myth. Holt concluded that the primary sense of the outlaw's surname was simply a reference to a hood [as an item of dress] and so not linked to Teutonic myth; that the May Games and place-names merely reflected the widespread popularity of the legend, not its origins; and that the tales, although fictional, contained no mythical or magic elements and were set in real geographical contexts.[17] Most recently, the leading contemporary literary scholar of the legend, Stephen Knight, considered that 'it is not easy to see why a limited English tradition, located in particular places and a restricted set of activities, would have first become national and then worldwide in its appeal'.[18] It should also be pointed out that none of the folklorists have yet found any historical evidence for their theories earlier than the May Games, and none of the sculptures of the Green Man yet identified include any hint of a visual representation of the outlaw himself in recognisable form.[19]

---

15   M. Keen, *The Outlaws of Medieval Legend* (London, 1961; revised edition, 1977; revised paperback edition, London, 1987), pp. 219–22.
16   D&T, p. 63.
17   Holt, *Robin Hood*, pp. 54–57.
18   Knight, *Complete Study*, pp. 13–14; and *Mythic Biography*, p. 203.
19   K. Basford, *The Green Man* (Cambridge, 1978, reprint 1996 and 2009). See also L. K. Stock, 'Lords of the Wildwood: The Wild Man, The Green Man, and Robin Hood', in Hahn, *Popular Culture*, pp. 239–49.

L. V. D. Owen: the outlaw in official documents

A lone and fleeting voice in the quest for an original Robin Hood among historical records between the two world wars was L. V. D. Owen (1888-1952), professor of history at University College Nottingham from 1920 until the year before his death. Owen was a member of the Council of the Pipe Roll Society, established at the Public Record Office in 1883 primarily to publish the texts of the early pipe rolls, which recorded the annual accounts of the sheriffs of the English counties, audited by the royal Exchequer.[20] In 1927 the Society published, out of sequence with the series, an edition of the pipe roll for the Exchequer year 1229-30, edited by the American scholar Chalfant Robinson of Princeton.[21] It was in that volume that Owen noticed an entry, in the Yorkshire account, which showed that the sheriff owed the sum of 32s 6d for the chattels of 'Robert Hod, fugitive'. In 1936 he mentioned it in a contribution he made in a supplement to *The Times* devoted to the economy of Nottingham. He made much of the fact that the pipe roll was an official document, and remarked that 'it is just possible that this lonely entry may be the only clue that we shall ever have as to the existence of the outlaw'. He concluded that 'the only likely source of authentic information about Robin Hood, as about much else, is in the records of the State'.[22]

Owen failed to follow up his discovery by searching for the first appearance of the entry in the preceding pipe rolls in the series. They were not in print, but were, and had long been, readily available in the Public Record Office in Chancery Lane. He republished his views again in *Chambers Encyclopaedia* in 1950, but in the same terms, so it was fifty years or so before this potentially important piece of evidence for the origins of the legend was fully brought to light. Owen's discovery was occasionally referred to by leading historians during the following decades, notably in 1947 when the eminent Oxford historian and Regius Professor, Sir Maurice Powicke, mentioned it in a footnote of his monumental work *King Henry III and the Lord Edward*, concluding that 'it is quite possible that thirteenth-century incidents lie behind legends afterwards applied to a definite person who had a fleeting notoriety'.[23] Powicke was attracted by the idea that the period following the battle of Evesham in 1265, when 'the Disinherited' were in rebellion in

---

[20] TNA, E 372.
[21] *The Great Roll of the Pipe for the Fourteenth Year of the Reign of King Henry III: Michaelmas 1230*, ed. Chalfant Robinson, PRS NS IV (1927).
[22] The Times, Trade and Engineering Supplement, xxxviii, no. 864 (new series), in February, 1936, p. xxix. I am grateful to Dorothy Johnston for supplying me with a copy of the article in 1993.
[23] F. M. Powicke, *King Henry III and the Lord Edward* (2 vols., Oxford, 1947), II, pp. 529-30.

various parts of England, was a likely time for the legend of Robin Hood to have originated, and was where the Scottish chronicler Walter Bower had placed him.

Joseph Hunter's theory: developed by J. W. Walker and P. V. Harris

During the decades following Hunter's death in 1861 there was significant development in the study of history in English universities, as it became more specialised and more clearly distinguished from other subjects, especially literature. Child's criticisms did not prevent the republication of Hunter's article, by local historian Robert White at Worksop in 1883. Nevertheless, during the nineteenth and the first half of the twentieth century academic historians were largely uninterested in Robin Hood, although in general histories they sometimes felt obliged to mention him. In the volume of the *Oxford History of England* covering the century and a half following the Norman Conquest, Austin Lane Poole briefly noted Owen's discovery, but was unsure whether 'the elusive and irresponsible sportsman' was an historical figure or 'merely a wood sprite of medieval folk-law'.[24] In the successor volume covering the fourteenth century, May McKisack failed to mention Robin at all.[25] Lady Doris Stenton, wife of the great historian of Anglo-Saxon England, Sir Frank Stenton, and a notable editor of early government financial and legal records in her own right, also made no reference to Robin Hood in an account of the forest laws.[26] It was left to a local historian from Wakefield, J. W. Walker, to elaborate on Hunter's ideas. In 1944 Walker published a long article in the *Yorkshire Archaeological Journal*, later developed into a book, *The True History of Robin Hood*, published in 1952. It was based essentially on further searching of the Wakefield manor court rolls, and he conjectured that Robin was born about 1290, the son of a forester called Adam Hood. He further surmised that he was baptised in Wakefield parish church and attended school there, and listed the references to him in the rolls. He also made use of a 'Contrariants Roll' preserved in the Wakefield Manor Office, listing confiscations made from tenants of the manor who had fought on the side of Thomas earl of Lancaster at the battle of Boroughbridge in 1322.[27] He considered that he had 'substantially proved' that Hunter's Robert Hood of Wakefield did fight on Lancaster's side and was outlawed. After that, Walker conjectured, he and Matilda changed their names to Robin and

[24] A. L. Poole, *From Domesday Book to Magna Carta* (2nd edition, Oxford, 1955), pp. 35–36.
[25] M. McKisack, *The Fourteenth Century* (Oxford, 1953).
[26] D. M. Stenton, *English Society in the Early Middle Ages 1066–1307* (London, 1951).
[27] Walker, *The True History of Robin Hood*, p. 11.

Maid Marian and fled into Barnsdale forest. He suggested this despite knowing that Marian was not mentioned in the *Gest*, his main source for the legend as it had been Hunter's. Walker also thought he had ascertained, from wardrobe books in the Public Record Office surviving from the five years before the date of the one used by Hunter, that the Robin Hood who was employed by the king in 1323–24 did not work for him in those years, so that he could not have been pensioned off for being worn out and unable to further perform his duties. He even managed to persuade Powicke that he had probably identified the original Robin Hood: 'I think your identification will be regarded as not merely very probable, but proved. I do think you have made Hunter's suggestion more likely than any other'.[28]

Walker was followed by P. Valentine Harris, who first published *The Truth about Robin Hood* in 1951. His book subsequently went through many editions, the last being published 'in the heart of the Robin Hood country' (Mansfield) in 1973. Harris claimed to have made new discoveries about the characters in the earliest Robin Hood ballads which vindicated Hunter's belief that he was a real historical figure. He ridiculed the beliefs of Thomas Wright and his successors that the outlaw was a myth, and sought to build on the discoveries of Walker by further researches in the Wakefield court rolls and other Yorkshire sources. He claimed to have identified a number of other minor characters in the legend.[29] The search for an original outlaw and study of his possible significance was, however, soon afterwards to pass from amateur enthusiasts like Walker and Harris to professional historians in a university setting, as the higher education sector expanded greatly in the late 1950s and 1960s. They began to debate aspects of the legend in ways which initially reflected the rival conservative and left-wing outlooks of some young British academics whose careers had begun in the aftermath of the Second World War.

Rodney Hilton and James Holt: the social origins of the legend and its audience

Academic debate over the social significance of the Robin Hood legend began in 1958 when Rodney Hilton published what soon became a very controversial article concerning 'The Origins of Robin Hood'. Born in 1916

---

[28] Walker, *The True History of Robin Hood*, p. 95, quoting Powicke's letter of 7 May 1944.

[29] P. V. Harris, *The Truth about Robin Hood: A Refutation of the Mythologists' Theories, with New Evidence of the Hero's Actual Existence* (Mansfield, 1973), pp. 78–93. For trenchant criticism of Harris's approach and his interpretation of this material, see Keen, *The Outlaws of Medieval Legend* (London, 1961), pp. 185–86; Holt, *Robin Hood*, pp. 48–49. See also D&T, p. 13 n. 3.

into a Lancashire working-class socialist family background, Hilton graduated from Oxford in 1938, and there he became a prominent member of the Communist Party, in which he remained until 1956. After war service, from 1946 he taught history at the University of Birmingham, where he continued until retirement in 1982. He concentrated on Marxist analysis of landlord–peasant relations in medieval England, especially during the period before and after the Peasants' Revolt of 1381, and his active membership of the Communist Party and later continuing left-wing views may have hindered the development of his career outside Birmingham. He was a co-founder in 1952 of the journal *Past and Present*, in which his article on Robin Hood was published.[30] It ignited a debate which continued in the pages of the journal for several years.

Hilton considered that Robin Hood, although more likely to be a 'literary creation' than a real individual, was the most popular English hero of the medieval period, perhaps originating in the thirteenth century at the time of the emergence of the ballad as a literary form. He was most renowned for robbing and killing landowners, especially ecclesiastical ones, and for maintaining 'guerilla warfare' against established authority as represented by the sheriff, and was a man 'who would now, of course, be described as a terrorist'. Hilton felt that he, as a social historian, could 'help to solve some Robin Hood problems which have so far mainly been considered by literary historians'. Dismissing the views of 'over-enthusiastic folklorists' like Thomas Wright that the legend originated in popular paganism, he looked at the evidence for what he called 'the recurring effort to manufacture an authentic, documented, individual' outlaw. He thought that the earliest ballads showed that the social milieu from which the legend emerged was mostly plebeian, in a period when 'peasants and landowners faced each other with mutual antagonism'. Robin's status as a yeoman, strongly emphasised in the *Gest*, was, Hilton argued, 'meant to imply neither a serving man ... nor a rich peasant, but simply a peasant of free personal status'. The surviving stories showed that the legend implied a thirteenth or early fourteenth century origin, before the Peasants' Revolt, when agrarian discontent was endemic in England. The main issue was the landlords' demands for rents and services, and after the Black Death of 1349 their attempts to control the wages of landless rural inhabitants. The county sheriffs supported aggrieved landowners, represented by the abbot of St Mary's, York against recalcitrant tenants. By contrast the king, the greatest landowner and the source of authority, was 'brave, strong, merciful and generous', but

---

[30] R. H. Hilton, 'The Origins of Robin Hood', *Past and Present* 14 (1958), pp. 30–44; reprinted in Hilton, *Peasants, Knights and Heretics: Studies in Medieval English Social History* (Cambridge, 1976), pp. 221–35.

their faith in him led to the downfall of the peasantry in 1381. The story of the life of the outlaws in the forest 'was an unconscious invention in poetic form of the life that those who enjoyed the ballads would have liked to have lived'.

Hilton's critic, James Holt (1922-2014), a Yorkshireman, was of a different cast of mind.[31] He only briefly espoused left-wing views, in early adulthood. After war service he graduated at Oxford in 1947 and taught at the universities of Nottingham and Reading before becoming Professor of Medieval History at Cambridge in 1978. In 1982 he published his monograph on Robin Hood, the result of twenty years of research since the controversy which followed his article of 1960.[32] Deploying a greater range of evidence than Hilton, he sought to establish why and when the legend emerged; the nature of the audience; the literary sources; and the identity of the outlaw. In contrast to Hilton, he regarded the ballads as the literature not of downtrodden peasants but of the gentry, and pointed out that the legend was northern, whereas the Peasants' Revolt was centred on the south-east and East Anglia. In the *Gest* the audience addressed was specifically gentle and free-born, containing no hint of hostility towards lay, as opposed to ecclesiastical, landlords. The abbot of St Mary's appeared in the *Gest* as a creditor and mortgagee, not a landlord, and his victim was a knight, not a peasant. Although he did take money from the rich, and in particular senior clergy, he did not do so in order to give it to the poor. His friends included knights and squires, as long as they were 'good fellows'. The administrators of the forest laws and harsh sheriffs were unpopular with all levels of society, not just the peasantry, and in the *Gest* Robin attacked the beasts in the royal forests. In similar stories such as Adam Bell and Gamelyn the heroes were of knightly or yeoman stock. Although some audiences were of peasants or servants, the central point of dissemination was in the households of the gentry, including servants. From them they would have spread to the local taverns, but 'the original audience was not concerned with ... class conflicts, of which the ballads are remarkably free, but with hospitality and its formalities, and with the precedence which arose from service and status'. Holt also concluded that the topics dealt with in the *Gest* related more closely to the thirteenth century than the fourteenth, and he suggested possible originals for the sheriff who held office in its earlier decades. He referred back to Owen's suggestion of 1936 that the original of the outlaw was the 'Robert Hod, fugitive' mentioned in the pipe roll for 1226, and noted that in the roll for the following year the same man was referred

---

[31] From the *ODNB* entry, by George Garnett, accessed on 12 June 2018, as well as personal knowledge of the author.

[32] J. C. Holt, 'The Origins and Audience of the Ballads of Robin Hood', *Past and Present* 18 (1960), pp. 89–110; reprinted in *Peasants, Knights and Heretics*, pp. 236–57.

to as 'Hobbehod', who lived in the right period and might possibly be the original outlaw. He was certainly to be preferred to the candidates suggested by Hunter and Walker, who had misinterpreted two crucial entries in the Wakefield manor court rolls of the reign of Edward II. Holt concluded that the legend was unlikely to be simply 'a literary tradition conjured up from nothing', and that the tales derived from a combination of fact and fiction, with 'Hobbehod' having the strongest claim to be an historical Robin Hood.

Maurice Keen and The Outlaws of Medieval Legend

In the following issue of *Past and Present*, Maurice Keen (1933–2012) contributed another article to the debate, in which he sought to identify the nature of the tyranny and injustice that the outlaws were fighting against, and argued that the legend derived from a different period than that indicated by Holt.[33] Keen graduated at Balliol College Oxford in 1957, and was a Fellow there from 1961 to 2000. He saw the dominant theme of the ballads as the righting of wrongs and the downfall of those who controlled the law by bribery and misuse of office; the need was to define what the outlaws were fighting against, most obviously rich clerics and secular officials such as sheriffs, lawyers and those who imposed the poll taxes. The lower orders were not enemies of a stratified society as such, but resented abuses by some of those in high official or social positions. Keen also disputed Holt's definition of the social status of yeomen, the audience addressed in the tales, as higher than that of peasants, being household servants slightly superior to a squire and possibly of 'gentle breeding'. He quoted references from the late fourteenth to the early sixteenth centuries in support of that view, concluding that, when the ballads were being composed, words such as 'yeoman', 'gentleman' or even 'poor man' implied sharp definitions of social status. In the context of corruption in the legal system, 'the interests of peasant, unprosperous knight and yeoman were at one'. His other main disagreement with Holt was the latter's association of the Robin Hood ballads with the thirteenth century. He argued that by then the longbow, 'the outlaw's long-distance weapon' had not yet been developed; that sheriffs were as much disliked in the fifteenth century as the thirteenth; and that the forest background was equally appropriate to both periods. Holt made a rapid rejoinder to some of Keen's arguments in the same issue of the journal.[34] He cited detailed evidence illustrating that bows were common in the early

---

[33] M. H. Keen, 'Robin Hood – Peasant or Gentleman', *Past and Present* 19 (1961), pp. 7–15. Earlier he had simultaneously advanced views similar to those of Hilton in 'Robin Hood: A Peasant Hero', *History Today*, October 1958.

[34] J. C. Holt, 'Robin Hood: Some Comments', *Past and Present* 19 (1961), pp. 16–18; reprinted in *Peasants, Knights and Heretics*, pp. 267–69.

thirteenth century and earlier, being commonly used by criminals, in warfare and in hunting. The Robin Hood ballads were not class literature, and could not have developed as they did without a mixed audience. They were in any case predominantly northern, while the peasant rebellion of 1381 and that of Jack Cade in 1450 took place in the south. The demands of the rebels of 1381 showed that they did not unquestioningly accept a stratified society, and that those demands were not reflected in the Robin Hood ballads.

Keen's interest in outlaws sprang from his early enthusiasm for literary evidence in history, and his research subsequently centred on topics other than Robin Hood. However, in 1961 he published an important book on outlaws generally, *The Outlaws of Medieval Legend*.[35] Its publication elicited a further brief comment by T. H. Aston, who agreed with Holt that 'the primary social significance of the Robin Hood ballads does not lie in the realm of peasant discontent'.[36] That view was coming to prevail, and eventually in 1976 Keen took the unusual step of recanting his original views on the outlaw in favour of broad agreement with those of Holt.[37] He repeated his change of view in greater detail in a new introduction added to the second edition of *The Outlaws of Medieval Legend* (1977), which included his chapter on 'The Outlaw Ballad as an Expression of Peasant Discontent'. The controversy over the social milieu of the legend initiated by Hilton in 1958 thus effectively came to an end, but much wider academic interest in Robin Hood had been aroused, and the chronological setting of the outlaw legend became a matter of further discussion. Keen argued, largely on the basis of the references to liveries and retaining in the *Gest*, that the stories fitted the context of the fourteenth and fifteenth centuries, not the thirteenth. The status of yeoman, prominent in the ballads, related more clearly to the period after the decline of unfree peasant status, so it seemed to him that the period between 1350 and 1450 was the most suitable context in which the ballads as we know them could have achieved such popularity. The most likely original of the King Edward to fit the tales was Edward III, although Edward I and IV might also fit, but the use of that name did not imply reference to any particular period, and the tales did not connect with any known event. He agreed with Child that the outlaw was a 'pure creation of the ballad muse', not an historical figure. Nevertheless, the discussion about the social significance of the legend had inevitably come to involve speculation as to the period of its emergence, and this related issue became of increasing interest and importance to several leading academic historians as the debate developed.

[35] M. Keen, *The Outlaws of Medieval Legend* (London, 1961; revised edition, 1977; revised paperback edition, London, 1987).
[36] T. H. Aston, 'Robin Hood', *Past and Present* 20 (1961), pp. 7–9; reprinted in *Peasants, Knights and Heretics*, pp. 270–72
[37] *Peasants, Knights and Heretics*, p. 266.

Dobson and Taylor: historical and literary study of the legend

During the early 1970s two northern historians, Barrie Dobson of the University of York and John Taylor of the University of Leeds, began a long collaboration in the study of Robin Hood. Dobson (1931-2013) spent most of his academic career at York, although in 1988 he moved to Cambridge as Professor of Medieval History in succession to his fellow Robin Hood scholar, James Holt. Their first article on the outlaw, a reassessment of the medieval origins of the legend, appeared in the journal *Northern History* in 1972, a decade after the controversy between Hilton, Holt and Keen, and it was in that publication that several more papers subsequently appeared as the study of the subject developed.[38] Some of the most important material in the first article related to the geography and history of Barnsdale, and they completed the precise identification of the location of 'the Sayles' in Barnsdale so nearly achieved by Hunter over a century earlier.[39] In 1976 they produced a full-length study of the legend, covering not only its medieval origins but also its subsequent evolution in later centuries. They also brought together many of the main texts, based on the work of Child, and compiled several appendices, including lists of all the known tales, Robin Hood proverbs, and Robin Hood place-names, the first methodical survey of that vital evidence.[40] The last section of the introduction consisted of a detailed and original historical account of the development of the legend from the sixteenth to the twentieth centuries, using many detailed works by literary scholars and cultural historians.

Dobson and Taylor considered in detail, and from a historical standpoint, the manuscript and printed contexts and contents of the earliest tales, their likely dates and audiences, and the manner of their performance, and concluded that any 'original' legend of the outlaw was lost beyond recall. Nevertheless, parallel examples of historical individuals who had been posthumously transformed into 'social bandits' made it tempting to believe that an 'original' Robin Hood had once existed, and that the performances of ballads were acts of remembrance of a primitive social rebel as well as entertainment. They discussed the search for the original outlaw through a variety of medieval English historical sources, giving examples of real men named Robert or Robin Hood, and three occurrences of the surname 'Robynhod' in lists of taxpayers and London coroners' records between 1296 and 1332. They also detected hints provided by details in the surviving tales to suggest that the legend might

---

[38] R. B. Dobson and J. Taylor, 'The Medieval Origins of the Robin Hood Legend: A Reassessment', *Northern History* 7 (1972), pp. 1–30.
[39] See p. 130.
[40] R. B. Dobson and J. Taylor, *Rymes of Robyn Hood: An Introduction to the English Outlaw* (London, 1976).

have originated in the thirteenth century rather than the fourteenth, as first indicated by Walter Bower. They also emphasised the dominance of Barnsdale over Sherwood in the legend, and suggested possible candidates for the original sheriff of Nottingham, while regarding the evidence as inconclusive. The importance of the sheriff suggested that originally there might have been two different cycles of stories, of a Yorkshire outlaw and a Nottinghamshire sheriff, that fused before the legend first appeared; the fusion might just possibly have been the work of the unknown compiler of the *Gest*. Extensive topographical and historical material about Barnsdale, and its notoriety as a place for ambushes and robberies around 1300, was noted, as well as the evidence for gentry gangs and official corruption in England as a whole. Dobson and Taylor's book provided, in their own phrase, the first 'introductory handbook' to the legend, and the fullest historical account of it written thus far. It remains, with the important modifications of their arguments in the subsequent editions (1989, 1997) and in separate papers, of fundamental importance in the literature about the Robin Hood legend.

John Maddicott: Robin Hood in the fourteenth-century

Dobson and Taylor's book was closely followed in 1978 by the publication of an article seeking to place the origins of the Robin Hood legend in the fourteenth century. The author, John Maddicott, a Fellow of Exeter College, Oxford, studied the practice of powerful individuals and institutions in retaining the legal services of royal justices for fees, and the corruption that sometimes resulted from it, which informed his views about the legend.[41] His interpretation was based on historical evidence and the *Gest*. The published form of the latter in the early sixteenth century was, he argued, 'something very close to its original form or to the form of its component ballads'.[42] Recent scholarly opinion had, with the notable exception of Keen, assigned the legend to the thirteenth century, but Maddicott considered that it was almost certainly a product of the first half of the fourteenth, not so long before the numerous and widespread references to the outlaw between 1377 and 1440, and that it was brought to birth by a particular set of circumstances. The *Gest* at several points used the language of bastard feudalism, of liveries and fees, characteristic of the fourteenth century and intelligible to audiences of that period, while distraint of knighthood, previously quoted as characteristic of the thirteenth century, was also frequently used during

---

[41] J. R. Maddicott, *Thomas of Lancaster, 1307–1322: A Study in the Reign of Edward II* (Oxford, 1970); and *Law and Lordship: Royal Justices as Retainers in Thirteenth and Fourteenth Century England*, Past and Present Supplement 4 (1978).

[42] J. R. Maddicott, 'The Birth and Setting of the Ballads of Robin Hood', *EHR* 93 (1978), pp. 276–99.

the reign of Edward III. Sheriffs and their misdeeds were as detested in the fourteenth and fifteenth centuries as they had been in the thirteenth, and the lack of references in the *Gest* to justices of the peace, created during the fourteenth century, was insignificant, because they were rarely complained about and lacked the capacity of the sheriffs for causing harm to others. The importance of the forest in the outlaw tales reflected the continuing oppressiveness of forest jurisdiction in the early decades of Edward III.

Maddicott focused on the first part of the *Gest*, the story of the indebtedness of the poor knight to the abbot of St Mary's York, to whom he had mortgaged his lands. The latter was supported and advised by a 'high justice' retained 'with cloth and fee', as well as the sheriff of an unnamed county. This, and the localisation of the events in Barnsdale and southern Yorkshire, suggested the identification of some of the individuals in the story and their activities. The abbot could be Thomas de Moulton (1332 to 1359), prominent in service to the king and his order. From 1332 to 1335, when the royal Chancery happened to be resident in York at the abbey, he is recorded in the Chancery close rolls compiled there as having lent sums totalling £362 to individuals and groups of men from the northern counties, including three knights.[43] A candidate for the high justice who was advising and helping the abbot was Sir Geoffrey le Scrope, chief justice of King's Bench from 1324 to 1338, a Yorkshireman who owned a house in York, and who the abbot might well have retained. Scrope's court was based in York for much of the time between 1332 and 1337. As to the identity of the sheriff of Nottingham, a possibility was John de Oxenford, in office for most of the period from 1334 to 1339, and whose activities were investigated by royal commissioners in 1341. The late 1320s and early 1330s were also the period when the criminal gangs of the Folvilles and Coterels were at large in the east midlands, among other offences kidnapping Sir Richard de Willoughby, then one of the junior justices of King's Bench, and holding him for ransom. Both gangs attracted some public sympathy, and the Folvilles in particular were, like Robin Hood, folk heroes in the eyes of some, because even if they did not give to the poor at least they robbed the rich. Mistrust of those who used office-holding under the crown for private profit led to a feeling that 'only the outlaw can execute true justice against the unscrupulous and extortionate'. Perhaps Robin Hood himself was a blend of fact and fiction:

> The compiler of the *Gest* may well have taken the career of some real outlaw ... given him a fictitious name and embroidered his progress in a series of episodes peopled with identifiable local villains and set

---

[43] J. W. Walker had already noticed that Moulton was a 'notorious money lender', but did not document this in detail: Walker, *The True History of Robin Hood*, p. 66.

against real backgrounds in Barnsdale and Sherwood Forest, and importing stock tales from other legends.

In the next major book on the outlaw legend, published by James Holt four years later, Maddicott's approach was critically appraised. Holt was a strong protagonist of the case for a thirteenth century original for the outlaw, and criticised Maddicott's method, which he likened to Joseph Hunter's. He characterised both as arbitrary attempts to fit pieces from the 'jigsaw of the legend' into the other jigsaw of documented historical events, so seeking to date material in the *Gest* through incidental rather than essential features. He regarded the relationship between the abbot and the justice and the involvement of the sheriff as of minor rather than essential importance, and thought that the strength of the cases for the identifications of the three characters with real individuals varied significantly. Holt did not, however, make a case for interpreting that story in the *Gest* as a fourteenth-century one, and without prejudice to the chronology of the interpretation he himself preferred, perhaps because of his focus on a possible thirteenth-century date for the origin of the legend.

James Holt: Robin Hood in the thirteenth-century

Since the controversy of the early 1960s, Holt had been intermittently engaged on research for a full-scale study of the Robin Hood legend, finally published in 1982.[44] In it he continued to argue that the legend was about yeomen, not the yeoman freeholder, but 'the yeoman servant of the feudal household', and was spread by minstrels employed in those aristocratic households to the audiences who frequented marketplaces and taverns. 'The tales were "talkyngs" ... said or told to listeners addressed as gentlemen or yeomen'. By the fifteenth century yeomen could be prosperous freeholders or household officials, with status in the royal household next below the status of a squire. Evidence from the records of monastic houses documented the existence of travelling minstrels in fifteenth century Yorkshire, many of them, but not all, from aristocratic households. Holt also gave a detailed account of the development and definition of social gradations in the later fourteenth and fifteenth centuries after the Black Death, and the more diverse social appeal of the tales in that period. This was aided by the rapid decline of French as the language of the upper classes from the mid-fourteenth century and the increased use of English, the language of the tales; there was no evidence that there were ever equivalents in French. He maintained his view that the tales originated in the thirteenth century, and now deployed evidence which, he argued, showed that the Robin

---

[44] J. C. Holt, *Robin Hood* (London, 1982).

Hood legend had reached southern England from its origin in Yorkshire before 1300, and that it did so via an aristocratic connection. In 1296 a man called 'Gilbert Robynhod' was recorded as paying a royal tax in the manor of Hungry Hatch at Fletching in Sussex. He argued that this occurrence of a 'Robin Hood' name on an estate belonging to the Lacy family of Yorkshire meant that the legend had reached Sussex via the feudal family connection between the two counties.[45] Dobson and Taylor had already identified a possible original of Friar Tuck, in the form of an outlawed robber active as the leader of a gang in Sussex between 1417 and 1429. When pardoned he turned out to be a chaplain in Lindfield, a parish neighbouring Fletching, and so reinforced the connection of the legend with a small area of the county.[46] Holt also added a newly-discovered fifteenth-century reference not only to Robin Hood and his men but also to the Cumberland outlaw heroes from the tale of *Adam Bell, Clim of the Clough and William Cloudesley*, written in 1432 by a Wiltshire clerk writing a parliamentary election return. The right-hand column included as usual a list of names of sureties for the elected members, but instead of real names he inserted a list of fictitious ones in place of the surnames, reading down on twenty lines: Adam, Belle, Clyme, Ocluw, Willyam, Cloudesle, Robyn, hode, Inne, Grenewode, Stode, Godeman, was hee, lytel, Joon, Muchette, Millersson, Scathelok, Reynoldyn'.[47] Its further significance was that it provided the earliest reference to Robin as a 'good man'.

Holt contended that from the beginning Robin Hood was believed to be a real historical personage, not a myth as later suggested by folklorists. He then dealt in detail with what writers from the fifteenth to the twentieth centuries knew, or thought they knew, about him. He made a critical re-evaluation of Hunter's discredited 1852 identification of the porter of Edward II's chamber of 1324 as a possible original of the outlaw.[48] While appreciative of Hunter's innovative although flawed use of original public records, and the Wakefield manor court rolls, to try to corroborate information given in the *Gest*, Holt criticised the more recent speculative ideas of Walker and Harris; they had erected 'a vast jerry-built structure' on Hunter's 'careful excavations' by misunderstanding and misinterpreting the information they took from the documents. Holt undermined their interpretation of the records, including the supposed evidence that they contained for the involvement of the outlaw in the revolt of Thomas earl of Lancaster against Edward II; they were guilty of 'mere guesswork inspired by wishful thinking'.[49] He also identified a damaged royal household account, covering April to July 1323, which

---

[45] For the details, see p. 174.
[46] D&T, p. 41 and note 2; Holt, *Robin Hood*, p. 59.
[47] TNA, C 219/14/3, part 2, no. 1; illustration on p. 70.
[48] See Chapter 3.
[49] Holt, *Robin Hood*, pp. 44–50.

showed that the porter Robyn Hode received wages in that period, so proving that he had worked for the king before he arrived in Nottingham later in that year, and before being finally paid off in 1324 because 'he can no longer work'. 'This was not the Robin Hood of the *Gest* who ... left the court through boredom to return to the greenwood where he lived for twenty-two years before his fatal journey to Kirklees'. Nevertheless, in the Wakefield court rolls, Holt was able to trace several Hood families who were tenants of the lordship in the fourteenth century, and a reference in an earlier foot of fine, a record of an agreement in the king's court, showed that one of them existed at least as early as 1202. These men all lived not far from Robin Hood's haunts in Barnsdale, and there were two 'Robin Hood' place-names of 1650 and 1657 near Wakefield. He suggested that 'the coincidence of family and place names in the vicinity of Barnsdale ... is unlikely to be accidental. Either the Hoods of Wakefield gave Robin to the world, or they absorbed the tale of the outlaw into their family traditions or their neighbours and descendants came to associate the two'. Holt went on to consider the credentials of Owen's candidate put forward in 1936, giving further details of the Yorkshire fugitive of 1225, 'Robert Hod, fugitive' alias 'Hobbehod, fugitive', from further pipe rolls that Owen had not consulted, and pointed out that he was the only Robert Hood so far discovered who was an outlaw. He concluded that the most likely candidate for the original outlaw was the Yorkshire fugitive of 1225, especially if he could be shown to have been a member of a Hood family living in the Wakefield area.

Dobson and Taylor, in a review article of Holt's book published in 1983, although recognising the importance of some of his documentary discoveries and their interpretation, were critical of some of the views expressed in his 'sustained attempt to establish the historical truth behind the legend'. This made him in some respects 'a true heir of Joseph Hunter', seeking out the possible historical significance of the surviving early poems, but without allowing for the possibility that their authors randomly invented or substituted the names and places that occurred in them, or that the tales as we have them did not reflect their nature at the time they originally emerged. Holt's approach was based on the evidence of written records, rather than on fifteenth-century literary sources, and, they thought, the danger of such an approach was that 'it runs the risk of implying that because a certain development is not documented it cannot have existed'. They considered that the discovery of the Wiltshire parliamentary return of 1432 was of great importance, not least because it showed that by that date the legend had already begun to be 'sentimentalised, satirised ... and exploited for commercial gain' before the date of the first surviving ballad text. Holt had also increased understanding of the importance of Barnsdale and the 'Sayles' in the legend, and indeed corrected their own earlier error as to the location of 'Robin Hood's Stone'. They also accepted that the importance of the 'Robinhood' compound surnames had not been taken seriously enough by previous scholars who had been aware of them, but that Holt's view that they were most likely to have been diffused by feudal links was less clear. They acknowledged that he had managed to show that there was nothing in the detail of the *Gest* to exclude the likelihood that it came from a thirteenth rather than a fourteenth century background, contrary to Maddicott's recent view. On the issue of the medieval audience for the tales, Dobson and Taylor doubted that even in the thirteenth century minstrels were so closely restricted to great households that they did not perform for other and larger popular audiences in towns and at markets and fairs.[50]

John Bellamy and another fourteenth-century Robin Hood

In 1985 John Bellamy, an established expert on crime in the later medieval period, produced a further study of the outlaw which sought to identify Sir John at the Lee, a courtier of the reign of Edward III, as the patron of the anonymous author of the *Gest* of Robin Hood.[51] Bellamy characterised his argument as 'an exercise in fourteenth-century prosopography tempered by frequent and close examination of the major literary source'. He noted that he had only taken into account the material in the *Gest*, ignoring the other tales known to date from the fifteenth century, because they consisted of nothing more than the development of particular themes which appear in the main Robin Hood text. When considering proposed candidates for the sheriff of Nottingham, he concentrated on those who held the office in the fourteenth century rather than the thirteenth, because they were chronologically nearer to the first literary references to the outlaw.[52] The role of the knight in the *Gest* was of prime importance, second only to Robin himself, and he sought through the use of detailed record evidence to show that the original of the knight was a real person, Sir Richard at the Lee. He was only named in the later part of the ballad, perhaps deliberately, so as not to give him too high a profile and so draw attention away from the outlaw leader. Bellamy worked backwards from the post-medieval story of *Robin Hood and Queen Katherine*, identified as Katherine Howard, the fifth wife of Henry VIII, in which a Sir Richard Lee appears, to a fourteenth-century Lee family of Hertfordshire which

---

[50] R. B. Dobson and J. Taylor, 'Robin Hood of Barnsdale: A Fellow Thou Hast Long Sought', *Northern History* 19 (1983), pp. 210–20.

[51] J. Bellamy, *Robin Hood: An Historical Enquiry* (London, 1985). See also J. G. Bellamy, *The Law of Treason in England in the Later Middle Ages* (Cambridge, 1970); and *Crime and Public Order in England in the Later Middle Ages* (Cambridge, 1973).

[52] For the details, see Chapter 9.

had strong connections with the royal household of Edward III. A Sir John Lee held a court office from which he was dismissed in 1368 for alleged maladministration, and Bellamy conjectured that he used the connection between his family name and that of the ally of the outlaw as family propaganda in an attempt to maintain his position, an idea which, as the author himself admitted, was not 'of any precision or certainty'. After another series of tenuous conjectures, Bellamy concluded that a Richard de la Lee who became parson of Arksey near Doncaster in 1319 appeared to be a strong candidate for recognition as the knight of the *Gest*. He also proposed further identifications of characters, all during the period in the 1320s in which Hunter's ideas were grounded, and were documented in government records. They included in particular a mariner called Little John, mentioned in the records of the royal Chamber between 1322 and 1323 at the same time as Hunter's Robin Hood, and various men with the surname 'Scathelock' and its variants mentioned in other records.

Bellamy's book was generally dismissed by historians of the outlaw legend, in particular Dobson, as being based on a series of unlikely assumptions. It was also 'a little curious that this supposedly deliberate piece of propaganda in the interests of the Lee family thereafter proved so cryptic and apparently self-defeating that it was never recognised as such until Bellamy himself came along to elucidate its message'.[53] His ideas were in any case out of date even by the time of the book's publication, since new documentary discoveries meant that in the mid-1980s the search by historians for the original outlaw moved back decisively from the fourteenth century to the thirteenth.

The 'Robinhood' names in historical sources

The publication of Holt's book in 1982, and his reassertion of the historicity of the legend, in particular the occurrence of the name 'Gilbert Robynhod' in Sussex in 1296, encouraged some younger historians to draw attention to a number of other previously unnoticed 'Robinhood' or 'Robehood' surnames found in documentary sources in the Public Record Office, in the records of the royal courts of law sitting at Westminster or on circuit. Most were identified by Henry Summerson, an historian of criminal law in the thirteenth century, in records of crown pleas; one was found in a civil case by Robert Palmer, an American legal historian; and another by the present author, then an assistant keeper at the Record Office. Those noted by Summerson came from Hampshire (two), Essex and Suffolk; that by Palmer from the borders of Huntingdonshire and Bedfordshire; and that by Crook from Berkshire.[54] These discoveries

---

[53] See in particular D&T, pp. xix–xx; and R. B. Dobson, 'Robin Hood: The Genesis of a Popular Hero', in Hahn, *Popular Culture*, pp. 70–71.

[54] For the full details and for the interpretation see Chapter 6. They are

were hailed by Holt in the second edition of his book in 1989, as showing that 'Robinhood' names were widespread in southern England, far from Barnsdale and Sherwood, and that, if they had been interpreted correctly, the legend had become a national one by the second half of the thirteenth century. The fact that five of them applied to men who were suspected or outlawed criminals left no real doubt that the interpretation was correct. The most important was the earliest, in which a member of a criminal gang active in Berkshire who was called 'William son of Robert le Fevere' in an entry in a plea roll of the justices in eyre in that county in 1261, was in 1262 named in an Exchequer memoranda roll as 'William Robehod, fugitive'. Whoever changed the name must therefore have heard about the legend. He probably did so because William, son of Robert, had Robert in his name and was a member of an outlaw gang; he therefore became William Robehod, and whoever changed the name knew of Robin as an exemplary outlaw. The original Robin Hood, if there was one, must therefore have lived some time before 1261-2, long enough for him to have become famous by that date. This new evidence suggested that the 'Hobehod' of 1226 'may well reflect the emergence of the legend'.[55] Holt maintained this view in his later publications, in 1995 and 2004, although he modified it by arguing that there was an alternative possibility that the legend might have emerged from more than one individual outlaw.

> In many other cases criminals could have used or attracted the nickname without its leaving any trace of itself in the record of their crimes. It is only through luck that the flash of illumination from the case of William, son of Robert le Fevre exists. So it could well be ... that the legend as it is now originated in multiple Robin Hoods, a composite person embodying real people and real incidents all brought together under the umbrella of a single persona. There were other outlaws with other names - some real, some legendary. This one snowballed, absorbing other legends and continuing to gather new material down to the present day.[56]

Not all medieval historians agreed, however. Colin Richmond considered that the discovery of the name 'Robehod' in 1262 was a 'liberating discovery'; the ballads had been 'released from their historical context (or cage) ... they are fictions purely'.[57] The view of Dobson and

---

mentioned by Holt, p. 188, though his reference to another Huntingdonshire case in 1285 seems to be an error.
55 Holt, *Robin Hood*, pp. 187–89.
56 J. C. Holt, 'Robin Hood: The Origins of the Legend', in Carpenter, *Robin Hood*, pp. 27–34, at 29; *ODNB* (2004): Hood, Robin (*supp. fl.* late 12th–13th cent.), legendary outlaw hero.
57 C. Richmond, 'An Outlaw and Some Peasants: The Possible Significance of Robin Hood', *NMS* 37 (1993), pp. 90–101, at 90, reprinted in Knight, *Anthology*, pp. 363–76.

Taylor was more nuanced. In 1989, in a foreword to the reprint of their original book, they concluded that there were two possibilities: to seek an original in the late-twelfth or early-thirteenth centuries, or to consider the possibility that 'by the 1260s the name 'Robehod' or 'Robin Hood' was in not uncommon use as a nickname for a fugitive or outlaw, without benefit of any fully developed legend at all'. The name of the outlaw might have preceded an actual man of that name.[58] In 1990, reviewing the second edition of Holt's book, published in the previous year, they concentrated on his interpretation of the 1262 'Robehod' reference, identified since the first edition was published. It had fully justified Holt's argument in his first edition of the significance of the 'Robinhood' surnames in showing that the name of the outlaw was already a nickname used to designate a notorious outlawed thief, and that the way forward was to discover more such names in official records, as Summerson had done in the preceding years. The names showed that the previous suggestions about the context of the genesis of the legend in the fourteenth century must be abandoned, with attention to be focused on the 1220s or even the 1190s, and that the chronological interval between the first reference to Robin Hood and the earliest surviving tales was now around two centuries. However, it also showed, disconcertingly, that the outlaw was capable of 'self-multiplication', and it might be that the nickname preceded rather than succeeded the later legend. Dobson and Taylor also pointed out the importance of Holt's suggestion that Robin Hood's role as a collector of money in the May Games under the early Tudor kings marked his emergence as a popular hero who may as a result have derived from this role his later reputation for taking from the rich to give to the poor.[59] As the 1990s began, therefore, historians were continuing to take the lead in investigating and re-interpreting the Robin Hood legend, but by the middle of that decade the debate was re-invigorated by a major change of direction and the emergence of a new leading writer on the subject.

Stephen Knight: Robin Hood as myth

Stephen Knight, a professor of English studies, introduced to the study of the subject a relatively new academic approach which had come to be known as 'cultural studies'. The nature of the discipline is difficult to define, but could be characterised as a multi-disciplinary approach to culture which blurs the boundaries between academic subjects and concentrates on the political dynamics of contemporary culture and its historical foundations; it views cultures not as fixed, bounded, stable, and discrete entities, but rather as constantly interacting and changing

---

[58] D&T, pp. xxi–xxii.
[59] R. B. Dobson and J. Taylor, 'General Review: Robin Hood', *Northern History* 26 (1990), pp. 229–32.

sets of practices and processes. These ideas originally emerged from the University of Birmingham in 1964, and developed further as the number of universities increased after 1992. In the new, more competitive environment, the academic leaders of some institutions, both old and new, were hungry for research output on popular and multi-faceted subjects like Robin Hood, and the publication of scholarly work in the subject area has in consequence increased exponentially in the last three decades.[60]

Knight was originally an Arthurian scholar, and became interested in Robin Hood when he joined De Montfort University in Leicester. He lived at Exton in Rutland, close to what he mistakenly described as 'the old royal forest' of Barnsdale.[61] His first book on the outlaw legend (although he has consistently referred to it as a myth) was published in 1994 as *Robin Hood: A Complete Study of the English Outlaw*; he said that it was prepared 'within bowshot of a fugitive place bearing just the name of his earliest location'.[62] A review in the *Times Literary Supplement* was therefore headed 'Robin of Rutland', while the book was prefaced by a map of supposed Robin Hood sites in Rutland and the neighbouring parts of adjacent counties. It included much interesting discussion and interpretation of the phenomenon of Robin Hood, but little new information about its origins.

Knight's literary and 'sociocultural' approach to the legend departed markedly from what he described as the 'historicism' of previous twentieth-century academic writers, who based their interpretations of the legend on the traditional cautious, rigorous, and contextualized interpretation of information by historical period, geographical place and local culture. Knight became the most combative and articulate critic of the approach of historians who had argued for the existence of a real original Robin Hood ('the "Real Robin Hood" industry'), whose practitioners excavate 'each load of empirical ore' but 'ignore the rich terrain of actual texts in favour of any crevices of fact into which they can thrust their empiricist pitons and so climb towards the peak of their faith, a historical progenitor of the legend'. In his treatment of the texts he remarked that the debate in the preceding decades about the nature of the audience had been affected by the fact that the commentators were historians who had little idea of 'the mediations and symbolisms that intervene between audience and material in the normal functioning of literature'. This intellectual divide was also apparent in his discussion of the reference to 'the Sayles' in the *Gest*, an 'empirical detail' whose 'quasi-precision' excited

---

60   For cultural studies generally, see J. Hartley, *A Short History of Cultural Studies* (London, 2003). For a partisan but informative account of the origins of the discipline, see S. Hall, 'The Emergence of Cultural Studies and the Crisis of the Humanities', MIT Press 53 (1990), pp. 11–23.
61   See pp. 133–34.
62   Knight, *Complete Study*. For the detailed textual material, see pp. 29–31.

some historians beyond its original causal significance, being 'an element that merely functions like the detail in a medieval painting whose mode as a whole remains general or allegorical'. Nevertheless, the outlook of the tale was, he thought, more anti-authoritarian than conservative historians like Holt believed, advocating appropriation from the church and rebellion against royal officials if not against the king himself. However, Knight's own lack of familiarity with and understanding of thirteenth-century legal records led him to a basic misunderstanding of the bureaucratic context, and therefore the significance of, the 'William Robehod' reference of 1262.[63]

Knight's volume was the subject of a short review article by Dobson and Taylor, published in 1997.[64] They hailed its appearance as the end of a long period during which literary critics had been reluctant to enter the Robin Hood debate. His approach was specifically 'sociocultural' as opposed to what he regarded as a defective 'historicist' standpoint, and Dobson and Taylor considered that it left him undecided as to how far the legend had emerged from a 'mythic' hero, many different outlaws, or the activities of one particular criminal in a specific temporal and geographical context. His suggestion that Robin Hood was active in a place in Rutland called Barnsdale, rather than the Barnsdale in Yorkshire, was highly improbable, particularly in view of the strong evidence in the *Gest* and historical sources in favour of the latter. Knight's disinclination to accept the significance of the 1262 reference, accepted by most historians as a major breakthrough in the dating and interpretation of the origins of the legend, by suggesting that it arose from 'scribal confusion', was not persuasive, and it now seemed most likely that the significance of the outlaw's name preceded rather than followed the evolution of the later legend. They also criticised his failure to make any real attempt to relate Robin Hood poems, plays and films to their audiences and their culturally determined expectations.

Kevin Carpenter: a touring exhibition of Robin Hood

In their review of Knight's book, Dobson and Taylor also considered another ground-breaking publication in the field, which they thought 'the most ambitious introductory guide to English greenwood literature, art and film ever produced', and important as the first 'detailed iconographical survey of the Robin Hood persona'. In 1995 Kevin Carpenter, an academic in the Faculty of Literary Studies in the University of Oldenburg, Germany, arranged an exhibition of a variety of artefacts

---

[63] See pp. 182–83.
[64] R. B. Dobson and J. Taylor, 'Merry Men at Work: The Transformation of Robin Hood from Medieval Outlaw to Heritage Hero', *Northern History* 33 (1997), pp. 232–37. See also D&T, pp. xxvii–xxx.

entitled *Robin Hood: The Many Faces of that Celebrated English Outlaw*, displayed in the library of the university. It was subsequently to go on tour to six other European cities, ending in Berlin in 1997, although it never actually visited the only intended British venue in the itinerary, York, planned for 1996. It was provided with a bilingual English and German illustrated catalogue, which also included contributory essays by historical and literary writers, although a main purpose of the exhibition was to illustrate the wide variety of children's books, toys, games, puzzles, comics, magazines, household objects and theatre posters about the outlaw.[65] One notable contributor, the literary scholar Thomas Ohlgren, even used the catalogue to offer methodological approaches to the teaching of undergraduate courses about the outlaw, from a literary and cultural rather than an historical standpoint. In doing so he asserted that Robin was the undoubted 'new hero of our post-Thatcher/Reagan era', and he contended that in the 1990s studies of Robin Hood had replaced the dominant Arthurian focus of the 1980s.

Dobson and Holt: later views

Dobson and Holt both continued to publish work on Robin Hood in their retirement. Dobson's last contribution was published in 2000, while Holt had his final say in the *Oxford Dictionary of National Biography* in 2004.[66] There was a continuing debate on the historicity of the outlaw between these two leading historians, while Holt produced a second edition of his book, with an important Postscript, in 1989. In the 1995 Robin Hood exhibition catalogue only a passing reference was made to the 1262 memoranda roll entry,[67] but in 1997 Dobson and Taylor gave a more detailed consideration of its value. They bore in mind the later 'Robehod/ Robynhod' references identified by Henry Summerson in the records of criminal trials from 1272 onwards, not all of them being the names of criminals. They considered that the names did not prove the existence of a fully developed greenwood legend by 1300, but at least they suggested 'the popularity of the concept as well as the name of an outstanding and perhaps quasi mythical outlaw figure', and believed that the search for an historical outlaw called Robin Hood in the late thirteenth or fourteenth

---

[65] K. Carpenter, *Robin Hood: The Many Faces of that Celebrated English Outlaw* (Oldenburg, 1995).

[66] R. B. Dobson, 'Robin Hood: The Genesis of a Popular Hero', in Hahn, *Popular Culture*, pp. 61–89; *ODNB*, J. C. Holt, 'Hood, Robin (supp. fl. late 12th–early 13th cent.), legendary outlaw hero' (2004); W. M. Ormrod, 'Robin Hood and Public Record: The Authority of Writing in the Medieval Outlaw Tradition', in *Medieval Cultural Studies: Essays in Honour of Stephen Knight*, ed. Evans (2006), pp. 57–74.

[67] Carpenter, *Robin Hood*, p. 40.

century was no longer worthwhile. Nevertheless, the possibility that there was such a man before 1262, and that he might, as had recently been suggested by the present author, have been a man called Robert of Wetherby, hunted down in Yorkshire by the sheriff of Nottingham in 1225, could not be ruled out. However, they contended that if a legend had emerged by 1262 it was surprising that no allusion to its popularity survived before the reference by William Langland in the 1370s, and that the case for a fourteenth-century origin for some of the themes and language of the *Gest* remained strong.[68]

Finally, in 1997, Dobson alone reiterated these points, and added others. One was that the legend seemed to have begun to expand in the 1320s and 1330s, was adapted to narrative form, and only then took on many of its critical defining features. It seemed most likely that under Edward II and III 'the adventures of a real Yorkshire highwayman and his gang stimulated a previously amorphous and very undeveloped outlaw legend into new heights of elaboration, into a full-scale saga rather than a reputation'. Dobson also took another detailed look at the 'William Robehod' reference of 1262, and the comments on the range of such names made by their principal discoverer, Henry Summerson, before offering three possible alternative explanations of the phenomenon of the names and their relationships to the genesis of the legend. Firstly, that 'some form of outlaw legend associated with a real, notable, and memorable robber called Robin Hood' was in existence by the mid-thirteenth century, and had become so popular that later criminals adopted the name. The second was that the suggestion that the 'Hobehod' of the 1220s, possibly the same man as the 'outlaw and evildoer of our land' executed in 1225, was the real original outlaw, if there was one at all; there was some doubt that his misdeeds were exceptional enough to become the focus of a local legend, never mind one that was known in southern England a generation later. The third was the possibility that before the 1260s the name of Robin Hood 'was in common use as a nickname for a fugitive or outlaw but without the benefit of any fully developed legend at all', a view with which Holt had disagreed because he thought that a criminal reputation could not exist without an accompanying legend. Dobson suggested that a popular medieval nickname rarely needed to imply a developed legend, but more often an eye or ear 'for its possible symbolism as well as its emotional appeal and resonance', like the aliases used by many rebels in the Peasants' Revolt. His conclusion was that future seekers of the birth of the legend 'must now at least contemplate the paradoxical possibility

---

[68] D&T, pp. xxx–xxxv; D. Crook, 'The Sheriff of Nottingham and Robin Hood: The Genesis of the Legend?', in *Thirteenth Century England II: Proceedings of the Newcastle upon Tyne Conference 1987*, ed. P. R. Coss and S. D. Lloyd (Woodbridge, 1988), pp. 59–69.

that names can come before things and that the original genesis of the outlaw hero may be not so much the appeal of his adventures as the coining of his name'.[69]

Anthony Pollard: the fifteenth-century world of Robin Hood

In 2007 Anthony Pollard, an historian of fifteenth-century England, wrote an account of the outlaw legend in that period.[70] Pollard defined scholarly interest in Robin Hood as 'a cultural phenomenon at the intersection of history, literature and media studies', and, noting that most published work in recent years had been produced by literary scholars, he sought to 'reclaim some of the ground for the historian'. His view was that in the fifteenth century Robin Hood was a 'literary creation', and although an original outlaw may have existed two centuries earlier, nothing was known of him. Stories about him certainly existed in the late fourteenth century, which may or may not have been like the stories in circulation in the fifteenth; they surely must have changed over time, as they certainly did after 1550. The Robin Hood of the tales was a literary creation of the fifteenth and early sixteenth centuries, and his intention was to write about how he was imagined then and how he fitted into contemporary society. His view of the temporal context of the Robin Hood of the *Gest* was to place it, in agreement with Ohlgren, Ayton and Maddicott, and latterly also Dobson, in the 1320s and 1330s. The King Edward of the tale was he thought probably a representation of Edward III, the ruler most likely to have been the 'Edward oure cumly king' of the *Gest*, whose reign was in the fifteenth century regarded as one of justice and social peace. In its hostility to the abbot of St Mary's, he considered that the *Gest* also articulated pre-Reformation anti-monastic feeling, already aroused in the second quarter of the fourteenth century by attacks by the men of some towns dominated by monasteries.

Stephen Knight and the 'rhizomatic Robin Hood'

Meanwhile, Stephen Knight had published his second book on the outlaw, *Robin Hood: A Mythic Biography*, in 2003. He had since the first produced several other important related publications.[71] In the 'mythic biography' Knight dealt with what he identified as the main four

---

69   R. B. Dobson, 'Robin Hood: The Genesis of a Popular Hero', in Hahn, *Popular Culture*, pp. 61–77.
70   Pollard, *Imagining Robin Hood*. Earlier, see R. Almond and A. J. Pollard, 'The Yeomanry of Robin Hood and Social Terminology in Fifteenth Century England', *Past and Present* 170 (2001), pp. 52–77.
71   S. Knight and T. Ohlgren, *Robin Hood and Other Outlaw Tales* (Kalamazoo, 1997); *Robin Hood: The Forresters Manuscript* (Cambridge, 1998), reviewed by

manifestations of Robin Hood, successively as a medieval outlaw, the earl of Huntingdon, a subject for playwrights and poets, and finally as a Hollywood phenomenon. The early stories about the outlaw did, he thought, 'give a remarkably consistent, overlapping, and self-supporting account of bold Robin Hood, the medieval outlaw', even though it included nothing about his birth and upbringing, or the reason for his outlawry. Knight's third volume on the outlaw, *Reading Robin Hood*, published in 2015, consisted of explorations and further treatment, from a cultural studies viewpoint, of individual areas not fully dealt with previously.[72] Once again, despite the energetic refutation by historians of its existence, the truly mythical 'forest of Barnsdale' 'in the heart of Rutland', 'one never noticed by the empiricist historians', appeared, and he also suggested that 'the historicist obsession with the real Robin Hood, so concerned with date and place, is a modern form of sentimental localism'. The book ended with a chapter entitled 'Rhizomatic Robin Hood', in which the author proposed that the Robin Hood tradition had the structure of a rhizome, 'a widely spread, invisible root-system which drives plants upwards through the ground at any point'; this was in contrast to an 'arborescent' or tree-like traditional 'rational foundation for order', involving 'coherence, interconnection, upward and onward movement and capacity to spread'. In this rhizomatic structure, 'the coherent determinants of time, place, class and power, as well as their servants in terms of literary tradition, operate only in a casual, not a causal way, [and] will help us to comprehend ... how the unusual features of this whole tradition can be seen as authentic to its meaning, mission and multiple validity'. Also, 'it appears that Robin Hood is today the über-outlaw, the archetype of resistance to the authorities, arborescent only in an essentially rhizomatic way'. It may be wondered what the original outlaw, if he ever existed, would have made of this.

Dobson and Taylor in 'Robin Hood Ballads', *Northern History* 35, pp. 237–39; and Knight, *Anthology*.

[72] S. Knight, *Reading Robin Hood: Content, Form and Reception in the Outlaw Myth* (Manchester, 2015).

Chapter 5

The Robin Hood Places

The development of the Robin Hood legend and the increase in its popularity over several centuries sometimes came to influence English local nomenclature, associating places with, in particular, the outlaw himself or Little John. This was mainly limited to minor geographical features, such as wayside crosses or distinctive rocks, not settlements, and these features did not always bear those names consistently or permanently. Such names were very numerous by the nineteenth century, and are found in quite significant numbers from the later sixteenth century onwards, although a large proportion of them are first recorded only on maps drawn in the later eighteenth century. They occur in many counties, not just in those most closely associated with the legend, that is, Yorkshire and Nottinghamshire. The fullest listing of them so far, specifically excluding street, inn and field names, was compiled by Dobson and Taylor and published in the first edition of their book on the outlaw legend in 1976.[1] It was reprinted without any modification or addition in subsequent editions, and made no claims to be comprehensive, providing 'only a small selection of what seem to us the most important in an enormous field', with the selection criterion being the appearance of the name in question on the Seventh Series of the One-Inch Ordnance Survey maps. The first appearance of any place-name in a document or on a map is accidental, and it may have existed for some time previously. Only the very earliest can be used to indicate the spread of the legend, and still less can they provide evidence for its origins. Nevertheless, the concentration of the early examples in the areas most associated with Robin Hood is striking. Many more may eventually come to light, especially as more detailed studies of field-names are carried out, although it seems unlikely that they will alter the general pattern of their distribution.

---

[1] D&T, pp. 293–311. There are significant Lancashire elements in the *Gest*, but no early Robin Hood place-names have been identified in the county.

The list includes only four names recorded before 1501, four more before 1601 and 13 more before 1701. Some early place-names were inherently more susceptible to modification by the widespread awareness of the legend than others. In particular, a handful of 'Robin' names were altered to 'Robin Hood' names subsequently. For example, 'Robin Hood Cross' near Bradwell in Derbyshire earlier occurred as the 'Robin Cross' in 1319 and still bore that name in 1640. A tower in the city walls of York, which was known as Bawing Tower in 1370 and Frost Tower in 1485 was called Robin Hood Tower by 1622.[2] These are probably examples of names changed by local etymology to fit local legends generated at a late stage in the development of the legend as a whole. Michael Evans has pointed out the striking example of 'Robynhill' in Nottinghamshire, which is first found in Henry II's foundation charter for Newstead priory, issued in about 1163, and only first appears as 'Robin Hood's Hills' over six centuries later in 1775.[3] The history of a place-name could be more complex and inconsistent. What is now Robin's Wood Hill at Matson in Gloucestershire, probably named after the Robins family who held it in 1526, became 'Robinhodes Hill' in 1624, but was again recorded as 'Robins-wood' in 1777, and then as 'Robin Hood's-hill' again only two years later.[4] The group of names in Richmond Park in Surrey and nearby in the vicinity of Kingston upon Thames seems clearly to have originated from Henry VIII's patronage of Robin's role in the May Games there, and the first appearance of Robinhood Walk in Richmond Park in 1548 may owe its origin to the presence nearby of Richmond Palace, built by Henry VII. The park also has a Robinhood Gate, at the entrance near Kingston upon Thames, but its existence as a gate cannot pre-date the enclosure of the great park by Charles I in 1637, and the name is not recorded until 1785, so the gate name more likely derives from that of the walk than directly from the May Games known to have taken place in Kingston in the early sixteenth century. The process continued even into the twentieth century with the application of the outlaw's name to a section of the Kingston bypass.[5]

Several kinds of feature recur in the names, most of which relate to remote, usually upland, sites, and are not often recorded before the nineteenth century. There are several rocks, hills and caves linked with the outlaw, none of them places of great resort. There are at least ten places in England called 'Robin Hood's Butts', or similar, but only one

---

[2] D&T, pp. 296, 305.
[3] M. R. Evans, '*Robynhill*, or Robin Hood's Hills? Place-Names and the Evolution of the Robin Hood Legends', *Journal of the English Place-Name Society* 30 (1998), pp. 43–53, at p. 43.
[4] D&T, p. 298; *The Place-Names of Gloucestershire* II, ed. A. H. Smith, EPNS XXXIX (Cambridge, 1964), p. 168.
[5] D&T, p. 304.

of them, near Brampton in Cumberland, is known to have had that name by 1600; others, at Bedworth in Cheshire and near Godalming in Surrey, are first mentioned in 1663 and 1673 respectively. The reference to archery contests, so prominent in the tales, is obvious. Most of them are small groups of two or more hills or prehistoric barrows or tumuli. Other names are also connected with archery, such as 'Robin Hood's Two Pricks', noted by Elias Ashmole in 1652, a prick being an archery target. Uniquely, the process of the emergence of a new fictional location for the outlaw can be observed in detail at Edwinstowe in Nottinghamshire, now at the centre of the Robin Hood legend in the county, in the first half of the nineteenth century. It resulted from the interest of Romantic writers and local enthusiasts in the extensive woods there, full of remarkable ancient oaks, and led by 1840 to the popular designation of a very large hollow oak as 'Robin Hood's Larder'.[6]

Naturally, it is mainly the earliest few recorded Robin Hood place-names which are of crucial importance to the origins of the legend and its development down to the time when the surviving early stories were being written down in the fifteenth century. At least two early place-names not mentioned by Dobson and Taylor, including one which is certainly the earliest so far discovered, have been identified since their list was compiled. Their significance will be discussed in the following account of the early place-names, arranged by their geographical locations and groupings.

Yorkshire

Barnsdale, the Sayles and Wentbridge

The place most associated with Robin Hood legend from its earliest manifestation is an area of southern Yorkshire called Barnsdale.[7] Its history was first properly investigated by the Rev. Joseph Hunter, the Yorkshire antiquarian, the second volume of whose great topographical work on the area covered by the ecclesiastical deanery of Doncaster was published in 1831. Over twenty years later he identified the approximate location of 'the Sayles', the place on 'Watling Street' to which in the *Gest* Robin sent Little John with Much and William Scarloke to wait for 'some unknown guest' to bring to dinner. It was referred to in a tax

---

[6] D. Crook, 'The Novelist, the Heiress, the Artisan and the Banker: The Emergence of the Robin Hood Legend at Edwinstowe, c1819 to 1849', *TTS* 119 (2015), pp. 1–13; and see also Holt, *Robin Hood*, p. 96, caption to plates 10–11.

[7] See Map 1. For a geographical sketch of Barnsdale, see Holt, *Robin Hood*, pp. 83–86. See D&T, pp. 21–23 for the details on which their identification of the Sayles was based, and Leland's description.

record recording its contribution, as part of the manor of Pontefract, to a feudal aid granted to Edward III in 1346-47 for the knighting of his eldest son and heir, Edward, the Black Prince, at a rate of one-tenth of a knight's fee. It was paid, at the sum of 4s, by Richard son of Adam of Sayles.[8] Hunter was unable to identify its precise location although, as a young student from Sheffield who travelled to theological college in York by stagecoach between 1805 and 1809, he must have passed close by it several times. In a letter of January 1807 he mentions that he and other passengers had to alight from a coach to York to walk up the hill just north of the village of Wentbridge, where the road crosses the River Went.[9] It was not until 1972 that Dobson and Taylor finally showed, confirming an earlier suggestion by J. W. Walker, that the name still survives in Sayles Plantation, south east of Wentbridge.[10] The name 'Watling Street' was in the fourteenth century applied to the section of what was later termed 'the Great North Road' which ran, from north to south, from the Aire crossing at Ferrybridge (Ferry Fryston) through Wentbridge, and its bridge over the River Went, to Barnsdale Bar and Doncaster.[11]

> From Sayles Plantation it was still possible, prior to the construction of the modern viaduct over the valley of Went, to observe all traffic crossing Wentbridge, and from Sayles it was easy to intercept southbound travellers in the high rolling country which they had to cross once they had ascended the winding road up the valley-side of the Went. For Robin and his men the setting was ideal, and this is registered in the legend: all the travellers he intercepts are travelling south. Modern traffic and the viaduct apart, the scene is still almost as it is described in the *Gest* and as it survives in the medieval place names.[12]

---

[8] J. Hunter, 'The Great Hero of the Ancient Minstrelsy of England, Robin Hood', *Critical and Historical Tracts IV* (London, 1852), pp. 15–16. The document in which he found it cannot now be identified among the records of the subsidy in E 179, to which it appears not to have been added. It is not in E 179/158/18 mm. 17–24, the only West Riding return, and was not printed in *Feudal Aids*, VI. It must be lost among the unsorted miscellanea in The National Archives.

[9] D. Crook, 'The Reverend Joseph Hunter and the Public Records', *Transactions of the Hunter Archaeological Society* 12 (1983), pp. 1–15, at p. 2. The bridge was already in existence by the reign of Henry II: *EYC* III, ed. W. Farrer (YAS RS, Extra Series, 1916), p. 200.

[10] R. B. Dobson and J. Taylor, 'The Medieval Origins of the Robin Hood Legend: A Reassessment', *Northern History* 7 (1972), pp. p. 18; and D&T, p. 22. See also J. W. Walker, *The True History of Robin Hood* (Wakefield, 1952), p. 60.

[11] An early reference to a section of the earlier line of the main road a little further north, between Castleford and Aberford, as 'Watling Street' (*chemino de Waplingestrete*), occurs in 1231: TNA, JUST 1/1043, rot. 12 [AALT-IMG 1338].

[12] Holt, *Robin Hood*, pp. 83–84.

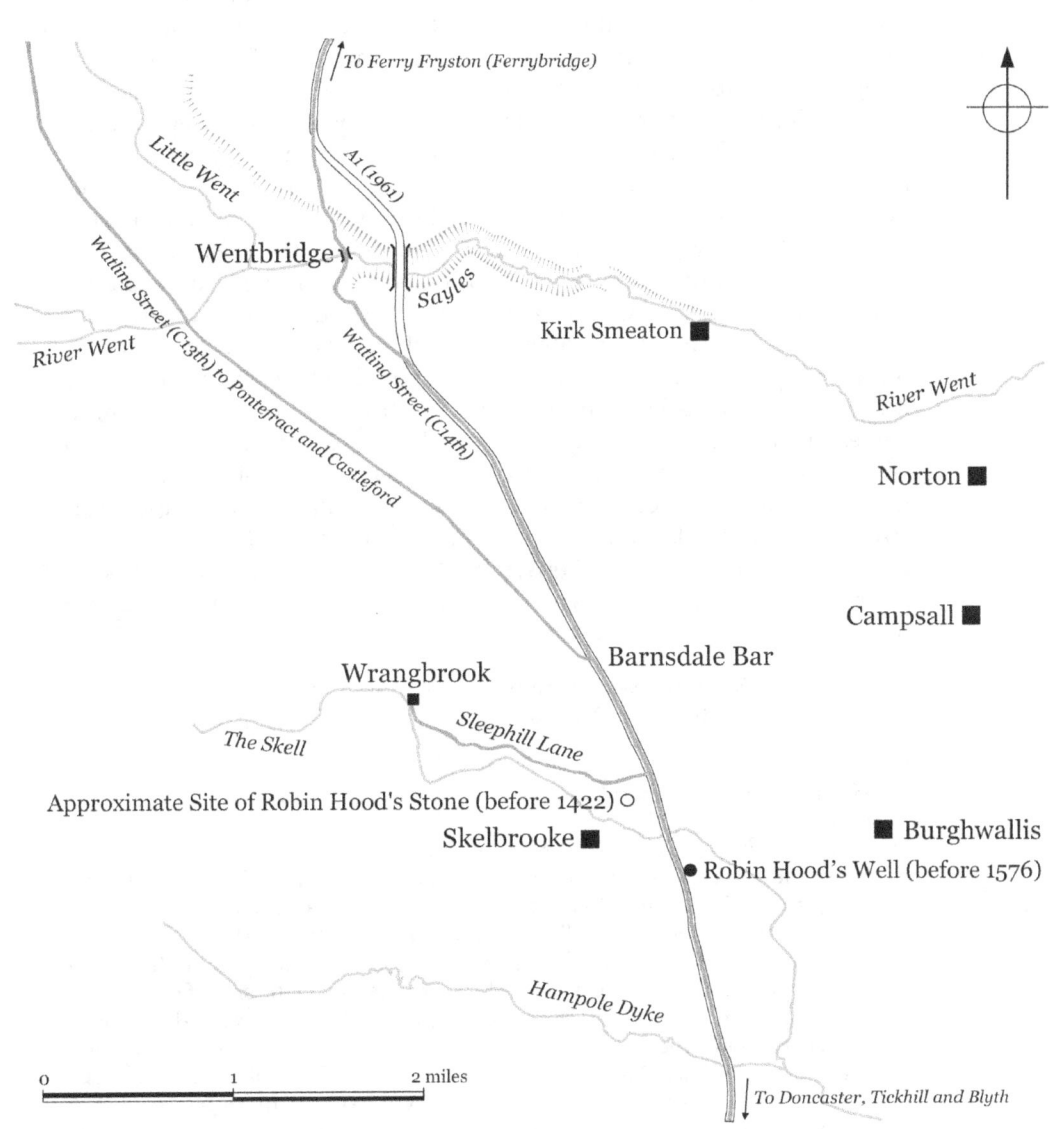

MAP 1. Medieval Barnsdale, showing places linked to the Robin Hood Legend.

Hunter regarded the River Went as the northern boundary of Barnsdale,[13] but Holt demonstrated that the definition of the area has never been precise or consistent. He argued that the original 'Beorn's valley' from which the name derived may have been that of the River Skell, about three miles south of the Went. The Skell is even a little to the south of Barnsdale Bar, the point at which the roads to Pontefract and the Aire crossing at Ferrybridge still divide. In 1806–7 Barnsdale Bar was referred to simply as Barnsdale in a petition for a turnpike road from there to Pontefract. Earlier, in the reign of Henry VIII, the poet, antiquary and traveller John Leland (c. 1503–1552) seems to have applied the name generally to the whole upland area south of Ferrybridge.[14] There is evidence for this more generalised definition of the area referred to as 'the Sayles' as early as the fourteenth century. A privy seal warrant for a commission of oyer and terminer in respect of a robbery at 'le Saylles', dated 23 June 1329, led on the same day to the issue of such a commission in the usual form of letters patent, but in the enrolment on the patent roll the robbery was said actually to have taken place at Skelbrooke, over a mile south of Barnsdale Bar and between three and four miles from 'the Sayles' as later precisely identified.[15] It looks very much as if the name of that notorious place was being used even then as shorthand for the location of any crime committed in the wider locality, and that the locality stretched from Skelbrooke to Wentbridge.[16] As the *Gest* says (stanza 27), as Robin's men 'loked into Bernysdale', they saw the knight who was to be their guest, i.e. victim. When he got to the outlaws' camp nearby he told them

> My purpose was to have dyned to day
> At Blithe or Dancastere

[13] Hunter, 'The Great Hero', p. 12.
[14] Holt, *Robin Hood*, p. 84.
[15] TNA, C 81/163/2703; *CPR 1327–30*, p. 432.
[16] For a more recent discussion of these issues by Henrik Thiil Nielsen, and a suggestion of an alternative site for the Sayles, near Barnsdale Bar, see the International Robin Hood Bibliography at http://www.irhb.org/wiki/index.php/Sayles_%28Barnsdale%29, accessed 10/2/2020. There was another 'Sailles' in Yorkshire, recorded as early as February 1225, when the sheriff of the county was ordered to give the prior of Worksop in north Nottinghamshire seisin of 36 acres of land there, formerly held by William son of Thomas, a tenant of the prior who had abjured the realm because he had killed a man: *RLC* II, p. 17. Its location is not known, and no Worksop cartulary has survived to show in detail where its Yorkshire lands were located; the cartulary is thought to have been destroyed by fire in 1761: G. R. C. Davis, *Medieval Cartularies of Great Britain* (London, 1958), pp. 124–25. A few places mentioned in *Monasticon* VI part 1 (London, Record Commission, 1846), pp. 119–22 and the *Valor Ecclesiaticus* V (London, Record Commission, 1825), p. 175, taken from transcripts, are in southern Yorkshire but none in or near Barnsdale.

When he met Robin's men he was, as we would say today, travelling south on the A1, intending to spend the night at Blyth in north Nottinghamshire or, if he ran out of daylight too soon, at Doncaster near the southern extremity of Yorkshire.

In 1994 Stephen Knight first suggested that the Barnsdale mentioned in the legend could equally well be the place of that name on the northern shore of Rutland Water, and produced a map identifying associated minor place-names in the region that he supposed supported his identification and which are not in Dobson and Taylor's list of Robin Hood place-names.[17] A decade later Douglas Gray colourfully remarked that in doing so he 'lobs one or two grenades into the lairs of historians'.[18] If so, they were badly aimed and rolled back into his own lair, because the error in the identification is easily demonstrated. The Rutland location now called 'Barnsdale' was until at least the early sixteenth century known as 'Bernard's Hill' (*Bernardeshull*, *Bernardishill*), and not as 'Barnsdale'. The latter form is unknown before the early seventeenth century, first recorded in 1602; its late alteration to 'Barnsdale' was almost certainly a reference to the legend, by then widely known.[19] Some of the supposedly related names on the accompanying map can be shown to have been very late in origin, and those not so easily traced probably are. Robin a (originally 'on') Tiptoe hill in Tilton, Leicestershire, is first so called on a tithe map of 1839; in the twelfth century it was known as *Riseberwe*.[20] Robin Hood's Stone in Leicester is first found in 1831.[21] Knight's 'royal forest of Barnsdale' in Rutland never existed, although the place to which he refers was once a park in the royal forest of Rutland. In the 1218 perambulation of the boundaries of the Rutland forest, and again in that of 1269, part of the boundary of the forest passed through the middle of 'the park of 'Bernardeshull'. In 1280 the park was part of the manor of Exton, which belonged to Bernard de Brus, and it was perhaps named after an earlier member of his family who bore the same name.[22] Knight's criticism that 'the allegedly empirical historians did not do their work well enough, never bothering to look up Barnsdale properly' could more appropriately

---

[17] Knight, *A Complete Study*, pp. 29–31; repeated most recently in S. Knight, *Reading Robin Hood: Content, Form and Reception in the Outlaw Myth* (Manchester, 2015), pp. 45–46.

[18] D. Gray, 'Everybody's Robin Hood', *Robin Hood: Medieval and Post-Medieval*, ed. Phillips, pp. 21–41, at 24.

[19] B. Cox, *The Place-Names of Rutland*, EPNS LXVII–LXIX (Nottingham, 1994), p. 20. The existence of the name is certainly not coincidental, as assumed by Michael Evans: Evans, '*Robynhill*, or Robin Hood's Hills', p. 49.

[20] B. Cox, *The Place-names of Leicestershire* III, EPNS LXXXI (Nottingham, 2004), p. 245; D. Crook, 'The Royal Forest of Leicestershire, c.1122–1235', *Leicestershire Archaeological and Historical Society Transactions* 87 (2013), pp. 137–59.

[21] Cox, *The Place-names of Leicestershire* I, EPNS LXXV (Nottingham, 1998), p. 136.

[22] CCR 1279–88, p. 61; Cox, *The Place-Names of Rutland*, p. 20.

have been applied to himself. An expert in English literature, he omitted to check so basic a work of reference as *The Place-Names of Rutland*, edited by a scholar living in Leicester, and published under the auspices of the English Department of the University of Nottingham. There could be no better illustration of the importance of empirical historical research, based on careful evaluation of the surviving evidence, in trying to understand the origins of the Robin Hood legend.[23]

Another late and probably derivative 'Barnsdale' name is what is now Eagle Barnsdale, in Eagle parish in northern Kesteven in Lincolnshire; as late as 1754, in the Customs of the Manor of Eagle, it was called 'Barnseede Moor'.[24] None of the Barnsdales was ever a royal forest.[25] The Yorkshire Barnsdale was mistakenly described as one by John Leland in the reign of Henry VIII, probably because of its well-known association with Robin Hood: 'the wooddi and famose forest of Barnesdale, wher they say Robyn Hudde lyvid like an outlaw'.[26] At the end of the sixteenth century someone much more knowledgeable about forest matters than Leland was in no doubt that Barnsdale was not a forest and had not been in the twelfth century. John Manwood, author of the standard account of forest law, published in 1598, related a story about Richard I's pursuit of a hart he was hunting in Sherwood forest in 1194. It fled from the forest into Barnsdale,

> and because he could not there recover him, he made proclamation at Tickhill in Yorkshire, and at divers other places there, that no person should kill, hurt or chase, the said Hart, but that he might safely retorne into the forest againe, which Hart was afterwards called a Hart royall proclaimed.[27]

Outside the forest the hart would be fair game for other hunters, and so it was necessary for the king to give him special individual protection there.

Whether or not 'the Sayles', however precisely defined, and Barnsdale generally, was a regular place for robberies during the earlier thirteenth century cannot be firmly established, and only two clear references to the

---

[23] See also D&T (1989), p. xxx note 1.
[24] I am indebted to Paul Cavill for this reference. The International Robin Hood Bibliography, at https://www.irhb.org/wiki/index.php/Eagle_Barnsdale (accessed 29 August 2018), includes no evidence for the name earlier than an Ordnance Survey map of 1886.
[25] Holt, *Robin Hood*, pp. 86, 194.
[26] *The Itinerary of John Leland, in England and Wales*, ed. L. Toulmin-Smith (London, 1906–10), IV, p. 13; D&T, p. 21.
[27] J. Manwood, *A Treatise on the Lawes of the Forest* (London, 1598), pp. 24–25; W. P. Marvin, *Hunting Law and Ritual in Medieval English Literature* (Cambridge, 2006), p. 99. The tale, according to Manwood, was found among ancient records 'in a maner defaced and hardly to be read by bad keeping of them' in the tower at Nottingham castle.

Barnsdale 'Sayles' before 1300 have yet been found. The first was part of the name of an individual from the Barnsdale village of Campsall, which lies less than five miles south-east of Wentbridge beyond Kirk Smeaton, and even less from the Sayles, which lies directly between the two places. William de Saylles de Campeshale is mentioned in a Common Bench writ file of 1281. The second was a reference to 'William the man of William del Sayles, living in Skelbrooke', mentioned among a list of men from villages to the north of Doncaster who were appealed by an approver in a gaol delivery by the justices in eyre sitting in York in 1293.[28] Barnsdale certainly had a reputation for being dangerous for travellers by 1306, when the Scottish bishops of St Andrews and Glasgow and the abbot of Scone, taken prisoner in Scotland, were being moved south. For the section of their journey from Pontefract to Tickhill the guard was increased to twenty archers 'on account of [*propter*] Barnsdale'. For other sections of their journey the number of archers was usually eight or twelve.[29] Doubtless most of the criminals who frequented the area were from places nearby. One fourteenth century robbery recorded as taking place there involved at least two men from the nearest important town, Doncaster. The commission of oyer and terminer issued in June 1329, already mentioned, concerned the robbery of William de Felton (described a royal valet, and probably a Northumberland man travelling along the north road) by two men of Doncaster, William Frere and William le Tavener, and five others, Thomas Frere, John Frere, Nicholas de Tykhull, Matilda de Clayton and John le Carter, whose places of domicile were not stated, and others unnamed.[30] The earliest reference to a robbery at 'the Sayles' yet discovered comes from the first decade of the fourteenth century in the record of the trial of an approver called John son of Henry of Wheatley.[31]

The village of Wentbridge itself is mentioned in the early tale of *Robin Hood and the Potter*, where Little John tells Robin that he had previously met the potter, and there is a possible play on the name in the first line of stanza 135 of the *Gest*, where 'a brydge' mentioned in the first line follows the reference to Barnsdale on the last line of the preceding stanza.[32] As the importance of the route of the north road passing through it increased during the fourteenth and fifteenth centuries, it became a recognised staging post for travellers. In 1330 and 1331 one of the bursars of Merton College Oxford travelled to and from the college's properties in Northumberland and Durham through Wentbridge, spending small sums there, 4½d (on

---

[28] TNA, CP 52/1/9/2/2, Common Bench writ file for Easter 3 weeks 9 Edward I, Yorkshire section, no. 311; JUST 1/1098, rot. 78 [AALT-IMG 7363].
[29] TNA, E 101/13/5.
[30] TNA, C 81/163/2703; CPR 1327–30, p. 432.
[31] TNA, JUST 3/55/2, rot. 1 [AALT-IMG 0015]. For the details of his robberies and fate see pp. 200–02.
[32] D&T, pp. 19, 21, 88 and n. 10, 124, 126.

horses), 3d and 2d (perhaps on refreshments), while in 1339 fellows of the college stayed there on another journey north. By 1487 at the latest the village had an inn providing overnight accommodation, and had four inns by the early seventeenth century.[33] By then two smaller local sites in Barnsdale were also firmly associated with the legend.

Robin Hood's Stone

Robin Hood's Stone in Barnsdale is first mentioned in a deed, dated 1322, in the cartulary of Monk Bretton priory, but it has long been generally accepted that this was an error for 1422. In 1831 Joseph Hunter noted a contemporary account of the first progress of Henry VII in the north of England after his coronation, in the spring of 1486, which he found in Thomas Hearne's edition of Leland's *Collectanea*. On 10 April Henry had left Doncaster with a great attendance of noblemen and gentlemen, and was met by the earl of Northumberland and 'a right great and noble company' 'by the Way in Barnesdale, a littil beyonde Robyn Haddezston'.[34] In 1852, however, Hunter also became the first of several writers to confuse the Stone with Robin Hood's Well.[35] Dobson and Taylor, following him and the later Yorkshire antiquary J. W. Walker, the editor of the cartulary, stated that the Well was on or very near the site of Robin Hood's Stone. Holt disputed that assumption and identified its approximate position by reinterpreting the topographical details given in the deed in the cartulary. He concluded that it must have stood to the west, not the east, of the Great North Road, in the fields of Sleep Hill adjacent to the 'ings' (a Norse word referring to water meadows) of Skelbrooke, between Wrangbrook and Skelbrooke.[36] Alternatively, it is possible that the 'lynges' mentioned in the deed refers to the type of heather called 'lyng' which frequently occurs in

---

[33] Holt, *Robin Hood*, pp. 84–5; G. H. Martin, 'Road Travel in the Middle Ages: Some Journeys by the Warden and Fellows of Merton College, Oxford, 1315–1470', *Journal of Transport History* 3 (1975–76), pp. 159–78, at pp. 167, 169, 175–76; D&T, p. 21; *York Civic Records*, ed. A. Raine, II, YAS RS CIII (1941), p. 5. For a further robbery, of a jeweller, at Wentbridge in 1466, see Pollard, *Imagining Robin Hood*, p. 92.

[34] BL Cotton Julius B XII, f. 10; *South Yorkshire* II, p. 487; from *Joannis Lelandi Antiquarii De Rebus Britannicis Collectanea*, ed. T. Hearne, 3rd edition (6 vols., London, 1774), IV, p. 186. See also Pollard, *Imagining Robin Hood*, p. 70.

[35] Hunter, 'The Great Hero', p. 61: 'It had the name, not indeed of Robin Hood's Well, but of Robin Hood's Stone, in the reign of Henry VII'. See also *The Place-Names of the West Riding of Yorkshire* II, ed. A. H. Smith, English Place-Name Society XXXII (Cambridge, 1961), pp. 36–37.

[36] D&T, pp. 23, 310; Holt, *Robin Hood*, pp. 106–07; *Abstracts of the Chartularies of the Priory of Monk Bretton*, ed. J. W. Walker, YAS RS LXVI (1924), p. 105.

Robin Hood Places

the place-names of Nottinghamshire and Yorkshire.[37] There is no known trace of the stone in the landscape today.

Robin Hood's Well

Dobson and Taylor list six Robin Hood's Wells in the West Riding of Yorkshire alone, but that located six miles north of Doncaster on the eastern side of the Great North Road, a mile south of Barnsdale Bar between Skelbrooke and Burghwallis, is the only one in the county of any antiquity. It used to be thought that it was first mentioned by the Yorkshire antiquary Roger Dodsworth in 1622, but it was certainly providing drinks for travellers nearly half a century earlier. By his will dated 19 May 1576, Robert Banister left to the poor of Skelbrooke 3s yearly, and a yearly rent of 4d 'to the repaire of Robin Hood well dish and cheine for poore travellers to drinke in both'.[38] By 1634 travellers were being feted there, for a fee. In August that year three unnamed soldiers, 'a captain, a lieutenant and an ancient [ensign], all three of the military company in Norwich', who were on a seven-week tour of parts of England, were travelling between Doncaster and Pontefract.

> Being thirsty, we tasted a cup at Robin Hood's Well, and there according to the usual and ancient custom of Travellers, were in his rocky chair of ceremony, dignify'd with the Order of Knighthood, and sworne to observe his Lawes. After our Oath we had no time to stay to heere our charge, butt discharg'd our due Fealtie Fee, 4d a peece to the Lady of the Fountaine, on we spur'd with our new dignitie to Pomfret, that day being Market-day.[39]

Richard Brathwait, the author of *Barnabee's Journal*, published in 1638, lamented in verse what he had to drink there, while travelling between Doncaster and Wentbridge:

> Thirst knows neither meane nor measure
> Robin Hoods Well was my treasure,
> In a common dish enchained,
> I my furious thirst restrained;
> And because I drank the deeper,
> I paid two farthings to the keeper.

He further noted, in an extra couplet:

---

37 MED V (ed. S. M. Kuhn and J. Reidy, Ann Arbor, 1968), p. 1034; *The Place-Names of Nottinghamshire*, ed. J. E. B. Gover, A. Mawer and F. M. Stenton, EPNS XVII (Cambridge, 1943), pp. 266, 338; *The Place-Names of the West Riding of Yorkshire* VIII, ed. A. H. Smith, EPNS XXXVII (Cambridge, 1963), p. 112.
38 TNA, C 93/7/4, m. 4.
39 BL, Lansdowne MS 213, f. 319.

A Well, thorne, bush, hung in an iron chaine,
For monuments of Robin Hood remaine.[40]

The diarist John Evelyn also stopped for a drink on 17 August 1654: 'We all now alighted in the high Way, to drink at a Christal Spring, which they call Robinhoods Well, neere it is a Stone Chaire, & an Iron Ladle to drink out of Chain'd to the Seate'.[41] By 1730 it was sheltered by a stone arch, built by Sir John Vanbrugh for the earl of Carlisle in about 1710. A printer and antiquarian of York, Thomas Gent, noted in 1730 that 'there is a very handsome stone-arch, erected by Lord Carlisle, where passengers from the coach frequently drink of the fair water, and give their charity to two people who attend there'. In 1740 the antiquary William Stukeley mentioned Vanbrugh's 'pretty ornament to the road' in his diary. A useful account of the well, dated as at Bath on May Day 1831, was given by Hunter at the end of his history of *South Yorkshire*.[42] He described it as being just south of Barnsdale, and noted that it boasted two inns 'for the convenience of the traveller', but they have long since disappeared. The arch was moved from its original site in about 1960, when the A1 road nearby was widened, but there is an official photograph showing the well-house in its original position next to the road in a Ministry of Transport file at The National Archives.[43] In 1964 the arch was re-erected adjacent to the new south-bound carriageway not far from its original site, the spring to its north being capped. The 'Little John's Well' in the same district near Hampole is only first mentioned in 1838, and may well be a late derivation from the proximity of Robin Hood's Well.[44]

Robin Hood's Bay

Robin Hood's Bay is on the north Yorkshire coast to the south of Whitby and twelve miles north of Scarborough, some distance away from the inland Robin Hood places in the county. The possible significance of the name for the legend was first pointed out by Joseph Ritson in 1795, mentioning that it was both a bay and a village, and quoting a reference by Leland, who described it as 'a fischer tounlet of 20 bootes caullid *Robyn Huddes bay*, a dok or bosom of a mile yn length'. Ritson went on to quote a story about the outlaw included in the history of Whitby written by Lionel Charlton (1720-1788). In it he is pursued by soldiers sent from London to

---

[40] R. Brathwaite, *Barnabees Journal* (London, 1774), p. 103; Hunter, *South Yorkshire* II, p. 488.
[41] Hunter, *South Yorkshire* II, p. 488; D&T, p. 310; Holt, *Robin Hood*, p. 178; *Memoirs of John Evelyn. 1641–1705–6*, II ed. W. Bray (London, 1827), p. 89.
[42] Hunter, *South Yorkshire* II, pp. 487–88.
[43] TNA, MT 121/86, taken in about 1957.
[44] D&T, p. 208.

capture him, and so flees from Whitby to the coast, where he kept fishing vessels to use as a refuge:

> His chief resort at these times, where his boats were generally laid up, was about six miles from Whitby, to which he communicated his name, and which is still called *Robin Hood's bay*. There he frequently went fishing in the summer season ... and not far from that place he had butts or marks set up, where he used to exercise his men in shooting with the long bow.[45]

Dobson and Taylor stated in their list of Robin Hood place-names that the earliest reference to the name is in a letter of 1544 among the State Papers in The National Archives.[46] They overlooked, however, a much earlier letter in the 'Ancient Correspondence' (SC 1) series there, which dated from up to two centuries earlier. Written in French, it is dated at Male in Flanders, near Bruges, on 1 March in an unspecified year, and was sent to Edward II or Edward III by a count of Flanders, Nevers and Rethel, either Louis I (1322-46) or Louis II (1346-84). In it, the place is called 'robin oeds bay', helping to confirm that the letter was, as would be expected, written by a Fleming.[47] The count forwarded a complaint from John Cullin, a burgess of Nieuport, one of the main centres for the Flemish herring trade, and his companions and fishermen.[48] They claimed that in the previous August, after they had succeeded in harvesting 14 lasts of herring from the sea, some men from Bury St Edmunds and other unspecified Englishmen in six ships had seized their ship and taken it to Robin Hood's Bay. From there the men of the country had taken the Flemish fishermen to Whitby to plead for their lives; there they were acquitted, but their ship and goods were not returned. They were now seeking, with the count's help, the restitution of their ship and goods by the king's command.

The involvement of the men of Bury St Edmunds in Suffolk in this incident is at first sight surprising, since the town was not a port and lies some distance from the sea, but its merchants were nevertheless involved in coastal trade in the North Sea during the fourteenth century. In 1310 John de Lenne and other merchants of Bury St Edmunds and their ship were given a royal safe-conduct for going on the king's service from Lynn to Scotland with corn and other victuals. The port from which the ship

---

45 *The Itinerary of John Leland the Antiquary*, ed. T. Hearn (London, 1710, 3rd edn., 1770), I, p. 53; Ritson, *Robin Hood*, pp. lxix–xx.
46 D&T, p. 306.
47 TNA, SC 1/33, no. 202; *PRO Lists and Indexes XV: List of Ancient Correspondence of the Chancery and Exchequer preserved in the Public Record Office* (Kraus Reprint, New York, 1968), p. 510. For the text, see the appendix at the end of this chapter. For a readily available image of the letter, see http://www.robin-hoodlegend.com/robin-hoods-bay-letter/
48 D. Nicholas, *Medieval Flanders* (London, 1992), p. 381.

departed, and the involvement of John 'of Lynn', presumably as its captain, indicates that the ship used by the merchants of Bury was from Lynn.

The men of Whitby seem during this period sometimes to have been involved in incidents of a piratical nature, well illustrated by a commission issued on 28 September 1326 at the Tower of London. A Flemish ship called *La Pelarym* had, despite a truce with Flanders then in force, been boarded at Whitby by persons who killed the master, named as Walter 'called Fosse', his sailors, nine Scottish merchants, 16 Scottish pilgrims and 13 women who were on board; they then removed the goods the ship carried before abandoning it; afterwards others took the abandoned ship 'and brought it with the goods remaining therein whither they would'. Clearly this cannot have been the same incident as that which resulted in the surviving letter from the count of Flanders, but it confirms the robust involvement by the men of Whitby in the herring trade, of which there is also other evidence later in the century. In 1352, after a shipwreck, 33 lasts of herrings were washed ashore at Whitby and seized by local men; in 1359 pirated goods, seized from a Scottish ship sailing from Sluys with a cargo worth £1000, were being sold at the port, while the ship was sunk off the Cleveland coast by pirates, some of whom were from Whitby.[49] In 1361 the men of Whitby petitioned the king for a grant on each 1,000 herring coming within the jurisdiction of their market, and on all goods coming by sea or land for 20 years, in aid of the repair of the bridge in their town, said to be ruinous. Probably in 1397 two Scots petitioned for the release of a Flemish ship containing their goods, which had been taken by men from Whitby, and the bailiffs and customers of Whitby were to be ordered to release the seized goods to them.[50]

Because of its importance, the full text of the letter is given in the appendix below. It is specifically addressed to 'Edward king of England and lord of Ireland', and so was sent sometime before the death of Edward III in 1377, but it is otherwise difficult to date. A terminus post quem is provided by the two subordinate titles held by the count, mentioned at the foot. Count Louis I inherited the county of Rethel from his mother Joan, who had brought the county to his father, Louis of Nevers, in marriage in 1290. Louis I succeeded his father as count in 1322, and acquired the title to Rethel on the death of his mother in 1328. He held the titles until his death at the battle of Crecy in 1346, fighting on the French side.[51] The covering dates of 1327-46 were given as the outside limits of the date of the letter by Dr Patricia Barnes of the Public Record Office, compiler of the revised *List and Index* of 'Ancient Correspondence', because she supposed that the letter

---

[49] CPR 1307–13, p. 215; CPR 1324–27, p. 354; CPR 1350–54, pp. 390–91: CPR 1358–61, pp. 217, 277.
[50] TNA, SC 8/171/8527; SC 8/218/10866; CCR 1396–99, p.165.
[51] On the Flemish background, see Nicholas, *Medieval Flanders*, chapter 9.

was written between the accession of Edward III and the death of Louis I.[52] As already noted, the one that refers to Robin Hood's Bay is dated 1 March at Male but no year is given. Three of the letters sent to Edward II were also issued at Male, all on specific dates in May 1324; they appear to be in the same hand, and have their filing holes in the same place.[53] The same hand wrote one dated to November 1322 from Ypres, but one from Amiens in 1334, over a decade later, is clearly, as one would expect, written in a different hand.[54]

Count Louis I was forced to flee to France in 1339 from the rebellion led by Jacob van Artevelde in Flanders, so the letter, if it was from him, could not have been written at Male after that date, and would therefore have been sent between 1328 and 1339.[55] There are difficulties here, however. The letter is in a different hand from the others, which is clearly later in date, and it is, very unusually, written on paper, whereas all the others were on parchment, as was the norm. It is therefore more likely to have been sent by Louis II, who succeeded his father in 1346, between that date and Edward's death in 1377.[56] 'Robin Hood's Bay' is therefore comfortably the earliest Robin Hood place-name yet discovered, at least 45 years and up to 75 years before the reference to Robin Hood's Stone in 1422. Significantly, it hints at a connection between the outlaw and piracy, the maritime equivalent of highway robbery. It has not even the remotest connection with the greenwood.[57]

Kirklees Priory

Kirklees Priory near Huddersfield has been linked to the Robin Hood legend at least since the lost original version of *A Gest of Robyn Hode* was composed, probably in the mid-fifteenth century. About a half a

---

[52] *List of Ancient Correspondence of the Chancery and Exchequer*, pp. 507–10. It comes at the very end of a large cache of letters to Edward II and Edward III in TNA, SC 1/33, nos. 149–202. They begin in the time of Count Robert de Bethune, running from 1306 and until 1321, and mostly concern complaints about the treatment of Flemish merchants trading with England (SC 1/33, nos. 149–194), followed by a smaller group of letters on similar matters from Count Louis I, five of which are dated between 1322 and 1324, and others probably or certainly to Edward III, one dated to 1334, which may have originally been filed together: SC 1/33, nos. 195–202.

[53] TNA, SC 1/33, nos. 197–99.

[54] TNA, SC 1/33, nos. 195, 201. There is another cache of four more letters from Count Louis I, two of which were also issued at Male: SC 1/38, nos. 42–45. Miss Barnes dated one of them to 1323–26 and the others to 1329, 1330 and 1331.

[55] Nicholas, *Medieval Flanders*, pp. 220–24.

[56] For my earlier view of the date, when I placed it in the period of Count Louis I before 1346, see Ohlgren, *Robin Hood: The Early Poems, 1465–1560*, pp. 123, 238.

[57] The text is given in the Appendix at the end of this chapter.

mile from the existing buildings at Kirklees there is an enclosed stone of a grave with an epitaph, supposedly at the place where Robin's last arrow, shot to determine the place where he was to be buried, fell. This element only first appears in the 'B' or Garland version of the story from the mid-eighteenth century, first published in York in about 1767 by Nicholas Nickson.[58] The arrow was supposedly fired from what is now 'the gatehouse', a mostly Tudor building next to the site of the priory, built with the old stone by Robert and Alice Pylkington before 1565.[59] Exactly when this legend began, and whether it was before the discovery of a grave of Robin Hood on the Kirklees estate or was invented to account for its existence, cannot now be determined. It is possible that the addition of the bow-shot to the tale was made to account for the distance between the buildings and the grave. It has also been suggested that the last five stanzas of this version of the tale were added specifically to establish a link with the epitaph on the tomb.[60]

The story of Robin's death at the hands of the prioress of Kirklees, said to have been a kinswoman of his, who was at the time having a close relationship with a Sir Roger of Doncaster, comes at the very end of the *Gest*, in its last six stanzas. Robin went to the priory to be bled, but the prioress deliberately bled him excessively ('whilst one drop of blood would run'), until he was near death.[61] In 1831 Hunter, in an account of the early history of the Stainton family (partly based on 'a kind of history of the family, drawn up in the reign of Elizabeth', but partly supported by surviving documents), noted the existence of an indenture, dated at Monk Bretton priory on 20 December 1344, confirming a family settlement. It involved the sending of two younger daughters under twelve, Elizabeth and Alice, to enter the nunnery at Kirklees. Elizabeth later became the prioress of Kirklees, her tomb being discovered in 1706; part of the inscription read *ayez mercy a Elizabeth Stainton, priores de cest maison*.[62] At that time Hunter made no connection between her and the death of Robin Hood. In 1852 he repeated what he had written in 1831, but went further: 'assuming that

---

58 D&T, pp. 134–39.
59 The whole story of the alleged grave of Robin Hood at Kirklees and the estate there has been studied by David Hepworth, whose work supersedes all previous accounts. Much of the detail given in the following paragraphs derives from D. Hepworth, 'A Grave Tale', in *Robin Hood: Medieval and Post-Medieval*, ed. Phillips, pp. 91–112; and 'Appendix: Written Epitaphs of Robin Hood', in the same volume, pp. 188–89. See also, in the same volume, R. F. Green, 'The Hermit and the Outlaw: New Evidence for Robin Hood's Death?', pp. 51–59.
60 D&T, pp. 134, 138.
61 D&T, pp. 111–12, stanzas 451–56.
62 Hunter, *South Yorkshire* II, pp. 384–85. He states that there were four copies of this indenture, one of them 'lately in the possession of the family of Cotton of the Haigh'.

there is so much reliance to be placed on the ballad testimony, ... we may believe that there was a relationship between the outlaw and the person who was Prioress of Kirklees at the time of his death, and that Elizabeth de Staynton was that prioress'.[63] The date of the discovery of her supposed grave was confirmed by him,[64] and it was later drawn by Joseph Ismay, vicar of Mirfield from 1739 to 1778, and by Richard Gough in his *Sepulchral Monuments in Great Britain*; nevertheless the editors of *The Heads of Religious Houses* were unable to find any contemporary documentary evidence of a prioress of that name.[65] However, John Watson, a Yorkshire antiquary, was in 1758 given a guided tour of the Kirklees estate, including Robin Hood's tomb and Elizabeth de Stainton's recently repaired tomb, by the agent for the owner. He left notes on his visit, which remain unpublished. Hepworth quotes a transcript by Watson of a royal licence under the statute of mortmain to the priory to acquire land, dated 1373/74, apparently endorsed with a note that the licence had been acquired 'in the time of Elizabeth de Staynton once prioress of Kirklees'.[66]

The first known quasi-historical reference to the burial of Robin Hood at Kirklees is given by the antiquary John Leland in his *Collectanea*, where he mentions 'Kirkley monastery of nuns, where the noble outlaw Robin Hood is buried'.[67] This note probably derives from one of his visits to Yorkshire in the 1530s, probably from 1534, just before the priory was surrendered and then dissolved in 1539, but does not provide any indication that there was an actual grave there before the Dissolution. The purchase of the Kirklees estate by the Armytage family in 1565 led to a long period of interest in the Robin Hood connection and the grave. The first evidence that there was a grave comes from Richard Grafton's chronicle of 1569, which states that the outlaw was buried at Kirklees at the side of the highway at the order of the prioress, and further that the names of 'Robert Hood, William of Goldesborough and others were graven', and that 'at eyther end of the sayde Tomb was erected a crosse of stone', which could now be seen there. Then, in 1589, John Saville, a member of a family who had briefly owned Kirklees after the Dissolution, wrote to William Camden to tell him that the outlaw was buried at Kirklees. Camden mentioned it in the fifth edition of

63 Hunter, 'The Great Hero', pp. 52–54.
64 Hunter, *South Yorkshire* II, p. 385.
65 Hepworth, 'A Grave Tale', pp. 98, 105; R. Gough, *Sepulchral Monuments in Great Britain* I, (London, 1786), p. cix plate 4, fig v; *The Heads of Religious Houses: England and Wales II, 1216–1377*, ed. D. M. Smith and V. C. M. London (Cambridge, 2001), p. 577.
66 Hepworth, 'A Grave Tale', pp. 98, 112; York Minster Archives, MS Add 203/2, 72. The document was earlier referred to by J. W. Walker, when it was in the possession of the Armytage family: J. W. Walker, *The True History of Robin Hood* (Wakefield, 1952), p. 124.
67 J. Leland, *De Rebus Britannicis Collectanea*, ed. T. Hearne (second edition, 6 vols., London, 1770), I, p. 54.

his *Britannia*, published in Latin in 1607, and the first English translation was published shortly afterwards in 1610.[68] It seems likely that Saville had seen the grave. In 1632 Robin's first fictitious epitaph was published by Martin Parker, at the end of his 'A True Tale of Robin Hood', with the assertion that it was set over Robin by the prioress of Kirklees before the Reformation, and so 'was to bee reade within these hundred yeares'; it named him as 'Robert Earle of Huntington', said that he sorely vexed 'these northerne parts' for thirteen years and more, and gave his date of death as 9 December 1198.[69] In the eighteenth century, by which time the grave was enclosed, there was a new epitaph claiming that Robin died on the '24 kalends of December 1247'. No such date exists in the Roman calendar, since the highest kalends of December was the eighteenth.

The connection of the legend with Kirklees therefore goes back to at least the fifteenth century and, if the evidence of the existence and date of the prioress Elizabeth de Stainton is reliable, to the latter part of the fourteenth century. It is therefore one of the most important geographical locations connected with Robin Hood.

Nottingham

Nottingham Castle and St Mary's Church

Local records confirm, in corroboration of the tale of *Robin Hood and the Monk*, that the borough of Nottingham, which became a county borough in 1449, by the later fifteenth century had become firmly associated with the legend. Nottingham castle appears in that tale as the centre of the sheriff of Nottingham's operations, and also as the place into the 'deep prison' of which Robin is cast before being rescued. In *Robin Hood and the Monk*, the parish church of St Mary is mentioned as the place in which Robin attends mass and where he is captured after being spotted by a 'great headed monk'. The incongruity of a monk being present in a parish church is obviated by the fact that St Mary's was from the first decade of the twelfth century the property of the Cluniac priory of Lenton, to the west of the town, and the priory's powerful position gave it an important role in the affairs of Nottingham. Rebuilt magnificently during the fifteenth century, St Mary's remained under the control of the priory until the Dissolution.[70] The rebuilding, and the prominence of its tower on a high hill overlooking the rest of the town, may have inspired the unknown author of the ballad in which it appears. (Figure 5) He would

[68] Hepworth, 'A Grave Tale', p. 96.
[69] Child (1889), pp. 227–33; D&T, pp. 187–90 (extracts only). See also above, p. 64.
[70] *Victoria County History of Nottinghamshire* II, ed. W. Page (London, 1910), pp. 91–100.

FIGURE 5. St Mary's Church, High Pavement, Nottingham, rebuilt in the fifteenth century when it was still the property of Lenton priory. It was here that, in *Robin Hood and the Monk*, Robin was recognised by a monk while attending mass, seized, and imprisoned in the dungeon of Nottingham castle, from which he was rescued by Little John and Much.

probably also have borne in mind that the church was dedicated to St Mary, to whom, as the *Gest* shows, Robin Hood was greatly devoted.

Robin Hood's Close and Robin Hood's Well/St Anne's Well

The earliest Robin Hood place-name in Nottingham is Robin Hood's Close, mentioned in the borough chamberlain's accounts in 1485, 1486 and 1500. On 12 May 1485 Richard Norys and John May were paid 2s 8d, at 4d a day each, for four days, for 'hedgyng at the Copy and at Robynhode Closse'. On 14 April 1486 Richard Norys was paid for two days, again at 4d a day, for hedging the close. In 1500 the close was described as a pasture rented by John Seliok and his son Richard for a number of years (there is blank space where the number should be) at 10s. per annum.[71] Robin Hood's Well, within the lordship and parish of Sneinton, less than two miles north-east of the centre of Nottingham, is first mentioned in a presentment made at Nottingham sessions on 20 July 1500 concerning the illegal digging up of a plot owned by the mayor and burgesses nearby. Robert Wyly of Sneinton, a husbandman, and 16 others unnamed, had on 24 April 1500 dug up the soil belonging to the mayor and burgesses in the holding of John Seliok, near 'Robynhode Well'.[72] It is clear from the inclusion of John Seliok in both the entries in 1500 that the close and the well were in the same place or at least very close together. Seliok was a prominent Nottingham townsman, serving as mayor in 1498 and as an alderman and justice of the peace in 1500 and 1501. He was one of the largest Nottingham contributors to a national tax levied in 1503-4. His son Richard, a bell-founder by trade, later served as one of the town sheriffs, and as mayor in 1506.[73] In 1548 another Richard Seliok and his son John granted two acres abutting upon the beck leading from the well called 'Robyns Wood Well', so the link between the family and the well lasted for over half a century.[74]

Although not within the town boundary itself, it is clear that the well was closely associated with Nottingham and should be regarded as geographically belonging with the town rather than the county of Nottinghamshire. It bore a dual name for several centuries, with the title 'St Anne's Well' the more often used. In the later years 'St Anne's Well' was invariably used, although the popular link with the outlaw remained. In 1597-8 it was referred to as 'Robin Hood's Well alias St Anne's Well'; the place appears again, as 'Robinhoodes Well', in the 1609 Sherwood Forest survey, and is named on the accompanying map.[75] In 1641 an anonymous

---

[71] *RBN* III, ed. W. H. Stevenson (London and Nottingham, 1885), pp. 66–67, 230, 254.
[72] *RBN* III, pp. 74–75.
[73] *RBN* III, pp. 299–300, 302–03, 309, 435; 144, 198–99, 437.
[74] *RBN* IV, ed. W. H. Stevenson (London and Nottingham, 1889), p, 441.
[75] *RBN* IV, p. 441; *Sherwood Forest in 1609: A Crown Survey by Richard Bankes*, ed.

writer reported that the supposed St Anne's chapel on the site had been founded in about 1409, and that only the east wall of the original building remained, as the east wall of the house there, and the only part of it that was built of stone. It was a dwelling house there for the woodward, who was an officer of the mayor, but there was also a 'Victualling House' and it was surrounded by summer houses as facilities for visitors from the town.[76] Although outside the town, the well had already by then played a significant part in civic and other activities for many years. From 1558 at least it was regularly visited by the mayor and burgesses of Nottingham on Easter Monday, and in 1601 it was ordered that each of the civic party, according to his degree, was to spend a prescribed sum of money on provisions provided there by the town woodward, and a discretionary amount with the keeper of Thorney Wood, one of the officials of Sherwood Forest; those not attending were to pay a fine to the mayor unless pardoned.[77] In 1627 the windows of the house there were being repaired, and other work being carried out with tiles and lime.[78] In 1630 the arrangements for the visit were reviewed, and those absent without leave were to make a charitable donation as well as to pay a fine. By then the coroners, sheriffs and the town clerk were also expected to attend. In 1635, because of the cold weather, the occasion was moved to Whit Monday, a date more closely associated with Robin Hood, although he was not mentioned as a reason for moving the event to that day.[79] Before the Reformation the corporation had visited Southwell Minster on Whit Monday to make the Pentecostal offering.

The event regularly held at the well between 1558 and the 1630s was a civic dinner, possibly with charitable connections and arranged in conjunction with forest officials. The references in the borough records which give the information usually call the well St Anne's Well, but in 1625 the meeting was said to have been held at Robin Hood's Well.[80] Nothing in the records directly connects the dinner with Robin Hood, but it was held in Sherwood Forest and at a well that had long been associated with him. Appropriately, many venison feasts were held there, according to the anonymous eye-witness writing in 1641. He also recorded that James I had once visited the well after hunting in the forest, when he and his companions 'drank the woodward and his barrels dry'.[81] In August 1634

S. Mastoris and S. Groves, Thoroton Society Record Series XL (Nottingham, 1997), no. 584, and Plate 1; TNA, MR 1/1142.

76 C. Deering, *Nottingham Vetus et Nova or an Historical Account of the Ancient and Present State of the Town of Nottingham* (Nottingham, 1751), p. 73.
77 RBN IV, pp. 117, 133, 163, 173, 256, 291, 356–59, 373, 381, 383, 386, 441. See also Deering, *Nottingham Vetus et Nova*, p. 125.
78 RBN V, ed. W. T. Baker (London and Nottingham, 1900), p. 123.
79 RBN V, p. 172.
80 RBN V, p. 102.
81 Deering, *Nottingham Vetus et Nova*, p. 74.

Charles I and Queen Henrietta Maria spent five nights in Nottingham and may have visited the well, because a sum was spent on tiling it 'against the king's coming'.[82] Whether any of the royal visitors was told of its supposed association with the outlaw is not known. It remained very popular, and the anonymous writer of 1641 noted that

> this well is all summer long much frequented, and there are but few fair days between March and October, in which some company or other of the town, such as used to consort there, use not to fetch a walk to this well ... and when any of the town have their friends come to them, they have given them no welcome, unless they entertain them at this well.[83]

The annual visit by the civic dignitaries does not seem to have survived the upheavals caused in Nottingham by the civil war, which was declared there in 1642. In 1645 it appeared that Sir John Byron, a leading royalist, had promised that if the king won the war, John Heywood would be given a lease of the well. However, following the victory of Parliament, in 1647 it was ordered that the well was not to be disposed of by the mayor alone, as it had been earlier, but only with the consent of the aldermen and council, and the house at the well was leased by the corporation throughout the period from the late seventeenth century to the nineteenth.[84] It was a popular general place of resort, at a walkable distance from the town. Before the end of the century we know for certain that it was a centre of Robin Hood tourism. In 1694, James Brome, a clergyman from Kent, published an account of a visit he made to Nottingham:

> Having pleasured ourselves with the antiquities of this town, we took horse and went to visit the well and ancient chair of Robin Hood, which is about a mile within the forest of Shirwood. Being placed in that chair, we had a cap, which, they say, was his, very formally put upon our heads, and having performed the usual ceremonies befitting so great a solemnity, we received the freedom of the chair, and were incorporated into the society of that renowned brotherhood, but that we may not receive such privileges without an honourable mention of the persons that left them to posterity; know we must that the patent was bequeathed to the inferior rangers of this forest, by Robin Hood and Little John, honourable personages indeed, being the chief lords of some most renowned robbers in the reign of King Richard I (...).[85]

---

[82] *RBN* V, p. 165. Similar precautions in respect of fencing had been ordered on 21 July 1624, during the reign of James I: *RBN* IV, pp. 385–86.
[83] Deering, *Nottingham Vetus et Nova*, p. 73.
[84] *RBN* V, pp. 240, 252.
[85] J. Brome, *Travels over England, Scotland and Wales* (London, 1694), pp. 90–91.

By 1702 there was a bowling green at the well, and by 1736 an orchard and two closes adjoining it.[86] There was also an alehouse, and in 1751 Charles Deering, a historian of Nottingham, described how the meaner inhabitants of the town now made use of the well and its neighbouring alehouse:

> The people who keep the green and public house to promote a holy-day trade, shew an old wickered chair, which they call Robin Hood's Chair, a bow, and an old cap, both these they affirm to have been this famous robber's property; this little artifice takes so well with the people in low-life, that at Christmas, Easter and Whitsuntide, it procures them a great deal of business, for at those times great numbers of young men bring their sweethearts to this well, and give them a treat, and the girls think themselves ill-used, if they have not been saluted by their lovers in Robin Hood's Chair.[87]

By the early eighteenth century, and probably earlier, the Chair was a piece of private property, passed on from one generation to the next. In 1713 Richard Jackson of St Anne's Well in his will left his worldly possessions to his wife Mary. The inventory list of these possessions included Robin Hood's Chair, and reference was also made to a summer house and bowling alley.[88] An added attraction was the presence on a nearby hill, an eighth of a mile east of the well, of a maze, cut out of turf, with the alternative names of 'Robin Hood's Race' (incidentally the name of a ballad first known to have been printed in 1663) or 'Shepherd's Race', which was used by people for exercising.[89] In 1795 the Mickletorn jury held its dinner as usual at the well, but by then the whole amenity was in decline.[90] The maze was ploughed up when Sneinton was enclosed in 1797. In his revised edition of Dr Robert Thoroton's *History and Antiquities of Nottingham* (1797), John Throsby gave a description of it as it then was. It was about 17 or 18 yards square, and at the angles were four oval projections facing the four cardinal points, the distance between the extremities of which were 34 yards or thereabouts.[91] Because it was ploughed up in the same year as the book was published, the maze he illustrated was actually another at nearby

---

Brome's reference was cited by Joseph Ritson in 1795, along with two much more recent ones of 1760 and 1785: Ritson, *Robin Hood*, pp. lxviii–ix.

86 *RBN* VI, ed. E. L. Guilford (Nottingham, 1914), pp. 8, 151.
87 Deering, *Nottingham Vetus et Nova*, p. 73.
88 Nottinghamshire Archives, PR/NW/6/15207. Jackson may be the man of that name who was one of the church wardens of St Nicholas's church in Nottingham in 1705: *RBN* VI, p. 32.
89 Deering, *Nottingham Vetus et Nova*, p. 75.
90 *RBN* VII, ed. E. L. Guilford (Nottingham, 1947), p. 312.
91 J. Throsby, *Thoroton's History of Nottinghamshire, Republished with Large Additions* (London, 1797), II, p. 171–72.

Clifton. Throsby also gave an account of the well and its surroundings, and the supposed relics of Robin Hood that were shown to visitors:

> Near Nottingham was, it is said, a sequestered haunt of Robin Hood, which tradition has given celebrity to for ages. It is situate within two miles North East of Nottingham, on the base of a hill, which a century ago, or less, was covered with fine ash trees and coppice, well as a great part of the adjacent fields, which are now cleared of wood, and is become good land; some portion of which still retains the name of coppice and belongs to the Burgesses of Nottingham. The house which is resorted to in the summer time, stands near the Well, both which are shaded by firs and other trees. Here is a large bowling-green, and a little neglected pleasure ground.
>
> The well is under an arched stone roof, of rude workmanship, the water is very cold, it will kill a toad. It is used by those who are afflicted with rheumatic pains; and indeed, like many other springs, for a variety of disorders. At the house were formerly shewn several things said to have belonged to Robin Hood; but they are frittered down to what are now called his cap, or helmet, and a part of his chair. As these things have passed current for many years, and perhaps ages, as things once belonging to that renowned robber, I sketched them.[92]

In 1802 the corporation was considering laying pipes to convey water from the well into the town, but social activities there continued, often in a disorderly fashion. In 1824 it was reported to the common council that 'great disorder, riot, drunkenness and fighting very frequently, as well on Sundays as on other days, take place at the Public House belonging to this Corporation called Saint Ann's Well Public House', and its licence was subsequently discontinued by the magistrates.[93] In 1838 a new coffee room was ordered to be built close to the northern bank of the garden, using the materials of the previous coffee room.[94]

Meanwhile, in 1804, a novel entitled *Sherwood Forest; or Northern Adventures*, was published in London by Mrs. Elizabeth Sarah Villa-Real Gooch, a self-styled 'Sherwood Forester', and an early romantic novelist, who was born at Edwinstowe in the forest. She began her story with the observation that

> upon a certain spot in the forest there now stands, in a deep dell, and by the side of a small rivulet, a house so ancient, that the foresters and neighbouring villagers are persuaded that it was heretofore one of the hiding places of Robin Hood himself. It is constructed principally

---

[92] Throsby, II, pp. 170–71
[93] *RBN* VIII, ed. D. Gray and V. W. Walker (Nottingham, 1952), pp. 22, 319–20.
[94] *RBN* IX, ed. D. Gray and V. W. Walker (Nottingham, 1956), p. 10.

of wood, long since black with age, and is of that antique form to give colour to the supposition; and the proprietor fails not to exhibit some warlike paraphernalia, as testimonies of his mansion being heretofore a residence of the renowned outlaw, who gave to Sherwood Forest much of its celebrity.

This proves however to have been a reference to St Anne's Well, as more explicitly does a comment by a character near the end of the story: 'Robin Hood has been dead for some years, but this is not his house. It stands on the other side of the forest, and is now called St. Anne's Well'.[95]

During the second half of the nineteenth century, the well was at first celebrated and then obliterated, as rapid population growth in Nottingham created a demand for suburban houses in the villages closest to the town. In 1855 the corporation ordered the old dwelling house, except the cottage at the back, to be pulled down, the cottage to be let to the tenant of the adjoining Coppice Farm.[96] A picture drawn in 1856 by Thomas Cooper Moore shows the well in a garden immediately to the rear of the cottage and not far from other buildings, and in 1857 expenditure of up to £100 was authorised for enclosing and covering in the well.[97] An early photograph of the cover, taken about 1860 and showing it to have been built of stone and surmounted by a pyramidal canopy, has survived in the Paul Nix collection of photographs of Nottingham. The building remained only until the well was filled up and its site covered by a railway embankment during the reconstruction of the Nottingham Suburban Railway in August 1887.[98] The station opened in 1889 and remained in use until 1954. The well was buried underneath the site of 'The Gardeners' public house, which later became derelict. The site, at the junction of Wells Road and Kildare Road, was in 2011 designated for new housing.

Nottinghamshire

Sherwood Forest

The earliest known mention of Sherwood, spelt *Scherewod*, as Robin's haunt comes in a scribbled poem, in both English and Latin versions, written about 1425 in a manuscript, produced somewhere in the east

---

[95] E. S. V. Gooch, *Sherwood Forest; or Northern Adventures*, 3 vols. (London, 1804), I, pp. 2–16; III, pp. 166–67.
[96] *RBN* IX, ed. D. Gray and V. W. Walker (Nottingham, 1956), p. 110.
[97] *RBN* IX, p. 124.
[98] *RBN* IV, p. 541.

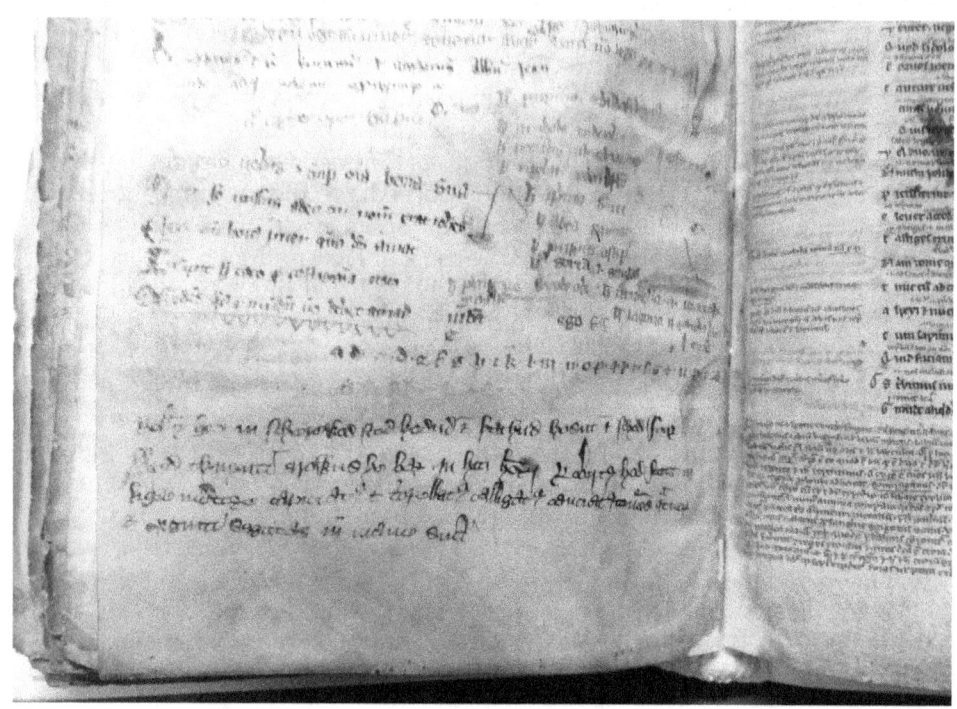

FIGURE 6. A short poem doodled in a 'pen trial' in an early fifteenth-century hand, one of the items on an unused page of a thirteenth-century liturgical manuscript now in the library of Lincoln Cathedral. It is the earliest known reference connecting Robin Hood with the Nottinghamshire forest of Sherwood. It reads, with inserted punctuation, 'Robyn hod in Scherewood stod, hodud & hathud, hosut & schod, Ffour and twynti arrowus he bar, in hit hondus'. The attempted Latin translation of the poem that follows in the same hand does not however mention Sherwood by name.

midlands and now in Lincoln Cathedral Library (Figure 6).[99] It is at the bottom of a verso page, previously blank and not containing any of the text of the volume, which was evidently used for writing practice by several scribes at a later date. The poem was first identified by G. E. Morris and published in the *Modern Language Review* in 1948.[100] It is difficult to judge the significance of the poem, other than that it shows that Robin Hood and his legend were, by the date it was written, linked in the popular imagination with Sherwood Forest.

There are no references to specific places within the forest in the surviving tales, and no early Robin Hood place-names have been found there. In the tale of *Robin Hood and the Monk*, Little John is said to know every path in Sherwood, but no topographical detail at all is given concerning Sherwood in that story or any of the others. As Holt commented, 'Sherwood differs from the idealised greenwood only in its name'.[101] During the nineteenth century the two ancient hays of Birkland and Bilhaugh, close to the village of Edwinstowe, came in themselves to be popularly regarded as Sherwood Forest. As a result of the influence of Romantic novelists like Sir Walter Scott and Thomas Love Peacock on the inhabitants of the locality, Edwinstowe itself became specifically associated with the legend between about 1820 and 1840. Its ancient parish church came to be identified as the place where Robin Hood and Marian married, and two large and hollow oak trees, called the Major Oak and Robin Hood's Larder, became associated in popular imagination with the outlaw legend.[102] These traditions have survived to the present, and the village, along with Nottingham itself, has become a recognised centre for Robin Hood tourism and commerce.

Robin Hood Cross, Pleasley

The earliest Robin Hood place-name so far discovered in Nottinghamshire relates to a point which is both on the border of Nottinghamshire and Derbyshire and also at the north-western boundary of Sherwood Forest, at Pleasley mill on the River Meden. It is however of quite a late date, recorded in a forest perambulation of 22-24 September 1589. The relevant passage in the description of the boundary reads

---

[99] Lincoln Cathedral MS 132, f. 100v. For a description of the volume as a whole, see R. M. Thomson, *Catalogue of the Manuscripts of Lincoln Cathedral Library* (Woodbridge, 1989), p. 102.

[100] G. E. Morris, 'A Ryme of Robyn Hode', *Modern Language Review* 43 (1948), pp. 507–08.

[101] Holt, *Robin Hood*, p. 88.

[102] D. Crook, 'The Novelist, the Heiress, the Artisan and the Banker: The Emergence of the Robin Hood Legend at Edwinstowe, c.1819 to 1849', *TTS* 119 (2015), pp. 1–13.

unto Plesley mylne, where stoode a crosse named Robyn Hoode Crosse, the streame goinge through the mylne damme by it ould course, and beneath the Milne damme the streame is put from it ould course to the north and descendeth still by the same water of Meden.[103]

The reference is retrospective, so we are told that the cross had existed some time earlier, but there is no knowing how long before 1589 that was thought to be. The previous perambulation, taken in 1538, and the last to be recorded in Latin, is generally less detailed than that of 1589, so it is possible that the cross may have existed and borne that name at that earlier date and beyond.[104] The final Sherwood Forest perambulation, taken in 1663, again in English and very detailed, mentions the cross in the same words.[105] None of the other Robin Hood names in the county, as distinct from the borough of Nottingham, are anywhere near as old as this cross. Robin Hood's Hills, near Mansfield, mentioned on a map of 1775, is the only one known before 1800.[106]

Lancashire

Lancashire places in the surviving tales appear only in the *Gest*, beginning with the story of the knight waylaid at the Sayles in Barnsdale by Robin's men. He is in financial difficulty because he had to sell his goods and mortgage his lands to the abbot of St Mary's York in return for a loan of £400, to buy pardon for his twenty-year-old son and heir, who 'slewe a knight of Lancaster and a squyer bold' in a joust (fytte one, stanzas 52-55). Much later, the king comes to Nottingham with his knights and, after asking local men about them, tries to capture both Robin and 'that gentyll knyght that was so bolde and stout'. He seizes all the knight's lands, and then moves through Lancashire ('alle the passe of Lancasshyre he went both ferre and nere'), until he came to Plumpton Park, where he found that many of his deer were missing. Where there were usually many herds, he could scarcely find one deer 'that bare ony good horne' (fytte seven, stanzas 354 to 357).

Plumpton Park

Despite the impression given by the progression of the text of the *Gest* that the park was in Lancashire, some have argued that it was not. Ritson stated that it was in Cumberland, but in 1852 Hunter wrote that

---

[103] TNA, E 101/534/1, f. 90r.
[104] TNA, E 36/77, f. 3r.
[105] *Fourteenth Report of the Commissioners of the Woods, Forests and Land Revenues of the Crown, 28 March 1793*, Appendix, no. 3, pp. 23–25; A. Stapleton, *The Last Perambulation of Sherwood Forest (A.D. 1662)*, (Newark, 1893), p. 7.
[106] D&T, pp. 301–03.

it was part of the Yorkshire forest of Knaresborough. In his first London edition of the *Gest* in 1861 Child noted that it was 'not in Cumberland, as Ritson states, but, says Hunter, a part of the forest of Knaresborough'.[107] In his later edition of 1889 he noted that the 1772 edition of Camden's *Britannia* had placed it 'on the bank of the Peterrel, in Cumberland, east of Inglewood', [that is, the river Petteril, a tributary of the Eden], but that Hunter, 'citing no authority', had said that it was part of the forest of Knaresborough in Yorkshire.[108] Much later, Dobson and Taylor proposed, following Hunter, that although it was usually located in Cumberland it could possibly be a reference to Plumpton Park near Knaresborough.[109] The park even found its way into the post-medieval tale of *The Noble Fisherman*, first entered in the Stationers' Registers in 1631, which its author set in Yorkshire at Scarborough, not far from Robin Hood's Bay, without suggesting any location for the park.[110]

If the Plumpton Park of the *Gest* is in Cumberland, it must be the hay of Plumpton in Inglewood Forest, in the parish of Plumpton Wall, north of Penrith, which by the sixteenth century was sometimes referred to as Plumpton Park.[111] If in Yorkshire, it must be Plompton in the parish of Spofforth, within Knaresborough Forest two miles south of Knaresborough; but Plompton is not referred to as a park in any of the references to the place garnered by the English Place-Name Society.[112] In Lancashire there are two Plumptons, Great Plumpton (formerly also known as Fieldplumpton) and Woodplumpton. Great Plumpton was not noted for its woodland, and it seems most likely that the Plumpton in question was Woodplumpton, a forest vill in Amounderness, which fits more easily into the narrative of the *Gest*.[113] Also, as Holt pointed out, it is adjacent to the king's demesne wood of Myerscough.[114] Nowhere in the sources was Woodplumpton described as a park. Myerscough, however, was many times called a park and many times a forest, and occasionally both, at various dates between 1323 and the Restoration.[115]

---

[107] Hunter, 'The Great Hero', p. 30; Child (1861), p. 106 note.
[108] Child (1889), pp. 54–55.
[109] D&T, pp. 78, 105 notes.
[110] D&T, p. 181, verses 12–14.
[111] *The Place-Names of Cumberland*, ed. A. M. Armstrong, A. Mawer, F. M. Stenton and B. Dickins, I , EPNS XXI (Cambridge, 1950), p. 234.
[112] *The Place-Names of the West Riding of Yorkshire*, ed. A. H. Smith, V, EPNS XXXIV (Cambridge, 1961), pp. 30, 77.
[113] R. Cunliffe Shaw, *The Royal Forest of Lancaster* (Preston, 1956), pp. 14, 90, 266, 322.
[114] Cunliffe Shaw, map between pp. 6–7; Holt, *Robin Hood*, p. 101.
[115] Cunliffe Shaw, *passim*. For a damaged seventeenth-century copy of a perambulation of its boundaries, made by a steward and forest officials sometime between 1338 and 1350, see p. 171. Several records in the archives of the Duchy of Lancaster, dated between 1614 and 1830, describe it as a park, this

It may well be, as Holt hinted, that the originator of this passage of the *Gest* had the general locality of Woodplumpton and Myerscough park/forest in mind. Myerscough was noted for the illegal hunting of wild deer, including before the Lancashire forest eyre of 1287 and during the disorder following the uprising of Thomas earl of Lancaster in 1322-3, although most of the damage on that occasion took place further south.[116]

Wyresdale

In fytte two of the *Gest*, stanza 126, it is revealed that the knight who Robin had befriended and rescued from financial exploitation by the abbot of St Mary's, lived in Lancashire. On his return from York, 'His lady met hym at the gate, at home in Verysdale'.[117] Following the original suggestion by Joseph Ritson, it is now generally agreed that this passage refers to Wyresdale, the valley of the river Wyre, in northern Lancashire beyond the Ribble, west of the forest of Bowland.[118] Holt made the most significant attempt to link the knight, identified, 'admittedly very artificially', as Sir Richard at the Lee, with real places in the landscape:

> In Wyresdale, where the road from Bowland to Lancaster crosses the Wyre, there stands the hamlet of Lee. Quite apart from that, Wyresdale was part of the forest of Lancashire and a family of Legh or La Legh, was involved in the administration of the forest, including Wyresdale.

They were sometimes themselves offenders against forest law, although none of them was a Richard.[119] A Nicholas of Lee, who was a forest offender arraigned in the Lancashire forest eyre of 1287, seems to have been just below knightly level, and one of his forest offences had taken place as far back as 1275. He had to be ransomed and released from prison.[120] A knight called Henry of Lee witnessed a document recording

---

being its normal appellation from the seventeenth century onwards: TNA, DL 42/202, 204, 206, 210; DL 49/42; E 317/Lancs/17.

[116] Cunliffe Shaw, pp. 113, 128–29, 143, 175.

[117] D&T, p. 88 and note.

[118] See, however, the speculative discussion of the form of the name and the possible other locations of the place in Nottinghamshire in J. Bellamy, *Robin Hood: An Historical Enquiry* (London, 1985), pp. 76–80. These suggestions have not so far attracted general support.

[119] Holt, *Robin Hood*, p. 100 and Plate 15. For a sketch map of Wyresdale Forest see Cunliffe Shaw, facing p. 145. Higher and Lower Lea stand virtually in its centre. An Elizabethan map of the forest in TNA, formerly DL 31/27 but now MPC 1/27, is illustrated in Cunliffe Shaw, facing p. 17, where it is said to be of seventeenth century date. For the Leghs' other involvements in forest matters, going as far back as the Lancashire forest perambulation of 1225, see Cunliffe Shaw, pp. 106, 247, 358–60, 384.

[120] Cunliffe Shaw, pp. 111, 114, 117–18, 155.

the relinquishment of the master forestership of Lancashire in 1280, and it was he who was bailiff of the forest of West Derbyshire in 1257 and sheriff of Lancashire between 1285 and 1291. He was the same Sir Henry who was lord of Charnock Richard.[121] A later Sir Henry of Lee of Charnock was a supporter of Sir Adam de Banastre in the Lancashire unrest of the reign of Edward II, and was executed with him in 1315.[122] However, the landed interests and activities of these men were in any case centred on an area of the county well south of Lee and Wyresdale, and no evidence has been found to show that Sir Richard at the Lee was a real person. In the tale of *Guy of Gisborne* the villain whom Robin fights and kills is named after the village of Gisburn, only ten miles from Wyresdale, which was in Yorkshire throughout its history before being placed in Lancashire in 1974. Gisburn, sometimes confused with Guisborough on the northern edge of the Yorkshire moors, seems to have no real significance in the topography of the legend.

Despite the great importance of tenurial links with Yorkshire, significant on the Lacy estates and emphasised by Holt,[123] Lancashire was never more than a minor outlier to Yorkshire and Nottingham in respect of the Robin Hood legend. The later predominance of Nottingham and its well over Yorkshire and its well in Barnsdale in the developing legend of Robin Hood was inevitable, given its position as an important county town and commercial centre, whose corporation owned property at the site of its well, a nearby place of popular resort, and was well established by the end of the seventeenth century. By comparison, Barnsdale Bar, despite the nearby well and its documented significance as an approach point to York, which lay over 30 miles to the north, was merely a wayside halt with amenities, a useful place at which to take refreshment while passing between market towns on the north road and nearby. It was only in the later twentieth century that a keen rivalry between the two areas claiming proprietary rights to the legend, came to its current prominence, typified by the choice of the title 'Robin Hood Airport' for the new airport close to Doncaster, on land in Finningley parish which was in Nottinghamshire until 1974. That rivalry looks set to continue.

---

[121] Cunliffe Shaw, pp. 16, 33, 39–40, 155, and see also 122–24; *List of Sheriffs for England and Wales*, PRO Lists and Indexes IX (London, 1898), p. 72. A Richard son of Roger de Lee, also of West Derbyshire, amerced in 1292, was clearly of much lower status: *Crown Pleas of the Lancashire Eyre 1292* II, ed. M. E. Lynch, Record Society of Lancashire and Cheshire CXLIX (2015), nos. 753, 1137.

[122] *South Lancashire in the Reign of Edward II*, ed. G. H. Tupling, Cheetham Society, 3rd Series I (Manchester, 1950), pp. xliii–xlvii, 12, 38, 42, 44–46, 49.

[123] Holt, *Robin Hood*, pp. 103–04.

Robin Hood: Legend and Reality

APPENDIX:
The First Robin Hood Place-Name, Robin Hood's Bay, Yorkshire

TNA, SC 1/33, no. 202

Trespoissans et treschers sires a nous ont esté Jehan Cullin bourgois de nuefport en Flandres et ses compaignons (et pescheurs *interlined*) complaignant et mostrant qe en/ cest aoust darrainement passé il se misent en mer a tout leur harnas pour gaaignier leur pain si avoient pris per l'aide de Dieu xiiij/ lastz de herens, puis vinirent gentz vostre terre S[aint] Emont et autres d'Engleterre a tout vj neifs et prisent la neif de nos bourgois dessus dis/ a tout lauoir qi dedens estoit et mener tout gentz et tout a robin oeds bay ou les gens dou paiis prisent nos bourgois dessus dis et les/ menerent a Witteby leur en plaida sur eux de leur vies, de quoy il furent iugiés quites sans calange par (bonnes *deleted*) cognissance par autres de/ bonnes gens, et ne leur fut leur neif ne biens point delivrez (ne renduz *interlined*) si comme plus a plain il declarront les choses dessus dictes. Pour qe/ trescher sires nous vous prions tant amiablement et de ceur qe nous plus poons qe a nos dessis dis burgois il uous plaise faire/ rendre et restituer leur neif et biens dessus dis ensi qe faire on le doit par droit et par raison quar vraiement che sont povrez gentz et/ qui il venendra mendyer se la dicte restitucion de leur neifs et biens ne leur est faite hastivement et par vous en ce en aide de droit/ souscouru. Treschers sires si vous en plaise tant faire en consideration de droit et a nostre pryere qe nous en soions tenuz a vous de/ faire le samblable et a votre requeste le quel nous feriemes volentiers et de ceur et assez plus grant se il avenoit. Nostre seigneur vous voelle/ garder corps et arme et vous donist bonne vie et longue. Escript a Male en Flandres le premier jour de March.

Le conte de Flandres et Nevers et de Rethel.

[*Endorsed*] A tres excellent et tres puissant p[rince] Monser Edward par la grace de dieu Roy d'Angletere et Seignur d'Irelond.

Most powerful and well beloved lords, Jehan Cullin burgess of Nieuwpoort in Flanders and his companions (and fishermen *interlined*) have come to us complaining and showing that in/ August last past they put to sea with all their equipment to earn their bread, then they caught by the aid of God 14/ lasts of herring, and then came men of your land from [Bury] St Edmunds and others from England, six ships in all, and captured the ship of our burgesses aforesaid mentioned/ and took possession of all that was inside and took all the men and everything to Robin Hood's Bay, where the men of the country arrested our burgesses mentioned above and /led them to Whitby, there to plead concerning these matters for their lives, of which they were judged quit without challenge by the acknowledgement of other /good men, and neither their ship nor their goods were delivered or returned to them even though they fully stated the matters above mentioned. Therefore/ most well beloved lords we pray you kindly and from the heart as we may that it please you to/ have returned and restored to our abovementioned burgesses their ship and goods aforesaid mentioned as well as to do according to the law, lawfully and reasonably, for they are truly poor men, and/ it will behove them to beg if the said restitution of their ships and goods be not made to them quickly, and help given by you in this matter to the assistance of the law. / Most dear lords be pleased to do in consideration of right and our prayer as much as we are bound to/ do likewise to you and to your request which we would do willingly and fervently and much more if the need arose. May our Lord willingly /protect you in body and soul and give you a good and long life. Written at Male in Flanders on the first day of March.

The count of Flanders and Nevers and of Rethel.

[*Endorsed*] To the most excellent and most powerful p[rince] sire Edward by the grace of God King of England and Lord of Ireland.[124]

---

[124] I am deeply indebted to Michael Jones for help in the transcription and dating of this document, and to Stephen O'Connor for assistance with the translation.

Part II

OUTLAW AND EVILDOER OF OUR LAND: THE ORIGINAL ROBIN HOOD

Chapter 6

The Robin Hood Names

Since the mid nineteenth century it has often been said that the occurrence of the surname of the legendary outlaw, and even of his Christian name and surname together, is not uncommon in historical sources, and examples were sometimes pointed out. Six were cited by Joseph Hunter in 1852 in his paper seeking to identify the original Robin Hood, and in 1861 his critic Francis Child also remarked on the frequency with which the surname 'Hood' and its variants occurred in medieval English documents already in print by that time; he cited three additional examples.[1] Until now, however, no-one has made a more systematic search for, and study of, such names in significant numbers, in spite of, or perhaps even because of, the richness of the available sources. These include the early records of the English state and courts of law, as well as local sources, especially deeds, from the end of the twelfth century onwards. The great increase in the number of documents published and indexed since the time of Hunter and Child has provided easier access to many more examples, in a variety of temporal and geographical contexts. A significant proportion of them are preceded by the Christian name 'Robert', whose diminutive form 'Robin' seems rarely if ever to have been used in documents written in Latin, although it could occasionally appear in ones using Anglo-Norman French.

The surname 'Hood', usually in the form Hod but sometimes Hodd, Hodde, Hoode, Houd, Hudde or Hude, was common in thirteenth and fourteenth century England, and occasionally also occurs in Scotland.[2] It

---

[1] Hunter, *Robin Hood*, pp. 10, 47–48; Child (1861), pp. xxi–xxii.
[2] In the following discussion, Hoods in general or in plural are described in that spelling, but in individual references the original spelling in the particular source cited is given. 'Hudde' is also occasionally used as a Christian name. In 1223 there is a reference to a 'Hudde' of Knaresborough: *RLC* I, p. 223b. Also, there were two of them in a gang of thieves indicted at Snaith in Yorkshire not long before 1231, mentioned in TNA, JUST 1/1043, rot.13d [AALT-IMG 1394].

can be explained as deriving originally from someone who made hoods (although the name Hoder or Hodere is a much less common alternative form), or, more frequently, who was noted for or characterised by the wearing of a hood.³ Occasionally, a name in the form 'de Hod' indicates an origin from a place called Hood, there being such locations in Devon and Yorkshire. It is possible that the Robert de Hod found in Richmond in Yorkshire in 1301 was one such individual, from the place of that name, now Hood Grange, in the parish of Kilburn, while the Devon place is in the parish of Rattery.⁴ Men called Robert Hod or one of the variants, with no implied connection with the legend, are not uncommon in early governmental and legal records even after the legend itself had already been widely disseminated, as it seems to have been by the 1260s.⁵ For example, in the earliest surviving coroners' rolls for Bedfordshire, a Robert Hude of Goldington, who in 1268 acted as a pledge, appears routinely among several other Hoods with different Christian names who were involved in other inquests dated between 1269 and 1276, and who do not appear to have been related since they lived some distance apart.⁶ The earliest Robert Hod so far identified was a Norfolk villein (*nativus*) who in 1206 was the subject of an agreement made before royal justices of assize in Lincolnshire, whereby Robert de Ver quitclaimed him and his family (*sectam*) to Alan son of Geoffrey for a payment of five marks.⁷

The best lists of names of relatively ordinary people in significant numbers for the late thirteenth and early fourteenth centuries are the surviving assessments for the lay subsidies levied by Edward I and Edward III to finance their wars against Scotland and France.

    For a Scottish 'Robert Hod', who received a pension and robe from Alexander III about 1264, see *The Exchequer Rolls of Scotland* I, ed. J. Stuart and J. Burnett (Edinburgh, 1878), p. 12.

3   P. H. Reaney, *A Dictionary of British Surnames* (London, 1958), p. 166; P. Hanks and F. Hodges, *A Dictionary of Surnames* (Oxford, 1988), p. 262. For interesting comments on the name Robert and its ramifications, by one whose own surname was the result of one of those ramifications, see also R. B. Dobson, 'Robin Hood: The Genesis of a Popular Hero', in Hahn, *Popular Culture*, pp. 71–72.

4   *The Place-Names of the North Riding of Yorkshire*, ed. A. H. Smith, EPNS IV (Cambridge, 1928), p. 195; *The Yorkshire Subsidy of 30 Edward I*, ed. W. Brown, YAS RS XXI (1897), p. 17; *The Place-Names of Devon* I, ed. J. E. B. Gover, A. Mawer and F. M. Stenton, EPNS VIII (Cambridge, 1931), p. 297.

5   D. Crook, 'Some Further Evidence Concerning the Dating of the Origins of the Legend of Robin Hood', *EHR* XCIX (1984), pp. 530–34; reprinted in Knight, *Anthology*, pp. 257–61.

6   *Bedfordshire Coroners' Rolls*, ed. R. F. Hunnisett, Bedfordshire Historical Record Society XLI (1960), nos. 28, 72, 114, 178, 243. See Map 2.

7   TNA, KB 26/480, rot. 1d [AALT-IMG 1323–5]; *The Earliest Lincolnshire Assize Rolls, A.D. 1202–1209*, ed. D. M. Stenton, Lincoln Record Society XXII, no. 1343.

MAP 2. The distribution of Hood surnames recorded in early Bedfordshire Coroners' Rolls, 1268–76, and the earliest Robin Hood surname, 1295.

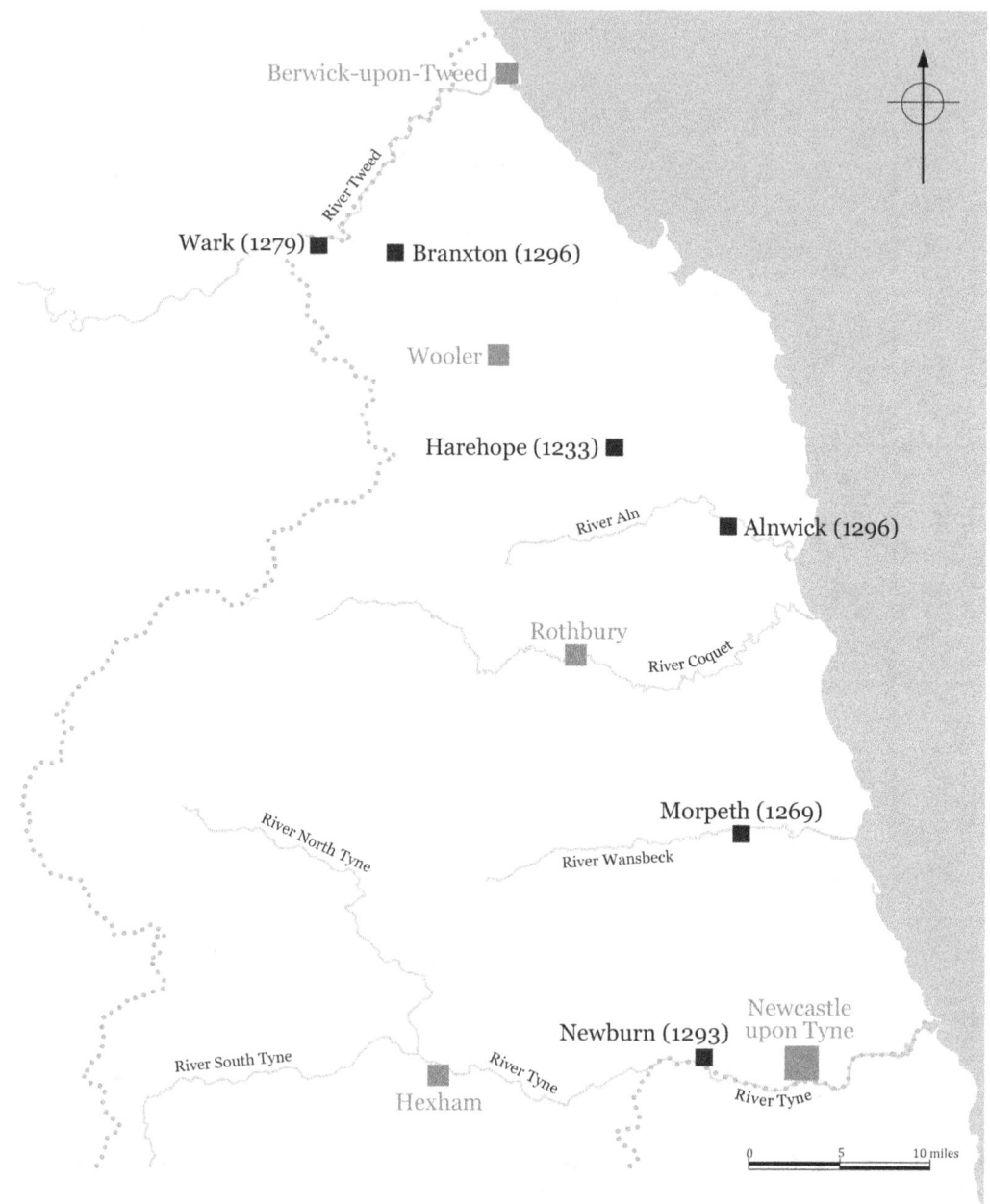

Map 3. The distribution of Hood surnames in Northumberland recorded in Legal and Tax Records, 1233–96.

These are now held at The National Archives in the E 179 series, and most of them have been printed by local record societies. The largest number of returns are for the taxes levied in 1327 and 1332, but there is also a handful from a few counties for 1296; these provide a significant cache of material, albeit from a limited geographical area, from before 1300. Between 1292 and 1332 many Hoods, from the south and centre as well as the north of England, appear in the records that have survived. A Robert Hod paid a subsidy in London in 1292.[8] In Sussex in 1296 there were four Hodes, Robert, Ralph, William and Simon, probably closely related, in the village of Petworth, and in 1327 there were John, Richard, Reginald and Agnes Hodes there, presumably their descendants. An isolated John Hod was living in Birchden in 1327 and 1332.[9] In 1327 three Hods, Henry, William and John, and also Robert Hude and John Houd, living in different places, paid the subsidy in Dorset, while Henry Hod of Wareham was one of the sub-taxers in that town. In 1332 in the same county, two John Hods appear, and Henry is found again, while there were also William, Matilda, John and Adam Houds.[10] In 1296 in Hertfordshire there were Thomas Hod in Sawbridgeworth, Walter Hudde in St Albans and John Hudd in Radwell, while one of the villeins of the abbot of St Albans in Cashio hundred was William Hudde.[11] In Essex, the 1327 subsidy was paid by Robert Hods in Ramsey and Southminster, and there were other Hods elsewhere.[12] In the midlands, at least three different Hoods paid taxes in Warwickshire in 1327 or 1332, while in Rutland in 1296 we find Hugh Hudde in Essendine, Walter and Nicholas Hod in Whissendine, and Simon and Henry Hudde in Clipsham.[13] In Northumberland, three Robert Hodes paid tax at Newburn, Alnwick and Branxton in 1296.[14] Two Yorkshire Hodes, William and Simon, did so in 1297 at Langton and Beverley in the East Riding, and in 1301 Robert Hode and Robert Hod occur in Ebberston and Aiskew in the North Riding.[15]

[8] *Two Early London Subsidy Rolls*, ed. E. Ekwall (Lund, 1951), p. 185.
[9] *Sussex Subsidies, 1296, 1327, 1332*, ed. W. Hudson, Sussex Record Society X (1910), pp. 75, 140, 187, 300.
[10] *The Dorset Lay Subsidy Roll of 1327*, ed. A. R. Rumble, Dorset Record Society VI (1980), pp. 14, 52, 70, 73, 76, 141; *The Dorset Lay Subsidy Roll of 1332*, ed. A. D. Mills, Dorset Record Society IV (1971), pp. 22, 36, 60, 65, 92, 103(2).
[11] TNA, E 179/120/3, mm. 10, 42, 43; E 179/120/5, m. 18d.
[12] *The Medieval Essex Community: The Lay Subsidy of 1327*, ed. J. C. Ward, Essex Record Office Publication 98 (1983), pp. 16, 35, 36, 90, 106, 109.
[13] I. Hjertstedt, *Middle English Nicknames in the Lay Subsidy Rolls for Warwickshire* (Uppsala, 1987), pp. 126–27; TNA, E 179/165/1, mm. 1, 6, 7.
[14] *The Northumberland Lay Subsidy Roll of 1296*, ed. C. M. Fraser (Society of Antiquaries of Newcastle upon Tyne, 1968), pp. 64, 96, 121. See Map 3.
[15] *Yorkshire Subsidy of 25 Edward I*, ed. W. Brown, YAS RS XVI (1894), pp. 148, 151; *Yorkshire Subsidy of 30 Edward I*, ed. W. Brown, YAS RS XXI (1897), pp. 63, 95.

Other Yorkshire examples come from the early court rolls of the large manor of Wakefield in the West Riding. Those from the years between 1274 and 1317 contain many references to Hoods, several of them called Robert.[16] Others appear incidentally in the records of cases in the royal courts, one of them sometimes suggested as a candidate for the original outlaw of the legend. In 1221 the jury of the town of Cirencester in the Gloucestershire eyre reported that a Robert Hod, who was in the mainpast of the abbot of Cirencester, had killed Ralph of Cirencester in the abbot's garden, the deed being witnessed by two other men in the abbot's household, Robert de Fermeria and Geoffrey Guf, who had also fled. Because the killer was in his household, the abbot at the time was accountable, and had made a fine of £100 with King John.[17] There are also numerous less striking examples in legal records, mostly but not always in those of civil rather than crown pleas. In 1225 in the Common Bench at Westminster, Robert Hod was the last-named of a number of men accused of throwing down the abbot of Ledbury's bercary at Shenley in Buckinghamshire and taking his wood.[18] In Northumberland, Robert Hod was a defendant in an assize of nuisance brought in 1233 against the prior of Tynemouth over the diversion of a stream in Harehope.[19] In the eyre of 1256 in the same county a fugitive who was present at a homicide caused by an arrow, and then absconded, was named Robert Hode. In the eyre of 1269 Robert Hode was mentioned in a civil case concerning land in Morpeth, involving the husband of his daughter Ascelina, and another of the same name was a juror for the vill of Wark in the eyre of 1279.[20] In

---

[16] *Court Rolls of the Manor of Wakefield* I, ed. W. P. Baildon, YAS RS XXIX (1901), pp. 86, 90, 92, 96, 104–05, 107, 142, 151, 166, 176, 194–95, 201, 204, 227, 238, 244, 246, 250, 266, 272–73, 276, 284–85, 289–91, 295, 298; II, ed. W. P. Baildon, YAS RS XXXVI (1906), pp. 8, 11–12, 20, 24, 27, 32, 36, 38, 40, 46, 51, 58, 64, 74, 77, 87, 94, 122, 132, 143, 156, 169, 177, 182, 184, 191, 198, 200, 204, 207, 216, 219, 227; III, ed. J. Lister, YAS RS LVII (1917), pp. 1, 5, 6, 8, 17, 25, 27, 33, 44, 53–54, 66, 70, 84, 94–95, 107, 109, 112, 132–33, 136, 148, 151, 154, 178; IV, ed. J. Lister, YAS RS LXXVIII (1930), pp. 1, 35, 68, 72, 77, 80, 89, 96, 107–09, 121, 129, 134, 136, 140, 165, 169, 172, 186, 190–91, 201.

[17] *Pleas of the Crown for the County of Gloucester 1221*, ed. F. W. Maitland (London, 1884), p. 65; *PRO Lists and Indexes IX, List of Sheriffs* (1898), p. 49; J. C. Holt, *Robin Hood* (1981), p. 54. The fine is not mentioned in the pipe rolls or the surviving fine rolls of John's reign, but, since Fermeria's chattels were to be accounted for by the heir of Gerard de Athée, the offence probably dates to 1207–09, when Gerard was sheriff of Gloucestershire, and not during the abbacy of Alexander Nequam (1213–16), as is sometimes said. There was no eyre in Gloucestershire between 1203 and 1221, so the killing could have taken place at any time between those dates.

[18] CRR XII, no. 520.

[19] TNA, C 66/43, m. 3d.

[20] *Three Early Assize Rolls for the County of Northumberland*, ed. W. Page, Surtees Society LXXXVIII (1891), pp. 120, 195, 395.

the 1293 Northumberland eyre, Robert Hod of Newburn was in one of two groups of men who allegedly disseised Robert of Throckley of a free tenement in Throckley, and also caused him a nuisance by erecting a stew in Newburn and blocking the road to Corbridge.[21] What may be the first references to Robin Hood's main accomplice, Little John, survive from 1292, when several men of that name, four in the form 'Parvus Johannes' and the other 'Petit Johan', were appealed of robbery in various places in southern England by three different appellors.[22]

Further Hoods are mentioned in land deeds either as principals or witnesses. Robert Hude of Plungar in Leicestershire was the first witness of a charter of unknown date issued by the prior of Belvoir leasing a cottage at Granby in Nottinghamshire.[23] In Yorkshire, in a Follifoot deed apparently from the first half of the thirteenth century, Robert Hod appears in the middle of the list of witnesses.[24] Robert Hode or Hudi is twice mentioned in undated deeds in the cartulary of the Percy family as having held land in the fields of Whitwell, near Wetherby.[25] Other Robert Hoods or Hoods with other Christian names can be found in the calendars of the patent and close rolls of the king's Chancery, like Robert Hode, whose son Thomas received a grant of property at Howden in the East Riding in 1336.[26] The best known of the examples from these rolls must be the Robert Hod who in 1354 was languishing in the forest gaol at Rockingham in Northamptonshire awaiting trial at the next forest eyre for trespass against the vert and venison; he was being considered for bail until the eyre.[27] Two examples from military records of 1346 and 1363 have been added by Andrew Ayton, in addition to the intriguing 'Robyn Hod', an archer added to the Isle of Wight garrison in 1338, mentioned in a document written in French.[28] The most famous of all these individuals

---

21 *The Northumberland Eyre Roll for 1293*, ed. C. M. Fraser, Surtees Society CCXI (2007), nos. 273–74. The second group also included an Elias Hod. For the distribution of the Northumberland Hod names, see Map 3.
22 TNA, JUST 2/254, rots. 1, 5. The roll lists appellors sent to Newgate for the trial of their appeals, or persons arrested on indictment and confined to Newgate, who subsequently became appellors there. I am indebted to Henry Summerson for this reference.
23 HMC, *The Manuscripts of the Duke of Rutland preserved at Belvoir Castle* IV (London, 1905), p. 135.
24 *Yorkshire Deeds* IV, ed. C. T. Clay, YAS RS LXV (1914), p. 67, no. 235.
25 *The Percy Chartulary*, ed. M. T. Martin, Surtees Society CXVII (1909), pp. 27 (no. XVIV), 91 (no. CCXXVII).
26 CPR 1334–38, p. 241. Earlier, in 1322 and 1323, Thomas made two feet of fines also relating to property in Howden: *Feet of Fines for the County of York from 1314 to 1326*, ed. M. Roper and C. Kitching, YAS RS CLVIII (2006), nos. 430, 524.
27 CCR 1354–60, p. 23.
28 A. Ayton, 'Military Service and the Development of the Robin Hood Legend in the Fourteenth Century', *NMS* 36 (1992), pp. 126, 129.

was the Robyn Hode, a porter in the Chamber of Edward II, who was paid off in 1324 because he could no longer work, and who Hunter suggested in 1852 was the original Robin.[29] Many further references from all these kinds of sources could readily be added. Hood was a very common surname in England, and a significant proportion of men with that surname were called Robert. It has been calculated that in about 1200 Robert was the second most common male Christian name in England, after William, and about 1300 the third, after John and William, in both periods standing at 11%; in the mid-fourteenth century Robert was the fourth most common, after John, William and Thomas.[30] Many of them must have been accustomed to being called by the diminutive or pet-form 'Robin' by their families and friends during their everyday lives.

It has been suggested by Robert Linley and David Pilling that the surname 'Ode', which is not uncommon, may be a variant of Hood. It is found in many counties. There was a Roger Ode at Anstey in Hertfordshire in 1296.[31] John, Thomas and Robert Ode paid tax in the East Riding of Yorkshire in 1297 and 1301.[32] A number of Odes paid subsidies in Huntingdonshire in the early years of Edward III, several of them being from Abbots Ripton and Morborne.[33] Ode could also be a Christian name. The 1297 Yorkshire tax roll included Matthew son of Ode, serving as a taxer for the subsidy at Wyton, near Beverley.[34] The Wakefield manor court rolls for the period between 1315 and 1317 include John son of Ode, Jordan son of Ode, and two references to William son of Ode, as well as a William son of Thomas Ode, all in Hipperholme, where there seems to have been an established Ode family.[35] Other Odes also appear in the earlier Wakefield manor court rolls, as do many Hoods, and the evidence they provide indicates that the Odes were clearly and consistently distinguished from the Hoods who are mentioned in the same documents. For example, between 1297 and 1307 there are a few appearances by members of the family of a Thomas Ode: his son William twice, an unnamed 'young daughter' once, and a probable other son, John, once.[36] During the same period there are far more frequent

---

[29] See pp. 90–92.
[30] E. G. Withycombe, *The Oxford Dictionary of English Christian Names* (3rd edition, Oxford, 1977), p. xxvi; Ayton, 'Military Service', p. 127 and n. 5.
[31] TNA, E 179/120/3, m. 17; E 179/120/5, m. 14.
[32] *Yorkshire Subsidy 25 Edward I*, pp. 119 (Halsam in Holderness), 134 (Garton on the Wolds); *Yorkshire Subsidy 30 Edward I*, p. 25 (Thrintoft).
[33] *Early Huntingdonshire Lay Subsidy Rolls*, ed. J. A. Raftis and M. P. Hogan (Toronto, 1976), pp. 74, 88, 95, 186, 249, 250.
[34] *Yorkshire Subsidy 25 Edward I*, pp. 119, 134, 156.
[35] *Wakefield* IV, pp. 16, 78, 118, 181, 194. William son of Ode had earlier appeared under Thornes in 1298 and Hipperholme in 1307, while the son of Thomas son of Ode is mentioned under Stanley in 1306: *Wakefield* II, pp. 33, 53, 65.
[36] *Wakefield* II, pp. 18(2), 33, 119.

appearances by a more prominent individual called Adam Hod, who sometimes served as a pledge for essoins and as a juror to judge indictments presented at the tourn.[37] Several other Hoods, John, Richard, Robert and Walter, also appear, all but the last quite frequently, from 1297 to 1309.[38] The clerks who collected the names of the taxpayers and wrote them on the rolls during those years were in no doubt that they were dealing with two quite different surnames, and nowhere did they confuse the two. The name Ode continued to be distinct from Hood in the succeeding centuries and was the ancestor of the modern surnames Odd, Odde, Oddy and Oddey.

The Hood surname could be, and frequently was, part of a compound surname. Two-syllable surnames in which 'hood' forms the second part are quite common in the records, especially those of the lay subsidies of 1296, 1327 and 1332, and also in legal sources. In many, the first element is a colour, such as black, grey, white, red or green. Robert Blachod paid tax in Northumberland in 1296, while William Greyhoud did so in Dorset in 1332.[39] In 1232 William Withod was bailed from the king's prison at Wallingford in Berkshire, and in 1258 William Whythod and his son Geoffrey were involved in a trespass at Steetley in north Nottinghamshire, while a John Whithod of the same county purchased an assize commission in 1272.[40] Henry Redhod was an accomplice of John Robehod in killing John son of Simon at Charford in Hampshire in 1272, and Roger Redhod was one of a number of men who broke into a park near Colchester in Essex in the same year and drove cattle from there into the town.[41] Thomas Redhode paid a subsidy in London in 1332.[42] John Redhod and Thomas Redhod were Northumberland taxpayers in Lee and Prudhoe respectively in 1296, and John Redhod at Bocking in Sussex, while the William Ridhoud and Nicholas Ridhoud who paid tax in Dorset in 1327 and 1332 were probably Redhoods too.[43] From 1274 to 1297 a William Grenehod and his relatives were living in Wakefield, while William Grenhod or Grenhoud of Ringmer was a taxpayer in Sussex in 1327 and 1332.[44] The John Pyhod of Coventry who purchased a

---

[37] *Wakefield* II, pp. 11–12, 20, 24, 27, 38 (2), 40, 46, 51(2), 58, 77, 94, 132.
[38] *Wakefield* II, pp. 8, 32, 36, 64(2), 74, 87(2), 122, 143, 156, 169, 177, 182(2), 184, 191(2), 198, 200, 204, 216, 219, 227.
[39] *Northumberland Subsidy 1296*, p. 75; *Dorset Subsidy 1332*, p. 80.
[40] CR 1231–34, p. 99; TNA, JUST 1/1187, rot. 19 [AALT-IMG 0046]; *Calendar of Fine Rolls 56 Henry III* (online), no. 961.
[41] TNA, JUST 1/780, rot. 18d. [AALT-IMG 8301]; JUST 1/238, rot. 57 [AALT-IMG 7728].
[42] *Two Early London Subsidy Rolls*, p. 318.
[43] *Northumberland Subsidy 1296*, pp. 4, 12; *Dorset Subsidy 1327*, pp. 11, 103; *Dorset Subsidy 1332*, p. 84; *Sussex Subsidies, 1296, 1327, 1332*, p. 43.
[44] *Yorkshire Subsidy 25 Edward I*, p. 113; *Wakefield* I, pp. 91, 131, 160, 250, 265; II, pp. 56, 60, 65, 68, 95, 108, 120–21, 128, 138, 146, 154, 175, 180, 191, 198, 200, 217;

licence to concord in a Warwickshire case in 1297, and a Nicholas Pyhod, also from Warwickshire, both had a black and white hood reminiscent of a magpie.[45]

Other compound surnames seem to derive from distinctive features of particular hoods. The Richard Stepelhode who paid tax at West Tanfield in Yorkshire in 1301 may have had a very tall hood, while Alan and Walter Straythode of Riccall may have had close-fitting ones; that of John Brodhoud, at Worth Matravers in Dorset in 1327, may have been broad, while that of John Litelhoud at Watford in Hertfordshire in 1296 was presumably small.[46] In London John Fairhod and Peter Feirhood, a collier (*Coliere*), both paid a subsidy in Baynard Castle ward in 1332, and the name also occurs in Warwickshire at the same time; it signifies someone with a fine hood.[47] John Furhode, taxed at Ayton in Yorkshire in 1301, may have had the same name, rather than one referring to a hood made of fur.[48] The name-elements 'cape' and 'cope' were evidently interchangeable, and may have been applied to men who habitually wore a small head-covering under a hood.[49] In 1327, Peter Capehoud (Charlton Marshal), William Copehoud (Combe Keynes) and Walter Copehoud (Wimborne) paid the subsidy in Dorset; five years later in the same county, Peter Copehoud and William Capehoud appeared again in the same places as before, and Richard Capehoud is listed under Combe Keynes.[50] Laurence Mundihod (protective hood) paid tax at Newbiggin in Northumberland in 1296.[51] Hobbe Ryvenhod, who appears in a list of outlaws in the 1292 Lancashire eyre roll, perhaps had a torn or ragged hood.[52] The plea roll of the Westmorland eyre of 1256 includes Adam Piledhod (spiked hood) among a long list of indicted suspected thieves whose chattels had been confiscated.[53] Similarly, 'Pik' could indicate a

---

III, pp. 2–3, 41, 51, 53–54, 59, 66, 92–93, 113, 146–47; IV, pp. 9, 26, 28, 33, 64, 95, 97, 154, 167, 170, 172, 174, 184, 193; *Sussex Subsidies, 1296, 1327, 1332*, pp. 197, 309.

45 Hjertstedt, *Middle English Nicknames*, p. 156.
46 *Yorkshire Subsidy 30 Edward I*, pp. 4, 50 (see also *Feudal Aids*, IV, p. 246, from 1346, and *CPR 1301–7*, p. 45, from 1302); *Dorset Subsidy 1327*, p. 87; TNA, E 179/120/3, m. 41; Reaney, *Surnames*, p. 48.
47 *Two Early London Subsidy Rolls*, pp. 339, 343; Hjertstedt, *Middle English Nicknames*, p. 106; Reaney, *Surnames*, pp. 113–14.
48 *Yorkshire Subsidy 30 Edward I*, p. 35.
49 *MED* II, ed. H. Kurath and S. M. Kuhn (Ann Arbor, 1959), p. 46.
50 Hanks and Hodges, *Surnames*, p. 122; *Dorset Subsidy 1327*, pp. 7, 41, 121; *Dorset Subsidy 1332*, pp. 4(2), 17.
51 *Northumberland Subsidy 1296*, p. 2.
52 *Crown Pleas of the Lancashire Eyre 1292*, II (Record Society of Lancashire and Cheshire, CXLIX, 2015), no. 409; *MED* VIII, ed. R. E. Lewis (Michigan, 1984), p. 758.
53 TNA, JUST 1/979, m. 13 (AALT-IMG 0310); *MED* VII, ed. S. M. Kuhn (Ann Arbor, 1980), pp. 920–21.

hood tapering to a point or peak, such as John Pikhod, another outlaw mentioned in the Lancashire eyre roll of 1292, and William Pykhod, who appears in Skyrack wapentake in the Yorkshire eyre of the same year.[54] William Colhod, a 'common depredator' hanged at Kingston upon Thames and mentioned in the roll of the 1263 Surrey eyre, was probably the wearer of a (coal) black hood, as also was Roger Colhod, who was one of those accused of breaking into a Middlesex manor house of the earl of Hereford in 1305 while the earl was on the king's service in Scotland.[55] John Bolthod appears in a Dorset civil case in 1296, and Robert Bolthoud paid tax in the same county in 1332. 'Bolt' was a west-country occupational name for a sifter of flour, so the name may refer to a style of hood characteristic of men who carried out that task.[56] Gilbert Tomehod, a payer of the 1327 subsidy at Bradle in Church Knowle in Dorset, seems to have had an empty or hollow hood.[57] It is more difficult to know what to make of the names of John Rachhoud, John Rechoud, John Fizhude, and Nicholas Blouccheboud, taxpayers in Dorset in 1327 and 1332, although the first two may have had 'pulled-off' hoods.[58]

The Wakefield Hoods were examined in detail by James Holt in his *Robin Hood*, originally published in 1982. After pointing out that a John Hood lived at Stanley as early as 1202, he identified several families bearing the name Hood and using the Christian name Robert, living not far from the outlaw's legendary haunt of Barnsdale, and in townships where there were 'Robin Hood' place-names by the mid seventeenth century. He suggested that some of the Wakefield Hoods had a role in the origins of the Robin Hood legend. 'Either the Hoods of Wakefield gave Robin to the world, or they absorbed the tale of the outlaw into their family traditions or their neighbours and descendants came to associate the two'.[59] This line of enquiry was not subsequently pursued by Holt, nor developed any further by more recent writers.[60] It has in effect been

---

[54] *Crown Pleas of the Lancashire Eyre 1292*, II, no. 409; TNA, JUST 1/1098, rot. 13d [AALT-IMG 7227]; *MED* VII, ed. S. M. Kuhn (Ann Arbor, 1980), p. 912; *Oxford English Dictionary* XI, ed. J. A. Simpson and E. S. C. Weiner (2nd edn., Oxford 1989), pp. 818–20.

[55] *The 1263 Surrey Eyre*, ed. S. Stewart, Surrey Record Society XL (2006), no. 623; *CPR 1301–7*, p. 349; Reaney, *Dictionary*, p. 74; *MED* II, p. 379.

[56] TNA, CP 40/113, rot. 59d [AALT-IMG 0459]; CP 40/121, rot. 30d [AALT-IMG 0763]; *Dorset Subsidy 1332*, p. 69; Hanks and Hodges, *Dictionary*, p. 61.

[57] *Dorset Subsidy 1327*, pp. 112; *MED* XI, ed. R. E. Lewis (Ann Arbor, 1993), p. 861.

[58] *Dorset Subsidy 1327*, p. 124; *Dorset Subsidy 1332*, pp. 56, 76, 101; *MED* VIII, ed. R. E. Lewis (Ann Arbor, 1984), p. 111.

[59] Holt, *Robin Hood*, pp. 50–51, 208.

[60] ...id Hepworth, however, has established a link between a neighbour of ...urteenth-century Wakefield Robin Hood, Thomas Alayn, and Kirklees the reputed burial place of the outlaw, where Alayn held a corrody:

put to one side after the discovery of a number of 'Robinhood' surnames in several counties in the south of England. Holt himself pointed to one in a list of Sussex taxpayers from 1296 and suggested how it came to be there. Gilbert Robynhod was a tenant of the liberty of Leicester in the county, which was centred on the manor of Hungry Hatch in the village of Fletching.[61] The liberty of Leicester was by 1294 settled on Thomas, son of Edmund earl of Lancaster, the brother of Edward I, who died in 1296. Thomas's wife Alice de Lacy, to whom he was betrothed in 1292 and married by 1294, brought with her the title to the honour of Pontefract, to which they would succeed on the death of her father, Henry de Lacy. 'In 1296, therefore, the heir to the Liberty of Leicester in Sussex, where Gilbert Robynhod was a tenant, was married to the heiress of the honour of Pontefract, within the southern bounds of which lay Barnsdale.' He speculated that

> perhaps Gilbert Robynhod was in the household of Alice de Lacy. Perhaps he played or recited the story and hence acquired the name. Perhaps he was an established Sussex tenant, the son of a Robert Hood, who now acquired a new surname from the outlaw hero whose deeds were set in the family lands of the new lady of the manor. By some such process the legend infected Sussex.

He went on to point out that

> the combination of Christian name and surname ... is most unusual. It is this exceptional formation of the name as well as its rarity which make it difficult to dissociate the surname 'Robinhood' from the tradition of the outlaw. This means that the legend was already known in Sussex by 1296.[62]

To this can be added a second example from a year earlier. In Trinity term 1295, in a lawsuit in the Common Bench at Westminster involving nine plaintiffs, the most significant being the prior of Stonely, a William Robynhod sued Roger son of Walter of Tilbrook to warrant to him 2s rent at Tilbrook in Huntingdonshire, which Richard son of Walter of Tilbrook, perhaps his brother, was claiming.[63] This suit continued in the following

---

see D. Hepworth, 'A Grave Tale', in *Robin Hood: Medieval and Post-Medieval*, ed. Phillips, pp. 91–112, at 111–12.

[61] G. A. Holmes, *The Estates of the Higher Nobility in Fourteenth-Century England* (Cambridge, 1957), p. 127.

[62] Holt, *Robin Hood*, pp. 52–53.

[63] TNA, CP 40/109, rot. 57 [AALT-IMG 0122]. The *Victoria County History* and other sources say that Tilbrook was in Bedfordshire until it was transferred to Huntingdonshire in 1888, and indeed in the lay subsidy of 1334 it was taxed under Bedfordshire, but in the plea rolls of the 1290s used here it is marginated as being in Huntingdonshire.

term, Michaelmas, when William's surname was spelt 'Robinhod', and there was then a further postponement to Easter term 1296.[64] It can therefore be equally confidently asserted that the legend was also known on the border of Huntingdonshire and Bedfordshire by 1295.[65] There is no doubt that, as Holt observed, this kind of surname, making clear reference to a universally familiar personality, was very rare indeed before 1300. Only three other early examples have so far been identified. In the Nottinghamshire eyre of 1280, Robert Jesucrist of Ratcliffe on Soar was involved in litigation over a small inheritance there, while in the Yorkshire eyre of 1231 a Henry Saladin, who reportedly accidentally drowned in a marsh, must have been named after the Saracen sultan and opponent of the crusaders in the late twelfth century, and who died in 1193.[66] The earliest was a 'Prestrejohan', who was sent to the king's court at Westminster in 1207 on behalf of the prior of Thornholme in Lincolnshire, to give his essoin (excuse for non-appearance) in a suit there, and appeared again on his master's behalf in 1219 before justices in eyre at Lincoln, this time as an attorney.[67] He was clearly named after the Christian priest-king Prester John who, according to twelfth-century legend, ruled in central Asia and fought against heathen rulers. To take a hypothetical contemporary equivalent, if someone called 'Kevin Waynerooney' existed among the English population today, it would be a reasonable assumption that the surname was somehow derived from, and was a reference to, that of the famous footballer.

Less straightforward are the several 'Robehod' surnames recorded in the last forty years of the thirteenth century, noticed by Dr Henry Summerson during his extensive research in the voluminous records of the royal criminal courts.[68] In chronological order they are as follows.

[64] TNA, CP 40/110, rot. 200 [AALT-IMG 1022]. In Hilary term 1296 Richard son of Walter of Tilbrook appointed an attorney against the prior of Stonely and others, but not all their names were recited: CP 40/111, attorneys rot. 8 [AALT-IMG 0357]. No further entries relating to the case in that Easter term or the two subsequent terms of 1296 have been found.

[65] By that time Robinhood may have become a heritable surname in London, but no evidence has survived before 1325: D&T p. 12 and note 3. At that time the authors considered that the surname 'could be used in late medieval England as a heritable family surname without benefit of any deliberate allusion to the outlaw legend', but later Dobson wrote that 'it now seems that we were probably seriously mistaken about that': R. B. Dobson, 'Robin Hood: The Genesis of a Popular Hero', in Hahn, *Popular Culture*, pp. 61–77, at p. 72.

[66] TNA, JUST 1/664, rot. 19d [AALT-IMG 3840]; JUST 1/1043, rot. 20 [AALT-IMG 1354].

[67] *Pleas Before the King or His Justices* III, ed. D. M. Stenton, Selden Society LXXXIII (1967), p. xxxiii; IV, Selden Society LXXXIV (1967), no. 2913; *Lincolnshire Eyre*, Selden Society LIII, no. 558 and introduction, p. lxxiv.

[68] For the details and references, see also D. Crook, 'The Sheriff of Nottingham and Robin Hood: The Genesis of the Legend?', in *Thirteenth Century England*

In the Hampshire eyre of 1272 the presenting jury for Fareham hundred said that John Robehod was one of four men in the tithing of Roger le Page of Compton who killed John son of Simon after a quarrel at an inn at Charford, after which he fled and was outlawed.[69] In the same year Alexander Robehod was one of many men indicted for burglary, homicide or larceny in Lexden hundred in Essex who failed to appear before the eyre justices and so were outlawed; unlike many of the others he was not reported as being in a tithing, and so may have been a wandering vagabond.[70] In the 1286 Suffolk eyre, in Blackbourne hundred, Gilbert Robehod was released to pledges by the justices after an unspecified charge in Suffolk had led to a steward taking 10s from him.[71] In 1294 in the Hampshire hundred of Evingar a Robert Robehod, who had been born at Sutton Scotney, was indicted for stealing four sheep.[72] To these criminal examples may be added a man recorded in a Suffolk assessment for the tax of a thirtieth in 1283 in Blackbourne hundred, where we have already met a Gilbert Robehod in 1286. One of the poorer taxpayers in Walsham le Willows in the same county was a Robert Robehod, whose crops and livestock, listed in detail, were valued at a total of £1 7s 1½d, on which he paid 10½d in tax.[73]

It might be argued that 'Robehod' is just another example of a '-hod' name like those already listed, such as 'Grenhod' or 'Stepelhode', because in thirteenth and fourteenth-century English the first element could mean 'robe'.[74] It would therefore be 'robe-hood', presumably with the meaning of a 'robe-shaped hood', but this is a combination which makes no sense. It is even less likely to mean the wearing of a robe and hood together. The form 'Robe' or 'Robbe' had been an established pet-form of 'Robert' since at least the later twelfth century, when it was already being used as a surname.[75] A recently-discovered example of its use as a Christian name from the first half of the thirteenth century is in a Cambridgeshire

---

II: *Proceedings of the Newcastle upon Tyne Conference 1987*, ed. P. R. Coss and S. D. Lloyd (Woodbridge, 1988), pp. 59–69, at 59. The entries are mentioned also in Holt's Postscript (1989), *Robin Hood*, pp. 187–88, but without references.

[69] TNA, JUST 1/780, rot. 18d [AALT-IMG 8301].
[70] TNA, JUST 1/238, rot. 58 [AALT-IMG 7730].
[71] TNA, JUST 1/827, rot. 41d [AALT-IMG 5457].
[72] TNA, JUST 1/1301, rot. 12 [AALT-IMG 4854].
[73] TNA, E 179/242/41, printed in E. Powell, ed., *A Suffolk Hundred in 1283* (1910), account sheet 33, skin 52. Much later, in 1327 another Suffolk Robert Robehod paid tax at Hacheston in Loes hundred: *Suffolk in 1327*, ed. S. H. A. Hervey, Suffolk Green Books IX (Woodbridge, 1906), p. 133.
[74] *MED* VIII, ed. R. E. Lewis (Michigan, 1984), p. 769.
[75] Reaney, *Dictionary*, p. 273; *Pipe Roll 24 Henry II*, PRS XXVII, p. 90 (Richard Robe, Sussex); *Chancellor's Roll 8 Richard I*, PRS NS VII, p. 28 (Robe coccus, Wiltshire); *Pipe Roll 1 John*, PRS NS X, p. 128 (Richard Robbe, Sussex); *Book of Fees* I, p. 79 (Richard Robbe, Somerset).

deed written sometime between 1216 and 1254. It is an acknowledgement by Martin Bricchnoth of Cambridge of his receipt from Prior Laurence and the convent of Barnwell of an acre and a half of land in the fields of Grantchester, with bounds mentioning 'the land of Robbe Hod'.[76] It was the equivalent of 'Robbie' in contemporary English personal nomenclature, and is now sometimes used even as a Christian name in its own right. Examples of its usage as a patronym or surname occur in the early subsidy rolls. In Yorkshire in 1301 John son of Robe and William son of Robe lived respectively at Marske cum Redcar, and in Kirkleatham, Yearby or East Coatham.[77] In Dorset in 1327, and again in 1332, Edward Robe paid tax in Bridport.[78] There is therefore no reason to doubt that the first element in the name 'Robehod' represents 'Robbie', and that such names are allusions to the Robin Hood legend in the same way as those in the form 'Robynhod'. In none of these examples do we know of any other name which might have been used by any of the men. In each case the information comes from a record of the administration of criminal justice, and it is possible that in some of these instances the 'Robehod' name was applied to the individuals concerned by the jurors responsible for indicting them because they connected them with the outlaw legend, in whatever form they were aware of it. However, this is unlikely to apply to William Robynhod or Robinhod, the plaintiff in the civil case relating to Tilbrook in 1295-6, who must have called himself, or was generally known by, that name when the group of fellow claimants sued out their writ. Likewise, the Sussex taxpayer Gilbert Robynhod at the same date would probably already have been known by that name in the locality before the assessors recorded it on their list. There is, however, one example, and earlier in date than any of those already mentioned, where the 'Robehod' surname was applied by an official to an individual criminal who in an earlier document had been identified by a different name, which he subsequently altered.[79]

Early in Easter term 1262, the barons of the Exchequer at Westminster received a writ notifying them that the king had pardoned the prior of Sandleford, a small house of Augustinian canons on the southern border of Berkshire, from the payment of a penalty of one mark that had been imposed on him during an eyre in Berkshire in the previous year. The prior's offence had been the seizure of the chattels of a fugitive called William Robehod, to which he was subsequently judged not to have been

---

[76] King's College Cambridge Archives, GRA/472. I am indebted to Nicholas Vincent for this reference.
[77] *Yorkshire Subsidy 30 Edward I*, pp. 34, 39.
[78] *Dorset Subsidy 1327*, p. 138; *Dorset Subsidy 1332*, p. 104.
[79] D. Crook, 'Some Further Evidence Concerning the Dating of the Origins of the Legend of Robin Hood', *EHR* XCIX (1984), pp. 530–34, reprinted in Knight, *Anthology*, pp. 257–61.

entitled. The original writ does not survive, but a note of it was made on one of the memoranda rolls kept by Exchequer officials called remembrancers. The eyre is known to have been held at Reading in February the previous year, because, as it happens, a plea roll of the justices who held it has survived. It contains the record of William Robehod's presentment by a jury of indictment, his conviction in absentia, and the seizure of his chattels, assessed as being worth 2s 6d. It appears that he was a member of a criminal gang, all of whom had fled from justice and were to be outlawed because they were suspected of having committed many unspecified larcenies and of harbouring thieves. The gang consisted of three men and two women, one of the men and the women evidently from the same family and from a village called Hannington, but William himself was said to be from the village of Enborne, which was close to the priory and in which it had property. He was a member of the frankpledge tithing of Alexander le Vyn there, and so Alexander was liable for an amercement for William's offences. The significant point is that in this earlier record William is referred to not as William Robehod but as William son of Robert le Fevere, i.e. Smith. At some point in the administrative process between the eyre record and the entry on the memoranda roll a year later, a clerk had altered the name of the individual concerned from 'William son of Robert Smith' to 'William Robehod'. We cannot know which clerk it was, because the documents recording the (probably four) intervening stages have not in this instance survived, but it must have been either a royal clerk working in the Chancery or the Exchequer, or a personal clerk of one of the justices in eyre. He could have originated from anywhere in England, so the Berkshire context may be no more than incidental. Whatever the geographical context in which he became aware of it, it seems certain that he knew something of the legend of Robin Hood, in whatever form it existed at that date. What did he know about Robin Hood? According to Holt, 'it must have been more than a simple criminal reputation because such can scarcely exist without an accompanying legend. The most likely answer is that the clerk already knew some of the tales which were later given literary form in the *Gest* and the other early ballads'.[80]

There seems to be no clear evidence of hereditary Robinhood surnames from the thirteenth century, but by the fourteenth 'Robinhood' or derivative names could be inherited by generations of the same family, and can occasionally be followed when detailed local records have survived, as in the case of the city of London.[81] A second example of 'Robynhod' occurs in a Sussex tax list of 1332, when Robert Robynhod was listed among the taxpayers in Harting, but so far distant from Fletching that

---

[80] J. C. Holt, 'Robin Hood: The Origins of the Legend', in Carpenter, *Robin Hood*, p. 34

[81] D&T, p. 12.

close kinship with the Gilbert of 1296 seems unlikely.[82] 'Robin Hood' and 'Robehod' names continue to appear in records after 1332, providing continuity with the thirteenth-century names discussed earlier in the chapter. Some of them have no obvious link with criminality. A Sussex man, John Robehoud, was one of the tenants of Richard earl of Arundel and Surrey at Houghton about 1380.[83] Other examples are from criminal records, and are more likely to be derived from the outlaw. In Hampshire in 1342 John Robynhoud of 'Cradefordbrigg' (possibly Crockford Bridge) and an accomplice, John Pubbel of Ringwood, were arrested after being indicted before the steward of the hundred court of Ringwood in the liberty of William de Montacute, earl of Salisbury, on 3 July 1342, for a robbery involving five cattle that had taken place on 11 June that year. They claimed benefit of clergy, and were found guilty by a jury before being handed over to the ordinary, the bishop of Salisbury, to be held in his prison.[84] The Hampshire coroner's roll of Thomas Canteshangre, covering the years from 1377 to 1393, mentions a Walter Robehoud, son of William Robehoud, who was said to have been the instigator of the homicide of John Dighere of Suffolk in the tithing of Hurstbourne. After Vespers on 24 May 1387, four men stabbed John Dighere in the chest with a knife called a 'basellard' at a place called, curiously enough, Rebehode. In another entry in the roll, a Robert Robehoud served as a pledge for Thomas King of Lymington, the first finder of the victim (his servant Henry) of another knife attack at Hurstbourne Regis (now Hurstbourne Tarrant), on 3 August 1389.[85] These entries suggest the existence of a Robehoud family at Hurstbourne at that time.

There was in the fourteenth century also a well-established 'Robhod' family at Walsham le Willows in Suffolk, where we have already come across the taxpayer Robert Robehod in 1283.[86] References in the surviving manorial court rolls run from 1317 to 1399, and cover several generations of the family.[87] The earliest, William Robhood, who was dead by 1317, was when he was first mentioned called William le Fenere, hunter or fen-dweller, or possibly Fevere, smith; and he may have been the first of the line to be called 'Robhood'.[88] A land transaction in 1376 involved

---

[82] *Sussex Subsidies 1296, 1327, 1332*, pp. 33, 236.
[83] *Two Fitzalan Surveys*, ed. M. Clough, Sussex Record Society LXVII (1969), p. 91.
[84] JUST 3/130, rot. 60 [AALT-IMG 0138]. I am grateful to Carrie Smith for this reference.
[85] JUST 2/155, rots. 13 (entry damaged) [AALT-IMG 0087], 16 [AALT-IMG 0093]. I am indebted to Carrie Smith for these references.
[86] E 179/242/41, printed in E. Powell, ed., *A Suffolk Hundred in 1283* (1910), account sheet 33; above, p. 176.
[87] R. Lock, ed., *The Court Rolls of Walsham le Willows, 1303–50*, Suffolk Records Society (1998), index (32 entries); R. Lock, ed., *The Court Rolls of Walsham le Willows, 1351–99*, Suffolk Records Society (2002), index (156 entries).
[88] *Walsham le Willows, 1303–50*, pp. 56 and n. 10, 59 and n. 12.

the transfer of 'the tenement Robhood', clearly an established family tenement, partible between male heirs according to the custom of the manor. John Robhood, the father, who died in 1365, had six sons, Robert, Nicholas, Peter, Walter, Richard and John, all villeins by blood.[89] The numerous offences committed against the lords between 1377 and 1397 by Peter Robhood, the third of the six sons, were serious in a manorial context. He caused considerable offence to them (including Robert and William de Ufford, successively earls of Suffolk, from 1360 to 1382) by breaking into their pound and removing livestock, often his own which had been impounded. He caused damage to the lord's demesne crops, pasture and woods, sometimes at night, with his animals; took hares and partridges in his warren; and sheared his sheep. He also withdrew labour services; ploughed in the lord's chase; cut down and sawed up his trees without permission; and forestalled a barrel of white herring on market day, the market belonging to the lord.[90] But Peter Robhood was no Robin Hood analogue, not a yeoman but an archetypal rebellious manorial villein of the age of the Peasant's Revolt of 1381, by which time the outlaw legend had long been a matter of general knowledge. His family name had been established at the latest by 1317, and Peter and his wife Catherine were villeins by blood, like all his brothers; one of them, Walter Robhood, listed as a fugitive villein in 1361, and who damaged the lord's close with horses in 1386, was respectable enough (if indeed he was the same man rather than a namesake) to be a juror in enquiries in 1396 and to be elected as reeve in the following year.[91] The family continued in Walsham le Willows at least until the reign of Henry VIII, because in 1524 John and Thomas Robhod paid a lay subsidy there.[92]

The alleged significance of the 'Robinhood' and 'Robehood' names for the early legend has not been universally accepted since Holt first opined that they showed that 'the legend must have been a national one by the second half of the thirteenth century', but on the other hand neither has there been any convincing alternative explanation of the names. There is a point of view, moreover, which contends that even the name of the outlaw himself is a literary, mythical concoction. Robert Pogue Harrison, an American literary and cultural historian, wrote that

---

[89] *Walsham le Willows, 1351–99*, pp. 78, 125.
[90] *Walsham le Willows, 1351–99*, pp. 128, 130, 132, 134–35, 143, 148, 151, 153, 159, 173–74, 177, 182, 185, 195, 200, 203–04.
[91] *Walsham le Willows, 1351–99*, pp. 61, 74, 78, 85, 145, 153, 162, 168, 171, 180, 182, 184, 187–88, 192, 196, 200, 202, 208.
[92] *Suffolk in 1524*, ed. S. H. A. Hervey, Suffolk Green Books X (Woodbridge, 1910), pp. 52–53. In 1327 another Suffolk Robehod, Robert, paid tax at Hacheston in Loes hundred, Suffolk: *Suffolk in 1327*, ed. Hervey, Suffolk Green Books IX (1906), p. 133.

the phenomenon of disguise appears in the very name of 'Robin Hood', which almost certainly derives from it. The *hood* is that which *hides*, providing a protective cover for the outlaw's head. The name 'Robin', in turn, derives from the French *robe*, the garment which cloaks the body.[93]

This is unconvincing, considering the abundance of real medieval men called Robert Hood before and after the emergence of the legend without any apparent implied connection with the outlaw, or any hint of the mythical. Among historians, Barrie Dobson accepted the relevance of the name but minimised its importance, and thought that, although the names might reasonably be seen as evidence that clerks working in the Exchequer and the royal law courts were well aware of the name and reputation of Robin Hood, this did not necessarily imply the existence of a developed and well-articulated legend by that date, which would underlie and explain the use of the 'Robinhood' surname in that way. 'Might it be that the nickname preceded rather than succeeded the myth? Interesting as it is to learn that criminals were styled 'Robinhood' by the 1260s, perhaps nearly everything that made and makes that name immortal followed thereafter'.[94] In his final review of the evidence, made in 1997, Dobson suggested that 'all attempts to discover the birth of the Robin Hood legend must now at least contemplate the paradoxical possibility that names can come before things and that the original genesis of the outlaw hero may be not so much the appeal of his adventures as the coining of his name'.[95] His cautious view had already been followed by Andrew Ayton, who remarked that Holt's conclusion 'is enticing, but not wholly convincing'. 'It may suggest no more than that by the 1260s Robin Hood had become a byword for outlawry'.[96]

In his own penultimate contribution to the debate, Holt himself took the view that 'it could well be … that the legend as we have it originated in multiple Robin Hoods. A composite person embodying real people and real incidents all brought together under the umbrella of a single *persona*'.[97] Holt's later contribution to the *Oxford Dictionary of National Biography* in 2004 noted that

> what the evidence of 1261–2 gives with one hand it takes away with the other. Certainly it provides a terminus ante quem for a prototype Robin Hood. Yet it also demonstrates how Robin Hoods were made. If

---

[93] R. P. Harrison, *Forests: The Shadow of Civilisation* (Chicago 1992), p. 79.
[94] R. B. Dobson and J. Taylor, 'General Review: Robin Hood', *Northern History* 26 (1990), pp. 229–32, at p. 231.
[95] R. B. Dobson, 'Robin Hood: The Genesis of a Popular Hero', in Hahn, *Popular Culture*, p. 76.
[96] A. Ayton, 'Military Service and the Development of the Robin Hood Legend in the Fourteenth Century', *NMS* 36 (1992), p. 130.
[97] J. C. Holt, 'The Origins of the Legend', in Carpenter, *Robin Hood*, p. 29.

William, son of Robert le Fevre, could become a Robin Hood, so could others. In the case of Robert Hod of 1226–7 the real name and nickname coincided; it is the only case where this is certainly so, and he could well have started the legend. But in many other cases criminals could have used or attracted the nickname without its leaving any trace of itself in the record of their crimes. It is only through luck that the flash of illumination from the case of William, son of Robert le Fevre exists. So it could well be, and almost certainly was, that the legend as it is now originated in multiple Robin Hoods, a composite person embodying real people and real incidents all brought together under the umbrella of a single persona. There were other outlaws with other names - some real, some legendary. This one snowballed, absorbing other legends and continuing to gather new material down to the present day.

Among other views, in 1998 Jeffrey Singman professed an interest in the possible significance of the Robin Hood names for the legend and its early diffusion, and regarded the evidence they provided as 'highly suggestive', because full names of this sort are rarely used as surnames'; but he concluded that 'regrettably, this evidence is not fully conclusive. In several cases the names take the form 'Robehod'; even if we regard this as a variant for 'Robinhood', it is by no means certain that the legendary outlaw lies behind the name'. He warns against 'too much confidence in our ability to interpret Middle English surnames', but goes on to cite the example of William Robehod in Berkshire, who he says, mistakenly, 'also appears as Hobbehod'.[98] Earlier, in 1994 Stephen Knight referred to 'Crook's distinctly optimistic reliance' on the significance of the 1262 name-change', and thought that

> some doubters might feel that the resemblance to 'Hobbehod' [which occurs in 1227 and 1228 in pipe rolls whose details would not have been known even to an Exchequer clerk in 1262, let alone a court clerk] is an influence on the renaming, either accidental or deliberate, and an ever-deeper sceptic might think the second reference, William Robehod, is just a miswritten or misunderstood version of name and patronymic.

If so, it is curious that so many other 'Robehod' names occur between 1272 and 1294, evidences that Knight does not seem to have taken account of, despite their having been listed by Holt in the second edition of his book in 1989. Knight's account of this issue was criticised by Dobson in his review of that edition in 1997:

> More challenging but even more questionable is Professor Knight's disinclination to accept the implications of Dr David Crook's recent documentary discoveries in the Public Record Office, accepted by most

---

[98] J. L. Singman, *Robin Hood: The Shaping of the Legend* (Westport, Conn. and London, 1998), p. 12.

historians as a major breakthrough in the interpretation of the origins of the legend. The fact that in 1261-62 some royal justice or clerk changed the name of a Berkshire thief called 'William, son of Robert le Fevere' into 'William Robehod, fugitive' is not of course to be denied: but Professor Knight's attempts to minimize the significance of that re-naming by invoking such possibilities as scribal confusion are a good deal less persuasive than Dr Crook's conclusion that whoever altered the name to 'Robehod' must have been well aware that this conflated sobriquet already carried the connotation of an exemplary outlaw. Since 1984 it has accordingly begun to seem more likely than not that the notoriety of the name of Robin Hood actually preceded rather than followed the evolution of the later well articulated outlaw legend'.[99]

By the time of his own second book, in 2003, Knight's misunderstanding had deepened, and he seems still to have had no awareness of the range of examples identified. He wrote that 'it is in fact extremely improbable that if there had been a developed myth of Robin Hood in the thirteenth century there would have been no references to it other than the 1262 one'.[100] By then he even seemed to think that the reference was found 'in the legal archives of Reading (a play-game town)', when it was in fact from the archives of the royal Exchequer. He even remarked that 'neither Crook nor Holt considers the more likely possibility that Gilbert derived his name from playing Robin's part in a local play-game'. By 2015 this possibility had been elevated to the level of probability,[101] even though he was well aware that there is no record of local parish Robin Hood play-games anywhere in England before 1475, and none in Reading before 1498; and that the earliest reference to a Robin Hood play occurs in the accounts of the receivers of the city of Exeter in 1427, when 20d was paid to 'the players playing the plays of Robin Hood'.[102] Such comments disclose a disturbing disregard for basic chronology and the careful evaluation of the surviving historical evidence.

Another writer, Jim Bradbury, seemed to misunderstand the details provided by the documents at several points, or what it is claimed that they signify.[103] The gang does not seem to have been William's, as Bradbury

---

[99] R. B. Dobson and J. Taylor, 'Merry Men at Work: The Transformation of Robin Hood from Medieval Outlaw into Heritage Hero', *Northern History* 33 (1997), pp. 232–37, at 234.

[100] S. Knight, *Complete Study* (Oxford, 1994), pp. 25–26; and *Mythic Biography*, pp. 194–96.

[101] S. Knight, *Reading Robin Hood: Content, Form and Reception in the Outlaw Myth* (Manchester, 2015), p. 240.

[102] D. Wiles, *The Early Plays of Robin Hood* (Cambridge, 1981), pp. 64–66; *REED Devon*, ed. J. M. Wasson (Toronto, 1986), pp. xvi, 89; D&T, p. xxviii; R. B. Dobson, 'Robin Hood: The Genesis of a Popular Hero', in Hahn, *Popular Culture*, pp. 61–77, 65.

[103] J. Bradbury, *Robin Hood* (Stroud, 2010), pp. 195–96.

assumes, and it appears to have been centred on the Tapping family of Hannington in a neighbouring county, while William seems to be a local, Berkshire, accomplice. There is no suggestion that he was the original Robin Hood, or descended from him, although Bradbury says that some historians believe that; in reality he simply serves to provide evidence that some form of legend had by 1262 come into existence. 'Robynhod' or 'Robinhod' is not a 'common surname', as Bradbury says, less than a dozen examples having come to light so far from the enormous amount of legal, financial and administrative documentation from the second half of the thirteenth century; nor is it particularly surprising that the examples so far identified all come, not from Yorkshire or Nottinghamshire, but from southern England, for which the surviving documentation is more extensive. He ends by suggesting that it may be that 'the real Robin Hood was actually someone surnamed Robinhood', which is to miss the point about the significance of the amalgamation of the two elements of the name by 1261-2, when it first appears; and he ignores the fact that there is no evidence for heritable Robinhood surnames before the first quarter of the fourteenth century, when Katherine Robynhod of London and the Robhoods of Walsham le Willows appear, to be followed by the Robhouds of Hurstbourne in the 1380s.

The personal-name evidence assembled in the earlier part of this chapter strengthens the case for placing the original outlaw, if one existed, in the thirteenth century. Robert, or Robin, Hood was a common name in that period and continued to be so for many years thereafter, without any apparent reference to the legend. The name could still be used in that straightforward way even in the twentieth century, despite the ubiquitous references to the legend broadcast in a variety of media readily available in most of the world. Of the many writers who have had to consider this idea since Holt's first forceful account of its significance, none has felt able to embrace it in the same way, but neither have they been able plausibly to deny the implication that the surnames provide for the existence of some kind of Robin Hood legend in the second half of the thirteenth century. The facts of the names and their contexts are not in doubt, and can only be denied by being ignored. To sustain a more cautious point of view requires a convincing alternative explanation as to why, in 1261-2, a robber whose name was originally supplied by an indictment jury who knew of him as William son of Robert the Smith, came a year later to be called William Robehod by an Exchequer, Chancery or eyre clerk who almost certainly did not know him. No-one has yet succeeded in finding one.

Chapter 7

Robin Hood and Criminality

In contemporary popular imagination the legendary outlaw Robin Hood is often associated with opposition to the forest laws of the Anglo-Norman and then Plantagenet monarchs who ruled England from 1066 onwards, and it is sometimes assumed that his outlawry arose from his offences against those laws. There is, however, a growing consensus among both historians and literary scholars that the original Robin Hood, if one existed, had nothing to do with the forest laws or the greenwood, but was a notorious highway robber whose supposed association with forests and woodland came about only after the genesis of his legend. According to Barrie Dobson and John Taylor,

> by a now familiar paradox the genesis of the most famous forest outlaw in English literature seems to lie in the exploits of "a strong thefe" of Barnsdale who may not even have been an outlaw and who apparently had little connection with a forest in any sense of that ambiguous word ... on the central question of how, and above all, when the highwayman of Barnsdale was transformed into an untransmutable forest outlaw the available evidence continues to remain obstinately imprecise.

Later, when discussing the significance of the first appearance of the surname 'Robehod' in 1262, the pair thought that 'a forest myth perhaps also engaged with the earliest associations which gathered round the name. There is no evidence that when first used the name Robin Hood had any greenwood associations. By some process that name was placed against a forest background'.[1] According to Stephen Knight, the idea of his opposition to the forest laws as the reason for his outlaw status only became firmly established in novels, with the influential *Robin Hood and*

---

[1] R. B. Dobson and J. Taylor, 'Robin Hood of Barnsdale: A Fellow Though Hast Long Sought', *Northern History* 19 (1983), pp. 213–14; and '"Rymes of Robyn Hood": The Early Ballads and the *Gest*', in Carpenter, *Robin Hood*, p. 40.

his Men of the Greenwood, by Henry Gilbert, published in 1912, being of particular significance in that respect.[2] Knight also pointed out that, because the criminality of killing deer contrary to the forest law does not appear in specific incidents in the medieval or later tales, episodes depicting it were only finally added to the legend in new Robin Hood stories devised for twentieth-century cinema, perhaps crucially in the 1938 film starring Errol Flynn, because the setting seemed to require it.[3] Tony Pollard, on the other hand, has shown that, by the time of the *Gest* in the fifteenth century, Robin was himself identified as an outlawed yeoman forester, supposed to be a maintainer of, rather than a trespasser against, the forest laws.[4]

Evidence firmly linking the outlaw with a forest, whether in general or with reference to Sherwood, does not appear until the first half of the fifteenth century. Perhaps the earliest known mention of Sherwood as Robin's haunt comes in a scribbled poem in an east midlands manuscript now at Lincoln Cathedral, written in about 1425, where he is said to be standing in Sherwood: it begins 'Robyn Hod in Scherewod stod'.[5] The phrase 'Robin Hood in Barnsdale stood' is a commoner version of this maxim, not linking him to the forest, and is first mentioned in a law report recording proceedings in the Common Bench in 1429, and subsequently repeated in the same context.[6] 'Greenwood' is a third alternative, used in an acrostic from a Wiltshire parliamentary election return of 1432. The relevant section reads 'Robyn, hode, Inne, Grenewode, Stode'.[7] The clearest evidence linking the outlaw with the forest comes from the end of the same decade, when Piers Venables and his followers, who fled to the woods in Derbyshire or Staffordshire in 1439 after rescuing a prisoner, were likened to Robin Hood and his 'meyne'.[8] By this time, however, we are almost, or even actually, into the period of the surviving tales. There is no explanation in them as to why Robin came to be linked with the greenwood; it was simply taken for granted. His criminality as related in the *Gest* consists to a minor extent of offences against the forest law. Robin and his dinner 'guest' the knight dine on the 'noumbles' (entrails) of the deer, as well as swans, pheasants and river fowl. That meal seems

[2] Knight, *Mythic Biography*, pp. 175–76; *Reading Robin Hood: Content, Form and Reception in the Outlaw Myth* (Manchester, 2015), pp. 123, 183, 208–89, 244; 'Robin Hood and the Forest Laws', *The Bulletin of the International Association for Robin Hood Studies* 1 (2017), pp. 1–14.

[3] Knight, *Mythic Biography*, pp. 20–21, 157, 164, 168, 178. See also Holt, *Robin Hood*, p. 65.

[4] Pollard, *Imagining Robin Hood*, chapter 2.

[5] Lincoln Cathedral Library, MS 132, f. 100v; R. M. Thomson, *Catalogue of the Manuscripts of Lincoln Cathedral Library* (Woodbridge, 1989), p. 102. See Figure 6.

[6] For the details, see p. 35.

[7] TNA, C 219/14/3, part 2, no. 101; Holt, *Robin Hood*, pp. 69–70.

[8] For the details, see below, p. 191.

to have been consumed in Barnsdale, where the knight was waylaid, but Barnsdale was not, and was not said to be, a royal forest, so the hunting of deer there would not have been illegal. The 'noumbles' of the deer were in any case the offal, usually (although this is not universally accepted) given to the servants of the hunters after the hunt, or to the lower orders of society generally. This is often regarded as the origin of the expression 'eating humble (umble) pie', signifying an acknowledgment by the person in question that he or she is in the wrong.[9] Elsewhere in the *Gest*, however, Robin is held to be responsible for the disappearance of deer from Plumpton park, and one passage shows him to be an habitual offender against the venison: he 'always slewe the kynges dere, And welt them at his wyll.'[10] This taking of deer from a royal park is plainly a forest offence, and here Robin is related by the story teller to real events that took place near the end of the reign of Edward II. There is some dispute as to which Plumpton, of three possible places of that name, in Lancashire, Yorkshire and Cumberland, is meant. Attacks on royal forests, particularly in Lancashire, but also in Yorkshire and to a lesser extent in Staffordshire and Derbyshire, took place at that time. These, however, were dealt with by the use of commissions of oyer and terminer and the itinerant court of King's Bench, not foresters or itinerant forest justices, or the sheriffs of those counties.[11]

There are no indications in the *Gest* or in the early tales generally that the sheriff was trying to hunt Robin Hood down for forest offences, and there are no references to forest justices or the local forest courts established to deal with offenders. The 'high justice' at York mentioned in the *Gest* was not a forest justice. His concern is the repayment of a debt, and debt litigation was under the jurisdiction of the courts of common law, especially the Common Bench. This court was normally resident in Westminster Hall, but sat at York for up to six years at a time on several occasions between 1298 and 1338, during the Scottish wars.[12] A forester,

---

[9] A detailed account of the dismemberment of the deer and of the use of the term 'noumbles' is given in *Sir Gawain and the Green Knight*: see W. P. Marvin, *Hunting Law and Ritual in Medieval English Literature* (Cambridge, 2006), pp. 150–51.

[10] *Gest*, stanzas 32, 357–66; D&T, pp. 81, 105.

[11] Holt, *Robin Hood*, pp. 101–02; *cf.* D&T, pp. 78 note 1, 105 note 1. For more detail about the places, see Chapter 5.

[12] D. M. Broome, 'Exchequer Migrations to York in the Thirteenth and Fourteenth Centuries', *Essays in Medieval History Presented to T. F. Tout* (Manchester, 1925), ed. A. G. Little and F. M. Powicke, pp. 291–300. The 'high justice' might possibly be based on Robert of Lexington, a justice of the Common Bench from 1221 onwards and its chief justice from 1236 to 1244. He came from Laxton (Lexington) in Nottinghamshire, but held the Yorkshire church of Rotherham from 1227 and was a protégé of the important Vescy family from that county. He was frequently commissioned to hear assizes in Yorkshire

however, does have an important role in bringing the king into personal contact with the outlaw who has plundered his deer. In the *Gest*, the plan to take the king and five knights into the forest to find Robin while disguised as monks is suggested by 'a proude fostere, That stode by our kynges kne'. When they do meet, Robin justifies his deer-poaching to the king, who is in the guise of an abbot, on the grounds of necessity: 'We lyve by our kynges dere, Other shyft have not we'. Even after the king's identity is revealed and Robin accepts his offer to enter his service, he adds the caveat that 'I wyll come agayne full soone, And shote at the donne deer, As I am wonte to done'.[13] The plea rolls of the justices in eyre of the forest, which survive in some numbers from the mid-thirteenth to the mid-fourteenth centuries, provide some instances of individuals or gangs of what might be called 'professional poachers'. The most habitual hunters were the aristocracy, the gentry and their servants, while foresters themselves were common offenders. Jean Birrell has suggested that some men appear in the eyre records so often, and in such circumstances, as to suggest that 'poaching was for them a major activity and at least a part of their means of livelihood'. She also found evidence that some of them regularly disposed of illicit venison to receivers. These poachers ranged from minor landowners and members of their families to men of near peasant status, operating mainly in very small numbers but sometimes in larger gangs.[14] The *Gest* does not place Robin Hood in this category. He and his men take deer to feed themselves or, as in the Plumpton park episode, out of bravado in defiance of the forest law. The only other reference to the venison in the early tales is in *Robin Hood and the Monk*, when Little John and Much are in Sherwood Forest watching out for a monk who is on his way to tell the king of Robin's capture. Either John, or possibly Much, makes an inconsequential remark that they should 'spare non of this venison, That gose in thys vale'.[15]

Robin, therefore, is an incorrigible hunter, but the tales provide no specific incident of an offence against the venison to set alongside the

---

during his career as an assize justice from 1223 to 1244: D. Crook, 'Dynastic Conflict in Thirteenth-Century Laxton', in *Thirteenth Century England XI*, ed. B. Weiler, J. Burton, P. Schofield and K. Stöber (Woodbridge, 2007), pp. 193–214; and 'Robert of Lexington, Chief Justice of the Bench, 1236–44', *Laws, Lawyers and Texts: Studies in Medieval Legal History in Honour of Paul Brand*, ed. S. Jenks, J. Rose and C. Whittick (Brill, Leiden and Boston, Mass., 2012), pp. 149–175. For the suggestion that the justice was Thomas de Moulton, who was resident in York from 1332 to 1335, see p. 113.

[13] *Gest*, stanzas 367, 377, 417; D&T, pp. 105–06, 109.
[14] D. Crook, 'The Records of Forest Eyres in the Public Record Office, 1179 to 1670', *Journal of the Society of Archivists* 17 (1996), pp. 183–193; J. Birrell, 'Who Poached the King's Deer? A Study in Thirteenth-Century Crime', *Midland History* 7 (1982), pp. 9–25, esp. 13–15.
[15] D&T, p. 118, stanza 37.

robberies in Barnsdale described elsewhere in the *Gest*. If an original Robin Hood were thought to have flourished in the period after the issue of the Charter of the Forest in 1217 and its reissue in 1225, he would not in any case have been liable to the severe corporal penalties of blinding, emasculation and even death that had been available as punishments for offences against the venison in the twelfth and early thirteenth centuries. In the Charter they were replaced by lesser penalties. Anyone convicted of taking deer could redeem himself by paying a fine. If he could not afford to do so, he was to remain in prison for a year and a day, after which he would be released if he could find pledges for his future conduct; if he could not he would have to abjure the realm, that is, go abroad and never return.[16] Severe as abjuration was, it was mild compared with the savage penalties that could have been imposed by forest justices in the previous century.

The forest, in the general sense of a wooded wilderness rather than specifically an area subject to the forest laws, was a favourite refuge for people who wanted to lie low or use it as a base for criminal activities.[17] It was on at least one occasion a place where significant numbers of people went to hide from the king's justices. When the first eyre for common pleas in Cornwall for over thirty years was announced in 1233, everyone, according to the annals of Dunstable, fled to the woods. They were ordered to return to the king's peace and live according to the laws of England, the only exception being made for homicides.[18] Ordinary criminals could escape to the forest to evade pursuit by hue and cry, as for instance did the thieves who burgled a house at Studley in Wiltshire in 1286 and escaped into the royal forest, probably Chippenham forest, nearby.[19] Forest or woodland areas were also useful places in which criminals could detain kidnap victims. On 31 October 1278 Nicholas de Leycester of Wath upon Dearne in Yorkshire was travelling south on the north road in Nottinghamshire to appear as a defendant in a civil case before the Common Bench at Westminster during the following week.

[16] J. C. Holt, *Magna Carta*, 3rd edition (Cambridge, 2015), appendix 13; translation in *English Historical Documents*, II, ed D. C. Douglas and G. W. Greenaway (London, 1981), pp. 337–40 (1217), 347–49 (1225). Two of the post-medieval ballads, closely similar, *Robin Hood Rescuing Three Squires from the Sheriff* (1670) and *Robin Hood Rescuing the Three Squires from Nottingham Gallows* (undated), referred, probably unwittingly, to the pre-1217 forest world, because a widow's three sons were in the tale condemned to die 'for slaying of the king's fallow deer': Child (1861), pp. 261, 263, 268.

[17] For some thirteenth-century examples, see *CR 1237–42*, pp. 137–38, 144–45, and C. R. Young, *The Royal Forests of Medieval England* (Leicester, 1979), pp. 105–06, 193.

[18] *AM* III, p. 135: omnes ad sylvas fugerunt.

[19] H. R. T. Summerson, 'The Enforcement of the Statute of Winchester, 1285–1327', *Journal of Legal History* 13 (1992), pp. 237, 247–48.

Between Muskham and Newark he was seized by unknown robbers and led into Sherwood. He was so badly treated by them that he lay ill in his bed for three weeks, or at least that was the excuse he later gave to the court, in January 1279, for his failure to appear at the due date.[20] The section of the road in question was about twelve miles from the nearest part of the royal forest, as defined in the perambulation of its boundaries in 1227, but it was the place of refuge for which the criminals naturally made with their victim. At a higher social level, after the senior royal justice Richard de Willoughby was kidnapped by the notorious Folville gang on the road between Melton Mowbray and Leicester in 1332, he was moved 'from wood to wood' while his captors negotiated for his ransom.[21]

More usually, the woods within royal forests were the refuges of fugitives who had committed, or were suspected of having committed, criminal acts, and who would be outlawed in the county court if they failed to return. In the early Robin Hood tales the forest woods serve mainly as a hiding place for criminals whose principal activity is highway robbery, like those whose views were expressed in the 'Outlaw's Song Of Trailbaston', dated to the time of the sessions of the justices of trailbaston in 1305-7. The author, professedly an old soldier of Edward I's Flemish, Scottish and Gascon wars, wrote in French and was clearly a cultured and well-informed individual, perhaps, in the view of comments about the process of ecclesiastical law, a minor cleric. He resolves to keep to the woods, characterised as 'the green wood (*vert bois*) of Belregard', where there is no bad law, although he insists that he is not an intentional killer or a bad robber who would harm ordinary people. The names of the four justices who are mentioned are those who were commissioned to visit the shires of south-west England, so the author was probably from one of those counties. Two of them he regarded as good men, but the other two were cruel, and he wanted to break their bones and cut out their tongues.[22] In 1390-1 William Beckwith, during a violent dispute with the forester of Knaresborough forest, was able to hide from a judicial commission established to deal with him by fleeing to the woods with his men.[23] As already mentioned, Robin Hood

---

[20] TNA, CP 40/28, rot. 11 [AALT-IMG 9992].

[21] E. L. G. Stones, 'The Folvilles of Ashby Folville, Leicestershire, and their Associates in Crime, 1326–1347', *Transactions of the Royal Historical Society*, 5th series 7 (1957), pp. 117–36, at 122.

[22] 'Per ce me tendroi antre bois sur le jolyf umbray; Là n'y a faucité ne nul male lay; Unque ne fu homicide, certes à moun voler, Ne mal robberes pur gent damager': *Thomas Wright's Political Songs of England*, with a new introduction by P. Coss (Cambridge, 1996), pp. 232, 234, 236. See also D&T, pp. 250–54, for comment and English translation.

[23] J. G. Bellamy, 'The Northern Rebellions in the Later Years of Richard II', *Bulletin of the John Rylands Library* 47 (1965), pp. 257; *Polychronicon Ranulfi*

himself had become firmly associated with flight to the woods by 1439. A petition to parliament mentioned the activities of Piers Venables, a Derbyshire gentleman from Aston who, after taking part in the rescue of a prisoner, John Forman of Snelston, at Sudbury, when he was being taken to Tutbury castle in Staffordshire, became a fugitive. 'After that tyme', according to the petition, and 'havinge no liflode ne sufficeante of goodes', he 'gadered and assembled unto him many misdoers, being of his clothinge, ... and in maner of insurrection, wente into the wodes in that contre, like as it hadde be Robynhode and his meyne'. They went on to terrorise the men of Scropton and made a foray into Cheshire, 'kepyn the wodes and strange contrays'.[24] Robin has been associated with the practice of using woods as a place of refuge ever since, but even in the mid-fourteenth century it was not inevitable that ambushes in woods would be thought of as related to him. In 1357 King John II of France, who had been captured following the battle of Poitiers in the previous year, was being led by his captor, Edward Prince of Wales, from Winchester to London. As they passed near a forest, perhaps the notorious Pass of Alton, 500 men dressed in green, like robbers or men of bad intent, and equipped with bows and arrows, swords and bucklers, ambushed them. The king marvelled greatly, and asked the prince what kind of men they were. He replied that they were English foresters living 'par sauvagine' by choice, and were accustomed to do so every day. It is to be assumed that the 'ambush' had been devised as an entertainment for the captive king, and that he took it as such. The chronicler, writing at St Mary's abbey in York up to forty years after the event, did not overtly connect the incident with Robin Hood, who according to the *Gest* ambushed and robbed the abbey's cellarer after earlier rescuing the poor Lancashire knight from the financial clutches of the abbot.[25]

The woods were where suspects fled to avoid prison, not necessarily where they committed crimes, although roads through them might of course provide good opportunities for robbery. The statute of Winchester

---

Higden, ed. J. R. Lumby (London, Rolls Series, 1886), p. 239: tandem cum paucis silvarum latibula expetiit ut ipsum de suis inimicis salvaret.

[24] *Rotuli Parliamentorum*, 7 vols. (London, Record Commission, 1783–1832), V, p. 16. Fifteen of his followers are named, all of them yeomen and seven of them from the village of Doveridge, near the Staffordshire boundary. Forman was arrested just after Christmas 1438.

[25] *The Anonimalle Chronicle, 1333–1381*, ed. V. H. Galbraith (Manchester, 1927), p. 41; and for the date of the passage, see pp. xxii–xxiv. For accounts of this episode, see Holt, *Robin Hood*, p. 158; Pollard, *Imagining Robin Hood*, p. 93; both give an incorrect page reference. It has recently been suggested that the story 'contained the kernel of the *Gest*: of men living outside the law, in the forest, making their living by robbing travellers, and dressed in green': R. W. Hoyle, 'A Re-Reading of the *Gest of Robin Hood*', NMS 61 (2017), pp. 71, 107–08.

of 1285 ordered that woods which lay alongside public highways were to be cut back for 200 feet on either side to reduce the risk of ambushes, and presumably this provision was intended to apply to woods in the king's forests as well as elsewhere.[26] Such a solution had been tried locally on royal instructions before 1285. For example, in 1258 the king, in response to complaints about murders and robberies perpetrated by malefactors lurking in his wood of Hopwas in Staffordshire, 'on account of the density of the trees there' (*propter spissitudinem eiusdem bosci*) ordered the keeper of Cannock forest to cause the underwood of the pass of Hopwas and adjacent parts to be cut back at his own expense, to secure the way through the pass.[27] A forest setting was the haunt of the early outlaw Eustace the Monk who, during his dispute with the count of Boulogne between 1203 and 1205, operated from the forest of Hardelot south of Boulogne.[28] Eustace was given lands in England by King John and was heavily involved in the cross-Channel warfare that eventually resulted in his death in 1217, so it may have influenced the development of the Robin Hood legend.[29] A forest was also the scene of the later story of *Adam Bell, Clim of the Clough and William of Cloudesley*, set in the Cumberland forest of Inglewood and the city of Carlisle, which has close parallels with the story of Robin Hood himself.[30]

Robin's enmity with the sheriff of Nottingham confirms that his most serious offences were not against the forest law. It was the duty of foresters and forest justices, not the sheriff, to enforce it, and the sheriff pursues Robin because he is an outlawed robber, not because he is a forest offender.[31] Thirteenth-century sheriffs had increasing responsibilities for the ever more complex processes of the common law, enforcing the observance of the king's peace, administering the local courts of shire and hundred, and accounting annually for crown income in their counties at the Exchequer. Their forest-related roles were only aspects of these duties.

[26] Summerson, 'The Enforcement of the Statute of Winchester', pp. 232–50.
[27] C 60/55, m. 11; *Calendar of Fine Rolls 42 Henry III*, no. 217 (online). See also CR 1237–42, p. 239.
[28] G. S. Burgess, *Two Medieval Outlaws: Eustace the Monk and Fouke Fitz Waryn* (Cambridge, 1997), pp. viii–ix. The tale was written down after 1223 and before 1284, perhaps between 1223 and 1235.
[29] Keen, *Outlaws*, pp. 53–63; Holt, *Robin Hood*, pp. 63–65.
[30] For the background and text, see D&T, pp. 258–73; Child (1861), V, pp. 124–159, and (1889), III, pp. 14–30; Keen, *Outlaws*, pp. 124–25; Holt, *Robin Hood*, pp. 69–74. See also T. Hahn in *Medieval Outlaws: Ten Tales in Modern English*, ed. T. M. Ohlgren (Stroud, 1998), pp. 239–52.
[31] H. Phillips, 'Forest, Town and Road: The Significance of Places and Names in Some Robin Hood Texts', in Hahn, *Popular Culture*, pp. 197–214, at 199, mistakenly states that one of the sheriff's main duties 'was to control forests, police them, and enforce forest laws'. This was only true very occasionally and in abnormal circumstances.

The collection of the financial penalties imposed by forest justices in their respective counties, and accounting for them, were only a small part of their wider collection and accounting work. Their activities in making the administrative arrangements for forest eyres were similar to but less important than the work they carried out before eyres for common pleas could take place. Their supervision of the election of forest verderers in the county court exactly paralleled the process for electing coroners to keep crown pleas, and later for the knights to represent the county in parliament. After the Charter of the Forest made imprisonment for a year and a day the punishment for offences against the venison, the sheriff was responsible for the imprisonment of some forest offenders awaiting trial or subsequently remaining in gaol, but their numbers must always have been far fewer than the normal prison population of offenders held while awaiting trial at common law. There were in any case special forest gaols from the late twelfth century to the fifteenth century, including by 1216 one in York for prisoners from Galtres forest. These probably held most forest prisoners, although they often required extra accommodation from county gaols where there was no local forest prison or the one available was not sufficient.[32] In 1354 the one in Rockingham, serving Rockingham forest in Northamptonshire, held one Robert Hod, imprisoned while awaiting trial before the forest justices.[33] The area with which Robin Hood's crimes were usually connected, Barnsdale, was never subject to the forest laws, but it was notorious for highway robbery. The circumstances of the stories of the robberies of the knight and the cellarer of St Mary's York in Barnsdale, as told in the *Gest*, are parts of the Robin Hood legend that have no analogues among the other medieval outlaw tales, and are related to a precise and identifiable place. They are the incidents whose details are most likely to have survived more or less unscathed from the origins of the Robin Hood legend until the time of the surviving tales, and indicate that the original Robin was primarily a highway robber, not an offender against the forest laws.[34]

The most certain thing about the original Robin Hood, if there was one, is that he was a hardened criminal, and, like others of his kind, his aim was to be successful in his criminal activities, and to avoid capture and the almost inevitable death that would follow. His domain was, as the surviving medieval tales indicate, the roads and forest hideouts, not towns, which he would nevertheless sometimes visit. The tales connect Robin with only a single large town, Nottingham, and his main enemy is the sheriff of Nottingham. The significance of Nottingham in the legend derives mainly from the facts that the sheriff's office was in the castle

---

[32] R. B. Pugh, *Imprisonment in Medieval England* (Cambridge, 1968), pp. 130–32; *CR 1234–7*, pp. 295, 499; *CR 1259–61*, p. 26; *CR 1247–51*, pp. 440, 457, 467.
[33] *CCR 1354–60*, p. 23.
[34] Holt, *Robin Hood*, chapter 4, especially pp. 74–75.

there, and that it was where the county gaol was located, but there is no historical evidence to connect Robin Hood with the town until as late as 1485.[35] The world of the rural criminal is increasingly well-documented in legal and administrative records as the thirteenth century goes on, and the surviving records become even more extensive in the fourteenth and early fifteenth centuries before declining sharply during the reign of Henry VI after 1422. It is the more remarkable, therefore, that until the 1980s scholars seeking the origins of Robin Hood paid little or no attention to the records of the criminal law, although it should be pointed out that the identification and classification of the records of itinerant justices holding crown pleas was very inadequate before the work of C. A. F. Meekings at the Public Record Office during the 1950s and 1960s. This neglect of the sources was despite the prescient and well-chosen words of Maurice Keen in 1961:

> Robin Hood the yeoman is not the kind of figure to catch the limelight of medieval historical writing. He has no part to play on the grand political stage; he is a forest robber of humble political origins and his cause has to do with the conditions of the everyday social world, not with the melodramatic conspiracies which troubled the sleep of kings. We must seek therefore for men of his stamp not in the chronicles but in the records of everyday business, in the rolls of forest administration, in the king's orders to his sheriffs and officers, and in the decisions of antique courts. It is here if anywhere that we will hear of the duties of his prototype, obscure bandits who had their hour of local fame and were then forgotten.[36]

The difference is that Robin Hood, one of these notorious local criminals, was remembered far beyond his own lifetime, because of an unusual combination of circumstances. His original personality and doings, perhaps not widely known in accurate detail in the first place, quickly became overlain by literary conceits and stock tales, either borrowed from the stories of other men of a similar type or from among a pool of stories in general circulation. These concoctions were then widely transmitted through the ever more sophisticated means of dissemination devised by successive generations. The records of Keen's 'antique courts', which, while not full enough in extent or content in the crucial decade to settle conclusively the identity of the original Robin Hood proposed in this book, nevertheless contribute significantly to that task, and provide a wealth of background material.

The desperation of the typical medieval criminal, probably starving and without an established social support network, has been discussed and documented by Henry Summerson in a number of articles since

---

[35] See p. 146.
[36] Keen, *Outlaws*, pp. 191–92.

the 1980s. Such men (and they were overwhelmingly men) sought anonymity and kept a low profile in order to maximise their chances of escaping detection. Others, far fewer in number, were not averse to the kind of celebrity brought about by notoriety, typified by the legendary gunslingers of the American 'Wild West' in the late nineteenth century, whether they deliberately set out to achieve it or, more likely, did so by accident. Robin Hood was one of the latter, perhaps developing the 'truculent independence' which led criminals to attack the more prosperous rather than ordinary people, many of whom were little better off than themselves.[37] Stripped of the later developments which provided him with other guises, it is most likely that the original Robin was a desperate criminal, one who seems to have achieved an essentially local or perhaps regional fame, and to have enjoyed success and freedom from capture for a long enough period to achieve that celebrity status. Despite this, by the fifteenth century, when some of the tales in their surviving form existed, his criminal status barely registered. As Tony Pollard has reminded us, by then a gang of hardened highwaymen and poachers had been transformed into 'jocular, heroic, swashbuckling adventurers'.[38]

Robin's reputation for violence did however survive into the fifteenth century tales, a few elements of criminal brutality remaining amongst the relative blandness of much of their content. They include ten killings, the sheriff suffering that fate twice, not counting the twelve men Robin is said to have dispatched when fighting his way out of the parish church of Nottingham in *Robin Hood and the Monk*.[39] The most brutal incident is the decapitation of the monk and the 'litull page' by Little John and Much in the same poem, to keep them quiet.[40] Both are more innocent, especially the child, than Guy of Gisborne, the bounty hunter, who receives the same treatment in *Robin Hood and Guy of Gisborne*, the most forbidding of the early tales, after Robin defeats him in combat.[41] There are other implied or actual references to Robin's criminality between the time of the origin of the legend and that of the earliest surviving tales. Several of the men with 'Robinhood' or 'Robehood' surnames identified in the plea rolls of the later thirteenth century were suspected criminals

---

[37] H. R. T. Summerson, 'Crime and Society in Medieval Cumberland', *Transactions of the Cumberland and Westmorland Antiquarian and Archaeological Society* 81 (1982), pp. 120–21.

[38] A. J. Pollard, 'Idealising Criminality: Robin Hood in the Fifteenth Century', in *Pragmatic Utopias: Ideals and Communities, 1200–1630*, ed. R. Horrox and S. Rees-Jones (2001), pp. 156–73; and Pollard, *Imagining Robin Hood*, chapter 4, especially p. 82.

[39] Pollard, *Imagining Robin Hood*, pp. 96–97.

[40] *Robin Hood and the Monk*, stanza 52; D&T, p. 119; Pollard, *Imagining Robin Hood*, p. 98; Holt, *Robin Hood*, p. 11.

[41] *Robin Hood and Guy of Gisborne*, stanza 41; D&T, p. 144.

or outlaws,[42] and in the fifteenth century there are incidents recorded in detail which make the point more clearly. Piers Venables and his followers were likened to Robin Hood and his 'meyne'. The yeomen and labourers, armed with jacks, swords, staves and cudgels, who lay in wait beside the road at South Acre in Norfolk (a non-forest county) in 1441, waylaying travellers and threatening to kill Sir John Harsyk, chanted the song 'We are Robynhodesmen men, war, war, war'.[43] Violence associated with the outlaw could also erupt in towns, as in the disorder in the Staffordshire town of Willenhall in 1498 connected with his developing role as a peaceful, although rumbustious, collector for church charities.[44] It continued even into the period of religious reform in the following century, when Robin's rule as a character in the May Games was at its height. The outlaw was still a criminal, despite the fact that his current activities were of financial help to many parish churches. His essential criminality, thus gradually obscured, was never fully recovered, as newer roles were foisted upon him as the centuries passed. By the late twentieth century it was even possible for a retired senior judge with a controversial reputation to write to his local newspaper in Nottinghamshire and complain about what he regarded as undue leniency shown to criminals against the will of the majority of the public. The solution was, he thought, to 'let the spirit of Robin Hood ride again for justice for the ordinary citizens'.[45] In his mind, Robin had become a potential solution to the problem of criminal activity rather than the problem itself.

Only a few thirteenth-century chronicles took any close interest in notable crimes and criminals. The annals of Dunstable priory in Bedfordshire, which had its own crown pleas jurisdiction (confirmed in 1219), its own coroners (from 1228) and its own gaol and gaoler, made frequent references to local offenders dealt with by royal eyre and gaol delivery justices sitting there. More occasionally they mention notorious incidents that occurred some distance away. Examples are the lynching in 1284 of Lawrence Duket, at the church of St Mary Arches in London, after he had wounded Ralph Crepin in Westcheap and taken sanctuary there; the robbery of the archdeacon of Richmond at one of his manors near Exeter in 1293; and the severe treatment of Simon le Constable, a 'noble', by the eyre justices in York in the same year, leading to his death in gaol.[46]

---

[42] D. Crook, 'The Sheriff of Nottingham and Robin Hood: The Genesis of the Legend?', in *Thirteenth Century England II: Proceedings of the Newcastle upon Tyne Conference 1987*, ed. P. R. Coss and S. D. Lloyd (Woodbridge, 1988), pp. 59–69 at 59.
[43] P. C. Maddern, *Violence and Social Disorder: East Anglia 1422–42* (Oxford, 1992), pp. 108–09.
[44] See Chapter 2.
[45] *Newark Advertiser*, 26 October 1990.
[46] *AM III*, ed. H. R. Luard (London, Rolls Series, 1866), pp. 54–55, 105, 108, 193,

Not far from Dunstable, at the abbey of St Albans in Hertfordshire, the great monastic chronicler Matthew Paris (d. 1259) gave full treatment to the trial of the robbers of the pass of Alton, in northern Hampshire, in 1249.[47] His interest in this case was exceptional, however, because of its wider importance. The victims were foreign merchants from Brabant, and attracted the attention of Henry III during two visits to Winchester, the city of his birth, where the trial took place. Paris did not take any interest in ordinary criminal trials heard in the eyres for common pleas held by royal justices visiting Hertfordshire, such as that in 1255, a session not even mentioned in his chronicle. However, in that same year he did make reference to the killing of Sir John de Seldeford, a knight of the liberty of St Albans, and his chaplain John, a regular canon, and the hanging of the killer, his son and heir William, in London. He was presumably attracted to this sensational case by the association of the victim with the abbey, the patricidal nature of the crime and the death of a cleric.[48]

The Worcester annals, on the other hand, record all the visits of the justices in eyre to Worcester under Henry III, in 1221, 1226, 1232, 1235, 1241, 1249, 1255 and 1275; those of the justices of the forest in 1232, 1240, 1247, 1262 and 1270; one by the justices of gaol delivery in 1271; and finally the sessions of the justices of trailbaston in Worcester, Hereford and Shrewsbury in 1305. They also mention, for no apparent reason, the visit of forest justices to the New Forest in Hampshire in 1280.[49] Despite this, no reference is made to any of the specific criminals who were tried before these courts, and the annals do not mention any of the local spots notorious for robberies, such as Linholt Wood in Feckenham forest.[50] Nevertheless, in the annal for 1283 attention is drawn to the fate of a certain William, a robber who had earlier been a monk at Wenlock before becoming a 'prince of thieves' (*princeps latronum*), and who was captured with a horse and brought to justice at Oswaldslow on 2 August that year 'with horses and arms' (probably meaning an armed escort) 'so that he could not be rescued by other thieves' (perhaps members of his gang), 'and there he got what he deserved'.[51] A notorious thief in the counties of the Welsh border who was a former monk was bound

---

231, 246–47, 261–62, 265–66, 278, 302, 321–22, 336, 342, 353–54, 395–96; 314, 377.

[47] M. T. Clanchy, 'Highway Robbery and Trial by Battle in the Hampshire Eyre of 1249', in *Medieval Legal Records Edited in Memory of C. A. F. Meekings* (London, 1978), pp. 26–61; Matthew Paris, *Chronica Majora* V, ed. H. R. Luard (London, Rolls Series, 1880), pp. 56–60.

[48] *Chronica Majora* V, p. 490.

[49] *AM* IV, ed. H. R. Luard (London, Rolls Series, 1869), pp. 413, 419, 423, 427, 431–33, 438, 443, 447, 460, 468, 477, 558.

[50] R. H. Hilton, *A Medieval Society: The West Midlands at the End of the Thirteenth Century* (Cambridge, 1966, revised edition 1983), p. 254.

[51] *AM* IV, p. 487: quidam Willelmus, prius frater de Wenlac, postea princeps

to attract the notice of a monastic writer at Worcester cathedral priory. Also, the chronicle of the foundation of Dale (also known as Stanley Park) abbey, in eastern Derbyshire, written by Thomas of Muskham in the mid-thirteenth century, mentions an unnamed 'very notorious outlaw' (*uthlagus famosissimus*), who frequented those parts on account of the road running between Nottingham and Derby through the forest, the whole of the country between Derby bridge and the River Erewash being within the royal forest at that time.[52] After having seen in a dream a vision of a golden cross on the future site of the abbey, from a hill called Lindrick beyond the abbey gate to the west, he repented of his misdeeds and lived out his life as a hermit in Deepdale, near the later abbey site and part of the manor of Ockbrook. This outlaw was placed in the reign of Henry II, at which time the area was indeed afforested, as the chronicle said.[53] It sounds as if this man was a highway robber, like Robin Hood, active on a road running through a royal forest. A version of this story was later associated with Robin Hood (Whood) by the Stamford antiquary Francis Peck, in a fanciful attempt to attach an early story of an unnamed twelfth-century outlaw to the legend of the man who was by then firmly established as the most famous outlaw of all.[54] In his case the presumably local fame of the outlaw was recorded simply because he was a small part of the story of the foundation of a monastic house. The references to these two men, only one of them named, preserve the memory of rare examples of criminals notorious for a short time in their own regions or localities, but whose memory faded away thereafter. Robin Hood was a similar but exceptional example, whose fame grew, rather than diminished, initially by chance, leading to widespread, and eventually global, fame.

In his trenchant criticisms of Joseph Hunter's proposed identification of the household porter of Edward II in 1323-4 as the original Robin Hood, Francis Child made much of the point that Hunter's candidate was

---

latronum, captus cum equo ducebatur ad judicium de Oswaldeslawe cum equis et armis, ne ab aliis latronibus eriperetur; et ibi prout meruit accepit.

[52] *Monasticon Anglicanum*, ed. W. Dugdale, rev. J. Caley, H. Ellis and B. Bandinel, 6 vols. in 8 (London, 1817–30), VI, pp. 892–95; F. Peck, *Desiderata Curiosa* (1735), liber xv, pp. 1–10, esp. p. 4 (London, 1779 edition, p. 563); W. H. St John Hope, 'Chronicle of the Abbey of St Mary de Parco Stanley, or Dale, Derbyshire', *Journal of the Derbyshire Archaeological and Natural History Society* 5 (1883), pp. 1–31, especially p. 7; and see H. M. Colvin, *The White Canons in England* (Oxford, 1951), pp. 170–78, 386 note 1. The passage reads: Fuit quidam uthlagus famosissimus partes istas frequentans propter iter commeantium inter Notingham et Darby per forestam. Erat enim tota patria inter pontem Darby et aquam de Yrewys afforesta eo tempore.

[53] D. Crook, 'The Forest between the Erewash and the Derwent, 1154 to 1225', *Derbyshire Archaeological Journal* 110 (1990), pp. 93–104.

[54] British Library, Add. MS 28638, f. 16, printed in Holt, *Robin Hood*, pp. 180–81. See also pp. 61–62.

not mentioned by any contemporary writer. 'It is altogether anomalous', he wrote, 'that a popular champion who attained so extraordinary a notoriety in song ... should be passed over without one word of notice from any authoritative historian'. He went on to mention a 'singularly exact parallel' case, the famous outlaw Adam Gurdon (curiously rendered as 'Gordon'), active during the aftermath of the Barons' War in 1267–67, in Hampshire and neighbouring counties.[55] This is exactly the chronological context in which Robin Hood was placed by Walter Bower, writing in Scotland in the 1440s, living 'amongst the woodland briars and thorns', but in no identified area. Gurdon had a refuge in Alton forest or wood, where he was eventually captured and then imprisoned by lord Edward, soon to become Edward I. He is referred to by several chronicles and mentioned in government records, but he was not anything approaching a parallel to the legendary outlaw.[56] As Child himself wrote, 'the Robin Hood of our ballads is neither patriot under ban, nor prescribed rebel', but 'an outlaw for venyson', like Adam Bell, 'and one who superadds to deer-stealing the irregularity of a genteel highway robbery'. The gulf between the two outlaws, one a highway robber of only local significance, and the other one among several regional anti-government rebels, was vast. By 1272, restored to favour, Gurdon was himself responsible for arresting notorious thieves, like Robin Hood, and taking them to prison in Winchester.[57]

The *Gest* locates Robin principally in Barnsdale, in southern Yorkshire north of Doncaster.[58] Barnsdale's importance principally derived from the fact that the section of the great north road running from Doncaster to York passed through it, as it still does today. By 1306 it had some notoriety as an unsafe place through which to travel, because the escort that attended the Scottish bishops of St Andrews and Glasgow, and the abbot of Scone, while they were travelling from Pontefract to Tickhill, was reinforced by twenty archers 'on account of Barnsdale' (*propter Barnisdale*).[59] The place-name 'the Sayles', on a hill adjacent to the north road just south east of Wentbridge in Barnsdale, and the place at which, according to the *Gest*, Robin robbed his victims, has been much discussed since it was conclusively identified by Dobson and Taylor in 1972. Whether or not 'the Sayles' was a regular site for robberies in the thirteenth century cannot be established, because no references to it before 1300 have been found. One fourteenth century robbery recorded

---

[55] Child (1861), V, pp. xiv–xxiv.
[56] *AM* II, p. 370 (Waverley); III, p. 241 (Dunstable); IV, pp. 187, 189 (Wykes). His family had land in Alton, and before his rebellion he had been keeper of Woolmer forest in Hampshire: *CR 1264–8*, p. 284; *CPR 1258–66*, p. 557.
[57] *CPR 1266–72*, p. 695.
[58] See Chapter 5 and Map 1.
[59] TNA, E 101/13/5.

as taking place there involved at least two men from the nearest large town. In 1329 a commission of oyer and terminer was issued in respect of the robbery at 'le Saylles' of William of Felton (probably a Northumberland man travelling along the north road) by two men of Doncaster and five others, including a woman, whose place of domicile was not stated.[60]

The earliest reference to a robbery at 'the Sayles' yet identified comes from the first decade of the fourteenth century, in the record of the trial of an approver called John son of Henry of Wheatley.[61] An approver was a captured criminal who 'turned king's evidence' against alleged former accomplices and fought judicial duels against them in the hope of saving himself from the gallows at their expense. As in this case, the testimony of such men often revealed the extent of criminal networks. Wheatley was a man either from the place of that name in north Nottinghamshire or, perhaps more likely, from Wheatley near Doncaster, and whose activities, significantly, link Nottinghamshire and Yorkshire, Sherwood and Barnsdale.[62] In Nottingham in 1307, at a gaol delivery held before Edmund de Eyncourt and William Inge, justices of trailbaston, Wheatley was sentenced to be hanged after a jury failed to convict those he had accused of complicity with him. One of his confessed crimes was committed at 'le Sailes' in Yorkshire, where he stole two blankets, two linen sheets and 15 ells of linen. Moving south into Nottinghamshire, under the administration of a different sheriff, he handed the stolen goods to Amice, the wife of William de Staveley of Alfreton (in Derbyshire), for disposal, and in company with her, her husband and their servant Robert, robbed a man of 17s. 6d. at Osland, which is still the name of a wood in Thoresby Park.[63] Then, to the south of Nottingham, in conjunction with William, a chaplain of Thorpe by Wysall, he took 9 marks and a bay horse from a brother of the Yorkshire abbey of Rievaulx at Bunny (*Boneye Rys*), on the road from Nottingham

---

[60] TNA, C 81/163/2703. *CPR 1327–30*, p. 432, gives the place of the robbery as Skelbrooke, a small hamlet in Barnsdale over a mile south of Barnsdale Bar and between three and four miles from the Sayles. See also Chapter 6.
[61] TNA, JUST 3/55/2, rot. 1 [AALT-IMG 0015].
[62] A. H. Smith, *The Place-Names of the West Riding of Yorkshire* I (EPNS XXX, Cambridge, 1961), pp. 36–37. The name of the Yorkshire place now survives only in the name of Wheatley Hall Road, a section of the A630, but Wheatley Hall, the subject of a licence to crenellate issued by Edward II in 1311 (*CPR 1307–13*, p. 340), and later the seat of the Cooke family from 1680, stood nearby until it was demolished in 1939. See http://www.sandallpark.org.uk/links/documents/BriefHistoryofWheatley_000.pdf.
[63] Osland was a small area of royal demesne land that in 1301 had for that reason been confirmed as a detached portion of Sherwood Forest: *The Sherwood Forest Book*, ed. H. E. Boulton, Thoroton Society Record Series XXIII (1965), p. 41.

to Leicester.⁶⁴ A criminal active in Barnsdale, and who like Robin Hood in the *Gest* robbed a monk from a large Yorkshire house, was thus tried at Nottingham because he was captured in Nottinghamshire. If he had been captured in Barnsdale, he would have been sent to York castle gaol to await trial, as the later highwayman Dick Turpin was in 1738 after being arrested in the East Riding.

Criminals like Wheatley, moving between two neighbouring counties along major roads, were common. The notorious approver Walter Bloweberme, who fought a judicial duel at Winchester in 1249 against one of those he had claimed to be an accomplice, had committed robbery at Salisbury in neighbouring Wiltshire as well as in Hampshire itself.⁶⁵ At about the same time an outlaw called Batinus, who seems to have come from the area around Bradford on Avon in Wiltshire, was pursued from that county into Somerset, where he was captured; he was taken to the county gaol in Ilchester and later died there.⁶⁶ In the Devon eyre of 1238, among the wandering thieves who had to abjure the realm, there were men from Cornwall, Somerset, Wiltshire and Gloucestershire, as well as an Irishman.⁶⁷ In about 1280, four thieves committed a robbery in Devon and then quarrelled over the spoils as they passed first into Somerset and then Gloucestershire, with the one remaining alive finally being taken back to Devon and hanged for the offence.⁶⁸ Some, however, were active over a much bigger area than neighbouring counties in the same region. The widespread crimes of the approver William Rose of Loughborough, at the end of the fourteenth century, show the range of some exceptional criminals. Rose, apparently in the few months in 1388 and early 1389 before his arrest and detention in Winchester castle gaol, was active in 17 different places in 12 counties as far apart as Hampshire, Norfolk and his native Leicestershire, and had 33 different accomplices, including one from Nottingham and others from Chester, Monmouth and Ireland, during that period.⁶⁹ Between 1298 and 1305 an earlier approver, Robert Nurry, probably originating from Nottinghamshire or Derbyshire

---

64 *The Place-Names of Nottinghamshire*, ed. J. E. B. Gover, A. Mawer and F. M. Stenton (London, 1940), pp. 141, 245. The most likely place for a robbery would have been on the road to the south of the village, at Bunny Hill.
65 Clanchy, 'Highway Robbery', pp. 50–51.
66 *Crown Pleas of the Wiltshire Eyre, 1249*, ed. C. A. F. Meekings, Wiltshire Archaeological and Natural History Society, Records Branch XVI (1961), nos. 144, 288, 422.
67 *Crown Pleas of the Devon Eyre of 1238*, ed. H. R. T. Summerson, Devon and Cornwall Record Society New Series XXVIII (1985), p. xxxv, nos. 34, 357, 420, 759, 771.
68 H. R. T. Summerson, 'Crime and Society in Thirteenth-Century Devon', *Transactions of the Devonshire Association* 119 (1987), p. 81.
69 J. B. Post, 'The Evidential Value of Approvers' Appeals: The Case of William Rose, 1389', *Law and History Review* 3 (1985), pp. 91–100.

but active all over the midlands and in Yorkshire, and as far south as Gloucestershire, Suffolk and Sussex, appealed 73 men of 43 crimes committed in 20 counties.[70]

It seems unlikely that many habitual criminals acted alone, and the examples of the approvers give evidence of accomplices acting with them, before eventually turning against them in an attempt to save their own skins. The largest number of accomplices involved in any of Nurry's crimes was seven, and often there was only one or two. John son of Henry of Wheatley had a small number of accomplices for the crimes he committed in Nottinghamshire, including a married woman. William son of Robert le Fevere, alias William Robehod, active in Berkshire in or before 1261, was himself from Enborne in southern Berkshire; but of his four accomplices, three, including the two women, probably came from a place called Hannington; there were two different places of that name, one in northern Hampshire, 14 miles from Enborne, the other in Wiltshire, over 30 miles from Enborne.[71] There is a great deal of information about criminal gangs, the overwhelmingly majority of which were small, in the voluminous records of justices of gaol delivery.[72] Basing her research on fourteenth-century gaol delivery rolls from Norfolk, Northamptonshire and Yorkshire, Barbara Hanawalt calculated that over half of all recorded crimes, and 78% of robberies, were committed by two or more people. Of the robber gangs, 41% had two members, 22% had three and 12% four, while 25% had more than four. Women were involved in 12% of gangs and accounted for 5% of named gang members; their role was usually unspecified, but it is likely that many were receivers of stolen goods or harbourers of male criminals. Kin groups were included in 21% of gangs, 47% of them brothers and 33% spouses, with fathers and sons accounting for 17%, but 33% of bandit gang members came from settlements over ten miles away from their associates, if their toponyms can be relied upon to indicate their true places of origin. Minor clergy were included in 13% of gangs and comprised 7% of the known criminals, while they acted as leader of 8% of gangs. Among their victims, 37% were women. 31% of robbers and burglars were convicted.[73]

---

[70] H. R. T. Summerson, 'The Criminal Underworld of Medieval England', *Legal History* 17 (1996), pp. 204–06.

[71] D. Crook, 'Some Further Evidence Concerning the Dating of the Origins of the Legend of Robin Hood', *EHR* 99 (1984), pp. 530–34; reprinted in Knight, *Anthology*, pp. 257–61. See also Chapter 6.

[72] For detailed examples, see Summerson, 'Criminal underworld', pp. 206–08.

[73] B. A. Hanawalt, *Crime and Conflict in English Communities, 1300–1348* (Cambridge, Mass., 1979), summarized in 'Ballads and Bandits: Fourteenth-Century Outlaws and the Robin Hood Poems', *Chaucer's England: Literature in Historical Context*, ed. B. A. Hanawalt (Minneapolis, 1992), pp. 154–75; reprinted in Knight, *Anthology*, pp. 265–84. Her conclusions should be used with some caution; see the criticism of her understanding and interpretation

In the Robin Hood tales, the outlaw is shown both as having a small gang close to himself and as being able to draw on far greater numbers of men when needed. His constant partner in crime is Little John, sometimes with Scathlock and Much as a third and fourth. The large numbers of unnamed followers that he could summon when he needed them, as many as 140 yeomen according to passages in the *Gest*, seem to have more of the characteristics of a late-medieval 'bastard feudal' retinue, complete with their livery of Lincoln green, than a normal band of robbers.[74] They are Robin's 'meyne', just as the abbot of St Mary's and the knight who comes to the abbey to repay his debt have theirs.[75] Robin's meyne is also referred to in *Robin Hood and the Potter*.[76] While Robin is at the king's court, he retains, like any bastard feudal lord, as many knights and squires as he can 'to gete hym grete renowne'.[77] Piers Venables and his men, 'being of his clothinge', were in 1439 likened to 'Robyn Hode and his meyne'. One isolated early example of a liveried gang is however recorded in Yorkshire as early as 1218.[78]

Some felons, those whose crimes were quickly discovered and who were captured still bearing the signs of their misdeeds (in the case of a homicide caught literally 'red-handed'), or in the case of a thief taken 'with the mainour' (*cum manuopere*), could be quickly and legally dispatched, in some circumstances without a court hearing.[79] Examples of the pursuit and decapitation of outlaws are rare in the records of the early thirteenth century, but when more crown pleas rolls from eyres and gaol deliveries survive far more information is available. It was established practice for fleeing thieves or homicides who were captured, or outlaws on the run, to be summarily dispatched and their chattels accounted for. When a fleeing outlaw was beheaded following pursuit by hue and cry, the coroner who held the inquest on his body was supposed to send the head to the county gaol. Fugitives were sometimes chased across county boundaries.

---

of the sources, in respect of an earlier work, by R. F. Hunnisett in *The American Journal of Legal History* 22, 3 (1978), pp. 257–59. He cites her 'inability to read and translate simple sentences and an alarming lack of understanding of legal procedure'.

74 *Gest*, verses 389, 448; D&T, pp. 107, 111.
75 Pollard, *Imagining Robin Hood*, pp. 142–43; *Gest*, stanzas 23, 95, 97, 262, 335; D&T, pp. 85–86, 98, 103.
76 *Robin Hood and the Potter*, stanza 4; D&T, p. 125. There are other references to Robin's 'men', which a medieval audience might have understood to mean 'meyne', stanzas 16, 19, 65, pp. 126–27, 131.
77 *Gest*, stanzas 433–34; D&T, p. 110; Holt, *Robin Hood*, pp. 80–81; Keen, *Outlaws*, pp. 136–38.
78 See p. 218.
79 F. Pollock and F. W. Maitland, *The History of English Law before the time of Edward I* (2nd edition, edited by S. F. C. Milsom, 2 vols., Cambridge, 1968), II, pp. 578–81.

For example, in 1271 some Lincolnshire men, led by their sheriff, and some from Huntingdonshire, pursued Hugh le Prest, a felon and outlaw in Lincolnshire and a homicide in Huntingdonshire, to a house at Little Staughton in Bedfordshire and there decapitated him, giving his head to the township to carry away, 'as by law should have been done'.[80] In the entries for Oswaldslow hundred in the 1275 Worcestershire eyre roll, lists of the chattels of thieves said to have been hanged are punctuated with the odd individual said to have been decapitated, presumably after immediate pursuit and without trial. This is explicitly confirmed in the case of a man mentioned under the pleas for the manor of Bromsgrove, one of a group of thieves pursued by some men from Warwickshire, who was beheaded while the others escaped. Another example occurs in the entry for the borough of Kidderminster.[81] In the roll of the 1292 Lancashire eyre, at least 57 men and women were recorded as having been beheaded by their pursuers, either being caught with stolen goods, or in circumstances where they were clearly guilty of homicide or theft, or were outlaws or escaped prisoners who were outside the protection of the law. In a few cases only was the legality of these beheadings called into question.[82]

Accused or suspected criminals who were not immediately apprehended and did not come forward to submit to justice, but went or remained on the run, were, after the completion of a procedure lasting five months, outlawed in the county court, and that fact recorded by a coroner.[83] Records of outlawry from county court rolls can be found fairly frequently in the records of the king's courts.[84] Outlawry process was carried out against fled forest offenders as well as those accused of common law offences.[85] In the thirteenth century, F. W. Maitland concluded, outlawry remained 'the law's ultimate weapon', even though

---

[80] R. F. Hunnisett, ed., *Bedfordshire Coroners' Rolls*, Bedfordshire Historical Record Society XLI (1960), no. 45, pp 20–21.

[81] *The Worcester Eyre of 1275*, ed. J. Rőhrkasten, Worcestershire Historical Society NS XXII (2008), nos. 749, 753, 846, 873.

[82] *Crown Pleas of the Lancashire Eyre 1292*, ed. M. E. Lynch with an introduction by H. Summerson (3 vols., Record Society of Lancashire and Cheshire CXLVIII, CXLIX, CL, 2014–15), I, pp. 17–18; II, nos. 65, 186, 204, 218b, 228, 307, 307a, 719; III, nos. 856, 886, 958, 1029.

[83] On the coroner and outlaws, see R. F. Hunnisett, *The Medieval Coroner* (Cambridge, 1961), pp. 61–68. In other jurisdictions outlawry did not involve this elaborate procedure. In the county of Boulogne, Eustace the Monk seems to have become an outlaw simply because of his failure to appear when summoned before the count of Boulogne at his castle of Hardelot to answer an accusation of maladministration while in the count's service: Burgess, *Two Medieval Outlaws*, pp. 54–55. Eustace was not, however, a common criminal but 'a peer of the Boulonnaise', as he described himself.

[84] See, for example, CRR XIX, no. 2423, in this case against an appellee.

[85] Turner, *Select Pleas of the Forest*, Selden Society XIII (1901), pp. 22, 23, 32, 36, 56, etc.

before 1300 a minor form of outlawry was also becoming available to coerce civil litigants who consistently failed to comply with the court's orders, after attempts at distraint had failed to achieve that end.[86] Maitland's observation that outlawry in the thirteenth century was becoming more a criminal process than a substantive punishment is not, however, confirmed by the judicial records, and it remained punitive.[87] Nevertheless, criminous outlaws suspected of felony continued to be in more serious danger, and proof of outlawry without a subsequent pardon was still enough in the mid and later thirteenth century to secure the hanging of any outlaw who subsequently came into custody, as examples from plea rolls show.[88] A man who defied the law was outside it, in conflict with the community that wished the law to be upheld, and it was 'the right of every man to pursue him, to ravage his land, to burn his house, to hunt him down like a wild beast and slay him'. The wild animal was the wolf, and the outlaw 'bears the head of the wolf' (*caput gerat lupinum*). As late as 1292 the Shropshire county court, as reported by a court pleader, proclaimed outlawry with the word 'wolfshead' (*e pus crie Wolveseved*).[89] If an outlaw was captured and brought before justices, his outlawry condemned him to the gallows without further process. It was for that reason that the only early treatise on the criminal law, *Placita Corone*, probably written in the mid-1270s, recommended that a pardoned outlaw carry his pardon with him, because if he were caught without it he might legally be beheaded (*serra decole cum home utlage solom la ley*).[90]

The status and consequences of outlawry, however, were greatly downgraded in the following centuries. By 1277 at the latest it was regularly being used as part of mesne process in civil disputes of a personal nature, especially trespass, where the original process was by attachment, although it was not used in purely civil pleas begun by

---

[86] *De Legibus et Consuetudinibus Anglie, Bracton on the Laws and Customs of England*, ed. G. E. Woodbine, translated, with revisions and notes, by S. E. Thorne (4 vols., Cambridge, Mass., 1968–77), II, p. 359; IV, p. 368; Pollock and Maitland, I, pp. 476–77; II, pp. 549, 593.

[87] H. R. T. Summerson, 'Criminal Law in the Age of Bracton', in *The History of English Law: Centenary Essays on 'Pollock and Maitland'*, ed. J. Hudson (Proceedings of the British Academy 89, Oxford, 1996), p. 123.

[88] *The Roll and Writ File of the Berkshire Eyre of 1248*, ed. M. T. Clanchy, Selden Society XC (1973), no. 862; and *Calendar of London Trailbaston Trials under Commissions of 1305 and 1306*, ed. R. B. Pugh (London, 1975), no. 305. There is much in detail about outlawry in that period in N. D. Hurnard, *The King's Pardon for Homicide before A.D.1307* (Oxford, 1969).

[89] Pollock and Maitland, I, pp. 447–48; II, pp. 449–50; *Select Pleas of the Crown*, ed. F. W. Maitland, Selden Society I (1887), p. 23; *Year Book 20–21 Edward I*, ed. A. J. Horwood (London, Rolls Series, 1866), p. 237.

[90] *Placita Corone, or La Corone Pledee Devant Justices*, ed. J. M. Kaye, Selden Society Supplementary Series IV (1966), p. 25.

summons, such as debt, covenant or account.[91] During the fourteenth century the summary execution of outlawed criminals became exceptional, although it was sometimes carried out when a coroner's roll was found to contain a record of their outlawry. By the fifteenth century, when the Robin Hood legend was fully developed, process to outlawry was more firmly established in proceedings against civil defendants than the earlier process by distraint.[92] Outlaws were in no danger of hanging and were able in practice to hold public office. In 1445 a Sussex coroner had to be replaced because he was, and long had been, an outlaw. Others, like the possible original of Friar Tuck in the same county, continued to lurk out of harm's way. A century later, in the reign of Elizabeth, an observer noted that, to the queen's offence, the inconvenience of outlawry was so slight that nearly a quarter of the members of the Commons in the most recent parliament were known to be outlaws. In 1618 the royal nominee for the office of recorder of London was a man who had been outlawed seventeen times.[93]

Some recent writers on the history of highway robbery have characterised Robin Hood as an early, or even the first, English highwayman. 'The Robin Hood of the original legend is a highway robber. He is usually represented as courteous, at any rate to those who take his fancy, but he is a robber just the same'.[94] There are instructive parallels and differences between the development of the legend of Robin Hood and that surrounding the eighteenth-century highwayman Dick Turpin (1705-39). Originally active in his home county of Essex as a member of the so-called 'Gregory gang', he moved north in 1737 to escape detection and capture. After horse stealing activities in north Lincolnshire and the East Riding he was arrested and sent to the gaol at York castle, and he was hanged there in 1739. The later date at which Turpin lived, and the consequent availability of factual information about him and his crimes from the records of his trial and those of his associates, added to the wealth of subsequent published material about him, makes it possible to establish

---

[91] D. W. Sutherland, 'Mesne Process upon Personal Actions in the Early Common Law', *Law Quarterly Review* 82 (1966), pp. 486–88.

[92] M. Blatcher, *The Court of King's Bench 1450–1550: A Study in Self-Help* (London, 1978), pp. 71–88; M. Hastings, *The Court of Common Pleas in Fifteenth-Century England* (Cornell, 1947), pp. 176–81; E. Powell, *Kingship, Law and Society: Criminal Justice in the Reign of Henry V* (Oxford, 1989), pp. 74–76.

[93] Hunnisett, *The Medieval Coroner*, pp. 67–68; Blatcher, *King's Bench*, p. 87; *Calendar of State Papers Domestic 1611–18*, p. 591.

[94] G. Spraggs, *Outlaws and Highwaymen: The Cult of the Robber in England from the Middle Ages to the Nineteenth Century* (London, 2001), p. 52. See also D. Brandon, *Stand and Deliver: A History of Highway Robbery* (London, 2001), chapter 1; J. Sharpe, *Dick Turpin: The Myth of the English Highwayman* (London, 2004), and D. Barlow, *Dick Turpin and the Gregory Gang* (London and Chichester, 1973).

with some accuracy how and when some of the later legends came to be attached to him. These led him for a time to a level of fame similar to that acquired by the medieval outlaw. As his biographer Derek Barlow put it, 'Turpin therefore is the classic example of a criminal who metamorphoses into mythical hero and then, by perpetuation in entertainment, fiction, and legend, achieves immortality'.[95] However, he only began to appear in chapbooks in about 1800, and a supposed ride from London to York to establish an alibi became attached to him, probably in 1808.[96] The 1834 novel *Rookwood* by Harrison Ainsworth (1805-82) added the now famous details of his heroic horse Black Bess dying from exhaustion when he reached York. This version of the tale became popular, and in 1836 a London print-seller, Martin Colnaghi (c.1792-1851), published six prints of famous incidents in Turpin's career, further establishing his lasting fame in legend. It is sometimes argued that an earlier notorious highwayman, John Nevison (sometimes called William), active in Yorkshire and Nottinghamshire, and who was also hanged at York, in 1684, was the man to whom the legend of the famous ride to York was originally attributed before it was transferred to Turpin.[97] Nevison, like the Robin Hood of the *Gest*, operated on the great north road, occasionally as far south as Grantham. He was also transformed by popular publications from his true nature into 'a more romantically acceptable gentleman of the road', and portrayed as a Robin Hood-type figure. Curiously, he was said in 1676 to have had a safe house in Wentbridge, as well as one further south on the road at Tuxford in Nottinghamshire; he also had a room in a public house in Newark in the same county, where he and his accomplices divided up their spoils. After his death he became a kind of literary hero in chapbook publications, and would doubtless have continued to be well-known had it not been for his being supplanted by Turpin in the early nineteenth century. Turpin himself eventually receded in popular imagination, while Robin Hood, through his continuing transformation and development, has survived them both and continues to flourish in the lore of the twenty-first century, his original criminality considerably diluted. However, the most likely candidate for the original outlaw, whose identity is suggested in the final part of this book, shared the same fate as his two notorious successors, albeit in very different circumstances: the bodies of all three were publicly hung in the city of York.

---

[95] Barlow, *Turpin, Richard [Dick] 1705–1739*, ODNB, accessed 10 November 2018.
[96] Barlow, *Dick Turpin and the Gregory Gang*, pp. 442–49.
[97] See Daniel Defoe, *A Tour through England and Wales*, introduction by G. D. H. Cole (2 vols., London, 1928), I, pp. 103–105, where the rider to York is described as 'one Nicks' and 'Swift Nicks', and may not refer to Nevison. This view is also that of Nevison's biographer in *ODNB*, Tim Wales.

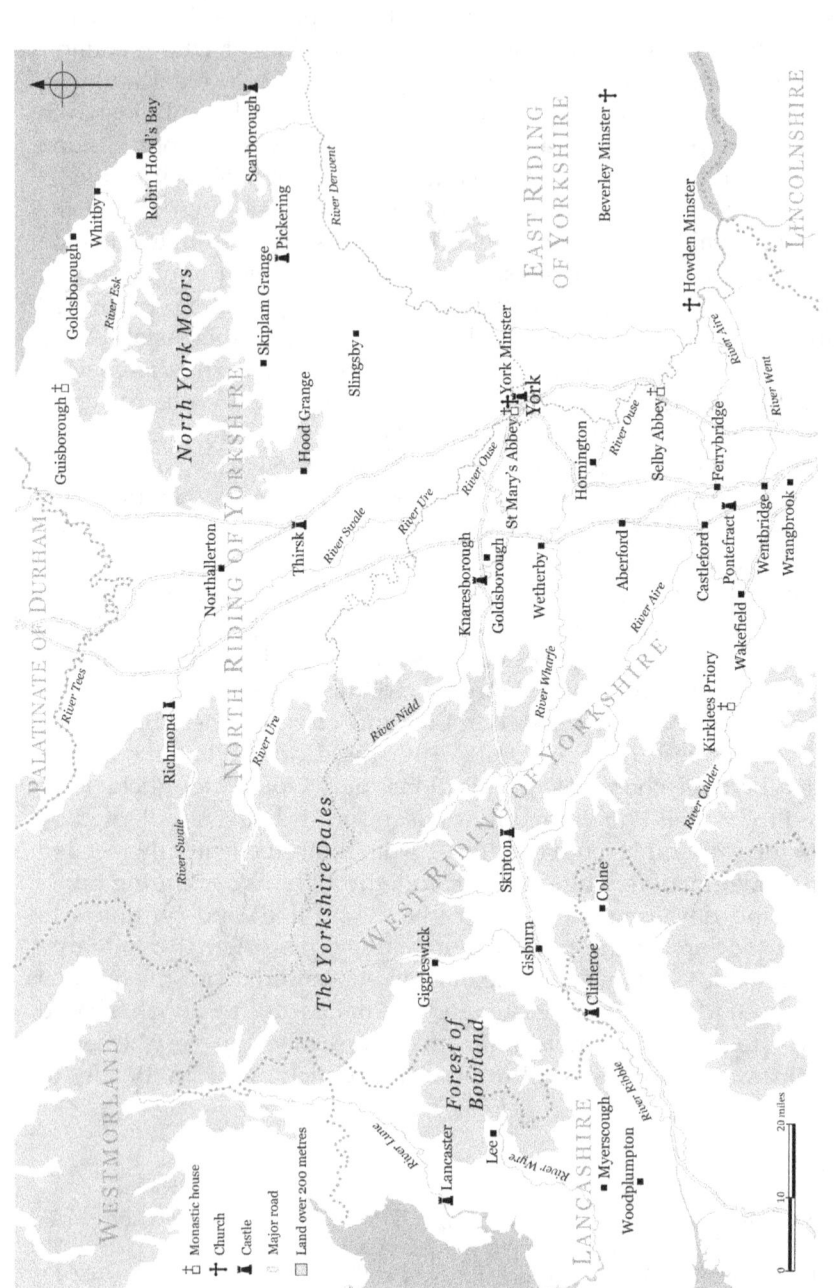

MAP 4. Places and routes connected with the Legend: North of Barnsdale.

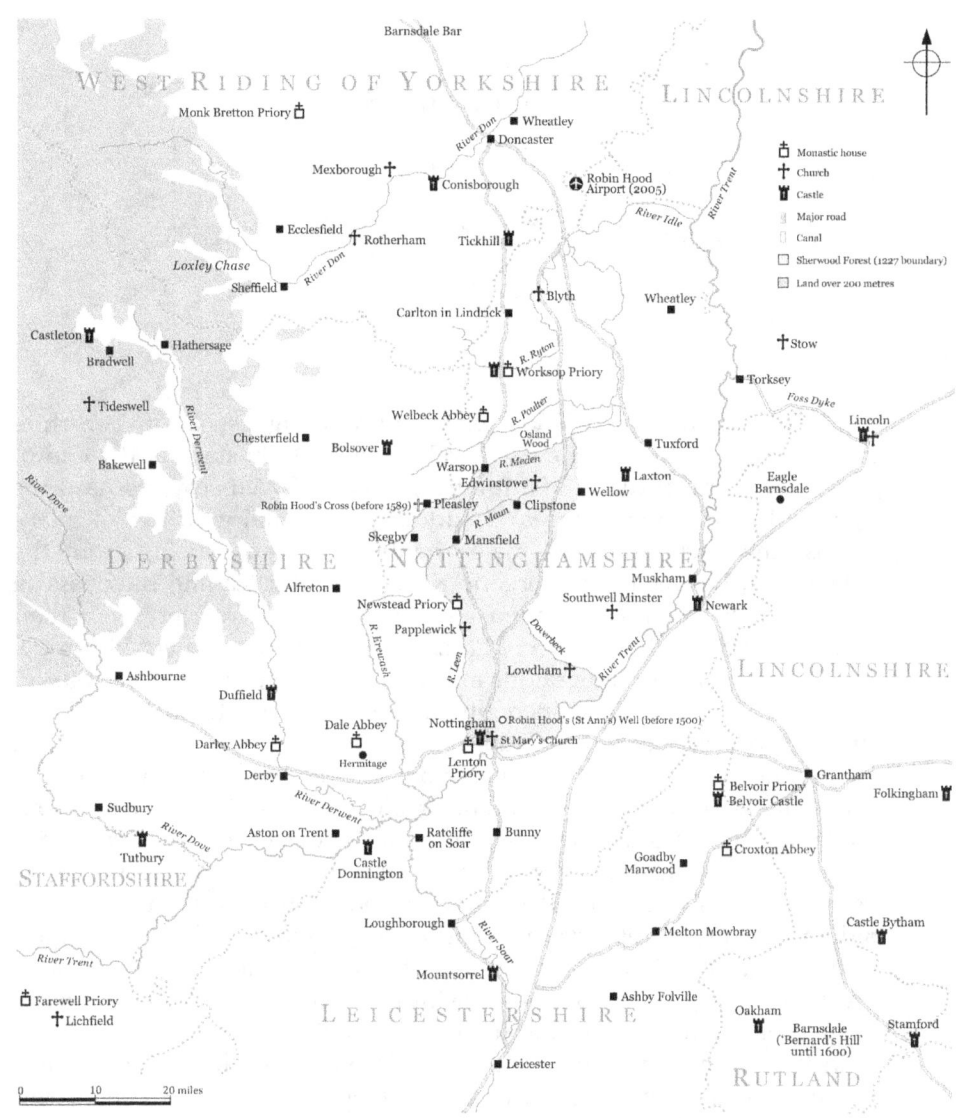

Map 5. Places and routes connected with the Legend: South of Barnsdale.

Chapter 8

Law and Disorder in Yorkshire, 1215–1225

The origin of the Robin Hood legend may, I suggest, lie in Yorkshire in the decade following the issue of Magna Carta in 1215, at the end of which the criminal career of a fugitive, Robert of Wetherby, perhaps the original Robin Hood, came to a sudden and brutal end. It took place against the background of major political tensions arising from the antagonism between the energetic King John and leading members of northern society, who were not used to forceful royal interference in their region. John visited the north of England far more than any of his predecessors, and tried to integrate it more fully with the rest of the country than ever before. His sustained attempts to do so eventually gave rise to strong opposition, and the northern counties were particularly unsettled during the later stages of his reign from 1212 onwards, when a series of events took place which eventually resulted in the king's concessions made in Magna Carta.[1] Despite the confirmations of the Charter in 1216 and 1217, the situation in the north remained hostile to the crown in the years following the accession of John's son, Henry III, then nine years old, in the autumn of 1216, and particularly so in Yorkshire, the largest county. The situation there was such, it will be argued, that it provided a suitable background for a successful and notorious criminal career to begin, flourish for a while and then be extinguished.

In the summer of 1212 there was a baronial plot against John's life, and a number of northern barons were suspected of involvement. One, Eustace de Vesci, fled abroad and, after a royal visit to the north, others gave the king hostages for their good behaviour. Yorkshire was thus the earliest focus of resistance to John's rule, and, after a short period during which the king was more conciliatory, their opposition continued to the

[1] J. C. Holt, *The Northerners* (2nd edition, Oxford, 1992), chapter 11, 'The Government of the North'.

end of his reign and beyond. Many of the leading rebels were lords with their main interests in Yorkshire, men such as de Vesci, Robert de Ros, William de Mowbray, Richard de Percy and Nicholas de Stuteville.[2] When war began, John's campaign in the north in January 1216 did nothing to reconcile leading Yorkshiremen to Plantagenet rule from Westminster, and probably further inflamed the situation. It was undertaken with a force consisting mainly of mercenary Flemish household knights, because of the desertion of many of his English knights.[3] The nature of the king's progress is graphically illustrated by a series of entries on a membrane of his last fine roll, and the recollections of a monastic chronicler. On 23 December 1215, at Melton Mowbray in Leicestershire, the men of the manor, tenants of William de Mowbray, felt constrained to offer John 100 marks as 'tenserie', a form of arbitrary wartime taxation, and to have royal letters of protection. After spending Christmas at Nottingham, John then forced the surrender of Belvoir castle nearby by threatening to starve to death its lord, William d'Aubigny, already his prisoner. On 1 January 1216 at Laxton in Nottinghamshire the men of Retford gave him another 100 marks as tenserie, and the men of Laxton itself gave him £100 to have his peace and for their houses not to be burnt. When he reached Yorkshire, the men of Thirsk, also Mowbray tenants, gave 80 marks for his protection and for their houses not to be burnt. Further north, the constable of Richmond castle gave 200 marks for his benevolence and his peace, and for his men who had been captured at the castle.[4] It is little wonder, therefore, that the chronicler of Crowland abbey, when recording John's death, characterised him as a 'despoiler of his own people' (*suorum depraedator*).[5] Yorkshire seems to have become brutalised by the effects of the war and John's harsh conduct during his campaign. The royalist victory over the rebels and their French allies in 1217, and the second reissue of Magna Carta that followed, did not immediately pacify the region, where baronial recalcitrance and political opposition to the crown's legal authority remained strong for some years after John's death. In 1222 some of the leading men of the county, including William de Mowbray and Richard de Percy, even committed contempt of court by not appearing at Brian de Lisle's Yorkshire forest eyre, although they had been summoned. Walter of Sowerby, steward of the younger Nicholas de Stuteville, who did attend, advocated an appeal

---

[2] Holt, *The Northerners*, pp. 79–85.
[3] S. D. Church, *The Household Knights of King John* (Cambridge, 1999), pp. 112–15.
[4] *Rotuli de Oblatis et Finibus*, ed. T. D. Hardy (London, Record Commission, 1835), pp. 568–69; *Rogeri de Wendover Flores Historiarum*, ed. H. G. Hewlett (3 vols., London, Rolls Series, 1886–89) II, p. 164.
[5] *Memoriale Fratris Walteri de Coventria* II, ed. W. Stubbs (London, Rolls Series, 1873), p. 232.

to the pope because he said that the forest pleas were contrary to the king's liberties.[6] Their action subsequently forced the government to suspend the holding of forest eyres for a full year. It required a lengthy struggle by the young king's ministers and council to bring the county back under a greater degree of royal control by the mid-1220s.

The evidence of letters recorded in the Chancery close rolls directed to the sheriff of Yorkshire, from the death of King John onwards, are revealing. In 1216 and 1217 there are only a handful, all connected with the restoration of lands to rebels returning to the royalist cause, and in July 1217 the government delegated to the archbishop of York powers to restore the forfeited lands. His importance derived not only from his status as a senior clergyman but also from his strong political authority in Yorkshire, the crown making use of his regional influence where its own was relatively weak.[7] Then, in May 1218, the sheriff of the county was instructed to give custody of the barony of Robert de Mesnill to the archbishop of Canterbury. The government must have anticipated some problems in this instruction being carried out, because the sheriff was told that if anyone resisted the transfer he was to take pledges from them for their appearance before the king's council at Westminster to explain why.[8] Whether the sheriff needed that authority, or was indeed able to carry out the order, is not known. As well as the council, the central royal court, the Common Bench, sitting at Westminster, assisted the sheriff from a distance as best it could. It too was trying to re-assert its authority after its suspension from Trinity term 1209 to 1214, and during the subsequent civil war. During that period royal justice had been exercised only by the court *coram rege* (later King's Bench), which travelled with the king, and by his itinerant justices in the counties. The days when King John had been involved personally in criminal cases before the court *coram rege* during the sessions of those years, some of them held in Yorkshire, were not and could not be repeated after 1217 by a king who was a minor and in a region where royal control was initially so weak. Under Henry III formal involvement in the proceedings of his own court did not begin until 1226, and the court *coram rege* itself was not revived until 1234.[9]

The government was also troubled by the threat posed to the king's authority by adulterine castles in Yorkshire. In February 1218 the sheriff

---

[6] *Pipe Roll 7 Henry III*, PRS NS LVI, p. 162.
[7] *PR 1216–25*, p. 77. Similar powers were given only to the bishop of Durham, the royal chancellor, at the same time, to deal with former rebels in his bishopric.
[8] *RLC* I, p. 361b.
[9] D. M. Stenton, *English Justice between the Norman Conquest and the Great Charter* (Philadelphia, 1964), pp. 101–14; C. A. F. Meekings and D. Crook, *King's Bench and Common Bench in the Reign of Henry III*, Selden Society Supplementary Series 17 (London, 2010).

was sent copies of Magna Carta and the Charter of the Forest, with instructions for their publication in the county court. The accompanying letter emphasised that special attention should be paid to the clause in Magna Carta about adulterine castles. Any that had been constructed or rebuilt since the beginning of the war were to be destroyed. This provision was said to have been made in the Charter 'by the counsel of the [papal] legate and our faithful men' to 'the maximum utility and tranquillity of us and our realm'.[10] These instructions were apparently sent only to Yorkshire, the former rebel stronghold still dominated by resentful barons, and confirms that the king's advisors saw the county as still in a state of disorder and requiring particular attention. Adulterine castles added to the general unrest as they had in earlier periods of civil war, particularly the 1140s and the mid 1170s. In July the sheriff was told to deal with the castle of Hood in the fee of Newburgh, which had been partly demolished but some of which was still standing. If he was able to establish that it had been erected since the outbreak of war he was to destroy it.[11] In political circumstances like these, when many of the natural leaders of society were still opponents of the king, and were not effectively restrained by the king's council and government even after the end of the war, it is easier to understand why crime could flourish among the lower orders of society in the same region.

The close rolls of the king's minority, in which letters sent to his officials were recorded, also show his council, and its local agent the sheriff, slowly beginning to reassume control of the system of criminal justice in Yorkshire. It is worth emphasising that significant royal involvement in the administration of criminal justice in much of the north of England, and the separate but related forest law, was only about 40 years old by the time King John died, and that during his reign it had far exceeded that of Henry II and Richard. As James Holt put it, 'Settled conditions could not be expected in the north. The line between stable government and administrative chaos, even civil war, was difficult to define'.[12] In March 1218 the sheriff was told to transfer an appeal of homicide, brought against three brothers for killing the uncle of Robert de Bailliol, before the Common Bench at Westminster at the end of April; however, this probably did not happen, since in September he was allowed to bail two of them until they could come before the eyre justices, whose visit to Yorkshire may by then have been at the planning stage. In early May the count of Aumale, the earl of Warenne, John constable of Chester, the constable of Tickhill, Robert de Ros and Hugh de Balliol were summoned to come before the barons of the Exchequer late in June to answer why they had hindered

---

[10] RLC I, p. 377.
[11] RLC I, p. 366b. The castle seems to have been at or near what is now known as Hood Grange, in Kilburn parish in the North Riding.
[12] Holt, *The Northerners*, pp. 199–201, 204–05.

the sheriff of Yorkshire in taking the king's pleas.[13] The Yorkshire eyre itself was eventually summoned on 3 November 1218, for a start on 25 November, and the county was the first to be visited in an eyre circuit which included only one other county, Northumberland.[14] This was the first eyre in the county since 1212, after six years largely of political crisis and war, and the justices had the difficult task of attempting to deal with all crown pleas since then.[15] The government must have been watching the progress of this eyre in particular, although they were being held in counties all over England, and eyres in seven other circuits began on the same day.[16] A crown pleas roll compiled for the Yorkshire justices has survived, as well as a memoranda roll of civil and criminal cases reserved for further discussion, presumably with the king's counsellors.[17] The latter is a unique record; nothing else of its type survives among the hundreds of records of general eyres covering all the counties of England for a period of over a century. The reference of a significant number of judicial matters from the provinces to the council was not a normal procedure, and its existence is a testimony to the uncertainty the justices felt in that time of disorder in Yorkshire and their need for support from Westminster.

The Yorkshire crown pleas roll deals as usual with the whole range of criminal offences, mainly responses to the articles of the eyre, arranged under the various wapentakes and recording the work of their juries of presentment. They include in particular homicides and suicides, appeals of homicide or robbery, misadventure, offences against royal prerogatives or regulations, offences of omission or commission by jurors, of first finders of bodies in suspicious circumstances, and by individual vills, coroners, and the sheriff. The outlawries of offenders who had fled and were to be dealt with by the normal processes in the county court are recorded, and their chattels accounted for. Brian de Lisle, one of John's most prominent northern officials had, it proved, been illegally retaining some of the latter.[18] All this was common form and took place at every eyre in every county. A few entries, however, give an impression of a level of public disorder unknown in the other four counties for which crown pleas rolls have survived. The dates of the offences are rarely given, so the chronology of offending since 1212 is in most instances

---

[13] *Calendar of Fine Rolls Henry III* I (Woodbridge and London, 2007), p. 15, 2 Henry III, no. 52.

[14] *RLC* I, pp. 369b, 378b, 380b, 403b.

[15] D. Crook, *Records of the General Eyre*, PRO Handbooks 20 (London, 1982), pp. 68–69, 75–76.

[16] Crook, *Records of the General Eyre*, pp. 71–76.

[17] TNA, JUST 1/1053, printed in *Rolls of the Justices in Eyre for Yorkshire 1218–19*, ed. D. M. Stenton, Selden Society LVI (1937), nos. 429–1095; and JUST 1/1041, printed in *Yorkshire Eyre*, nos. 1096–1153.

[18] *Yorkshire Eyre*, nos. 754, 762, 766, 796, 829.

impossible to establish, although particular cases arising from events in 1209, even before the 1212 eyre, and in 1213, are mentioned.[19] The main indication of date is that an incident is said to have happened 'in time of war', which must be defined as between September 1215 and the peace of September 1217, or 'in time of peace'. Those who committed offences 'in time of peace' had transgressed before or after those dates, although there was naturally confusion about whether some particular offences fell inside or outside the 'time of war'.[20] The jury of Doncaster was uncertain, or at least said that it was uncertain, of the dates of the war. It reported that a force led by two of King John's former household servants had attacked the town on 19 September 1217, killed two men, burned five houses and two brattices, and pillaged, causing £500 damage. This attack took place only a week after the peace, so the margin was fine. News of the conclusion of hostilities may not have reached Yorkshire in time to prevent it; but, given the state of affairs in the county, it might not have made any difference if it had.[21]

More general and significant than ordinary entries in the crown pleas section of the roll is the first recorded under the pleas of the Strafforth wapentake jury: 'Speak about those who were put in gaol and delivered in time of war'.[22] Other entries indicate that this was a general release of prisoners, not their trial before the sheriff, which would have been contrary to chapter 24 of Magna Carta 1215, a provision retained in the later versions.[23] Roger son of Adam of Boulton was accused of homicide, arrested and taken to York prison, but 'he escaped on account of the war'. This came about 'because it was attested that Geoffrey de Neville allowed all the prisoners to leave the gaol on account of the war'. As a result, Boulton was to be outlawed; he had no chattels because he had eaten them in prison.[24] He was not the only prisoner to be released by Neville in that way; one female and two suspected male homicides were described as being 'let go' (*dimissa fuit abire*), one by Peter fitz Herbert, who had been sheriff from about April 1214 to June 1215, but who temporarily defected from John's side in 1216.[25] During the war the administration of justice broke down and offences committed during it could not effectively be punished. In two cases in the eyre, the trial

---

[19] *Yorkshire Eyre*, nos. 570, 724.
[20] *Yorkshire Eyre*, nos. 455, 468, 476.
[21] *Yorkshire Eyre*, p. xxv, no. 516.
[22] *Yorkshire Eyre*, no. 459.
[23] J. C. Holt, *Magna Carta* (3rd edition, Cambridge, 2015), pp. 385, 423.
[24] *Yorkshire Eyre*, no. 499.
[25] *Yorkshire Eyre*, nos. 502, 631, 656, 737, 758, ?864, 901, 990, 1034–35, 1056, 1059, 1081, 1136; Holt, *The Northerners*, pp. 97–98, 139, 229n; *List of Sheriffs*, PRO Lists and Indexes IX (1898), p. 161.

juries had to decide whether an offence had taken place in war or peace; if during the former, 'nothing was, or could be, done'.[26]

The reason why Geoffrey de Neville as sheriff released the prisoners in the county gaol during the war, and when it happened, is unclear. Lady Stenton suggested that he did so in the spring of 1216, not long after he took office in February, when rebel troops besieged York and forced the citizens to purchase a truce.[27] If so, it would have been a spur of the moment decision, like the infamous one he made when he hanged a prisoner convicted of homicide in the county court on a wife's appeal when no royal justices were present; he justified this on the basis that he had already done it to two malefactors in Gascony, where he had been the king's seneschal.[28] In fact, however, he may have been ordered to release the prisoners in York gaol by King John on 17 April 1215, in other words before what was later defined as 'the 'time of war', when he and three others were instructed to let go in peace (*quietos abire permittatis*) all their prisoners who were not knights or men of good birth (*gentiles*).[29] Whatever his motive, and whenever it took place, the release of the prisoners can only have added to the lawlessness in the county already fuelled by the unrest prior to the issue of Magna Carta itself. A reference in the roll to the progress of appeals indicates that the county court ceased to meet during the war,[30] and its suspension must also have meant that the process of outlawry, which required five summonses in different sessions of the court, also could not be carried out. However, the county court was certainly meeting again by the time the eyre began to sit on 25 November 1218, over a year after the peace.

The memoranda roll produced by the justices' clerks begins with a list of 13 points to be discussed (*loquendum de*), suggesting that they are queries to be referred to the king's council for advice.[31] Second among these is 'Speak about those who were put in prison and were delivered by G[eoffrey] de Neville in time of war'. The third membrane of the roll is headed 'suits put in respite to the great court', that is, the Common

[26] *Yorkshire Eyre*, nos. 972, 1022.
[27] *Yorkshire Eyre*, p. liv, followed by Holt, *The Northerners*, p. 135.
[28] *Yorkshire Eyre*, no. 744.
[29] *RLP* I, p. 133. There are considerable difficulties about this, because Neville was not officially sheriff of Yorkshire at that time and was addressed as 'chamberlain'. Peter fitz Herbert eventually accounted as sheriff of Yorkshire for the period up to Easter 1215, Easter falling on 19 April in that year: *Pipe Roll 17 John*, PRS NS 37, pp. 39, 55. Neville was not appointed sheriff until 4 February 1216, after two short-term holders of the office were appointed in July and August 1215 respectively: *List of Sheriffs*, p. 161; Holt, *The Northerners*, p. 122 note 1. The possibility that he controlled York castle gaol in April 1215 should be considered.
[30] *Yorkshire Eyre*, no. 939.
[31] TNA, JUST 1/1041.

Bench,[32] and the material in this roll deals with civil pleas, often with proceedings and judgments made in the Bench added in a later hand at the end of the entry. Some of the pleas involved important people, lay and clerical, like the earl of Chester, Robert de Percy, the widow of Robert de Stuteville the elder, the bishop of Durham and the abbot of St Mary's York. The continuing reliance of the government on the efforts of the archbishop in the county even after the eyre was over appears from the order to the sheriff in October 1219 to hand over the cash from the amercements levied in the eyre, together with the proceeds of debts, fines and farms, and anything else to hand, to the archbishop to enable him to do what the king had instructed. He was also forbidden to surrender or deliver any of the money arising from his bailiwick, whether from amercements, fines, debts, farms or other things, save to the king at the Exchequer or to the archbishop.[33]

The Bench itself had begun to sit at Westminster again half-way through Michaelmas term in November 1217.[34] The number of Yorkshire civil cases was at a reasonable level, but even by 1220 the court had some difficulties in enforcing its instructions in the county. In Hilary term that year the sheriff told the Bench justices that a group of Robert de Ros's men, armed with bows and arrows, had prevented his bailiffs from executing a judgment against Robert by the justices in eyre in respect of common of pasture in Latham, claimed by the prior of Ellerton. He was told to arrest anyone who resisted its execution and bring them before the justices at Easter One Month (27 April), and if they withdrew and refused to stand trial they were to be exacted and outlawed in the county court.[35] It is not known whether Ros relented; certainly he does not appear in the Bench plea roll for Easter term. Ros had been one of the leading northern rebels against King John, and like others remained recalcitrant during the minority of Henry III. He had acted as baronial sheriff of Yorkshire, and made the life of his royalist successor very difficult.[36] On 5 June 1220 the papal legate Pandulf wrote to the justiciar Hubert de Burgh from Lincoln asking for the sheriff of Yorkshire to be

---

[32] *Yorkshire Eyre*, p. 413.
[33] RLC I, p. 402; see also 405b; *Calendar of Fine Rolls Henry III* I, 3 Henry III, nos. 423–25, p. 120.
[34] *Bracton's Note-Book*, ed. F. W. Maitland, 3 vols. (London, 1887) III, heading before no. 1295.
[35] CRR VIII, pp. 198–99, 325; *Yorkshire Eyre*, pp. xxxviii–xxxix, nos. 304, 423, 1151; *Yorkshire Feet of Fines 1218–31*, ed. J. Parker, YAS RS LXII (1921), p. 33. The working sheriff at this time was Simon de Hale, a Lincolnshire man, who as under-sheriff substituted for Geoffrey de Neville, following his reappointment as seneschal of Poitou in May 1218, when he insisted on retaining the shrievalty: D. A. Carpenter, *The Minority of Henry III* (London, 1990), p. 80.
[36] Holt, *The Northerners*, especially pp. 24–26, 65–68, 120 note 7.

released 'according to justice and the law of the land...since you are bound to observe this to everyone, acting in such a way that the honour of the king may be preserved unharmed'.[37] The implication is that the sheriff had been actually detained during the course of carrying out his duties. Burgh acted by holding pleas of novel disseisin in York himself, where Ros was convicted of nine disseisins and amerced 200 marks.[38] Pressure from lords in favour of a particular defendant or plaintiff could be a threat to the dispensation of justice even after the war had ended. In the eyre Thomas of Rydale, who had appealed John de Chinum of robbery at Weaverthorpe, was accused of a malicious appeal. Because of the dispute between their lords, respectively Peter of Weaverthorpe and Peter fitz Herbert, a former rebel, Thomas was reluctant to submit himself to the verdict of jurors 'because some of them are Peter fitz Herbert's men'. Another lord feared the possible consequences of his own self-confessed disreputable conduct. Robert de Percy refused to accept jurors from the wapentakes of Richmondshire because he had committed many evil deeds there in the war, presumably concerned that this would influence their verdict.[39]

The most significant entry in the eyre roll, however, concerns the activities of John de Thorenton (John of Thornton), 'who goes about the country with fifteen horsemen and is received in Richmond castle as peacefully as any honest man in his house'. He was said to have come to Richmond at Christmas (probably the most recent, 1218) with 100 marks worth of cloth, and clothed his men with it 'as if he were a baron or an earl', and 'went through the whole country (*patriam*) robbing wherever he can'. As to his reception at the castle, the constable, Nicholas of Stapleton, admitted that 'he was once in the castle before Christmas and left immediately'.[40] This was one of the cases referred to the king's council in the memoranda roll. Here we have a man who, presumably 'in time of peace', since the war is not mentioned, led a criminal gang of fifteen men, clad in his own livery, who terrorised the countryside. This was in one of the areas that had been a centre of rebellion in 1215-16.[41] Nothing is known of what, if anything, the council and the central judicial administration did immediately to try to counter this. The neighbouring pleas in the memoranda roll, all civil cases, were adjourned to

---

[37] *Royal Letters of Henry III* I, ed. W. W. Shirley (London, Rolls Series, 1862), no. cxi.

[38] *Pipe Roll 4 Henry III*, PRS NS XLVII, pp. 36–37; *Pipe Roll 5 Henry III*, PRS NS XLVIII, pp. 133–34, 137. For some of his disseisins see *Yorkshire Eyre*, nos. 137, 301, 424, 425, 889, 894. See also TNA, E 163/1/8B, m. 7d, where his debts are brought together.

[39] *Yorkshire Eyre*, nos. 939, 1140.

[40] *Yorkshire Eyre*, no. 1149.

[41] Holt, *The Northerners*, pp. 46–49.

the Bench at Westminster in Easter term 1219,[42] but Thornton's activities were more difficult to deal with.

Of even greater significance is the context in which Thornton next appears in the records. On 2 May 1221 letters patent authorised by the justiciar and council proclaimed to all the senior men of Yorkshire, from the archbishop downwards to free tenants, that, although John of Thornton had been accused in the eyre of 'arson, robbery and the death of men', he was to be left in peace because he had given pledges to stand to right in the king's court. His pledges were impressive: the two most senior earls in England, Ranulph, earl of Chester and Lincoln and William earl of Salisbury; Robert de Ferrers, brother of the earl of Derby; and three significant men below comital rank, Walter de Deyville, Robert Marmiun and Henry de Trubleville, with no obvious Yorkshire connections.[43] He had no lack of friends in high places. Little more than a month later, on 18 June, the men of Yorkshire, down to the level of free tenants, were informed by letters patent that Thornton had been appointed to pursue and capture robbers and wandering malefactors in the county, and to enquire into who harboured them, during the king's pleasure, and the men of the county were told to help him in this endeavour.[44]

Thus was the poacher first rehabilitated and then almost immediately turned into a gamekeeper. His remit was countywide and comprehensive, and such arrangements were recorded in no other county at this time. The government was desperate to use any means possible to restore order in Yorkshire, and prepared to employ whatever instrument was to hand. Detailed evidence of criminal activities in the county in the early 1220s, when Thornton should have been active, is sparse, but there is a little in the records of the Bench at Westminster. In Easter term 1221, just prior to the date of his commission, there is a record of a series of crimes committed by a gang of thieves consisting of eleven men, five of whose names are known. Firstly, they stole three loads of salmon worth 8s, and killed the men on whose cart the goods were being carried. Then they robbed another cart in which they hoped to find fish, but which was in fact carrying cups, and, after tying up the carters, killed them. Finally, they robbed eighteen men from York of five swords and 10s. These events only came to light because Robert son of Ives, who admitted to being a thief himself, appealed Adam Lal (or Laf) of belonging to the gang and being involved in these offences, of which his and his sons'

---

[42] *Yorkshire Eyre*, nos. 1145, 1147–48, 1150–53.
[43] *PR 1216–25*, p. 288. Trubleville (Turberville) was a former household knight of King John: Church, *Household Knights*, p. 44.
[44] *PR 1216–25*, p. 293: ad persequendum et capiendum predones et malefactores itinerantes per comitatum Eboraci…et ad inquirendum receptatores eorum per eundem comitatum. Official payments to individuals to seek out outlaws were rare; see pp. 242–43.

share consisted of 8s for the salmon and a mark for the cups. Robert son of Ives was an approver, although that word is not used, and agreed to fight Lal in a judicial duel in the hope of avoiding punishment for his own offences.[45] The duel was to be held in the presence of Geoffrey de Neville and colleagues, appointed as justices for that purpose. Much further detail is given, but the ultimate outcome of the case is uncertain since it is not recorded in surviving plea rolls. However, it seems that Robert son of Ives lost the duel. It is briefly referred to in the legal treatise *De Legibus et Consuetudinibus Anglie* (Concerning the Laws and Customs of England), to illustrate procedure following the outcome of a case where the approver lost his appeal.[46] It is also recorded in 'Bracton's Note Book', a volume of transcripts of important cases from plea rolls.[47]

The general significance of this case is that it is only recorded in a roll of the Bench because Robert son of Ives turned king's evidence and accused his former criminal colleagues in order to save himself. There must have been more, perhaps many more, robberies of this kind in Yorkshire in the early 1220s that have left no trace; there are very few crown pleas in the surviving Bench rolls of those years. Another indication is the appointment in August 1223 of four commissioners to hold judicial duels between approvers in prison at York and those they accused.[48] Thornton's commission in itself indicates a climate of criminal lawlessness in Yorkshire. He was evidently not successful, at least not immediately, for on 13 January 1223 his commission was renewed in the same terms by the justiciar and council, the only difference being that he was said now to be assisted by eight sergeants, who were also to receive the aid of the men of the county.[49] This force was numerically just more than half of the fifteen men, clad in his own livery, who had been criminally active under him in the years immediately after the civil war. It would be interesting to know if any of them were in both groups, and whether or not they expected to receive a bounty for any criminal they took. Nothing is known of the success or otherwise of Thornton's group during the following period. If they had been notably successful one might have hoped for some slight indication of that fact among the fairly extensive records of those years.[50]

45 CRR X, pp. 67–68; The passage about the carters being killed is cancelled in the roll, however (note 9).
46 *De Legibus et Consuetudinibus Anglie, Bracton on the Laws and Customs of England*, ed. G. E. Woodbine, translated, with revisions and notes, by S. E. Thorne, 4 vols. (Cambridge, Mass., 1968–77), II, p. 432. Traditionally associated with the senior justice Henry Bracton (d. 1268), *De Legibus* is now thought to have been produced earlier in the circle of William Raleigh.
47 *Bracton's Note-Book*, ed. F. W. Maitland (London, 1887) III, p. 424, no. 1517.
48 PR 1216–25, p. 347.
49 PR 1216–25, p. 364.
50 A few isolated references to criminals, their custody and outlawry between

While men of the lower orders of society in Yorkshire were carrying out robberies involving homicide, some of those of higher social status continued to carry out violent activities for their own ends, adding to the general disorder. In 1219, when the king's justices evidently were unable to deal effectively with disputes between important men, recourse was made to arbitrators on at least one occasion. On 24 August 1219, five months after the departure of the justices in eyre from the county, a lengthy arbitration by a number of leading men, led by the abbot of St Mary's York, the dean of York, Robert de Percy and Simon de Hale, the sheriff, was promulgated in an attempt to settle a series of disputes, including forest trespasses, between Richard de Percy and his nephew and rival for the Percy barony William de Percy, which had arisen during and since the war.[51] The arbitration did not end the disputes within the Percy family, which were in the following years dealt with in the king's central court as it re-established its authority in the county. In 1224 the Common Bench at Westminster dealt with a dispute in which Robert de Percy used the procedure known as an appeal to initiate a suit against Henry de Percy, his brother William de Percy's son, and eleven others for unspecified robbery and breach of the peace. Robert alleged that on 9 February 1224 William came 'with horses and arms, armed with hauberks and other arms and with banners unfurled and pennants and barded horses' to his mill at Hornington, and many armed men broke the mill and removed all the timbers; they carried one of his millstones away in a boat, while the other fell into the water and was then broken with iron hammers. He also broke open Robert's chests and carried them away, taking away also his corn, and the iron and wood of the mill. Jordan de Stokes, Robert's sergeant in the village, raised the alarm, so William and his men beat him and robbed him of his cloak, a sword and felt hat. William offered to prove his case by a judicial duel, if the court agreed; and, if not, he offered the king 3 marks for an inquiry to be made. In addition, three of Robert's servants appealed Henry, also offering judicial combat, because of specified acts of violence and robbery committed against them during the same incident. The defendants denied all the accusations, and in the end were discharged on a technicality, after Robert de Percy conceded that when the attack and robbery had been committed he had been ill and had not witnessed them, and so was only liable to a fine. There seems little reason to doubt therefore that the events described actually occurred.[52]

This was perhaps an isolated violent act in the continuing struggle between Richard and William de Percy, uncle and nephew, over a

---

1221 and 1224 are in *RLC* I, pp. 462b, 470b, 555b, 586b, 634, 636b–7.
[51] *The Percy Chartulary*, ed. M. T. Martin, Surtees Society CXVII (1911), no. C, pp. 54–57.
[52] *CRR* XI, nos. 1483, 2037.

number of manors which comprised the Percy fee, divided between them, which would normally be pursued through civil litigation in the Common Bench.⁵³ Perhaps, however, it was an example of the frequent violence engendered by the self-help hidden behind the conciliatory tones of the feet of fines with which the court tried to resolve conflict, but which rarely reached the attention of the Bench at Westminster. Here even the attempt of an aggrieved party whose protest reached as far as the Bench could not obtain satisfaction for his opponent's extreme behaviour, albeit because of a technical flaw in his case in using a procedure in which very precise rules had to be followed.⁵⁴ There may have been many less determined Yorkshiremen who did not attempt to seek redress for such criminal acts, so this case may illustrate social fracture at the upper levels of county society. Below them, ordinary criminals could thrive in the atmosphere of disorder in which some of their superiors indulged themselves to an equivalent degree.

By 1225, therefore, Yorkshire still faced severe difficulties with public order. Then, on 12 July that year, at Winchester, the king and the justiciar, Hubert de Burgh, authorised a writ to the barons of the Exchequer to allow to the sheriff of Yorkshire on his account the sum of 40s he had spent by royal order to hire sergeants to 'seek and take and behead Robert of Wetherby, outlaw and evil-doer of our land'.⁵⁵ The manhunt mentioned in this writ may have already been completed by the time it was issued. The sheriff's account for the year in which it was claimed was audited at the Exchequer on 27 November 1225 and recorded in the pipe roll for the ninth year of the reign. In the section for expenses set against his county farm, the writ was mentioned and its amount

---

⁵³ In Trinity 1225 William de Percy was suing the four assize justices and the jurors in an assize of novel disseisin between him and Richard de Percy about a pond (*stagnum*), possibly a millpond, at Hornington, probably part of the same dispute: CRR XII, no. 655. For other details of the various disputes between Richard and William, which continued until at least 1228, see *Yorkshire Feet of Fines 1218–31*, pp. 1–2, 108–11; *The Percy Chartulary*, pp. 6–10; CRR VIII, pp. 38, 87, 360; IX, pp. 175–76, 189, 308, 326; XI, nos. 46, 317, 696, 1303, 1685, 2432, 2498, 2726; XII, nos. 87, 656, 1444, 1959, 2311; XIII nos. 570, 586, 856, 1161, 1224, 1546; *EYC* XI, ed. C. T. Clay, YAS RS, Extra Series IX (1963), pp. 6–7; *Yorkshire Eyre*, pp. xxviii–xxxii; *Complete Peerage*, ed. V. Gibbs and H. A. Doubleday (London, 1945), X, pp. 448–52.

⁵⁴ For process in appeals, see C. A. F. Meekings and D. Crook, *The 1235 Surrey Eyre* I, Surrey Record Society XXXI (1979), pp. 116–25, especially 122–23.

⁵⁵ RLC II, p. 50: Rex Baronibus de Scaccario salutem. Computate vicecomiti Ebor' quadraginta solidos quos posuit per preceptum nostrum in quibusdam servientibus ad Robertum de Werreby utlagatum et malefactorem terre nostre querendum et capiendam et decapitandum. Teste Rege apud Winton' xij die Julii anno nono. Coram Justiciario. This was a writ of *computate*, as described in the official account of Exchequer procedure, written in 1177–78: *Dialogus de Scaccario*, ed. C. Johnson (London and Edinburgh, 1950), p. 33.

entered. Among other expenses claimed and allowed without any writ of authorisation was a further sum of 2s 'for a chain to hang Robert of Wetherby'.[56] Since he had presumably already been decapitated, it must have been his body that was hung up. In the account for the following year the sheriff made a further claim, by a writ that was not enrolled in the close roll, for a further 28s spent on the pursuit of Wetherby by William Vinitor and associates, who had been instructed to lie in wait for him and take him.[57] It is not absolutely clear, but very probable, that both payments authorised by writ were made to William Vinitor's group of sergeants, not two different groups. The total cost of the manhunt was therefore 68s.

Any attempt to estimate the number of men involved and the time it took can only be speculative. There is a good deal of information about the rates of pay of sergeants in the pipe roll for the first year of King John (1199-1200), which shows that they were very inconsistent and were most likely negotiated for each individual task. In Surrey, for example, a group of twenty foot sergeants engaged in an unspecified task for twenty days were paid only 1d a day each, while in Lincolnshire nine sergeants were paid 6d a day, another ten were paid 2d a day, six mounted sergeants received 4d a day, and six foot sergeants 1½d a day. In London 23 mounted sergeants were paid 9d a day each, while in Kent another group of ten men received 4d a day each.[58] We do not know whether Vinitor's men were mounted or not, and how much he as leader was personally paid. At a flat rate of 3d a day per man, however, the total sum accounted for would have paid for 232 man-days, giving some indication of the scale of the undertaking. Whatever their number, the sergeants employed by the sheriff were paid to decapitate Robert of Wetherby when they had captured him, not to hold him so that he could be brought to trial. Vinitor, apparently a paid bounty hunter, was clearly a man of lesser standing than Thornton, who was able to produce such significant pledges when he needed to, and his group had been given a specific commission by the sheriff to track down a particular criminal, not the unrestricted licence given to Thornton two years earlier.[59] It may be that Wetherby's head was what the authorities thought was needed to

---

[56] E 159/8, m. 10 [AALT-IMG 0031]; E 372/69, rot. 9 [AALT-IMG 1221]: Et pro j cathena ad suspendendum Robertum de Wereby ij s.'.

[57] E 372/70, rot. 1 [AALT-IMG 6997]: Et in custo quem idem Eustachius [the sheriff] posuit in Willelmo vinitore et sociis suis assignatis ad insidiendum et capiendum Robertum de Werreby malefactorem xxviij s. per breve regis.

[58] *Pipe Roll 1 John*, PRS NS X, pp. 56, 60, 129, 133.

[59] It is possible but very unlikely that the William Vinitor who led the hunt for the outlaw was the same man as the William Vinitor who was fined for selling wine in Yorkshire in the pipe roll for 1224–25: TNA, E 372/69, rot. 9 [AALT-IMG 1224].

bring the crime wave in Yorkshire to an end, or at least symbolise their determination to do so to anyone tempted to imitate him.

The display of Wetherby's body at a prominent place in York may already have been the accepted practice for prominent criminals successfully hunted down in Yorkshire. It was not only criminals who could have their dead bodies displayed in public in the county. In 1191 Roger de Lacy, constable of Chester and lord of Pontefract, hanged Peter de Bovencourt, without judgment, on a gibbet with an iron chain (*in patibulo cum catena ferrea*) for handing over Tickhill castle to Count John during the latter's rebellion against the ministers of his brother King Richard, who was away on crusade. Three days later Lacy also hanged a squire who had driven away birds that were tearing at Bovencourt's body with their claws and beaks.[60] The pursuit of Robert of Wetherby in 1225 was carried out by a professional posse, rather different from other cases when it appears that the usual hue and cry was successful in apprehending the suspected criminal. In the eyre of 1218-19 it was reported that Robert Burtham, who had been outlawed for the death of Herbert, Richard de Percy's sergeant, was afterwards taken and beheaded.[61] The eyre roll records that six fleeing thieves were beheaded, but there is no mention of their heads being sent to York.[62] However, it was certainly common practice for fleeing thieves or homicides who were captured to be decapitated and their heads sent there, perhaps for public display. There are some good examples in the roll of William Raleigh's Yorkshire eyre of 1231.[63] No plea roll has survived for the 1226 eyre, but the procedure then must have been the same. The practice of beheading fleeing thieves who were apprehended is well illustrated by two entries in the roll of the Northumberland eyre of 1256, the first to survive for that county, the beheadings being carried out in the presence of the king's bailiff. In the first, the local custom is stated by the sheriff and coroner: 'the custom of the county is this, that as soon as anyone is taken with stolen goods, he shall immediately be beheaded, and those who followed because of the chattels taken from himself has his chattels for beheading the same'.[64] This principle is apparent in other entries. In one, the person who raised the hue was rewarded with the horse of a

---

[60] *Gesta Henrici Secundi Benedicti Abbatis*, ed. W Stubbs, 2 vols. (London, Rolls Series, 1867), II, p. 233.
[61] *Yorkshire Eyre*, no. 856.
[62] *Yorkshire Eyre*, nos. 535, 538, 617, 712, 761.
[63] See pp. 241–43.
[64] TNA, JUST 1/642, rot. 13 [AALT-IMG 2310]; *Three Early Assize Rolls for the County of Northumberland*, ed. W. Page, Surtees Society LXXXVIII (1891), p. 70: consuetudo comitatus talis est, quod quamcito aliquis capiatur cum manuopere, statim decolletur, et ipse qui sequitur pro catallis ab ipso depridatis, habuit catalla sua pro ipso decollando.

decapitated horse-thief.⁶⁵ How appropriate, therefore, in the tale of *Robin Hood and Guy of Gisborn*, that the situation is reversed, with the hunted outlaw, Robin Hood, decapitating Guy and disfiguring his head with an Irish knife, which he later uses to cut Little John's bonds.⁶⁶

In 1225 Yorkshire was visited, as part of a countrywide series of circuits, by justices commissioned to take assizes and deliver gaols. Their instructions for the gaol delivery were to do justice on the king's part, and to ensure the observation of his peace 'concerning those who are believed to be bad or indicted of larcenies, robberies or homicide'.⁶⁷ The annalist of Dunstable priory in Bedfordshire regarded these commissions as a reaction to a national crime wave, which he described in dramatic terms: 'through all the provinces of England thieves are more abundant. Not only do these transients plunder goods but they also slay innocents, so that no-one can sleep securely in townships, nor safely travel from borough to borough'.⁶⁸ Many of the criminals were hung, he continued, and he named the two justices who served in Bedfordshire. The Yorkshire justices were Robert of Lexington, William d'Aubigny, Brunus son of Alan and the abbot of Selby, who were to hold their session at York on 20 July. Afterwards Robert of Cockfield and Theobald de Valeines, archdeacon of Essex, were added to the list of justices. The justices who actually sat are recorded in feet of fines made in civil cases in the session.⁶⁹ The sheriff was kept fully occupied by the presence of the justices, to the extent that in early September he secured government agreement that he should not have to appear in the Exchequer at Michaelmas to render his account. He was fully engaged in 'great affairs', including 'inquiring into the lands of those who had been outlawed, those hanged for larceny and other malefactors of the county', taking them into the king's hand because of the presence there of the assize and gaol delivery justices. His crime-fighting activities were a more urgent priority than having his account audited, because the situation in Yorkshire was more serious than elsewhere.⁷⁰

---

65 TNA, JUST 1/642, rot. 14 [AALT-IMG 2312]; *Three Early Assize Rolls*, pp. 73, 78–9, 80.
66 D&T, p. 145, stanzas 41–42.
67 RLC II, p. 76: de hiis qui male creduntur vel indictantur de latrociniis roberiis vel de morte hominum.
68 *AM* III, ed. H. R. Luard (London, Rolls Series, 1866), p. 95: Per omnes provincias Angliae, latrones adeo abundabant. Et non solum transeuntes bonis spoliabant, sed innocentes occidebant, ita quod nemo securus in villis dormiebat, neque de burgo in burgum tutus incedebant.
69 RLC II, p. 76; *Yorkshire Feet of Fines 1218–31*, p. 60.
70 *Calendar of Fine Rolls of the Reign of Henry III, II, 1224–1234*, 9 Henry III, no. 313, p. 48. By contrast, the sheriff of Oxfordshire, who was given a similar respite a few days later, was said to be seeking to expedite the collection of the taxation of a fifteenth granted to the king earlier in the year (no. 315).

The loss of the plea roll of the 1226 eyre in Yorkshire is unfortunate because, although there would have been no record of a trial since Wetherby was immediately executed when captured, it is likely that it would have included at least side-lights on the events of 1225. It might have provided evidence to add to the meagre amount of information we have about the activities of John of Thornton and Robert of Wetherby between the 1218 eyre and that in 1226.[71] The loss is particularly disappointing because the chief professional justice of the eyre was Martin of Pattishall, whose rolls survive in considerably greater numbers than those for any other justice in this period. Pattishall took part in ten of the 24 eyres held between 1218 and 1222, and in six of the eight for which rolls survive, including of course those of the Yorkshire eyre of 1218 to which extensive reference has already been made. He took part in nine of the eyres of 1226-9; rolls survive from four of the last five of them, but not that in Yorkshire.[72] Over 50 civil pleas from the Yorkshire eyre were extracted from the roll by the compiler of 'Bracton's Note Book', a collection of extracts from the plea rolls mainly of Pattishall and William Raleigh, Pattishall's clerk and his successor as a justice.[73] Raleigh's successor Henry de Bratton ('Bracton') held Pattishall's and Raleigh's rolls until 1257, when he was ordered to deliver them to the Exchequer.[74] This order must be the reason why we still have so many of Pattishall's and Raleigh's rolls, preserved in the Exchequer until the nineteenth century and subsequently from 1838 in the Public Record Office. It is not certain whether that collection still included the 1226 Yorkshire roll; if it did, it must have been lost subsequently. Ten civil cases in the roll were also referred to in the *De Legibus et Consuetudinibus Anglie*.[75] We therefore only know what the pipe rolls and Chancery rolls tell us about these matters, that is, very little indeed.

After the events of 1225 and the eyre of 1226 the situation in Yorkshire seems to have settled down, judging from the absence of anything in government records to indicate the contrary. In July 1226 repairs were ordered at York gaol, and in July 1227 four justices headed by the sheriff and William le Constable (possibly the constable of York castle) were commissioned to do justice to those appealed of larceny and felony by two named approvers who were held in the gaol.[76] This may represent

---

[71] The long lists of amercements collected by the sheriff appear in the two overlapping receipt rolls for Easter 10 Henry III (TNA, E 401/8, rots. 6–6d and E 401/9, rots. 6–6d) do not shed any light on these matters.
[72] Crook, *Records of the General Eyre*, p. 15.
[73] *Bracton's Note Book* III, nos. 1844–90.
[74] *Close Rolls 1256–9*, p. 281; *Select Cases in the Court of King's Bench under Edward I*, I, ed. G.O. Sayles, Selden Society LV (1936), p. cliv.
[75] *De Legibus et Consuetudinibus Anglie, Bracton on the Laws and Customs of England* II, p. 94; III, pp. 107, 267, 307, 316, 362, 378; IV, pp. 193, 287, 300.
[76] RLC II, p. 130b; PR 1225–32, pp. 159–60.

a tidying up of outstanding crimes from a few years previously. The government was now able to exert more direct control over criminal matters in Yorkshire. In October 1227 the sheriff of Yorkshire brought two prisoners who had been arrested at York to London at the king's order, to be kept in custody by the gaoler of Newgate [77] There is nothing in the roll for the Yorkshire eyre of 1231, led by the justiciar Stephen of Seagrave and Robert of Lexington, to indicate any large-scale criminal disorder in the county during the period since 1226.[78] Soon afterwards regular gaol deliveries at York are first recorded, beginning with the first enrolled gaol delivery commission, issued in May 1232.[79]

By disposing of Wetherby, Vinitor's men and their paymaster may have brought a period of particular lawlessness in Yorkshire to an end. This prominent offender thus seems to take on greater importance than might otherwise have been supposed. The next significant bout of unrest in the country as a whole began in 1231-2 as a result of the actions taken by a Yorkshire knight, Marmaduke of Thwing, alias 'William Wither', against foreign clerics to whom benefices had been given, including one of his own at Kirkleatham, near Guisborough.[80] Here, however, we are in different territory, when the uncertainties of the civil war of 1215-17 and the minority of Henry III had given way to the development of the political themes which characterised the personal rule of the king. The extensive criminal activity that took place in Yorkshire in the early and mid-1220s in Yorkshire could well have provided the background to the activities of the original Robin Hood and the context for the origin of his legend.

---

[77] *RLC* II, p. 202b.
[78] TNA, JUST 1/1043; Crook, *Records of the General Eyre*, p. 86. The most notable incident was an attack on the park of the royal servant and former sheriff Robert de Cockfield at Hazlewood, which prompted a royal instruction to the justices for a jury of enquiry (rot. 16; AALT-IMG 1347). See also the criminal cases mentioned in Chapter 9.
[79] *PR 1225–32*, p. 518.
[80] H. Mackenzie, 'The Anti-Foreign Movement in England 1231–1232', in *Anniversary Essays in Medieval History by Students of C. H. Haskins*, ed. C. H. Taylor and J. L. LaMonte (New York, 1929), pp. 183–203; N. Vincent, 'Thwing [Thweng], Sir Robert (III) of [alias William Wither] (d. 1245x57), knight', *ODNB*.

Chapter 9

The Sheriff, the Fugitive and the Civil Servant

In the five surviving early tales of Robin Hood the outlaw has various enemies, but the only one who appears in all of them is a sheriff, and all the tales refer to one particular sheriff only, the 'sheriff of Nottingham'. In none of them, however, does the sheriff appear as anything like a character with a personality (with the slight exceptions of *Robin Hood and the Potter*, where he briefly becomes a figure of fun, and the third fytte of the *Gest*, when he complains of the discomfort of spending a night in the forest wearing only his breeches and shirt). He seems simply to be an archetype, an anti-hero representing the enforcement of authority against the heroic outlaw, and no specific information or suggestion about the origins and nature of the enmity between them is given in any of the early tales. According to Dobson and Taylor, he

> plays so fundamental a role in the legend that he may have been more crucial to its origins than Robin Hood himself. In the *Gest* ... one is left with the overall impression that it was the sheriff's presence in Nottinghamshire that drew Robin to that county rather than that it was Robin's activities in Sherwood which compelled the local royal agent to move into the centre of the legend.

They also speculatively suggested that stories about him 'arose independently from and perhaps even preceded those concerning Robin Hood', and that the legend was 'an amalgam of two originally distinct story cycles', one centred on a Yorkshire outlaw from Barnsdale and one on a Nottinghamshire sheriff.[1] It is difficult, however, to imagine a type of popular story in which a sheriff was heroic, and the idea does not fit with the plot of that other tale of yeomen outlaws, *Adam Bell, Clim of the Clough*

---

[1] D&T, pp. 14–15.

and William of Cloudesley, the earliest text of which dates from 1536 but which is certainly of medieval origin. The three heroes were 'outlawed for venyson' and lurked in Inglewood Forest in Cumberland, near the town of Carlisle, whose justice and sheriff jointly play the role of official villain, although in this tale the justice is the senior figure. Both are killed by the arrows of the outlaws.[2] The nearest approximation to a tale of an 'evil hero' is that of *Eustace the Monk*, a poem in French composed probably not long after 1223 and surviving in a manuscript of 1284 or slightly later. It is based on the real life of Eustace Busquet (c.1170-1217), a monk from the abbey of St Samer in the Boulonnais who, after the murder of his father, became an outlaw in the forest of Hardelot and an enemy of the count of Boulogne, his former employer, who in the poem he frequently tricks through his mastery of disguise. Later, as a pirate in the English Channel, he was involved in the war between King John and King Philip II of France, first working for the one and then the other, and was beheaded after being captured at a naval battle off Sandwich in 1217, regarded by some as an act of God. The tale describes how, early in his life, he was taught black magic and evil tricks and charms by the Devil in Toledo, and the epilogue was on the theme that 'no-one can live a long life if he always attempts to do harm'. He has been described as 'the Robin Hood of the sea' and even as a possible predecessor of Friar Tuck.[3]

It seems inherently most likely that the Robin Hood legend originally derived from a set of circumstances in which a Yorkshire outlaw was pursued by a sheriff somehow connected with Nottingham, but not specifically with Sherwood Forest. Sherwood is not mentioned by name in the *Gest* or any of the early tales except *Robin Hood and the Monk*, whose provenance is from the midland region rather than Yorkshire.[4] A twelfth or thirteenth-century sheriff was an individual appointed by the king for an undefined period to administer a county, or in some cases more than one county, on the monarch's behalf, and account for the shire revenues at the royal Exchequer once a year. He also presided over local justice in the courts of the shire and hundred, and assisted the judges of the king's central courts when they visited his county or counties to hold their judicial eyres or forest eyres. He was responsible for public order, and occasionally, in times of civil war or unrest, was expected to assemble what we might call the 'county militia' to undertake military

---

[2] D&T, pp. 258–73. For the historical background to this tale, see H.R.T. Summerson, *Medieval Carlisle* (Cumberland and Westmorland Antiquarian and Archaeological Society, Extra Series XXV, 1993), pp. 432–34.

[3] G. S. Burgess, ed., *Two Medieval Outlaws: Eustace the Monk and Fouke Fitz Warin* (Cambridge, 1997), pp. 3–82; D. J. Conlon, ed., *Li Romans de Witasse le Moine*, University of North Carolina, Studies in Romance Languages and Literature 126 (1972). See also Holt, *Robin Hood*, chapter 4.

[4] See above, pp. 11–12.

activity of a local or regional nature on behalf of the crown, such as to assist in the siege of a castle being held by the king's enemies. The tales connect Robin with Nottingham, a county town, and his main enemy is the sheriff of Nottingham. It is in Nottingham castle gaol that Robin is imprisoned by the sheriff, and from which he is rescued by Little John. The significance of Nottingham in the legend derives mainly from the facts that the sheriff's office was in the castle there, and that it was where the county gaol was located. It was established as part of the programme to create a network of county gaols, initiated as a result of the assize of Clarendon in 1166, which remained in place for centuries thereafter. Nottingham's gaol is first recorded in 1169-70, probably very soon after it was built.[5] During the period in which the conflict between Robin and the sheriff is supposed to have taken place, the official known for convenience as the 'sheriff of Nottingham', and usually referred to as such in official documents in the thirteenth century, was the joint sheriff of two neighbouring counties, Nottinghamshire and Derbyshire. It was only in 1567 that Derbyshire first had a sheriff of its own, although in 1256 the men of Derby purchased, for a fine of 60 marks, the establishment of a separate county court, administered by the sheriff of Nottingham, who held separate meetings in Nottingham and Derby on different days of the same week.[6] From 1449, when Nottingham became a county borough, with powers, institutions and officials separate from the county of Nottinghamshire, it had its own sheriff, who was also known, with greater accuracy, as the sheriff of Nottingham. During the period when the *Gest of Robyn Hode* was first being printed, therefore, the title related to two quite distinct offices, both of which still exist today.[7] It is also worth noting that, although the town itself lay within the boundaries of the royal forest, its growing legal privileges as a borough from the time of its first charter in 1155 made it a privileged enclave in reality little affected by the forest laws.[8]

In both the *Gest* and *Robin Hood and Guy of Gisborne* the sheriff is killed, but no real medieval sheriff of Nottingham is known to have died while in office. Several suggestions have been made as to which of the many sheriffs of Nottinghamshire and Derbyshire was the original opponent of the outlaw. In 1960 James Holt first proposed Philip Marc, sheriff of

---

[5] W. Stubbs, *Select Charters*, 9th edition (Oxford, 1913), p. 171; R. B. Pugh, *Imprisonment in Medieval England* (Cambridge, 1968), pp. 64-65; *Pipe Roll 16 Henry II*, PRS XV, p. 80.

[6] D. Crook, 'The Establishment of the Derbyshire County Court, 1256', *Derbyshire Archaeological Journal* 103 (1983), pp. 98–106; TNA, C 60/53, m. 12.

[7] *Public Record Office, Lists and Indexes IX, List of Sheriffs of England and Wales* (1898), pp. 31, 102–04, 218.

[8] D. Crook, 'The Exemption of Nottingham from the Forest Laws in the Twelfth and Thirteenth Centuries', *TTS* 109 (2005), pp. 69–73.

those two counties from 1209 to 1224 and, curiously, Brian de Lisle, never a sheriff except briefly in Yorkshire (1233-4) and whose chief employment under both King John and Henry III was as the senior forest administrator north of the Trent.[9] In 1976 Dobson and Taylor reviewed the evidence, declining to propose a candidate of their own, but two years later John Maddicott suggested that the original sheriff of Nottingham might have been John de Oxenford, an unpopular outsider from Oxford, who held the office for most of the period from 1334 to 1339. He was outlawed in 1340, indicted for many offences against the men of the county in royal judicial proceedings in Nottinghamshire in 1341, and was detested both by the gentry and men of lower rank.[10] In 1978 further candidates active in the fourteenth century were suggested by John Bellamy, the only other writer to give extended treatment to the subject. Like Maddicott, he directed his attention towards the second quarter of the fourteenth century, and suggested Sir Robert Ingram, sheriff of Nottinghamshire and Derbyshire for about three years and of Yorkshire for much of the period between 1322 and 1334, and also mayor and member of parliament for Nottingham on several occasions; he had earlier been mentioned in passing by Dobson and Taylor.[11] Early in his career, at Nottingham in the 1960s, Bellamy had written about the activities of the notorious Coterel gang of criminal gentry, with whom Ingram was associated.[12] He also for the first time put forward, at considerable length, the claims of Henry de Fauconberg, sheriff of Nottinghamshire and then Yorkshire at dates between 1318 and 1330, and was struck by the fact that he served one of his periods as sheriff of the former county at the time when Edward II was concerned about the shortage of deer in his parks and when Hunter's 'original Robin Hood' left the king's service to return to the greenwood. He further conjectured that Fauconberg's appointment as sheriff of Yorkshire in 1325 was to place him 'where he could keep a watch on Robin's future activities', which 'were indeed nefarious and centred on Barnsdale'. Bellamy also researched Fauconberg's significant landholdings and activities in both counties, as well as possible financial and legal misconduct, using both central government and local sources, including the Wakefield manor court rolls for a period when a Robert

[9] J. C. Holt, 'The Origins and Audience of the Ballads of Robin Hood', *Past and Present* 18 (1960), pp. 89–110; reprinted in *Peasants, Knights and Heretics: Studies in Medieval English Social History*, ed. R. H. Hilton (Cambridge, 1976), at pp. 253–54.

[10] J. R. Maddicott, 'The Birth and Setting of the Ballads of Robin Hood', *EHR* 93 (1978), pp. 276–99, at 286–93. For the record of these proceedings, see TNA, JUST 1/691. See also p. 113.

[11] J. Bellamy, *Robin Hood: An Historical Enquiry* (London, 1985), chapter 4; D&T, pp. 15, 29.

[12] J. G. Bellamy, 'The Coterel Gang: An Anatomy of a Band of Fourteenth-Century Criminals', *EHR* 79 (1964), pp. 698–717.

Hood was active in the manor. Fauconberg's original landed estate was in Holderness, and in the *Gest* Little John, when he was seeking to enter the sheriff's employment, claimed to come from there. Bellamy concluded that his case for identifying Fauconberg with the sheriff of the *Gest* remained substantial, while admitting that there was no positive evidence for it. His view did not, however, receive support among other historians, particularly since his book was published a year later than an article by the present author, using name evidence which showed that the Robin Hood legend existed in some form by 1262 and was already known by then to at least one royal clerk.[13]

A much more plausible suggestion for the original sheriff of the legend was made by Jeffrey Stafford, of Hyde in Cheshire, in correspondence with James Holt in 1977, after his interest in the subject had been aroused in 1970 and subsequently further stimulated by the publication of Dobson and Taylor's book in 1976.[14] Stafford suggested that Eustace of Lowdham, a Nottinghamshire sheriff who was briefly sheriff of Yorkshire, from 29 April 1225 to 26 May 1226, was the best candidate. Influenced by the earlier suggestion of Dobson and Taylor that the sheriff and the outlaw were originally the subject of different tale cycles, Holt saw Lowdham as helping to bring together what were perhaps originally separate Yorkshire and Nottinghamshire stories, although 'the identity of the prototype of the villainous sheriff of Nottingham, if indeed there was one, need not depend at all on his intervention in Yorkshire'.[15] He wrote shortly after the publication in 1988 of an article in which the present author attempted to put the fullest case then possible for Lowdham's candidature. In this the fact that he was the sheriff of Yorkshire who in 1225 sent the sergeants to 'seek, take and behead' Robert of Wetherby was crucial.[16]

Eustace of Lowdham, the son of a man named Herbert about whom nothing further is known, took his name from the village of Lowdham in the Trent valley in Nottinghamshire. He was a clerk, presumably in minor orders, and probably connected in some way with the parish church in Lowdham. (Figure 7) He was, however, important enough to be the first witness to two undated local charters, in both of which his son Walter was the second witness, showing that by the time they were

---

[13] D. Crook, 'Some Further Evidence Concerning the Dating of the Origins of the Legend of Robin Hood', *EHR* 99 (1984), pp. 530–34. See Chapter 4.
[14] I am grateful to Jeffrey Stafford for this information, supplied in late 2018.
[15] Holt *Robin Hood*, pp. 60–61, 209.
[16] Crook, 'The Sheriff of Nottingham and Robin Hood: The Genesis of the Legend?' in *Thirteenth Century England II: Proceedings of the Newcastle upon Tyne Conference 1987*, ed. P. R. Coss and S. D. Lloyd (Woodbridge, 1987), pp. 59–69. What follows is based on that article, with some corrections and new material.

FIGURE 7. Lowdham parish church, Nottinghamshire. The lancet windows on the west and south sides of the tower are of the late 12th century; the buttresses were added in 1822 to prevent its collapse. The tower must have been well-known to Eustace of Lowdham, 'the sheriff of Nottingham', who may in his youth have witnessed its construction and may also have been a priest at the church before becoming a sheriff.

issued Eustace was already middle-aged. One was given to John chaplain of Lowdham by William Spichfat of Caythorpe, where he is referred to as 'Eustace of Lowdham, clerk'; the second, in which he is not called 'clerk', was granted by Geoffrey the Angevin to Fulk of Lowdham.[17] In 1207, as 'Eustace parson of Lowdham', he owed King John a fine of 15 marks for creating what was deemed to be an unlicensed deer-leap at Lowdham, presumably on the boundary of a park he had established there.[18] This may have brought him into direct personal contact with King John, who visited Lowdham in August that year and took a close personal interest in forest matters. He next appeared, as 'Eustace clerk of Lowdham', before the king's eyre justices at Derby in November 1208, as the defendant in a case brought by Thomas son of Geoffrey concerning half a carucate of land at Lamcote in the parish of Radcliffe on Trent. The case concluded with an agreement by which he paid Thomas 3 marks as an acknowledgment that the land was the latter's property, in return for an agreement that he himself would hold it for an annual rent of 2s.[19] It is clear that by the middle of John's reign Eustace was an established man of property and deeply involved in affairs in his native village and the surrounding district. It is therefore not surprising that he became involved in county administration under Philip Marc, an exiled Tourangeau, probably from Chenonceaux near Tours. Marc had followed John to England, as a follower of Gerard d'Athée, after the loss of Normandy in 1204. He became sheriff of Nottinghamshire and Derbyshire in 1209, remaining in office for a decade and a half, serving John throughout the rebellion against him in 1215, during the civil war that followed and most of the minority of the young King Henry III after the death of John at Newark in 1216.

Marc was supported as sheriff by an entourage of several of his close relatives who had crossed the Channel with him, but he also needed able, literate and experienced English officials familiar with the locality to help carry out his heavy administrative and fiscal responsibilities.[20] Eustace of Lowdham had become one of them by 1212, when 'Eustace the clerk' vouched for the sheriff's expenditure of £107 in obtaining wine, grain and pork for the king and transporting them to York, Chester and Nottingham.[21] Before September 1213, and probably for several years

[17] UNMASC, Middleton Mi D714, and Mi D870, printed in HMC, *Middleton MSS* (London, 1911), pp. 38–39, 54–55.
[18] *Pipe Roll 9 John*, PRS NS 22, p. 124. In 1275 the jurors of the Hundred Rolls enquiry confirmed that he had created a park in Lowdham: *Rotuli Hundredorum*, II (London, 1818), p. 311.
[19] TNA, CP 25/1/182/2, no. 43 [AALT- IMG 0057].
[20] J. C. Holt, 'Philip Mark and the Shrievalty of Nottinghamshire and Derbyshire', *TTS* 56 (1952), pp. 8–24.
[21] *Pipe Roll 14 John*, PRS NS XXX, p. 27.

previously, he rented from the king a house in Nottingham, situated in St Mary's parish below the gaol, presumably as a convenient dwelling close to his office in the castle.[22] By 1214 Lowdham was Marc's clerk and undersheriff, since after Michaelmas that year he accounted for the first time at the Exchequer, on his master's behalf, for the shrievalty of Nottinghamshire and Derbyshire.[23] During the civil war between King John and the rebel barons in 1215–16, when Marc at Nottingham was the mainstay of the royal cause in the east midland counties, Lowdham temporarily deserted him, taking the side of his lord, John de Lacy, constable of Chester, a leading rebel, who had been appointed commander of the rebel forces in Yorkshire and Nottinghamshire in 1215. In May 1216 John notified Marc that, at the request of Lacy, he had pardoned Lowdham for the arrears in payment of the fine that he had made with the king for supporting Lacy against the monarch.[24] Although the manor of Lowdham was held by Emma de Beaufey, whose other estates were in Norfolk, Lacy had a mesne holding there of the honour of Chester, the result of a grant to his ancestor Henry de Lacy by an earlier earl of Chester during the reign of King Stephen in about 1143–4, and it must have been through that tenurial link that Eustace was connected with Lacy.[25]

In the event, his temporary disloyalty to King John made little difference to his career under the young Henry III; he was too valuable to Marc. The Nottinghamshire and Derbyshire accounts in the pipe rolls for the early years of the new reign, the earliest being heard in 1217, are headed by Marc's name, giving the impression that he rendered the accounts in person, but this is often misleading. By 1177–8 it was already officially acknowledged that if a sheriff was unable to account in person and had to appoint a deputy, the wording of the account

---

[22] *RLC* I, p. 149.
[23] *Pipe Roll 16 John*, PRS NS 35, p. 156.
[24] *Memoranda Roll 10 John*, PRS NS 31, p. 144. Peace between the king and Lacy was made in January 1216: J. C. Holt, *The Northerners* (2nd edition, Oxford, 1992), p. 1. For Lacy's changes of sides in 1215–17, see also N. Vincent in *ODNB*, 'Lacy, John de, Third Earl of Lincoln (c. 1192–1240)', accessed 16 December 2018.
[25] *The Charters of the Anglo-Norman Earls of Chester, c. 1071–1237*, ed. G. Barraclough, Record Society of Lancashire and Cheshire CXXVI (1988), no. 69; *EYC* III, ed. W. Farrer (YAS Record Series, Extra Series, 1916), pp. 190–91; W. E. Wightman, *The Lacy Family in England and Normandy, 1066–1194* (Oxford, 1966), p. 91. For the Beaufey manor in Lowdham see *The Thurgarton Cartulary*, ed. T. Foulds (Stamford, 1994), pp. 316–18; *Calendar of Charter Rolls* I, pp. 49, 212, 223. Lowdham was also later said to have assarted and held 2½ acres *in castellario* of the fee: *The Sherwood Forest Book*, ed. H. E. Boulton, Thoroton Society Record Series XXIII (1965), p. 96.

would be the same as if he was sitting at his account in person.[26] The memoranda rolls of the two remembrancers, king's and treasurer's, officials who were present at the accounts and taking notes, survive in broken series from the beginning of Henry III's reign. During the latter part of the time that Marc held the shrievalty, when the names of those actually rendering the accounts begin to be recorded in them, they show that from 1222 until the end of 1224 he only once appeared in person to render his account; they were regularly rendered in his name by 'Eustace of Lowdham, clerk'.[27] During that period Marc was in many respects a regional military overlord, continuing in the role he had performed with such success in Nottinghamshire and its region during the civil war of 1215-17.[28] Under him, Lowdham served as the working sheriff of the two counties, and would normally have been referred to as 'sheriff of Nottingham' during that time, although documentary references to him as such survive only from his later tenure of the office.[29] (Figure 8) By the mid-1220s he may have been closely enough associated with the office to be popularly known as 'the sheriff of Nottingham'.

Eustace of Lowdham accounted at the Exchequer on behalf of Philip Marc for the last time, for the eighth year of Henry III (Michaelmas 1223 to Michaelmas 1224) on 27 October 1224.[30] Marc was very last of King John's Poitevin administrators to lose his office, on 28 December 1224, when Ralph fitz Nicholas, a household steward of the king, was appointed as the new sheriff of Nottinghamshire and Derbyshire. This left Lowdham without an official position, because the new sheriff employed a new clerk and undersheriff, Hugh le Bel. However, only four months later, on 29 April 1225, he was appointed sheriff of Yorkshire.[31] He was in office as a custodian (*ut custos*) only for just over a year, and rendered his only preliminary view of account for the county

---

[26] *Dialogus de Scaccario*, ed. C. Johnson (London and Edinburgh, 1950), pp. 82–84.

[27] TNA, E 159/5, m. 14d [AALT-IMG 0072]; E 368/4, m. 17d [IMG 2461]; E 159/6, mm. 10, 15d [IMG 0023, 0078]; E 368/6, mm. 17d, 23d [IMG 2631, 2647]. The single exception was that Marc accounted in person for the sixth year of Henry's reign on 1 May 1223: E 368/5, m. 3 [IMG 2472].

[28] D. Crook, 'Philip Marc, Robert de Gaugy and the First Siege of Newark, July 1218', *TTS* 122 (2018), pp. 103–20, at 113.

[29] CRR XV, no. 508; *Descriptive Catalogue of Derbyshire Charters*, ed. I. H. Jeayes (London and Derby, 1906), nos. 501, 503; HMC *Middleton MSS*, pp. 55–56 (referring to what is now UNMASC, Mi D.940); *Rufford Charters*, ed. C. J. Holdsworth, Thoroton Society Record Series XXIX, XXX, XXXII, XXXIV (1972–81), nos. 174–75, 551, 631. There are occasional specific references to an 'under-sheriff' (*subvic'*), such as one to Simon de Hale, under-sheriff of Yorkshire, in 1224: TNA, E 368/6, m. 6d [AALT-IMG 2257].

[30] TNA, E 368/7, m. 25 [AALT-IMG 2743].

[31] *PR 1216–25*, pp. 500, 524.

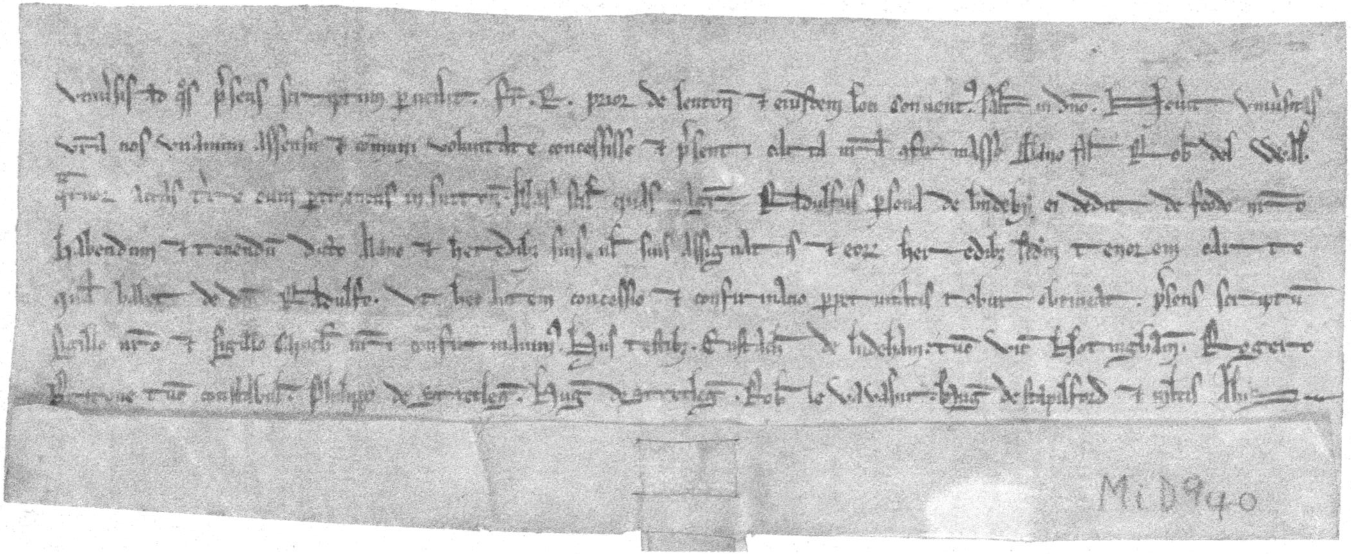

FIGURE 8. Eustace of Lowdham is the most likely real individual to have been the sheriff of Nottingham in the Robin Hood tales. Only one surviving document so far identified describes him as holding that office, a charter of the prior of Lenton Priory, granting four acres of land in Sutton (unidentified, Notts) to Alan son of Robert del Wal, undated but probably of about 1233, in which he appears as the first witness. His name, in the form 'Eustace of Lowdham, then sheriff of Nottingham', occupies the second half of the penultimate line.

on 16 July 1225, and his first annual account on 27 November 1225.[32] When his second Yorkshire account was rendered, on 16 May 1227, he accounted as custodian for only three-quarters of the fiscal year 1225-6 (being given over £87 for his expenses), since he had been replaced on 25 May 1226 by Robert of Cockfield, the steward of the justiciar, Hubert de Burgh, the king's principal advisor.[33] During his relatively short period in office, Eustace of Lowdham carried out the usual tasks performed by all sheriffs, such as administering routine justice, maintaining the county gaol in York, collecting the regular farms, paying his officials, making purchases, and carrying out his written instructions. His first account included the reference to the purchase of a chain to hang up the body of Robert of Wetherby, and the second the costs of the men he had sent to kill the fugitive. Not long after he left office the Exchequer ordered the new sheriff of Yorkshire to distrain those who were in debt to Lowdham to render their arrears from the time he was sheriff.[34] He was still in debt to the king to the extent of more than £125; over £30 of that amount was pardoned in two stages in 1228-9, and he continued to pay off the rest at a fixed rate of £10 per annum, although in 1232 he was threatened with distraint because he was not serving his repayment terms.[35] Such arrangements were perfectly normal, and did not prevent him from briefly holding office as a sheriff again, in his native Nottinghamshire. About 24 April 1233, for unknown reasons, he temporarily replaced Ralph fitz Nicholas; the arrangement seems to have come to an end by mid-October in the same year. No record exists of any shrieval activity he undertook during those months, and he never served as a sheriff again.[36] He did, however, continue to carry out other governmental tasks, as a justice of gaol delivery and special assize commissioner in Nottinghamshire, and as late as 1241 he was appointed to assess tallage in Nottinghamshire, Derbyshire, Lincolnshire and Yorkshire.[37] He was dead by the early

---

[32] E 159/8, mm. 10–10d [AALT-IMG 0031, 0082]; E 368/8, m. 20 [IMG 0060]; E 372/69, rot. 9–9d [IMG 1221–24, 1281–4].

[33] *PR 1225–32*, p. 38; E 372/70, rot. 1 [AALT–IMG 6997–99, 7058–61]; E 368/9, m. 7 [IMG 2869]. Many sheriffs had been described as custodians in the pipe roll for the previous year, including Philip Marc, but not the sheriff of Yorkshire, Simon de Hale: *Pipe Roll 8 Henry III*, PRS NS LIV, pp. 8, 204, 260 and *passim*.

[34] E 368/9 m. 5d [AALT-IMG 2901].

[35] E 372/72, rot. 14d [AALT-IMG 1540]; 73, rot. 17d [IMG 3515]; 74, rot. 14 [IMG 3578]; *CR 1227–31*, pp. 61, 156; *Memoranda Rolls 16–17 Henry III*, ed. R. A. Brown (London, 1991), no. 281.

[36] *CR 1231–34*, p. 212; *CRR*, XV, no. 508; TNA, E 368/12, m. 1 [AALT-IMG 0027].

[37] TNA, CP 25/1/283/10, no. 107 [AALT-IMG 0012]; *Yorkshire Fines 1232–46*, YAS RS LXVII (1925), p. 171; *PR 1225–32*, pp. 160, 306, 443, 516; *1232–47*, p. 263; *CLR 1240–45*, p. 63; *CR 1237–42*, p. 303.

autumn of 1246, when in the latest Exchequer records the regular references to him were hurriedly amended to refer to his heirs.[38]

In the later years of his life Eustace continued to accumulate property in Lowdham and other places in south-eastern Nottinghamshire, but he also acquired an interest further north in the county, at Carlton in Lindrick near the Yorkshire boundary, on the road between Worksop and Tickhill. In 1234 the king granted him and his heirs the rent of 30s formerly held by Henry Corbin there, for which he was to render 6d yearly at the Exchequer.[39] He is not known to have had property in Yorkshire until 1241, when he held part of the royal demesne at Kilham, a member of the soke of Driffield in the East Riding. This property was apparently held on a similar basis to his holding at Carlton in Lindrick, since they were both exempted from tallage on the same terms.[40] His appointment as sheriff of Yorkshire in 1225 may have been no more than the calling in of an experienced but currently unemployed professional administrator to undertake the task; it is possible although less likely that he was brought in specifically to deal with the fugitive Robert of Wetherby. He did in any case have a close connection of long standing with the county through the Lacy lordship, centred on the castle of Pontefract, which had led him briefly to rebel against King John. [Figure 9] It may have been John de Lacy's influence which in 1225 helped to secure the Yorkshire shrievalty for his protégé. It is possible that Lowdham also served as an honorial official of the Lacy estates, although no evidence of that has been found. What is certain is that his son and heir, Walter, did so, and in a senior capacity.

In 1232 John de Lacy was made earl of Lincoln, and the title was inherited on his death in 1240 by his son Edmund, a minor.[41] Edmund's steward was Walter of Lowdham, who before John de Lacy's death had received from him a grant of timber, and who had earlier witnessed some of John's charters.[42] Early in 1248, at the Exchequer, and described as Edmund's bailiff, Lowdham acknowledged receipt from the archbishop of York of all Edmund de Lacy's lands which the archbishop had held at farm.[43] He had managed Edmund's lands on his behalf while he was

---

38 TNA, E 368/19, m. 1 [AALT-IMG 3754]; E 372/89, rot. 1 [IMG 5364].
39 On Eustace's lands in Nottinghamshire, see also *The Thurgarton Cartulary*, ed. T. Foulds (Stamford, 1994), nos. 7 and note, 8, 15n, 58n, 476n, 485n, 524n.
40 *Calendar of Fine Rolls 25 Henry III*, no. 559; online at finerollshenry3.org.uk/content/calendar/roll_037.html.
41 GEC *The Complete Peerage*, ed. H. A. Doubleday and Lord Howard de Walden (London, 1929), VII, p. 680.
42 CR 1237–42, p. 281; TNA, DL 25/54, 55. Other references to him as Edmund's steward are in *EYC* VIII, ed. C. T. Clay, YAS RS, Extra Series VI (1949), pp.197, 247; and *The Chartulary of St John of Pontefract*, I, ed. R. Holmes, YAS RS XXV (1899), pp. 198, 268.
43 TNA, E 368/20, m. 6 [AALT-IMG 3844].

FIGURE 9. Painting of Pontefract castle by Flemish artist Alexander Keirincx, 1639-40, a decade before it was demolished in 1649, by order of the Commonwealth, after a lengthy siege. It had ceased to be the centre of the Lacy estates in 1311, and was greatly enlarged by the dukes of Lancaster thereafter, taking on palatial characteristics and eventually having eight towers. It did not look nearly so impressive during the lifetimes of Eustace of Lowdham and his son Walter, but its importance as a centre of baronial power was even then considerable.

under age, as illustrated by an undated charter which must have been issued in or before 1248, when the young earl was allowed to succeed to his lands at the age of only 18.[44] Some of the demesne lands of the Lacy honour and the holdings of his subtenants lay in or near Barnsdale.[45] As Edmund's steward, Walter of Lowdham agreed to exchange with Adam de Neufmarché a small piece of land (twenty perches of 22 feet long by 10 feet wide) next to a windmill, below Adam's garden in Campsall, a village on the eastern fringe of Barnsdale, subject to Edmund's confirmation when he should come of age.[46] Walter of Lowdham may by then already have inherited Eustace's park at Lowdham and land in Carlton in Lindrick.[47]

In 1225, therefore, Eustace of Lowdham, 'sheriff of Nottingham', within less than three months after he became sheriff of Yorkshire, sent sergeants paid for by the king to 'to seek, take and behead' the notorious criminal Robert of Wetherby. As demonstrated in the previous chapter, the pursuit and decapitation of fleeing criminals was common enough, and their respective fates had to be reported to royal justices in the county when they next held an eyre there, in the *veredicta* presented by the jurors for the various wapentakes. Examples of the procedure recorded in the next surviving Yorkshire eyre roll help to set the task performed by the sheriff's men in 1225 in context. The eyre was held before Stephen of Seagrave, Robert of Lexington and five other justices between early June and the middle of July 1231, mainly at York. The executions recorded in the plea roll must have taken place since the previous eyre, which ended in February 1227 and was the first in the county since that of 1218-19, from which examples have already been given.[48] The beheadings listed in 1231 therefore all took place within a few years of 1225. In Ryedale wapentake Walter Guyt killed a cleric and fled to a church to claim sanctuary and abjure the realm, acknowledging his crime. When he left the church he was pursued by five men, the first named possibly being the victim's son Stephen, another cleric. They captured him at Skiplam, led him back three leagues to the gallows of Slingsby, and there cut off his head. In Gilling Adam de Stoclive was decapitated by Richard de Tyndal after the hue was

---

44 N. Vincent in *ODNB*, 'Lacy, John de, third earl of Lincoln (c. 1192–1240)', accessed 16 December 2018.
45 *EYC* III, pp. 230–31 (Skelbrooke); 231–32 (Sleephill in Skelbrooke); 232 (Campsall); 254–55 (Skellow); 260–61 (Smeaton); 298, 300 (Wentbridge); 326–27, 377–79 (Wrangbrook); 401 (Kirk Smeaton); 402–03 (Hampole). See also Wightman, *Lacy Family*, p. 23 map.
46 TNA, DL 25/2156.
47 *Rotuli Hundredorum*, ed. R. Illingworth, 2 vols. (Record Commission, 1812, 1818), II, p. 311; TNA, C 132/2, no. 16; *Calendar of Inquisitions Post Mortem*, I, no. 36.
48 TNA, JUST 1/1043; D. Crook, *Records of the General Eyre*, Public Record Office Handbooks 20 (London, 1982), pp. 75–76, 79, 87. See Chapter 8.

raised, and the four nearest vills testified that he was a thief. In Ryedale again, Henry of Washington and Simon son of the chaplain beheaded two thieves between 'Marewde' and Langlands, and their heads were sent to York. In Richmond town Richard Scalle was reported to have been decapitated in the forest of Wandale because he was a thief, and his head was carried to York. In Ainsty wapentake John son of the priest (*presbiter*), a malefactor, was found beheaded on Monkton Moor, and a pregnant woman found with him was handed to the sheriff; she was not suspected of any offence, and so was released. Once more in Ryedale, Albinus Firguiling was imprisoned at Pickering after committing larceny; he escaped, but three months later he was captured with the stolen goods at Howden and beheaded. In Morley wapentake William Brun and William Malot killed Richard son of William and fled; they were followed by another Richard, the victim's brother, who beheaded them and himself fled. It was testified that the hue had not been raised before Richard carried out his punishment, and, since he could not be found, he was outlawed. Under Staincliffe wapentake it was reported that, after a robbery at Wrangbrook, the hue and cry was raised and the thieves were pursued. One of them, Adam de Scocia, fled into the church at distant Giggleswick, acknowledged himself to be a thief and abjured the realm. Robert the chaplain and Thomas Marscall were, while fleeing, found in possession of the stolen goods. Marscall was immediately beheaded, but the chaplain was imprisoned at York, pleading his clerical state to avoid trial in a lay court. A jury swore that he was a thief, captured with the stolen goods, and his case was referred to the archbishop. In Staincross wapentake Osbert Brodun was reported to have killed Matilda of Carlecotes on Stamford moor and fled; afterwards he was found and beheaded. In Agbrigg wapentake Geoffrey Berefot of Wakefield was said to have killed Roger Sherewind; he was beheaded while fleeing.[49]

These cases illustrate the usually reactive nature of pursuits, often made by relatives or friends of the victim, sometimes without following the correct procedure while raising the hue and consequently risking outlawry themselves. Some pursuits could be very lengthy. The distance between Wrangbrook, near Skelbrooke in Barnsdale, where Adam de Scocia committed his crime, and Giggleswick, where he took sanctuary, is about 66 miles. Perhaps he was a Scot and was trying to escape back over the border before his pursuers caught up with him. The distance from Ryedale to Howden, where Firguiling was captured months after his crime, is around 50 miles. The heads of three of the fugitives were said to have been sent to York, and others may have been. The pursuit of Robert of Wetherby in 1225 by the sergeants sent by the sheriff and paid a significant sum of money for carrying out their task was

[49] TNA, JUST 1/1043, rots. 7, 3d (3), 5d, 7d, 12d, 14d, 15d, 16d; [AALT-IMG 1327, 1371 (2), 1372, 1375, 1380, 1392, 1395, 1396, 1398].

altogether different and, as far as can be judged after an examination of the extensive surviving records, totally unprecedented. In Exchequer records from before 1225, there are only very occasional entries about the pursuit and killing of outlaws. In the pipe roll for the ninth year of Richard I (1196-7), in the Leicestershire account, there are examples in two successive and probably related entries. In the first, Robert the sergeant of the earl of Leicester and his two companions, 'pursuers (*persecutoribus*) of outlaws', had been paid 15s., authorised by a writ of the king's justiciar. The second is a payment of 5s. to the sergeants for the head of an outlaw named Geoffrey, who they had killed, authorised by the king's writ.[50] Earlier, in the Worcestershire account in the roll for Richard's seventh year (1194-5), Thomas de Prestewude was given 2 marks for taking the head of an outlaw called William de Elleford to Westminster, authorised by another writ, which may or may not mean that he was the man who killed him.[51] There are no other similar entries in the ten pipe rolls of Richard's reign. In those of John's reign (1199-1216), all but one of which survive, there is only a single reference to a payment to someone to hunt down outlawed men in this way. In the king's third year (1200-01), the sheriff of Shropshire was allowed in his account the significant sum of 4 marks paid to one Simon de Lenz 'to sustain him in seeking outlawed men'.[52]

How common were such deadly pursuits? During John's reign royal letters patent and, more important, letters close, which conveyed private instructions from the monarch to his officials, began to be recorded in parchment rolls kept by the royal Chancery, and although some are missing the majority still survive at The National Archives and have been available in print for nearly two centuries.[53] It has been estimated that the eighteen surviving close rolls from 1204 to 1225 (those for the tenth to the thirteenth years of John are lost) contain the texts of approximately 14,000 letters close. Before the order of 12 July 1225 concerning the payment for the hunting down of Robert of Wetherby, there is not even a single letter of a similar nature, and there is none in the patent rolls either. It can therefore be argued that the circumstances which led to its being issued were unprecedented, and consequently that the pursuit of Wetherby had exceptional significance. Barrie Dobson's comment in 1997 that there was no evidence that his misdeeds 'were quite exceptional enough to become the focus of a local legend, let alone ones which were spectacular enough to be widely known ... a generation

---

[50] *Pipe Roll 9 Richard I*, PRS NS VIII, p. 169.
[51] *Pipe Roll 7 Richard I*, PRS NS VI, p. 9.
[52] *Pipe Roll 3 John*, PRS NS XIV, p. 277: Et Simoni de Lenz [or Lens] iiij m. ad sustentationem suam ad querendos utlagatos homines.
[53] RLC I; RLC II.

later' therefore seems very questionable.[54] Not only are these events of 1225 unique in the substantial surviving record, but they took place in the county where it is generally accepted that the legend of Robin Hood had its origin, and during the brief period when the sheriff of that county was the former sheriff of Nottingham.

Robert of Wetherby was not the only, or indeed the first, candidate for the original Robin Hood, living in or around the year 1225, to be proposed by historians during the twentieth century. Another trail of references among the records of Henry III's government, this time restricted to the financial records produced by the king's Exchequer and not found amongst the letters recorded in the rolls of his Chancery, was noticed by L. V. D. Owen in the pipe roll of 1230, and first mentioned in the unlikely context of an engineering supplement printed in *The Times* newspaper in February 1936.[55] Owen did not trouble to trace the entry concerned systematically from its first appearance in the Yorkshire account in the pipe roll for the tenth year of Henry III (1225-6) until its final one in the roll for the eighteenth year of the reign (1233-4), and its disappearance from the roll for the following year. These entries need to be considered in detail. In the pipe roll for 1225-6, which was audited before the barons of the Exchequer on 16 May 1227, a reference to the confiscated chattels of a fugitive called Robert Hod, valued at 32s 6d, appears among the financial issues arising from the visit of a group of justices to the county in July the previous year.[56] The debt was not cleared in that account, so the name continues to appear in the Yorkshire account in the nine subsequent pipe rolls from 1226-7 to 1233-4, six times as Robert Hod, once (in 1229-30) as Robert Hood, and twice (in 1227-8 and 1228-9) as Hobbehod.[57] In 1227-8 'St Peter' is inserted in the margin of the roll next to the entry referring to him, and in 1233-4 his name is preceded by a mark like a 'plus' sign, written cursively, apparently inserted after the entry was first written. In that year it is one of a number of debts in a paragraph again preceded in the margin by an inserted 'St Peter'; in the following year it does not appear at all, having been removed from the roll, although all the other debts that had been in the same paragraph still remain.[58] The reason for its removal was not mentioned in any of the surviving memoranda rolls of the Exchequer. That reason might possibly be related to the long-standing claim of the

---

[54] R. B. Dobson, 'Robin Hood: The Genesis of a Popular Hero', in *Robin Hood in Popular Culture*, ed. T. Hahn (Cambridge, 2000), p. 76.

[55] See p. 104.

[56] E 372/70, rot. 1d [AALT-IMG 7060].

[57] TNA, E 372/70, rot. 1d [AALT-IMG 7060]; E 372/71, rot. 4d [IMG 1375]; E 372/72, rot. 14d [IMG 1540]; E 372/73, rot. 17 [IMG 3447]; E 372/74, rot. 14 [IMG 3578], the one noticed by Owen; E 372/75, rot. 11 [IMG 3714]; E 372/76, rot. 3 [IMG 3827]; E 372/77, rot. 4 [IMG 3974]; E 372/78, rot. 2 [IMG 4067].

[58] TNA, E 372/79, rot. 2 [AAALT-IMG 4208].

archbishop of York, whose cathedral was dedicated to St Peter, to be entitled, in the terms of a supposed charter of Henry I early in his reign, 'to have his pleas in his own court concerning his moneyers and robbers and all other causes'.[59] If so, it may imply, as Holt suggested, that Robert Hod was a tenant of the archbishop, but this cannot be certain.[60] In January 1226 the archbishop and the dean and chapter of York claimed the chattels of their men who were fugitives in Yorkshire, and were given a respite from the demands of Martin of Pattishall and his fellow eyre justices for payment until after Easter. This may suggest a continuing dispute between the Exchequer and the church of York over the matter, which continued until the Robert Hod entry was deleted from the pipe roll account in 1234 or 1235.[61] No records of the archbishop's court survive until much later, so nothing further can be done to clarify this issue.

The reason why Robert Hod's name, in its various forms, appeared in the Exchequer pipe rolls for nine successive years was because it had been reported to the king's justices who held a session for assizes and gaol delivery at York, under the leadership of Robert of Lexington, beginning on 20 July 1225. Hod would have been due to stand trial before them because he had been accused of committing an unknown criminal offence, but he had not been caught and had, like many others, become a fugitive; he was not, therefore, in gaol at York awaiting an appearance before them. The plea roll for the session, which would have given brief details of the offence of which he was accused, has, like all Lexington's other eyre and assize rolls, failed to survive, almost certainly because they were never handed in to the treasury after his death in 1250; no general order to hand in such rolls is recorded until 1258, after which they survive in far greater numbers.[62] All the pipe roll records about him is that his chattels, his moveable goods, had been seized, and that they were valued at 32s 6d, which the sheriff, at that time Eustace of Lowdham, was liable to pay into the treasury and to account for it at the Exchequer.[63] The

---

[59] *Regesta Regum Anglo-Normannorum* II, ed. C. Johnson and H. A. Cronne (London, 1956), no. 518, dated by the editors to 21 April [1101] at Winchester, but which could have been issued at any Easter between 1101 and 1104. Richard Sharpe has recently concluded that the charter is a forgery concocted in the thirteenth century. It survives in many copies, including several in archbishopric of York sources, but it was also produced before the king's justices in eyre, holding *quo warranto* pleas at York in 1279–81, and confirmed by Edward III in 1338: *CPR 1338–40*, p. 166. I am indebted to Dr Sharpe, and also to Nicholas Vincent, for advice about the charter.

[60] Holt, *Robin Hood*, p. 54.

[61] *Calendar of Fine Rolls Henry III*, II, ed. P. Dryburgh and B. Hartland (2008), 11 Henry III, no. 71 (p. 124).

[62] Crook, *Records of the General Eyre*, pp. 16–17.

[63] An indication of the significance of the sum is that it was only 1s more than was paid in 1218 for the expenses of 30 miners, and a horseman who guided

pipe roll shows that he did not pay it, nor did his successors during the eight years after he ceased to be sheriff, until the sum was written off and removed from the pipe roll of 1234–5, a perfectly normal practice.

If Hod was still alive by the time the account was heard, in May 1227, he would almost certainly have by then been outlawed, after being summoned to five successive sessions of the county court. These courts were already accustomed to keeping plea rolls by John's reign, and in them outlawries must have been recorded, but none has survived for the thirteenth century for any county, and certainly no record of Robert Hod's outlawry now exists.[64] If he was outlawed, he may subsequently have been captured and executed without trial, but no record of that has survived. His description as 'fugitive' belonged to the time of the assize and gaol delivery session in Yorkshire in 1225, possibly even earlier, when the records for the session were being prepared. Once written down, the original entry would have remained unaltered in the estreat, the name given to the list of penalties sent by the justices to the Exchequer, and used by the treasurer's clerk to draw up the summons to be sent to the sheriff, listing the sums to be collected at Easter and Michaelmas.[65] Whatever had happened to the fugitive subsequently, the sheriff was still bound to answer for his chattels. Even though the estreat could have been handed in as early as September 1225, just after the assizes session at York ended, it is most likely that there was a delay. The debt for Hod's chattels was first included only in the summons for Easter 1226, because it does not appear in the Yorkshire account for 1224–5, held at the Exchequer on 27 November 1225. It first occurs in the county account for 1225–6 which, as already noted, was not heard until 16 May 1227.[66] For some time after the later entry for the same debt in the 1230–1 pipe roll was first noticed and pointed out by Owen, Hod was regarded by some as the most likely candidate for the original Robin Hood.[67] He was an outlaw; he bore the right Christian name; and he lived in the right county, at a time when it had serious problems with law and order, some of them resulting from the activities of Robert of Wetherby.

The most intriguing aspect of the run of entries in the pipe rolls relating to Robert Hod during those nine years is the fact that on the second and third occasions the clerk who wrote the entry referred to the outlaw as 'Hobbehod'. In 1989 Holt suggested that the appearance of the name

---

them, for travelling from Gloucester to Stamford, a journey that took six days: *RLC* I, p. 365; *Pipe Roll 3 Henry III*, PRS NS XLII (1976), p. 8.

[64] *CRR* VI, p. 230.
[65] For the entry into Exchequer summonses of the penalties imposed by the king's justices, see *Dialogus de Scaccario*, p. 70.
[66] E 372/69, rot. 9d (AALT-IMG 1284); E 368/8, m. 20 (IMG 2788); E 368/9, m. 7 (IMG 2869).
[67] Holt, *Robin Hood*, pp. 53–54, 189, 196.

in that form 'may well reflect the emergence of the legend', and later continued to regard it as 'a hint that he became legendary'.[68] Even more significant in its implications is the fact that in the following, fourth, year in which it appeared, the name reverted back to its original form, albeit initially with a doubling of the vowel. Evidence exists to indicate who it was that altered the name to 'Hobbehod' in the second roll, and suggests an explanation as to why it returned to 'Robert Hod' in the last six. For the years 1220–23 and 1226 there are some valuable entries in the receipt rolls and issue rolls of the Exchequer which supply information about its officials and their expenses.[69] There were two senior clerks and scribes, responsible for writing the records of the accounts rendered by the sheriffs, the pipe roll and its duplicate the chancellor's roll. They were jointly paid 10s. for obtaining the parchment needed for a full year, presumably for making the pipe roll, the chancellor's roll, which they were also responsible for preparing, and other needs.[70] The individuals named as receiving the payments were Richard of Barking and Robert of Bassingbourn, who presumably took their names from the places with those names in Essex and Cambridgeshire respectively. Bassingbourn was, in all but the first entry, named first, so it may be assumed that he was the senior of the two, the king's scribe, who wrote the main roll, the pipe roll, while Barking was the treasurer's scribe, who wrote the chancellor's roll.[71] Bassingbourn was also named first in various entries concerning payments for the robes of the Exchequer clerks between 1218 and 1224.[72] His seniority is apparently confirmed by an entry for Easter term in 1222, which states that Robert of Bassingbourn was paid 4s 2d (5d a day, his normal salary) for ten days while he wrote summonses.[73] The *Dialogue of the Exchequer*, written about 1177–8 by the then treasurer Richard Fitz Neal, and which described the constitution and workings of the Exchequer in great detail, stated that this task was normally performed by the chancellor's scribe. It seems that for some reason he was unable to carry out this essential duty at Easter 1222, so the work fell on that occasion to his colleague, who had therefore to work and be paid for ten extra days during the vacation. This entry therefore confirms

[68] Holt, *Robin Hood*, p. 189; Carpenter, *Robin Hood*, p. 29; ODNB.
[69] TNA, E 401, E 403.
[70] *CLR* VI, Appendix I, nos. 2157–58, 2163, 2167, 2182. They also, in 1222, received half a mark for the parchment for writing the rolls of the Jewish Exchequer: *RLC*, I, p. 517b.
[71] TNA, E 372, E 352 respectively. On the remembrancers in the thirteen century, see D. Crook, 'The Early Remembrancers of the Exchequer', *Bulletin of the Institute of Historical Research* 103 (1980), pp. 11–23.
[72] *RLC* I, pp. 402, 441b, 473, 517b, 523b, 574; II, p. 8b. In 1222 Bassingbourn alone received a gift of 5 marks from the king, and in 1223 a prest (imprest) of 3 marks (pp. 446, 556b).
[73] *CLR* VI, Appendix I, no. 2163, gives the total as 3s 2d, an error in transcription.

that Bassingbourn was the treasurer's scribe and Richard of Barking the chancellor's.[74] As such, Bassingbourn was responsible for writing the annual pipe roll for the years between the beginning of Henry III's reign and 1229, since they are all clearly written in the same hand, and he also wrote the earliest surviving roll of foreign accounts, containing material from the mid–1220s.[75] His tenure approximately coincided with the treasurership of Eustace of Fauconberg, which began in 1217. Fauconberg, who was also bishop of London from 1221 onwards, worked assiduously as treasurer, restoring royal finances after the disruption caused by the civil war of 1215–17, spending much of his time at Westminster for that purpose, until he died in 1228.[76] Bassingbourn acted as treasurer's scribe under him, writing the pipe roll which recorded the annual accounts of the sheriffs, before retiring not long after his master's death, before the roll which began to be compiled at Michaelmas 1229 was begun. At that point, the pipe rolls began to be written in the hand of another, unidentified, scribe, who changed the name of the fugitive 'Robehod' back to 'Robert Hod'.[77]

A little is known of Robert of Bassingbourn's earlier career. It is likely that he was related to, or at least personally acquainted with, two other royal servants from his native village: Humphrey of Bassingbourn, an ecclesiastic who became archdeacon of Salisbury, and Warin of Bassingbourn, a prominent counsellor of King John. He certainly once held land there.[78] Robert's first appearance in record, described as 'clerk', is in an entry in the pipe roll for 1203, relating to Heydon in Cambridgeshire and to London, a debt of 15 marks in the account for Essex and Hertfordshire, with which his connection is uncertain; he paid off the debt in instalments by 1212.[79] He is first referred to as a royal clerk in 1204, when King John granted him the churches of Grimsby, Bradley and Scartho in Lincolnshire, to hold them as soon as they fell vacant.[80] He certainly came to hold the last two, but may never have held the church of Grimsby.[81]

---

74 D. Crook, introduction to *Pipe Roll 5 Henry III*, PRS NS XLVIII, pp. xxiv–xxvi; *Dialogus de Scaccario*, pp. 17–18, 26, 28–32, 69–75, 104.
75 TNA, E 372/62-72; TNA, E 364/1, printed in PRS NS XLIV.
76 ODNB. Bassingbourn witnessed a Lincolnshire charter concerning Neville land in Redbourne whose witnesses were headed by the chancellor and Fauconberg, enrolled on a Common Bench roll in 1221: CRR X, pp. 216–17.
77 TNA, E 372/73. The new hand is more upright than the one it replaced.
78 ODNB, Bassingbourn, Humphrey of (d. 1238x41), by Nicholas Vincent; CRR VIII, no. 1482.
79 *Pipe Roll 5 John*, PRS NS XVI, p. 136; finally quit in *Pipe Roll 14 John*, p. 52. He retained some interests in the south of England into the 1220s: in 1221 he sued for a debt in Bedfordshire, and in the same year received a gift of 5 oaks from just outside the royal park of Havering in Essex: CRR X, p. 155; RLC I, p. 465.
80 RLP I, p. 47b.
81 PR 1216–25, p. 438; *The Letters and Charters of Cardinal Guala Bicchieri, Papal*

However, he certainly acquired important lay interests in Grimsby, which was rapidly developing and had received two charters from King John in 1201; the building of a royal castle there was also being planned.[82] In 1200 a man called Ralph of Bradley was beginning to withdraw from his leading role in Grimsby, and by 1206 Bassingbourn had taken his place, later obtaining a royal charter. In 1208 Bassingbourn's property, briefly forfeited like that of many other secular clergy because of the imposition of the papal interdict, was restored, and in the following month he was given, by another charter, all the property in Grimsby that Bradley had forfeited.[83] In 1212 he made another fine for the farm of the demesne of Grimsby, and two years later bought from the king all the stone and lime originally intended for building the castle.[84] His interests there continued during the reign of Henry III after the war of 1215–17, but on 9 October 1225, before the barons of the Exchequer in session at Westminster, he surrendered the lands he had in Grimsby under King John's charter, probably in favour of his nephew, Alan the almoner. Bassingbourn, however, was still rector of Bradley and Scartho in about 1226–1228, and in 1232 still had a tenement in Bradley and Grimsby, held by him and his nephew.[85] In 1231 he was in the process of resigning from the church of Scartho, being replaced by Hugh of Bassingbourn, probably another relative.[86] He was no longer described as a royal clerk when, early in 1230, Henry III gave him a gift of £5 to discharge his debts, and this probably confirms his retirement from the king's service at the Exchequer.[87]

Robert of Bassingbourn's property interests therefore remained predominantly in the Grimsby area into his later years, but he had before then also acquired a lesser connection with the county and diocese of York. He had become the joint holder of the church of Mexborough in southern Yorkshire, in which he was in the process of being replaced on 26 June 1234, perhaps soon after his death. It is not known when he had been presented to that living, but his successor was presented by the prior and monks of Monk Bretton, at that time a Cluniac house, a few miles away from Mexborough to the north-west, and it is probable that he also had been.[88]

Legate in England 1216–18, ed. N. Vincent, Canterbury and York Society LXXXIII (1996), no. 33 and note.

[82] S. H. Rigby, *Medieval Grimsby: Growth and Decline* (Hull, 1993), pp. 8, 38–40; E. Gillett, *A History of Grimsby* (Hull, 1970), pp. 10–11.

[83] *Rotuli de Oblatis et Finibus*, pp. 107, 338, 347; RLC I, p. 112b; *Rotuli Chartarum*, ed. T. D. Hardy (Record Commission, 1837), p. 177b.

[84] *Pipe Roll 14 John*, p. 112; *Pipe Roll 16 John*, PRS NS XXXV, p. 154.

[85] *Pipe Roll 8 John*, PRS NS XX, pp. 87, 103, to *Pipe Roll 16 John*, p. 146; TNA, E 372/69, rot. 13 (AALT-IMG 1237); TNA, E 368/8, m. 1 [AALT-IMG 2751]; CRR XII, no. 216; *Book of Fees*, pp. 361–62.

[86] PR 1225–32, p. 437.

[87] CLR I, p. 169.

[88] *The Register, or Rolls, of Walter Gray, Lord Archbishop of York*, ed. J. Raine Surtees

Like other royal clerks and justices required to be at Westminster during most of the year to carry out his official duties, Bassingbourn would doubtless have spent some of the intervals between terms, especially the long vacation in the summer, visiting his properties in places far from his workplace. Such visits can only usually be documented in the case of the justices of the central courts, who were often commissioned to take assizes of novel disseisin, or serve as justices of gaol delivery, in the areas where their own interests lay, particularly in the summer vacation; the commissions were recorded on the dorses of the patent rolls.[89] This is illustrated by a remarkable series of personal letters from William of York to his patron Ralph de Neville, the king's chancellor, written in 1226–28. William probably began his career as a Chancery clerk, but in 1226 he was just beginning to serve as a justice in eyre. The letters show his concern to visit his property in his native Yorkshire; in 1226, for instance, he wanted to visit a living there to which he had recently been presented, probably at Kirk Deighton.[90]

It is therefore possible to speculate, and it is pure speculation, that during one of those vacations from his work in the Exchequer at Westminster, most likely that of the summer of 1227, Robert of Bassingbourn visited his church at Mexborough, which lies only nine miles south of Barnsdale Bar. There perhaps he found the country alive with stories about a notorious criminal, popularly known to some as 'Hobbehod', who had formerly been at large in the southern parts of Yorkshire. After a successful career, perhaps as a highway robber, during which he managed for a time to evade capture, he had in 1225 at last succumbed to a group of professional man-hunters employed by the sheriff at the king's expense. They had, as instructed, hunted him down and beheaded him, and the sheriff had displayed his body by hanging it in chains in York as an example to others. It is even conceivable that the parson of Mexborough saw the remains of it if he visited the cathedral city. Returning before Michaelmas to work at Westminster, and preparing the Yorkshire account for the pipe roll for the eleventh year of the reign (1226–7), Bassingbourn guessed, rightly or wrongly, that the Robert Hod whose name he had entered in the previous roll was the criminal about whom he had heard so much during his recent visit to Yorkshire. The audit was actually made

---

Society LVI (1872)) p. 66. The other half of the church seems to have belonged to Nostell priory, whose early benefactors were the Lacy family: *EYC* III, nos. 1428, 1435.

[89] 'Robert of Lexington, Chief Justice of the Bench, 1236–44', *Laws, Lawyers and Texts: Studies in Medieval Legal History in Honour of Paul Brand*, ed. S. Jenks, J. Rose and C. Whittick (Brill, Leiden and Boston, 2012), pp. 149–175, at 166–71.

[90] C. A. F. Meekings, 'Six Letters Concerning the Eyres of 1226–8', *EHR* 65 (1950), pp. 492–504; Meekings and D. Crook, *King's Bench and Common Bench in the Reign of Henry III* (London, Selden Society, 2012), pp. 63–65; *ODNB*.

before the barons of the Exchequer on 12 March 1228.[91] After that year Bassingbourn did not write another pipe roll, because a new treasurer's clerk with a very different hand began to compile the record in 1229, and he changed the name back to its original form. Bassingbourn may have retired from the Exchequer at that point, possibly because the new treasurer appointed late in 1228, Walter Mauclerc, bishop of Carlisle, wanted to appoint a treasurer's clerk of his own choosing. His successor, whose name is not known, then altered the name back from 'Hobbehod' to 'Robert Hod', and it remained in that form in the rolls from 1229 to 1234, when it was removed.

If an outlaw had made such an impact in the country south of York and as far as Doncaster, it is reasonable to wonder, as did Francis Child in his criticism of Hunter, why his criminal career had been 'passed over without one word of notice from any authoritative historian', a point subsequently also made by other critics. This is however relatively easy to explain. Although none of the surviving early thirteenth-century chronicles makes any reference to an outlawed highway robber called Robin Hood or anyone else, it does not mean that this is not the right period in which to try to place the original outlaw. No general chronicles were being written in the east midlands or southern Yorkshire in the early part of the reign of Henry III, with the exception of the *Flores Historiarum* of Roger of Wendover. Roger, a St Albans monk and the predecessor of Matthew Paris as the abbey chronicler, was prior of the abbey's cell at Belvoir in Leicestershire for about a decade before 1226, but he gives no local information about events in the area further north than Newark and Lincoln, and had no interest in reporting crime.[92] The same applies to the chronicle written at Crowland abbey in the south Lincolnshire fens, which comes to an end in 1225.[93] A later monastic chronicle written by Thomas Burton (d. 1437) at Meaux abbey in Holderness, an isolated part of the East Riding of Yorkshire, mainly between 1388 and 1396, includes an account of the whole period from the abbey's foundation in the mid-twelfth century down to his own time. However, its local history material is very much confined to the area around the abbey, and consists overwhelmingly of documents relating to the abbey's affairs and estate, and the fortunes of its lay patrons.[94] The outlaw therefore received no

---

[91] TNA, E 159/9, m. 6 [AALT-IMG 0013]; E 372/71, r. 4d [IMG 1375].

[92] D. Crook, 'Roger of Wendover, Prior of Belvoir, and the Implementation of the Charter of the Forest, 1225–1227', in D. Crook and L. J. Wilkinson, eds., *The Growth of Royal Government under Henry III* (Woodbridge, 2015), pp. 166–78.

[93] The chronicle has previously mainly been referred to as the 'Barnwell' annals, and has only been firmly associated with Crowland in the last few years; Cristian Ispir, *A Critical Edition of the Crowland Chronicle*, King's College London Ph D (2015), available at file:///F:/Lincs%20misc/2015_Ispir_Cristian_Nicolae_1068129_ethesis.pdf

[94] A. Gransden, *Historical Writing in England II, c.1307 to the Early Sixteenth*

mention by monastic historians during his brief career, not because he was not notorious in the region, but because no-one chanced to record his activities, or, if anyone did, what they wrote has not survived.

However, a much less dramatic and more prosaic explanation of the brief appearance of the name 'Hobbehod' in the two pipe rolls seems more likely, and one may be suggested. 'Hobbe' sometimes appears in record as a name in its own right, presumably one of several pet forms of 'Robert'. It was certainly not coined at the point at which 'Hobbehod' appears in the pipe roll for 1226–7. It occurs on several occasions in judicial records during the preceding decades, among the 'humble nicknames of the countryside' given to those who served litigants in the king's court at Westminster as essoiners. They were representatives of litigants delegated to cast essoins, allowable excuses for non-appearance, at the court when a hearing was due in a plea involving one of their clients.[95] In Easter term 1198, 'Hobbe the man of Geoffrey de Say' failed to appear or to cast an essoin.[96] It was probably again he who in Hilary term 1205 essoined on behalf of Roger de Lenz in a Worcestershire case, and in Trinity term 1208 for Henry de Aubigny in a Wiltshire one.[97] In Hilary term 1209 'Hobbe' essoined a Warwickshire litigant, and a 'Hobbe of Skirbeck' in Lincolnshire essoined a Lincolnshire one. Three years later a 'Dobbe son of Dobin', a different form of the name, performed the same role for a Bedfordshire litigant.[98] The name continued to be used throughout the thirteenth century, to judge by the appearance, for example, of a 'Hobbe Ryvenhod' in a list of outlaws in the 1292 Lancashire eyre roll.[99] Much later, in the Peasants' Revolt of 1381, it was popularly applied to senior royal ministers, probably with the deliberate intention of implying that they were no better than thieves themselves. John Ball, in a letter addressed to the rebels, urged them to 'chastise wel Hobbe the Robbere', and this was echoed in another letter of Jakke Carter instructing them to 'lokke that Hobbe robbyoure be wele chastysed'. In the context of the Revolt it might have referred either to the royal treasurer or to one of two royal justices who all happened, conveniently for the rebels, to be named 'Robert', and became, as Holt suggested, 'simply another folk version of Robert the Robber as the archetypal criminal'.[100] Robert of

---

Century (London, 1982), pp. 355–71.
[95] D. M. Stenton, Introduction to *Pleas Before the King or His Justices 1198–1212* III, Selden Society LXXXIII (1967), pp. xxxii–xxxvi.
[96] CRR I, p. 47. The entry is damaged, so many of the details are missing, including the county from which the case originated.
[97] CRR III, p. 266; CRR V, p. 256.
[98] Stenton, *Pleas Before the King or His Justices 1198–1212* IV, Selden Society LXXXIV (1967), nos. 2589, 2639, 4636.
[99] *Crown Pleas of the Lancashire Eyre 1292* II (Record Society of Lancashire and Cheshire CXLIX, 2015), no. 409.
[100] Holt, *Robin Hood*, pp. 156–57.

Bassingbourn, who altered 'Robert Hod' to 'Hobbehod' in the pipe roll for 1226–7, and repeated it in the one for the following year, was almost certainly aware of the name. He may even have had personal knowledge of the Hobbe who appears several times in the records and was perhaps a familiar figure in the environs of the king's court during the first decade of the thirteenth century. Bassingbourn himself had served on at least one occasion as an attorney in the court, and so may have known about, or even have seen, Hobbe working there in his humbler role of essoiner. In Hilary term 1205 he represented Guiomar of Bassingbourn as his attorney in a plea of land in Cambridgeshire, brought against Guiomar by Robert de Saham. Another case brought by Saham at the same time was against a Muriel of Bassingbourn, so the property in question is very likely to have been in or at least near his native village. Robert of Bassingbourn may therefore, according to one possible explanation, merely have been playing with the name 'Robert Hod', putting the two elements of it together and replacing the Christian name with a colloquial version with which he was well acquainted.[101] Perhaps, despite his senior official position and his long tenure of it, he was a man with a whimsical or jocular side to his character, and could not resist the temptation to alter the form of the name in the roll to create a nickname that amused him. He may have coined the combination of the two elements for the first time or, perhaps more likely, used the name because it was one that was already current among his colleagues and in his wider social milieu. The new treasurer's clerk who succeeded him may have been of a different cast of mind, ignorant of the significance of, or disapproving of, his predecessor's alteration. For whatever the reason, he reverted to the original form of the name, after referring either to the original estreat received from the justices or the first pipe roll in which it appeared.

It is conceivable, but impossible to prove or indeed to disprove, that Robert of Wetherby, whose fate is known in a little detail, and the fugitive Robert Hod, who is just a name in a financial record, were one and the same man. If so, he could have been Robert Hod of Wetherby. The possibility is not ruled out by the different ways in which the two are described. Robert of Wetherby had been outlawed by July 1225, and possibly quite some time before that, while Robert Hod alias Hobbehod was described in the repeated pipe roll entry merely as a fugitive. That would usually be taken to mean that he was a suspect who had fled, but the confiscation of his chattels could have been noted at a time when he had not yet been outlawed, a process which would have taken some time. If Robert of Wetherby's toponym meant that he did in fact come from Wetherby, he is likely to have been a man of the Percy lordship, for it

---

[101] D. M. Stenton, ed., *Pleas Before the King or his Justices 1198–1212* III (Selden Society LXXXIII, 1967), nos. 1349, 1363.

was a Percy manor.[102] His connection with the place may not, however, have been close, and there is no reason why he should not in some way have been claimed to be subject to the legal jurisdiction of the archbishop of York, as Robert Hod may have been. It is quite within the bounds of possibility that the area in which he was hunted was, or included, Barnsdale itself. All that can be said for certain is that the two men shared the same, very common, forename, and broke the law in the same, very large, county at about the same time. Robert of Wetherby was probably captured before 12 July 1225, when the first retrospective claim was made for the expenses of his pursuers; the matter of his chattels could therefore have come before the justices, led by Robert of Lexington, at York on 20 July, dealing with the crown pleas brought before them.[103] Although not 'justices for all pleas', their commission obliged them to take presentments from local juries 'concerning those who are suspected of larcenies, robberies and homicides'; and the only surviving plea rolls from any of the circuits, for Berkshire, Somerset and Surrey in Martin of Pattishall's circuit, confirm that the justices dealt with the chattels of suspects who had fled, and of those already dealt with.[104]

The search for the legendary outlaw in and around the year 1225 therefore runs through two separate but just possibly related trails among the detailed but incomplete administrative and financial records of the early thirteenth-century English state. The loss of key documents, especially Robert of Lexington's plea roll for the Yorkshire assizes and gaol delivery of 1225 and Martin of Pattishall's roll for the Yorkshire eyre of 1226, may well have deprived us of valuable evidence. The two trails never coalesce, but they do lead to two real criminals with different names, one a toponym and the other based on a common characteristic item of clothing, who shared the same, very common, Christian name. Both were active in the same English county, the largest of them all, at about the same time. It is not beyond the bounds of possibility that they were one and the same man, but it is most likely that they were not. If not, there is nevertheless a further possibility that they could have become confused with each other in the popular imagination at a very early stage in the development of the legend. They were both at large in the county with which the legend was originally associated, at a time

[102] *EYC* IX, ed. C. T. Clay, YAS RS, Extra Series IX, 1963, pp. 252–54.
[103] *RLC* II, p. 77. They held another session there on 31 August after visiting other northern counties in the interval: TNA, CP 25/1/262/17, no. 11 [AALT-IMG 0223].
[104] TNA, JUST 1/36, rots. 2, 4–7, 10; 755, rots. 1–3, 8, 11–12 (translation in *Somersetshire Pleas, Civil and Criminal*, I, Somerset Record Society XI, 1897); 863, rots. 4–6, 7. The latter roll, for Surrey, includes a detailed list of confiscated chattels of those who had fled or been hanged; only two of them had chattels worth more than Robert Hod, and nearly all the rest very much less than his [AALT-IMG 8713].

when the king's government was worried about crime within it, and was prepared to take unusual measures to deal with it. These facts, although they can never form the basis of an unquestionable identification of the original outlaw, nevertheless offer the most intriguing and suggestive coincidence of names, events, time and place that it is possible to derive from the historical evidence that has survived to the present day. It seems unlikely that any more convincing case could be made in the future, so it is probably the nearest we will ever be able to get to the original outlaw, if he ever existed. Although it will never be possible to prove, we may look for the origins of the legend of Robin Hood in those summer days in Yorkshire in 1225, when the sheriff of Nottingham's men, hired at the king's expense, hunted down and decapitated Robert of Wetherby, 'outlaw and evildoer of our land', before his body was hung in public on a chain in York as an example to others.

Conclusion

The radical ideas about the origins of the legend of Robin Hood proposed in this book were made possible only by the results of the painstaking work of generations of archivists and record scholars of the earliest surviving records of English government. That work was carried out between the beginning of the nineteenth century and the early years of the twenty-first, and took place initially under the auspices of the six Record Commissions between 1800 and 1837, before the establishment of the Public Record Office in 1838.[1] The Rev. Joseph Hunter, already a noted antiquary, became one of the first generation of assistant keepers of public records. From 1843 to 1858 he was, in the words of his distinguished colleague Henry Cole, 'employed on the highly important business of arranging the 4,000 bushels of miscellaneous records of the Queen's Remembrancer's Office of the Exchequer', an enormous archive which included many detailed accounts. His fellow assistant keepers, including Cole, carried out similar work on the records of other departments of the Exchequer, and of the Chancery and courts of common law, in other record offices in the capital, until they were finally brought together in the new Public Record Office building on the Rolls Estate in Chancery Lane in 1859.[2] Among the records under his charge and which came to light as he worked, Hunter made what he thought was a very exciting discovery. In an account of the king's Chamber under Edward II he found records of payments to Robert Hod, a lowly porter, which he thought might relate to both a section of the *Gest* of Robin Hood and to real events which took place in the early 1320s. He wrote a lengthy paper based upon them, published in 1852, suggesting that they might refer to the original legendary outlaw, Robin Hood.[3] His ideas, initially received

[1] For the history of the Record Commissions, see P. Walne, 'The Record Commissions 1800–37' in F. Ranger, ed., *Prisca Munimenta: Studies in Archival and Administrative History presented to Dr A. E. J. Hollaender* (London, 1972), pp. 19–26.

[2] For the detailed history of the PRO as an institution, see J. D. Cantwell, *The Public Record Office 1838–1958* (London, 1991), and J. D. Cantwell, *The Public Record Office 1958–1969* (London, 2001).

[3] See Chapter 3.

Conclusion

with interest among fellow antiquaries, were within a decade savagely criticised and ridiculed, and this may have had the long-term effect of discouraging any others who might have been tempted to undertake further research into the subject in documentary sources. When he moved from his former office at Carlton Ride into the new repository in Chancery Lane, these early records that had for centuries been stored on several sites in London were now for the first time together in one place and so physically accessible to him. He might, with sufficient time and leisure, have found in these sources further information relevant to the origins of the outlaw legend, had he sought to do so. He was, however, a sick man, already in his mid-70s and frequently on leave of absence, and probably had no such inclination. The dictum of Francis Child, Hunter's most articulate critic, that the outlaw was 'absolutely the creation of the ballad muse', thereafter became, and in many quarters remains today, the received wisdom on the matter.

Hunter's colleague Thomas Duffus Hardy (1804–78), earlier the keeper of the records at the Tower of London, was the most important of the scholars who were initially involved in the publication of some of the most important early documents of English government. These included, in particular, the close rolls of the royal Chancery down to the year 1227, and the patent and charter rolls down to the death of King John in 1216. Hunter himself had been responsible for several volumes produced by the Commissions, including the texts of five of the early pipe rolls of the Exchequer and the earliest feet of fines for several counties, made in the king's court at Westminster. Following the foundation of the Public Record Office, such publications ceased for a considerable period because of constraints on public expenditure, after a few volumes already in progress had been completed and published by 1844.[4] Work on early Exchequer documents only recommenced after four decades, when the Pipe Roll Society was founded by another assistant keeper, Walford Selby (1845–89), within the Office in 1883. Financed by members' subscriptions, it resumed the publication of the pipe rolls begun by Hunter.[5] By 2005 all those rolls down to the year 1224 had been published, and two others transcribed in preparation for publication in coming years. The Selden Society, founded in 1887, and also subscription-based, began to publish early records of the courts of common law; its first volume, edited by the great Cambridge legal historian F. W. Maitland (1850–1906), dealt with *Select Pleas of the Crown, 1200–1225*. In 1891 Maitland also edited a volume of plea rolls from the reign of Richard I for the Pipe Roll Society. It was only in the 1890s, under the deputy keepership of Henry Maxwell Lyte, that work on the publication of the royal letters recorded in the Chancery rolls, suspended since 1844, was resumed in the form of transcripts of the

[4] Cantwell, *The Public Record Office 1838–1958*, Appendix VI, pp. 541–44.
[5] Pipe Roll Society NS XLI (1976), p. 8.

Patent Rolls (published from 1901 onwards) and the *Close Rolls* (from 1902). Finally, the systematic official transcription and publication of the texts of the early plea rolls of the central courts of common law, under the title *Curia Regis Rolls*, was initiated by Cyril Flower (1879–1961) at the Public Record Office in 1910. The publication of the rolls from the 1190s onwards began in 1922, and made significant progress in that area for the first time in over eighty years. The series came to an end only in 2006 when the year 1250 had been reached, in twenty volumes. In the meantime, many eyre rolls dealing with legal proceedings held in individual counties by itinerant royal justices had been published by local record societies, work which still continues. Since the beginning of the new millennium access to these legal sources has, as a result of the creation of the Anglo-American Legal Tradition website by Robert Palmer, increased exponentially. Much credit is due to all those who made this huge amount of source material so readily available to contemporary scholars.

At an early stage in the sorting, cataloguing and publication of the vast treasures of the archives, in which he was so deeply involved, Joseph Hunter enthusiastically snatched at a small group of suggestive and intriguing references that he chanced to find during the course of his work on the records of the Exchequer. He soon suffered the consequences of his temerity. Today, after over 150 years of further work by his successors, he would not have been so precipitate. He was looking, in what might have been one of the right places, for the legendary outlaw, but the archival landscape in his time lacked most of the signposts and maps that generations of his successors have subsequently provided. It was all but a century after Hunter's death, and over six decades after that of Child, before study of the Robin Hood legend first attracted the serious interest of academic historians. Moreover, that interest was initially focused on the interpretation of the social significance of the tales, and their date, rather than the identification of specific candidates for the original outlaw and other individuals among the contents of the public records. Literary scholars and some historians have tended not to engage fully with the historical evidence on that matter, or to offer serious alternative interpretations of it. It is now clear that an original outlaw, if he lived at all, did so a little while before the year 1262, and the argument has here been made that the crucial year may have been 1225, when a Yorkshire outlaw called Robert of Wetherby was hunted down by a group of men employed by a former sheriff of Nottingham and financed by the government of King Henry III. This book has sought to stretch to the limit, and even occasionally to speculate beyond that limit, of the highly suggestive but tendentious evidence for the origin of the legend that can be found among the early records of the English state, now far more easily accessible than they have ever previously been. It has for the first time fully exposed two sequences of references in the early records of the Chancery

Conclusion

and the Exchequer which, while not coalescing at any point, nevertheless do intersect in that they share a very narrow temporal and geographical context; and which, further illuminated by background information from the near contemporary records of the royal courts of common law, provide the most promising locus yet proposed for the identification of an original Robin Hood.

Bibliography

Original Manuscript Sources

The National Archives (formerly the Public Record Office)

Chancery: Charter Rolls
Chancery: Close Rolls
Chancery: Fine Rolls
Chancery: Liberate Rolls
Chancery: Patent Rolls
Chancery: Warrants for the Great Seal, Series 1
Chancery: Commissioners for Charitable Uses: Inquisitions and Decrees
Chancery: Parliamentary Writs and Returns
Court of Common Pleas: Feet of Fines
Court of Common Pleas: Plea rolls
Court of Common Pleas: Brevia Files
Duchy of Lancaster: Maps and Plans
Duchy of Lancaster: Parliamentary Surveys
Duchy of Lancaster: Court of Duchy Chamber: Papers in Lawsuits
Exchequer: Treasury of the Receipt: Miscellaneous Books
Exchequer: King's Remembrancer: Accounts Various
Exchequer: King's Remembrancer: Memoranda Rolls
Exchequer: King's Remembrancer: Miscellanea
Exchequer: King's Remembrancer: Miscellaneous Books, Series I
Exchequer: King's Remembrancer: Particulars of Account, Lay and Clerical Taxation
Trustees for Crown Lands and Fee Farm Rents: Parliamentary Surveys
Exchequer: Pipe Office: Foreign Accounts Rolls
Exchequer: Lord Treasurer's Remembrancer: Memoranda Rolls
Exchequer: Pipe Office: Pipe Rolls
Exchequer of Receipt: Receipt Rolls
Exchequer of Receipt: Issue Rolls
Justices in Eyre, of Assize, and of Oyer and Terminer: Rolls and Files

Bibliography

Coroners' Rolls and Files
Justices of Gaol Delivery: Gaol Delivery Rolls and Files
Courts of Common Pleas and King's Bench, and Justices Itinerant: Early Plea and Essoin Rolls
Court of King's Bench: Plea Rolls
Maps and Plans Extracted to Rolled Storage from Various Series of Records
Ministry of Transport: Roads Files
Ancient Correspondence of the Chancery and the Exchequer
Ancient Petitions
Court of Star Chamber: Proceedings, Henry VII
Court of Star Chamber: Proceedings, Henry VIII
Court of Star Chamber: Proceedings, James I

British Library

Additional MSS 28638 and 27879
Cotton Faustina C 11
Cotton Julius B XII
Cotton Otho A 18
Harley 3601 and 4866
Lansdowne 213
Sloane 780 and 5141

Society of Antiquaries of London, Minute Books and Records of Fellows
Bodleian Library, Oxford, Dodsworth MSS
Brotherton Library, University of Leeds, Special Collections, YAS/MS 166
Cambridge University Library, MSS Ee.4.35.1 and Ff.5.48
Corpus Christi College, Cambridge, MSS 171 and 618
King's College Cambridge Archives, GRA/472
Trinity College Cambridge, MS R.2.64
King's College London Archives, Furnivall 6/1–3
University of Nottingham Manuscripts and Special Collections, Middleton MSS
York Minster Archives, MS Add. 203/2
Berkshire Record Office, Reading St Lawrence Churchwardens Accounts, D/P 97/5/2
Kingston History Centre, Kingston Borough Archives, Churchwardens Accounts, KG 2/2/1
Nottinghamshire Archives, Records of the Borough of Nottingham; Probate Records, PR/NW/6/15207
Oxfordshire Archives, MS DD Par Woodstock
Somerset Heritage Centre, Quarter Sessions Roll 1607–8, QSR 2, f. 7v; Consistory Court Ex Officio Book 1607, D/D/Ca 155, ff. 40v–41

Bibliography

Printed Primary Sources

Place of publication is London unless otherwise stated

Abstracts of the Chartularies of the Priory of Monk Bretton, ed. J. W. Walker, Yorkshire Archaeological Society Record Series LXVI (1924)
Annales Monastici, ed. H. R. Luard (5 vols., Rolls Series, 1864–69)
Annals of England, J. Stow (1603)
The Anonimalle Chronicle, 1337–1381, ed. V. H. Galbraith (Manchester, 1927)
Apophthegmes of Erasmus, ed. R. Roberts (Boston, Mass., 1877)
Appendix to the Memoirs of Thomas Hollis, F. Blackburne (1780)
Bacon's History of the Reign of King Henry VII, ed. J. R. Lumby (Cambridge, 1885)
Barnabees Journal, R. Brathwaite (1774)
Bedfordshire Coroners' Rolls, ed. R. F. Hunnisett, Bedfordshire Historical Record Society XLI (1960)
Bishop Percy's Folio Manuscript: Ballads and Romances, ed. J. W. Hales and F. J. Furnivall (3 vols., 1867–8)
The Book of Fees, ed. H. C. Maxwell Lyte (3 vols., 1920–31)
Bracton on the Laws and Customs of England, ed. G. E. Woodbine, translated, with revisions and notes, by S. E. Thorne (4 vols., 1968–77)
Bracton's Note Book, ed. F. W. Maitland (3 vols., 1887)
Calendar of Charter Rolls, Henry III–Henry VIII, 1226–1516 (6 vols., 1903–27)
Calendar of Close Rolls, Edward I–Henry VI (42 vols., 1892–1947)
Calendar of Inquisitions Post Mortem, Henry III (1904)
Calendar of Liberate Rolls, Henry III (6 vols., 1916–64)
Calendar of London Trailbaston Trials under Commissions of 1305 and 1306, ed. R. B. Pugh (London, 1975)
Calendar of Patent Rolls, Henry III–Henry VI, 1232–1461 (55 vols., 1891–1938)
Calvin's Sermons on the Epistles to Timothy and Titus, L. Thomson (London, 1579)
The Cartulary of Dale Abbey, ed. A. Saltman, Derbyshire Archaeological Society Record Series II (1967)
A Catalogue of Letters and Other Historical Documents Exhibited in the Library at Welbeck, ed. S. A. Strong (1903)
The Charters of the Anglo-Norman Earls of Chester, c.1071–1237, ed. G. Barraclough, Record Society of Lancashire and Cheshire CXXVI (1988)
The Chartulary of St John of Pontefract, I, ed. R. Holmes, YAS RS XXV (1899)
Chronica Majora, Matthew Paris, ed. H. R. Luard (7 vols., Rolls Series, 1872–83)
Chronica Monasterii de Melsa, a Fundatione ad Annum 1396, ed. E. A. Bond (3 vols., Rolls Series, 1866–8)
A Chronicle at Large, Richard Grafton (2 vols., 1809)
Close Rolls of the Reign of Henry III (14 vols., 1902–38)

Bibliography

Complete Peerage, ed. H. A. Doubleday and Lord Howard de Walden, VIII (1929); ed. V. Gibbs and H. A. Doubleday, X (London, 1945)

Court Rolls of the Manor of Wakefield I, ed. W. P. Baildon, Yorkshire Archaeological Society Record Series XXIX (1901); II, ed. W. P. Baildon, Yorkshire Archaeological Society Record Series XXXVI (1906); III, ed. J. Lister, Yorkshire Archaeological Society Record Series LVII (1917); IV, ed. J. Lister, Yorkshire Archaeological Society Record Series LXXVIII (1930)

The Court Rolls of Walsham le Willows, 1303–50, ed. R. Lock, Suffolk Records Society (Woodbridge, 1998)

The Court Rolls of Walsham le Willows, 1351–99, ed. R. Lock, Suffolk Records Society (Woodbridge, 2002)

Crown Pleas of the Devon Eyre of 1238, ed. H. R. T. Summerson, Devon and Cornwall Record Society, NS XXVIII (Torquay, 1985)

Crown Pleas of the Lancashire Eyre 1292, ed. M. E. Lynch with introduction by H. Summerson (3 vols., Record Society of Lancashire and Cheshire, vols. CXLVIII, CXLIX, CL, 2014–15)

Curia Regis Rolls, c. 1199–1250 (20 vols., 1922–2006)

Descriptive Catalogue of Derbyshire Charters, ed. I. H. Jeayes (London and Derby, 1906)

Desiderata Curiosa, II, Francis Peck (1735)

Dialogus de Scaccario, ed. C. Johnson (London, Edinburgh, Paris, Melbourne, Toronto and New York, 1950)

The Diary of Henry Machyn, ed. J. G. Nichols, Camden Society XLII (1848)

A Dictionary of British Surnames, P. H. Reaney (1958)

A Dictionary of Surnames, P. Hanks, and F. Hodges (Oxford, 1988)

The Dorset Lay Subsidy Roll of 1327, ed. A. R. Rumble, Dorset Record Society VI (1980)

The Dorset Lay Subsidy Roll of 1332, ed. A. D. Mills, Dorset Record Society IV (1971)

The Earliest Lincolnshire Assize Rolls, A.D. 1202–1209, ed. D. M. Stenton, Lincoln Record Society XXII (1926)

Early Yorkshire Charters, III, ed. W. Farrer, Yorkshire Archaeological Society Record Series (1916)

Early Yorkshire Charters, VIII, ed. C. T. Clay, Yorkshire Archaeological Society Record Series, Extra Series VI (1949)

Early Yorkshire Charters, XI, ed. C. T. Clay, Yorkshire Archaeological Society Record Series, Extra Series IX (1963)

English Royal Documents, King John–Henry VI, 1199–1461, P. Chaplais (Oxford, 1971)

The English and Scottish Popular Ballads, ed. F. J. Child, 8 vols. (London, 1861), vol. V

The English and Scottish Popular Ballads, ed. F. J. Child, 5 vols. (Boston, Mass., and New York), vol. III (1889)

Bibliography

Excerpta e Rotulis Finium I, ed. C. Roberts (2 vols., Record Commission, 1835–6)

The Exchequer Rolls of Scotland, I, ed. J. Stuart and J. Burnett (Edinburgh, 1878)

The Family Memoirs of the Rev. William Stukeley, ed. W. C. Lukis, Surtees Society, LXXIII (1882)

Feudal Aids, 1284–1431, 6 vols. (1899–1920)

Fine Rolls Henry III, 1226–42, ed. P. Dryburgh and B. Hartland (3 vols., 2007–9); 1242–1272 available online

Fouke Le Fitz Waryn, ed. E. J. Hathaway, P. T. Ricketts, C. A. Robson and A. D. Wilshere, Anglo-Norman Text Society (Oxford, 1975)

Fourteenth Report of the Commissioners of the Woods, Forests and Land Revenues of the Crown, 28 March 1793, Appendix

The Heads of Religious Houses: England and Wales II, 1216–1377, ed. D. M. Smith and V. C. M. London (Cambridge, 2001)

Historia Majoris Britanniae, John Major, ed. R. Fairbairn (Edinburgh, 1840)

A History of Greater Britain, John Major, ed. A. Constable, Scottish History Society X (Edinburgh, 1892)

The Itinerary of John Leland the Antiquary, ed. T. Hearn (3rd edn., 1770), I

Le Jeu de Robin et Marion par Adam le Bossu, ed. E. Langlois (Paris, 1896)

King's Bench and Common Bench in the Reign of Henry III, C. A. F. Meekings and D. Crook, Selden Society Supplementary Series XVII (2010)

De Legibus et Consuetudinibus Anglie, Bracton on the Laws and Customs of England, ed. G. E. Woodbine, translated, with revisions and notes, by S. E. Thorne (4 vols., Cambridge, Mass., 1968–77)

The Letters and Charters of Cardinal Guala Bicchieri, Papal Legate in England 1216–18, ed. N. Vincent, Canterbury and York Society LXXXIII (1996)

List of Ancient Correspondence of the Chancery and Exchequer preserved in the Public Record Office, Public Record Office Lists and Indexes XV (Kraus Reprint, New York, 1968)

List of Various Common Law Records, C. A. F. Meekings, Public Record Office Lists and Indexes, Supplementary Series I (1970)

The Manuscripts of the Duke of Rutland preserved at Belvoir Castle, IV, Historical Manuscripts Commission (1905), section I, charters and cartularies, J. H. Round

The Manuscripts of Lord Middleton preserved at Wollaton Hall, Nottinghamshire, Historical Manuscripts Commission (1911)

Medieval Cartularies of Great Britain, ed. G. R. C. Davis (1958); second edition edited by C. Breay, J. Harrison and D. M. Smith (2011)

The Medieval Essex Community: The Lay Subsidy of 1327, ed. J. C. Ward, Essex Record Office Publication 98 (1983)

Medieval Latin Dictionary from British Sources, various editors, British Academy, 17 fascicules (Oxford and New York, 1975–2013)

Memoirs of John Evelyn 1641–1705–6, II, ed. W. Bray (1827)

Memoranda Rolls 16–17 Henry III, ed. R. A. Brown (1991)
Middle English Dictionary, various editors, 13 vols. (Ann Arbor, 1954–1999)
Monasticon Anglicanum, ed. W. Dugdale, rev. J. Caley, H. Ellis and B. Bandinel, 6 vols. in 8 (1817–30)
The Northumberland Eyre Roll for 1293, ed. C. M. Fraser, Surtees Society CCXI (2007)
The Northumberland Lay Subsidy Roll of 1296, ed. C. M. Fraser, Society of Antiquaries of Newcastle upon Tyne (1968)
The Original Chronicle of Andrew of Wyntoun, ed. F. J. Armours, Scottish Text Society (5 vols., 1903–14)
Paston Letters and Papers of the Fifteenth Century, ed. N. Davis, 2 vols. (Oxford, 1971, 1976)
Patent Rolls, Henry III, 1216–32 (2 vols., 1901, 1903)
Patronymica Britannica: A Dictionary of the Family Names of the United Kingdom, M. A. Lower (1860)
The Percy Cartulary, ed. M. T. Martin, Surtees Society CXVII (1911)
Phillip Stubbes' Anatomy of the Abuses in England in Shakspere's Youth, part 1, ed. F. J. Furnivall (1877)
Pipe Roll 5 Henry III, ed. D Crook, Pipe Roll Society New Series XLVIII (1990 for 1984–86), introduction
Pipe Rolls 2 Richard I to 8 Henry III, Pipe Roll Society New Series I–LVI (1925–2008), various editors
The Place-Names of Cumberland, ed. A. M. Armstrong, A. Mawer, F. M. Stenton and B. Dickins, I, English Place-Name Society XXI (Cambridge, 1950)
The Place-Names of Devon I, ed. J. E. B. Gover, A. Mawer and F. M. Stenton, English Place-Name Society VIII (Cambridge, 1931)
The Place-Names of Gloucestershire II, ed. A. H. Smith, English Place-Name Society XXXIX (Cambridge, 1964)
The Place-Names of Leicestershire I, ed. B. Cox, English Place-Name Society LXXV (Nottingham, 1998)
The Place-Names of Leicestershire III, ed. B. Cox, English Place-Name Society LXXXI (Nottingham, 2004)
The Place-Names of the North Riding of Yorkshire, ed. A. H. Smith, English Place-Name Society IV (Cambridge, 1928)
The Place-Names of Nottinghamshire, ed. J. E. B. Gover, A. Mawer and F. M. Stenton, English Place-Name Society XVII (Cambridge, 1943)
The Place-Names of Rutland, ed. B. Cox, English Place-Name Society LXVII-LXIX (Nottingham, 1994)
The Place-Names of the West Riding of Yorkshire I, ed. A. H. Smith, English Place-Name Society XXX (Cambridge, 1961)
The Place-Names of the West Riding of Yorkshire II, ed. A. H. Smith, English Place-Name Society XXXII (Cambridge, 1961)

Bibliography

The Place-Names of the West Riding of Yorkshire V, ed. A. H. Smith, English Place-Name Society XXXIV (Cambridge, 1961)

The Place-Names of the West Riding of Yorkshire VIII, ed. A. H. Smith, English Place-Name Society XXXVII (Cambridge, 1963)

Placita Corone, ed. J. M. Kaye, Selden Society Supplementary Series IV (1966)

Placita de Quo Warranto, ed. W. Illingworth (Record Commission, 1818)

Pleas of the Crown for the County of Gloucester 1221, ed. F. W. Maitland (1884)

'Proceedings of the Ecclesiastical Courts in the Archdeaconry of Leicester, 1516–1535', ed. P. A. Moore, *Associated Architectural Societies' Reports and Papers* (1905–6)

PRO Lists and Indexes, IX, List of Sheriffs for England and Wales from the Earliest Times to A.D. 1831 (1898)

De Rebus Britannicis Collectanea, John Leland, ed. T. Hearne (second edition, 6 vols., London, 1770), I

Receipt Rolls 4, 5 and 6 Henry III, ed. N. Barratt, L. Napran and D. Crook, Pipe Roll Society New Series LII (2003)

Records of the Borough of Nottingham, various editors, vols. 1–9 (1882–1956)

Records of the General Eyre, 1194–1348, D. Crook, Public Record Office Handbooks XX (1982)

Records of Plays and Players in Kent, 1450–1642, ed. G. E. Dawson, Collections Volume VII (Malone Society, Oxford, 1965)

Regesta Regum Anglo-Normannorum II, ed. C. Johnson and H. A. Cronne (1956)

Register, or Rolls, of Archbishop Gray, ed. J. Raine, Surtees Society LVI (1872)

Register of Walter Giffard, Lord Archbishop of York, ed. W. Brown, Surtees Society CIX (1904)

Reliques of Ancient English Poetry, Consisting of Old Heroic Ballads, Songs and other Pieces of our Earlier Poets (Chiefly of the Lyric Kind) together with some few of Later Date, ed. T. Percy, 3 vols. (1765)

Ritson, J., *Robin Hood: A Collection of All the Ancient Poems, Songs and Ballads, now extant, relative to that Celebrated Outlaw* (1795)

Rogeri de Wendover Flores Historiarum, ed. H. G. Hewlett (3 vols., Rolls Series, 1886–9)

Roll of Divers Accounts for the Early Years of the Reign of Henry III, ed. F. A. Cazel, Jr, Pipe Roll Society, New Series XLIV (1982)

Rolls of the Justices in Eyre for Lincolnshire 1218–19 and Worcestershire 1221, ed. D. M. Stenton, Selden Society LIII (1934)

Rolls of the Justices in Eyre for Yorkshire 1218–19, ed. D. M. Stenton, Selden Society LVI (1937)

The Roll and Writ File of the Berkshire Eyre of 1248, ed. M. T. Clanchy, Selden Society XC (1973)

Li Romans de Witasse le Moine: Roman de Trezième Siècle, ed. D. J. Conlon, University of North Carolina Studies in Romance Languages and Literatures, 126, Chapel Hill, University of North Carolina (1972)
Rotuli Hundredorum, ed. W. Illingworth (2 vols., Record Commission, 1812, 1818)
Rotuli Litterarum Clausarum, ed. T. D. Hardy (2 vols., Record Commission, 1833, 1844)
Rotuli Litterarum Patentium, ed. T. D. Hardy (Record Commission, 1835)
Rotuli de Oblatis et Finibus, ed. T. D. Hardy (Record Commission, 1835)
Rotuli Parliamentorum, ed. J. Strachey and others, 7 vols. (Record Commission, 1767–77, 1832)
Rotuli Selecti ad Res Anglicas et Hibernicas Spectantes, ex Archivis et Hibernicas Spectantes, ex Archivis in Domo Capitulari Westmonasteriensi, ed. J. Hunter (Record Commission, 1834)
Royal Letters of Henry III, I, ed. W. W. Shirley (Rolls Series, 1862)
Rufford Charters, ed. C. J. Holdsworth, Thoroton Society Record Series XXIX, XXX, XXXII, XXXIV (4 vols., 1972–81)
Scotichronicon by Walter Bower, ed. S. Taylor, D. E. R. Watt, with B. Scott, V (Aberdeen, 1990)
Select Cases in the Court of King's Bench under Edward I, I, ed. G. O. Sayles, Selden Society LV (1936)
Select Charters, ed. W. Stubbs, 9th edition (Oxford, 1913)
Select Pleas of the Crown, ed. F. W. Maitland, Selden Society I (1887)
Select Pleas of the Forest, ed. G. J. Turner, Selden Society XIII (1901)
Seven Sermons before Edward VI, by Hugh Latimer, ed. E. Arber (1869)
The Sherwood Forest Book, ed. H. E. Boulton, Thoroton Society Record Series XXIII (1965)
Sherwood Forest in 1609: A Crown Survey by Richard Bankes, ed. S. Mastoris and S. Groves, Thoroton Society Record Series XL (Nottingham, 1997)
South Lancashire in the Reign of Edward II, ed. G. H. Tupling, Cheetham Society, 3rd Series I (Manchester, 1950)
A Suffolk Hundred in 1283 (1910), ed. E. Powell
Suffolk in 1327, ed. S. H. A. Hervey, Suffolk Green Books IX (Woodbridge, 1906)
Suffolk in 1524, ed. S. H. A. Hervey, Suffolk Green Books X (Woodbridge, 1910)
The 1235 Surrey Eyre, I, C. A. F. Meekings and D. Crook, Surrey Record Society XXXI (1979)
Sussex Subsidies, 1296, 1327, 1332, ed. W. Hudson, Sussex Record Society X (1910)
Testamenta Eboracensium III, ed. J. Raine, Surtees Society XLV (1865)
Thomas Wright's Political Songs of England, with a new introduction by Peter Coss (Cambridge, 1996)

Three Early Assize Rolls for the County of Northumberland, ed. W. Page, Surtees Society LXXXVIII (1891)
The Thurgarton Cartulary, ed. T. M. Foulds (Stamford, 1994)
Travels over England, Scotland and Wales, J. Brome (1694)
Two Early London Subsidy Rolls, ed. E. Ekwall (Lund, 1951)
Two Fitzalan Surveys, ed. M. Clough, Sussex Record Society LXVII (1969)
Valor Ecclesiasticus Tempore Henr. VIII V, ed. G. Eyre and A. Strahan (Record Commission, 1825)
Victoria County History of Nottinghamshire II, ed. W. Page (London, 1910)
The Vision of William concerning Piers the Plowman in Three Parallel Texts, ed. W. W. Skeat (3rd edition revised, Oxford, 1879)
Visitations in the Diocese of Lincoln, 1517–31, ed. A. H. Thompson, Lincoln Record Society XXXVII (1947)
William Worcestre Itineraries, ed. J. H. Harvey (Oxford, 1969)
Wistasse le Moine (Halle, 1891), ed. W. Foerster and J. Trost
The Worcester Eyre of 1275, ed. J. Röhrkasten, Worcestershire Historical Society NS XXII (2008)
Year Book 20–21 Edward I, ed. A. J. Horwood (Rolls Series, 1866)
York Civic Records, II, ed. A. Raine, Yorkshire Archaeological Society Record Series CIII (1941)
Yorkshire Feet of Fines 1218–31, ed. J. Parker, Yorkshire Archaeological Society Record Series LXII (1921)
The Yorkshire Subsidy of 25 Edward I, ed. W. Brown, Yorkshire Archaeological Society Record Series XVI (1894)
The Yorkshire Subsidy of 30 Edward I, ed. W. Brown, Yorkshire Archaeological Society Record Series XXI (1897)

Secondary Works

Place of publication is London unless otherwise stated

Almond, R. and Pollard, A. J., 'The Yeomanry of Robin Hood and Social Terminology in Fifteenth Century England', *Past and Present* 170 (2001), pp. 52–77
Anglo, S., 'An Early Tudor Programme for Plays and Other Demonstrations Against the Pope', *Journal of the Warburg and Courtauld Institutes* 20 (1957), pp. 176–79
Aston, T. H., 'Robin Hood', *Past and Present* 20 (1961), pp. 7–9; reprinted in Hilton, *Peasants, Knights and Heretics*, pp. 270–2
Ayton, A., 'Military Service and the Development of the Robin Hood Legend in the Fourteenth Century', *Nottingham Medieval Studies* 36 (1992), pp. 126–47
Barczewski, S. L., *Myth and National Identity in Nineteenth Century Britain: The Legends of King Arthur and Robin Hood* (Oxford, 2000)

Bibliography

Barlow, D., *Dick Turpin and the Gregory Gang* (London and Chichester, 1973)
Barnard, J., 'Keats's "Robin Hood", John Hamilton Reynolds, and the "Old Poets"', *Proceedings of the British Academy* 75 (1989), pp. 181–200, reprinted in Knight, *Anthology*, pp. 123–40
Basford, K., *The Green Man* (Cambridge, 1978, reprint 1996 and 2009)
Beckett, J., ed., *A Centenary History of Nottingham* (Manchester, 1997)
Bellamy, J. G., 'The Coterel Gang: An Anatomy of a Band of Fourteenth-Century Criminals', *English Historical Review* 79 (1964), pp. 698–717
—— 'The Northern Rebellions in the Later Years of Richard II', *Bulletin of the John Rylands Library* 47 (1965), pp. 254–61
—— *The Law of Treason in England in the Later Middle Ages* (Cambridge, 1970)
—— *Crime and Public Order in England in the Later Middle Ages* (1973)
—— *Robin Hood: An Historical Inquiry* (London and Sydney, 1985)
Bessinger, J. B., Jr, 'Robin Hood: Folklore and Historiography, 1377–1500', *Tennessee Studies in Literature* 11 (1966), pp. 61–9
—— 'The *Gest of Robin Hood* Revisited', in *The Learned and the Lewed*, ed. L. D. Benson (Cambridge, Mass., 1974), pp. 355–69, reprinted in Knight, *Anthology*, pp. 39–50
Birrell, J., 'Who Poached the King's Deer? A Study in Thirteenth Century Crime', *Midland History* 7 (1982), pp. 9–25
Blackmore, H. L., *Hunting Weapons from the Middle Ages to the Twentieth Century* (1971)
Blatcher, M., *The Court of King's Bench 1450–1550: A Study in Self-Help* (1978)
Bradbury, J., *The Medieval Archer* (Woodbridge, 1985)
—— *Robin Hood* (Stroud, 2010)
Brandon, D., *Stand and Deliver: A History of Highway Robbery* (2001)
Bronson, B. H., *Joseph Ritson: Scholar at Arms* (2 vols., Berkeley, 1938)
Broome, D. M., 'Exchequer Migrations to York in the Thirteenth and Fourteenth Centuries', in *Essays in Medieval History Presented to T. F. Tout*, ed. A. G. Little and F. M. Powicke (Manchester, 1925), pp. 291–300
Burd, H. A., *Joseph Ritson: A Critical Biography* (University of Illinois, 1916)
Burgess, G. S., *Two Medieval Outlaws: Eustace the Monk and Fouke Fitz Waryn* (Cambridge, 1997)
Cantwell, J. D., *The Public Record Office 1838–1958* (1991)
—— *The Public Record Office 1958–1969* (2001)
Carpenter, D. A., 'The Decline of the Curial Sheriff in England, 1194–1258', *English Historical Review* 101 (1976), pp. 1–32, reprinted in his *The Reign of Henry III* (London and Rio Grande, 1996), pp. 151–82
—— *The Minority of Henry III* (1990)
Carpenter, K., *Robin Hood: The Many Faces of that Celebrated English Outlaw* (Oldenburg, 1995)

Bibliography

[Carter, James], *A Visit to Sherwood Forest, including the Abbeys of Newstead, Rufford & Welbeck; Annesley, Thoresby and Hardwick Halls; Bolsover Castle and other interesting places in the locality with a critical essay on the life and times of Robin Hood* (London, Mansfield and Nottingham, 1850)

Chambers, E. K., *English Literature at the Close of the Middle Ages* (Oxford, 1945)

Church, S. D., *The Household Knights of King John* (Cambridge, 1999)

Clanchy, M. T., 'Highway Robbery and Trial by Battle in the Hampshire Eyre of 1249', in *Medieval Legal Records Edited in Memory of C. A. F. Meekings* (1978), pp. 26–61

Clawson, W. H., *The Gest of Robin Hood* (Toronto, 1909)

Colvin, H. M., *The White Canons in England* (Oxford, 1951)

Coss, P. R., 'Aspects of Cultural Diffusion in Medieval England: The Early Romances, Local Society and Robin Hood', *Past and Present* 108 (1985), pp. 35–79

Cressy, D., *Literacy and the Social Order* (Cambridge, 1980)

Crook, D., 'The Struggle over Forest Boundaries in Nottinghamshire, 1218–1227', *Transactions of the Thoroton Society* 83 (1979)

—— 'The Early Keepers of Sherwood Forest', *Transactions of the Thoroton Society* 84 (1980)

—— 'The Early Remembrancers of the Exchequer', *Bulletin of the Institute of Historical Research* 103 (1980), pp. 11–23

—— *Records of the General Eyre*, Public Record Office Handbooks 20 (1982)

—— 'The Establishment of the Derbyshire County Court, 1256', *Derbyshire Archaeological Journal* 103 (1983)

—— 'The Reverend Joseph Hunter and the Public Records', *Transactions of the Hunter Archaeological Society* 12 (1983), pp. 1–15

—— 'Some Further Evidence concerning the Dating of the Origins of the Legend of Robin Hood', *English Historical Review* 99 (1984), pp. 530–34; reprinted in Knight, *Anthology*, pp. 257–61

—— 'The Sheriff of Nottingham and Robin Hood: The Genesis of the Legend?', in *Thirteenth Century England II: Proceedings of the Newcastle upon Tyne Conference 1987*, ed. P. R. Coss and S. D. Lloyd (Woodbridge, 1988), pp. 59–69

—— 'The Forest between the Erewash and the Derwent, 1154 to 1225', *Derbyshire Archaeological Journal* 110 (1990), pp. 93–104

—— 'The Archbishopric of York and the Boundaries of the Forest in Nottinghamshire in the Twelfth Century', in *Law and Government in Medieval England and Normandy: Essays in Honour of Sir James Holt*, ed. G. Garnett and J. Hudson (Cambridge, 1994)

—— 'The Records of Forest Eyres in the Public Record Office, 1179 to 1670', *Journal of the Society of Archivists* 17 (1996), pp. 183–93

—— 'The Records of Taxation in England in the Public Record Office', in *Crises, Revolutions and Self-Sustained Growth: Essays in European Fiscal History, 1130–1830*, ed. W. M. Ormrod, R. Bonney and M. Bonney (Stamford 1999), pp. 427–35

—— 'The Exemption of Nottingham from the Forest Laws in the Twelfth and Thirteenth Centuries', *Transactions of the Thoroton Society* 109 (2005), pp. 69–73

—— 'Dynastic Conflict in Thirteenth-Century Laxton', in *Thirteenth Century England XI*, ed. B. Weiler, J. Burton, P. Schofield and K. Stöber (Woodbridge, 2007), pp. 193–214

—— 'Robert of Lexington, Chief Justice of the Bench, 1236–44', in *Laws, Lawyers and Texts: Studies in Medieval Legal History in Honour of Paul Brand*, ed. S. Jenks, J. Rose and C. Whittick (Leiden and Boston, 2012), pp. 149–75

—— 'The Royal Forest of Leicestershire, c.1122–1235', *Leicestershire Archaeological and Historical Society Transactions* 87 (2013), pp. 137–59

—— 'The Novelist, the Heiress, the Artisan and the Banker: The Emergence of the Robin Hood Legend at Edwinstowe, c.1819 to 1849', *Transactions of the Thoroton Society* 119 (2015), pp. 1–13

—— 'Roger of Wendover, Prior of Belvoir, and the Implementation of the Charter of the Forest, 1225–1227', in *The Growth of Royal Government under Henry III*, D. Crook and L. J. Wilkinson, eds. (Woodbridge, 2015), pp. 166–78; reprinted in paperback 2020

—— 'Philip Marc, Robert de Gaugy and the First Siege of Newark, July 1218', *Transactions of the Thoroton Society* 122 (2018), pp. 103–20

—— 'Nottingham, Robin Hood, and the Coronation of Charles II', *Church, Land and People: Essays Presented to John Beckett*, ed. R. A. Gaunt (Nottingham, 2020), pp. 31–35.

Cunliffe Shaw, R., *The Royal Forest of Lancaster* (Preston, 1956)

Davenport, E., 'The Representation of Robin Hood in Elizabethan Drama: *George a Greene* and *Edward I*', in *Playing Robin Hood*, ed. Potter (1998), pp. 45–62

Deering, C., *Nottingham Vetus et Nova or an Historical Account of the Ancient and Present State of the Town of Nottingham* (Nottingham, 1751)

Defoe, D., *A Tour through England and Wales*, introduction by G. D. H. Cole (2 vols., London, 1928)

DeVille, O., 'The Deyvilles and the Genesis of the Robin Hood Legend', *Nottingham Medieval Studies* 43 (1999), pp. 90–109

de Vries, K., 'Longbow Archery and the Earliest Robin Hood Legends', in *Robin Hood in Popular Culture*, ed. Hahn (2000), pp. 41–59

Dobson, R. B. and Taylor, J., 'The Medieval Origins of the Robin Hood Legend: A Reassessment', *Northern History* 7 (1972), pp. 1–30

—— *Rymes of Robyn Hood: An Introduction to the English Outlaw* (London, 1976; 2nd edition, Stroud, 1989; 3rd edition revised, Stroud, 1997)

—— 'Robin Hood of Barnsdale: A Fellow thou Hast Long Sought', *Northern History* 19 (1983), pp. 210–20

—— 'General Review: Robin Hood', *Northern History* 26 (1990), pp. 229–33

—— 'Merry Men at Work: The Transformation of Robin Hood from Medieval Outlaw into Heritage Hero', *Northern History* 33 (1997), pp. 232–37

—— 'Robin Hood Ballads', *Northern History* 35 (1999), pp. 237–39

Dobson, R. B., 'Robin Hood: The Genesis of a Popular Hero', *Robin Hood in Popular Culture*, ed. Hahn (2000), pp. 61–77

Evans, D., 'Joseph Hunter, Assistant Keeper of the Records, 1838–1861', *Transactions of the Hunter Archaeological Society* 8 (1960–63), pp. 263–71

Evans, M. R., '*Robynhill*, or Robin Hood's Hills? Place-Names and the Evolution of the Robin Hood Legends', *Journal of the English Place-Name Society* 30 (1998), pp. 43–53

—— 'Robin Hood in the Landscape: Place-Name Evidence and Mythology', in *Robin Hood: Medieval and Post-Medieval*, ed. H. Phillips (2005), pp. 181–87

Evans, R., Fulton, H., and Matthews, D., eds., *Medieval Cultural Studies: Essays in Honour of Stephen Knight* (Cardiff, 2006)

Falls, C., *Elizabeth's Irish Wars* (1950)

Fisher, K., 'The Crying of Ane Playe: Robin Hood and Maying in Sixteenth-Century Scotland', in *Medieval and Renaissance Drama in England* 12, ed. J. Pitcher (1999), pp. 19–58

Fowler, D. C., *A Literary History of the Popular Ballad* (Durham, North Carolina, 1968)

Foulds, T., 'The Foundation of Lenton Priory and a Reconstruction of its Lost Cartulary', *Transactions of the Thoroton Society* 92 (1988), pp. 34–42

Friedman, A. B., *The Ballad Revival: Studies in the Influence of Popular on Sophisticated Poetry* (Chicago, 1961)

Gillett, E., *A History of Grimsby* (Hull, 1970)

Godfrey, J. T., *The History of the Parish and Priory of Lenton in the County of Nottingham* (1884)

Gooch, E. S. V., *Sherwood Forest; or Northern Adventures*, 3 vols. (1804)

Gransden, A., *Historical Writing in England* [I], *c.550–c.1307* (1974)

—— *Historical Writing in England II, c.1307 to the Early Sixteenth Century* (London and Henley, 1982)

Gray, D., 'The Robin Hood Poems', *Poetica* 18 (1984), pp. 1–19, reprinted in Knight, *Anthology*, pp. 3–37

—— 'Everybody's Robin Hood', in *Robin Hood: Medieval and Post-Medieval*, ed. Phillips (2005), pp. 21–41

Green, R. F., 'The Hermit and the Outlaw: New Evidence for Robin Hood's Death?', in *Robin Hood: Medieval and Post-Medieval*, ed. Phillips (2005), pp. 51–68

Gregory, E. D., *Victorian Songhunters: The Recovering and Editing of English Vernacular Ballads and Folk Lyrics, 1820–1883* (Lanham, Maryland, Toronto and Oxford, 2006)

Groom, N., *The Making of Percy's Reliques* (Oxford, 1999)

Gutch, J. M., *A Lytell Geste of Robin Hode, with other Ancient and Modern Ballads and Songs* (2 vols., 1847, and second edition, 1850)

Hahn, T. G., ed., *Robin Hood in Popular Culture* (Cambridge, 2000)

—— 'Robin Hood and the Rise of Cultural Studies', in *Medieval Cultural Studies: Essays in Honour of Stephen Knight*, ed. Evans (2006), pp. 39–54

Hales, J. W. and Furnivall, F. J., *Bishop Percy's Folio Manuscript: Ballads and Romances* (3 vols., 1867–68)

Hall, S., 'The Emergence of Cultural Studies and the Crisis of the Humanities', MIT Press 53 (1990), pp. 11–23

Hanawalt, B. A., *Crime and Conflict in English Communities, 1300–1348* (Cambridge, Mass., 1979)

—— 'Ballads and Bandits: Fourteenth-Century Outlaws and the Robin Hood Poems', *Chaucer's England: Literature in Historical Context*, ed. Hanawalt (Minneapolis, 1992), pp. 154–75; reprinted in Knight, *Anthology*, pp. 263–84

Harland-Haughey, S., 'Forest Law Through the Looking-Glass: Distortions of the Forest Charter in the Outlaw Fiction of Late-Medieval England', *William and Mary Bill of Rights Journal*, 25, issue 2 (2016), pp. 548–89; available online at http://scholarship.law.wm.edu/cgi/viewcontent.cgi?article=1800&context=wmborj

Harris, P. V., *The Truth about Robin Hood: A Refutation of the Mythologists' Theories, with New Evidence of the Hero's Actual Existence* (Mansfield, 1973) (first edition published in London by the author, 1951)

Harrison, R. P., *Forests: The Shadow of Civilisation* (Chicago, 1992)

Hartley, J., *A Short History of Cultural Studies* (2003)

Hastings, M., *The Court of Common Pleas in Fifteenth-Century England* (Ithaca, 1947)

Heaney, M., 'The Earliest Reference to the Morris Dance?', *Folk Music Journal* 8, no. 4 (2004), pp. 513–15

Hepworth, D., 'A Grave Tale', and 'Appendix: Written Epitaphs of Robin Hood', both in *Robin Hood: Medieval and Post-Medieval*, ed. Phillips (2005), pp. 91–112, 188–89

Hilton, R. H., 'The Origins of Robin Hood', *Past and Present* 14 (1958), pp. 30–44; reprinted in Hilton, *Peasants, Knights and Heretics*, pp. 221–35, and also in Knight, *Anthology*, pp. 197–210

—— *A Medieval Society: The West Midlands at the End of the Thirteenth Century* (Cambridge, 1966, revised edition 1983)

—— ed., *Peasants, Knights and Heretics: Studies in Medieval English Social History* (Cambridge, 1976)

Bibliography

Hjertstedt, I., *Middle English Nicknames in the Lay Subsidy Rolls for Warwickshire* (Uppsala, 1987)

Hobsbawm, E., *Bandits* (1969)

Hodgart, M. J. C., *The Ballads* (1950)

Holmes, G. A., *The Estates of the Higher Nobility in Fourteenth-Century England* (Cambridge, 1957)

Holt, J. C., 'Philip Mark and the Shrievalty of Nottinghamshire and Derbyshire', *Transactions of the Thoroton Society* 56 (1952), pp. 8–24

—— 'The Origins and Audience of the Ballads of Robin Hood', *Past and Present* 18 (1960), pp. 89–110, reprinted in Hilton, *Peasants, Knights and Heretics*, pp. 236–57, and in Knight, *Anthology*, pp. 211–32

—— 'Robin Hood: some Comments', *Past and Present* 19 (1961), pp. 16–18; reprinted in Hilton, *Peasants, Knights and Heretics*, pp. 267–69

—— *Robin Hood* (1982); revised and enlarged edition, 1989

—— *The Northerners* (second edition, Oxford, 1992)

—— 'The Origins of the Legend', in K. Carpenter, ed. *Robin Hood: The Many Faces of that Celebrated English Outlaw* (Oldenburg, 1995), pp. 27–34

—— *Oxford Dictionary of National Biography* (2004): Hood, Robin (*supp. fl.* late 12th–13th cent.), legendary outlaw hero

—— *Magna Carta*, 3rd edition (Cambridge, 2015)

Holt, J. C., and Toshiyuki Takamiya, 'A New Version of "A Rhyme of Robin Hood"', *English Manuscript Studies* I (1988), pp. 213–21

Hope, W. H. St John, 'Chronicle of the Abbey of St Mary de Parco Stanley, or Dale, Derbyshire', *Journal of the Derbyshire Archaeological and Natural History Society* 5 (1883)

Hoyle, R. W., 'A Re-Reading of the *Gest of Robyn Hode*', *Nottingham Medieval Studies* 61 (2017), pp. 67–113

Hunnisett, R. F., *The Medieval Coroner* (Cambridge, 1961)

Hunter, J., *Hallamshire: The History and Topography of the Parish of Sheffield* (1819)

—— *South Yorkshire: The History and Topography of Deanery of Doncaster*, 2 vols. (1828, 1831)

—— 'The Great Hero of the Ancient Minstrelsy of England, Robin Hood', *Critical and Historical Tracts IV* (London, 1852); reprinted, with different pagination, by Robert White, Worksop (1883)

Hunter, S. J., *A Brief Memoir of the Late Joseph Hunter, F.S.A.*, privately printed (1861)

Hurnard, N. D., *The King's Pardon for Homicide before A.D.1307* (Oxford, 1969)

Hutton, R., *The Rise and Fall of Merry England: The Ritual Year 1400–1700* (Oxford, 1994)

Ikegmi, Masa,'The Language and Date of "A Geste of Robyn Hode"', *Neuphilologische Mitteilungen* 96 (1995), pp. 271–81

Bibliography

Jacobs, A., *The Book of Common Prayer: A Biography* (Princeton and Oxford, 2013)

Johnson, A. F., 'The Robin Hood of the Records', in *Playing Robin Hood*, ed. Potter (1998), pp. 27–44

Kane, S., 'Horseplay: Robin Hood, Guy of Gisborne, and the Neg(oti) ation of the Bestial', in *Robin Hood in Popular Culture*, ed. Hahn (2000), pp. 101–10

—— 'The Outlaw's Song of Trailbaston, the Green Man, and the Facial Machine', in *Images of Robin Hood*, ed. Potter (2008), pp. 41–50

Keen, M. H., 'Robin Hood: A Peasant Hero', *History Today* 8 (1958), pp. 684–89

—— 'Robin Hood – Peasant or Gentleman', *Past and Present* 19 (1960), pp. 7–15; reprinted, with a disclaimer, in Hilton, *Peasants, Knights and Heretics*, pp. 258–66

—— *The Outlaws of Medieval Legend* 1961; revised edition, 1977; revised paperback edition, 1987

Kelly, W., *Notices Illustrative of the Drama* (1865)

Knight, S., *Robin Hood: A Complete Study of the English Outlaw* (Oxford, 1994)

—— Robin Hood: *The Forresters Manuscript (British Library Additional MS 71158)* (Cambridge, 1998)

—— *Robin Hood: An Anthology of Scholarship and Criticism* (Cambridge, 1999)

—— *Robin Hood: A Mythic Biography* (Cornell, Ithaca and London, 2003)

—— 'Robin Hood: The Earliest Contexts', in *Images of Robin Hood*, ed. Potter (2008), pp. 21–40

—— *Reading Robin Hood: Content, Form and Reception in the Outlaw Myth* (Manchester, 2105).

—— 'Robin Hood and the Forest Laws', *The Bulletin of the International Association for Robin Hood Studies*, 1 (2017), pp. 1–14 (online)

Knight, S. and Ohlgren, T., *Robin Hood and Other Outlaw Tales* (Kalamazoo, 1997)

Lawes, A., 'Publishing the Public Records: 1800–2007', in *Foundations of Medieval Scholarship: Records Edited in Honour of David Crook*, P. Brand and S. Cunningham, eds., pp. 115–32 (York, 2008)

Lees, J., *The Quest for Robin Hood* (Nottingham, 1987)

Luxford, J. M., 'An English Chronicle Entry on Robin Hood', *Journal of Medieval History* 35 (2009), pp. 70–76.

Mackenzie, H., 'The Anti-Foreign Movement in England 1231–1232', in *Anniversary Essays in Medieval History by Students of C. H. Haskins* (New York, 1929), pp. 183–203

Maddern, P. C., *Violence and Social Disorder: East Anglia 1422–42* (Oxford, 1992)

Maddicott, J. R., *Thomas of Lancaster, 1307–1322: A Study in the Reign of Edward II* (Oxford, 1970)
—— *Law and Lordship: Royal Justices as Retainers in Thirteenth and Fourteenth Century England*, Past and Present Supplement 4 (1978)
—— 'The Birth and Setting of the Ballads of Robin Hood', *English Historical Review* 93 (1978), pp. 276–99; reprinted in Knight, *Anthology*, pp. 233–55
Manwood, J., *A Treatise on the Lawes of the Forest* (1598)
Marshall, J., '"Goon in Bernysdale': The Trail of the Paston Robin Hood Play', *Leeds Studies in English* 29 (1998), pp. 185–217
—— 'Playing the Game: Reconstructing *Robin Hood and the Sheriff of Nottingham*', in Hahn, *Popular Culture* (2000), pp. 161–74
—— 'Picturing Robin Hood in Early Print and Performance: 1500–1590', in *Images of Robin Hood*, ed. Potter (2008), pp. 60–81
Martin, G. H., 'Road Travel in the Middle Ages: Some Journeys by the Warden and Fellows of Merton College, Oxford, 1315–1470', *Journal of Transport History* 3 (1975–76)
Marvin, W. P., *Hunting Law and Ritual in Medieval English Literature* (Cambridge, 2006)
Matthews, D., 'What was Medievalism? Medieval Studies, Medievalism and Cultural Studies', in *Medieval Cultural Studies: Essays in Honour of Stephen Knight*, ed. Evans (2006), pp. 9–22
Matthews, J., *Robin Hood: Green Lord of the Wildwood* (Glastonbury, 1993)
—— *Robin Hood* (Stroud, 2016)
McKisack, M., *The Fourteenth Century* (Oxford, 1953)
Meekings, C. A. F., 'Six Letters concerning the Eyres of 1226–8', *English Historical Review* 65 (1950), pp. 492–504
Meekings, C. A. F. and Crook, D., *King's Bench and Common Bench in the Reign of Henry III*, Selden Society Supplementary Series 17 (2010)
Meisel, J., *The Barons of the Welsh Frontier: The Corbet, Pantulf, and Fitz Warin Families, 1066–1272* (Lincoln, Nebraska, 1980)
Mill, A. J., *Medieval Plays in Scotland* (Edinburgh, 1927)
Morris, G. E., 'A Ryme of Robyn Hode', *Modern Language Review* 43 (1948), pp. 507–08
Murray, M., *The Witch-Cult in Western Europe* (Oxford, 1921)
—— *The God of the Witches* (1931)
Nelson, M. A., 'The Earl of Huntington: The Renaissance Plays', in *The Robin Hood Tradition in the English Renaissance*, Salzburg Studies in English Literature, Elizabethan Studies 14 (Salzburg, 1973), reprinted in Knight, *Anthology*, pp. 99–121
Nicholas, D., *Medieval Flanders* (London, 1992)
Ohlgren, T. H., ed., *A Book of Medieval Outlaws: Ten Tales in Modern English* (Stroud, 1998)
—— 'The '"Marchaunt" of Sherwood: Mercantile Ideology in *A Gest*

of Robyn Hode', in *Robin Hood in Popular Culture*, ed. Hahn (2000), pp. 175–90

―― 'Edwardus Redivivus in *A Geste of Robyn Hode'*, *Journal of English and German Philology* 99 (2000), pp. 5–9

―― '*Robin Hood and the Monk* and the Manuscript Context of Cambridge University Library, MS Ff.5.48', *Nottingham Medieval Studies* 48 (2004), pp. 80–115

―― 'Merchant Adventure in *Robin Hood and the Potter'*, in *Robin Hood: Medieval and Post-Medieval*, ed. Phillips (2005), pp. 69–78

―― *Robin Hood: The Early Poems, 1465–1560: Texts, Contexts, and Ideology, with an Appendix: The Dialects and Language of Selected Robin Hood Poems by Lister M. Matheson* (Newark, Delaware, 2007)

―― '"Pottys, gret chepe!": Marketplace Ideology in *Robin Hood and the Potter* and the Manuscript Context of Cambridge, University Library MS Ee.4.35', in Ohlgren, *Robin Hood: The Early Poems*, pp. 68–96

―― 'From Script to Print: Robin Hood and the Printers', in Ohlgren, *Robin Hood: The Early Poems*, pp. 97–134

―― 'The "Marchaunt" of Sherwood: Mercantile Adventure in *A Lytell Geste of Robyin Hode'*, in Ohlgren, *Robin Hood: The Early Poems*, pp. 135–82

―― '"Lewed peple loven tales olde"': *Robin Hood and the Monk* and the Manuscript Context of Cambridge, University Library MS Ff.5.48', in Ohlgren, *Robin Hood: The Early Poems*, pp. 28–67

Ohlgren, T. H. and Matheson, L. M., eds., *Early Rymes of Robyn Hood: An Edition of the Texts, ca. 1425 to ca. 1600*, Medieval and Renaissance Texts and Studies 428 (Tempe, 2013)

Ormrod, W. M., 'Robin Hood and Public Record: The Authority of Writing in the Medieval Outlaw Tradition', in *Medieval Cultural Studies: Essays in Honour of Stephen Knight*, ed. Evans (2006), pp. 57–74

Owen, L. V. D., 'Robin Hood in the Light of Research', *Times Trade and Engineering Supplement* 28, part 864 (1936), p. xxix

Oxford Dictionary of National Biography (Oxford, 2004–19), online

Page, W., ed. *Victoria County History of Nottinghamshire* II (London, 1910)

Pearsall, D., 'Little John and the Ballad of *Robin Hood and the Monk'*, in *Robin Hood: Medieval and Post-Medieval'*, ed. H. Phillips (2005), pp. 42–50

Petzold, D., 'Der Rebell im Kinderzimmer: Robin Hood in der Kinderliteratur', in Carpenter, *Robin Hood* (1995), pp. 65–86

Phillips, H., ed., *Robin Hood: Medieval and Post-Medieval'* (Dublin, 2005)

―― 'Forest, Town and Road: The Significance of Places and Names in some Robin Hood Texts', in *Robin Hood in Popular Culture*, ed. Hahn (2000), pp. 197–214

―― '"Merry" and "Greenwood": A History of Some Meanings', in *Images of Robin Hood*, ed. Potter (2008), pp. 83–101

Plant, M., *The English Book Trade* (1939)

Pollard, A. J., 'Idealising Criminality: Robin Hood in the Fifteenth Century', in *Pragmatic Utopias: Ideals and Communities, 1200–1630*, ed. R. Horrox and S. Rees-Jones (2001), pp. 156–73
—— *Imagining Robin Hood: The Late-Medieval Stories in Historical Context* (2007)
—— 'Robin Hood, Sherwood Forest and the Sheriff of Nottingham', *Nottingham Medieval Studies* 52 (2008), pp. 113–30
—— 'Political Ideology in the Early Stories of Robin Hood', in *Outlaws in Medieval and Early Modern England: Crime, Government and Society*, ed. J. C. Appleby and P. Dalton (Farnham, 2009), pp. 111–28
Pollock, F., and Maitland, F. W., *The History of English Law before the Time of Edward I* (2nd edition, edited by S. F. C. Milsom, 2 vols., Cambridge, 1968)
Poole, R. L., *From Domesday Book to Magna Carta* (2nd edition, Oxford, 1955)
Post, J. B., 'The Evidential Value of Approvers' Appeals: The Case of William Rose', *Law and History Review* 3 (1985), pp. 91–100
—— 'Public Record Office Publication: Past Performance and Public Progress', *The Records of the Nation: The Public Record Office 1838–1988* (1990)
Potter, L., *Playing Robin Hood: The Legend as Performance in Five Centuries* (Newark, Delaware, 1998)
Potter, L., and Calhoun, J., *Images of Robin Hood: Medieval to Modern* (Newark, Delaware, 2008)
Powell, E., *Kingship, Law and Society: Criminal Justice in the Reign of Henry V* (Oxford, 1989)
Powicke, F. M., *King Henry III and the Lord Edward* (2 vols., Oxford, 1947)
Pringle, P., *Stand and Deliver: The Story of Highwaymen* (1951), chapter 15, 'Who rode to York?'
Pugh, R. B., *Imprisonment in Medieval England* (Cambridge, 1968)
Raglan, Lady, 'The Green Man in Church Architecture', *Folklore* 50 (March, 1939)
Raglan, Lord, *The Hero: A Study in Tradition, Myth and Drama* (1936)
Reaney, P. H., *A Dictionary of British Surnames* (1958)
Records of Early English Drama (REED), 1979–2017
Richards, J., *Swordsmen of the Screen* (1977)
—— *Robin Hood of the Screen*, in Carpenter, *Robin Hood* (1995), pp. 135–44; reprinted in Knight, *Anthology*, pp. 429–40
Richmond, C. F., 'An Outlaw and Some Peasants: The Possible Significance of Robin Hood', *Nottingham Medieval Studies* 37 (1993), pp. 90–101; reprinted in Knight, *Anthology*, pp. 363–76
Rigby, S. H., *Medieval Grimsby: Growth and Decline* (Hull, 1993)
Sargent, H. C., and Kittridge, G. L., *English and Scottish Popular Ballads, Student's Cambridge Edition* (1904)
Sharpe, J., *Dick Turpin: The Myth of the English Highwayman* (2004)

Simone, W. E., 'The Games and the Robin Hood Legend', *Journal of American Folklore* 64 (1951), pp. 265–74; discussion in *ibid.*, 65 (1952), pp. 304–05, 418–20
Singman, J. L., *Robin Hood: The Shaping of the Legend* (Westport, Connecticut, 1998)
—— 'Munday's Unruly Earl', in *The Legend as Performance in Five Centuries*, ed. L. Potter (Newark, Delaware, 1998), pp. 63–76
Southey, R. and C., *Robin Hood, A Fragment, By the Late Robert Southey and Caroline Southey* (Edinburgh and London, 1847), pp. 1–37
Southworth, J., *The English Medieval Minstrel* (Woodbridge, 1989)
Spraggs, G., *Outlaws and Highwaymen: The Cult of the Robber in England from the Middle Ages to the Nineteenth Century* (2001)
Stapleton, A., *The Last Perambulation of Sherwood Forest (A.D. 1662)* (Newark, 1893)
Stenton, D. M., *English Justice between the Norman Conquest and the Great Charter* (Philadelphia, 1964)
Stock, L. K., 'Lords of the Wildwood: The Wild Man, the Green Man, and Robin Hood', in *Robin Hood in Popular Culture*, ed. Hahn (2000), pp. 239–49
Stokes, J. D., 'Robin Hood and the Churchwardens in Yeovil', *Medieval & Renaissance Drama in England: An Annual Gathering of Research, Criticism and Reviews* 3 (Madison, 1986), pp. 1–25
—— 'Processional Entertainments in Small Towns', in K. Ashley and W. Hüsken, *Moving Subjects: Processional Performance in the Middle Ages and the Renaissance* (Amsterdam-Atlanta, 2001), pp. 239–57
Stones, E. L. G., 'The Folvilles of Ashby Folville, Leicestershire, and their Associates in Crime, 1326–1347', *Transactions of the Royal Historical Society*, 5th series, 7 (1957), pp. 117–36
Strickland, M., and Hardy, R., *The Great Warbow* (Stroud, 2005)
Summerson, H. R. T, 'The Structure of Law Enforcement in Thirteenth Century England', *American Journal of Legal History* 23 (1979), pp. 313–27
—— 'Crime and Society in Medieval Cumberland', *Transactions of the Cumberland and Westmorland Antiquarian and Archaeological Society* 81 (1982), pp. 111–24
—— 'The Early Development of *Peine Fort et Dure*', in A. H. Manchester and E. W. Ives, eds., *Law, Litigants and the Legal Profession* (1983), pp. 117–25
—— 'Crime and Society in Thirteenth-Century Devon', *Transactions of the Devonshire Association* 119 (1987), pp. 67–84
—— 'The Enforcement of the Statute of Winchester, 1285–1327', *Journal of Legal History* 13 (1992), pp. 232–50
—— *Medieval Carlisle*, Cumberland and Westmorland Antiquarian and Archaeological Society, Extra Series XXV (1993)

—— 'The Criminal Underworld of Medieval England', *Journal of Legal History* 17 (1996), pp.197–224

—— 'Criminal Law in the Age of Bracton', in *The History of English Law: Centenary Essays on 'Pollock and Maitland'*, ed. J. Hudson (Proceedings of the British Academy 89 (Oxford, 1996)

—— 'Suicide and Fear of the Gallows', *Journal of Legal History* 21 (2000), pp. 49–56

—— 'Attitudes to Capital Punishment, 1200–1350', in *Thirteenth Century England VIII*, ed. M. Prestwich, R. Britnell and R. Frame (Woodbridge, 2001), pp. 123–33

Sutherland, D. W., 'Mesne Process upon Personal Actions in the Early Common Law', *Law Quarterly Review* 82 (1966), pp. 486–88

Sutherland, J., The Longman Companion to Victorian Fiction (London, 1988)

Swan, G., "Robin Hood's 'Irish Knife'", *University of Mississippi Studies in English*, New Series 11–12 (1993–95), pp. 51–80

Thale, M., 'The Robin Hood Society: Debating in Eighteenth-Century London', *London Journal*, vol. 1, no. 22 (1997), pp. 33–50

Thomas, K., *Religion and the Decline of Magic* (1971)

Thompson, K. A., 'The Late Medieval Robin Hood: Good Yeomanry and Bad Performances', in *Images of Robin Hood*, ed. Potter (2008), pp. 102–10

Thomson, L., *Calvin's Sermons on the Epistles to Timothy and Titus* (1579)

Thomson, R. M., *Catalogue of the Manuscripts of Lincoln Cathedral Library* (Cambridge, 1989)

Thoroton, R., *The History and Antiquities of Nottinghamshire* (1677)

Throsby, J., *Thoroton's History of Nottinghamshire, Republished with Large Additions* (1797)

Todd, H., *Illustrations of Gower and Chaucer* (1810)

Truesdale, M., *The King and the Commoner Tradition: Carnivalesque Politics in Medieval and Early Modern Literature* (New York and Abingdon, 2018)

Tupling, G. H., ed., *South Lancashire in the Reign of Edward II*, Cheetham Society, 3rd Series I (Manchester, 1950)

Underdown, D., *Revel, Riot, and Rebellion: Popular Politics and Culture in England 1603–1660* (Oxford, 1985)

Vincent, N., *Peter de Roches: An Alien in English Politics, 1205–1238* (Cambridge, 1996)

Walker, J. W., *The True History of Robin Hood* (Wakefield, 1952)

Walne, P. F., 'The Record Commissions 1800–37' in *Prisca Munimenta: Studies in Archival and Administrative History presented to Dr A. E. J. Hollaender*, ed. F. Ranger (1972)

Wheare, M., '"From the Castle Hill they came with Violence": The Edinburgh Robin Hood Riots of 1561', in *Images of Robin Hood*, ed. Potter (2008), pp. 111–20

Bibliography

Wightman, W. E., *The Lacy Family in England and Normandy, 1066–1194* (Oxford, 1966)
Wiles, D., *Early Plays of Robin Hood* (Cambridge, 1981)
Wilson, R. M., *The Lost Literature of Medieval England* (1952)
Winnick, S. D., 'Reynardine and Robin Hood: Echoes of an Outlaw Legend in Folk Balladry', in *Images of Robin Hood*, ed. Potter (2008), pp. 51–59
Wright, T., *The Vision and the Creed of Piers Ploughman: With Notes and a Glossary* (1842)
—— 'On the Popular Cycle of the Robin Hood Ballads', *Essays on Subjects Connected with the Literature, Popular Superstitions and History of England in the Middle Ages* (2 vols., 1846), II
Young, C. R. *The Royal Forests of Medieval England* (Leicester, 1979)

INDEX

Counties are the historical counties before boundary changes made in the last two centuries, appropriately abbreviated. In the many Yorkshire entries, the Ridings are given in the format WR, ER and NR, but in entries for Scottish towns their counties are not given.

Abbots Ripton, Hunts   170
Aberdeen, Scotland   36, 48
Abingdon, Berks   44
Abjuration of the realm   243
   for forest offences   189
   for homicide   132 n.16, 241–42
   for robbery   201, 241–42
Adam Bell, Clym of the Clough and William Cloudesley   36, 61, 67, 79, 81, 108, 115, 192, 228–29
Agbrigg wapentake, Yorks WR   242
Ainsty wapentake, Yorks WR   242
Ainsworth, Harrison   207
Aiskew, Yorks NR   167
Alayn, Thomas   173 n.60
Allen a Dale   60, 68
Alnwick, Northumb   166, 167
Alton, Hants, pass of   191, 197, 199
Amounderness, Lancs   155
Angevin, Geoffrey the   234
Anstey, Herts   170
Antony, Cornwall   44
Antwerp, Flanders   17
Approvers   135, 199, 200–02, 219–20, 221, 226
Archery and archery contests   12, 15, 24, 25–26, 28, 31, 32, 58, 60, 99, 129
Arksey, Yorks WR   118
Armytage family, Kirklees   143
Ashburton, Devon   44
Ashmole, Elias   129
Aston, T. H.   109–10

Aston, Derbys   191
Attercliffe, Yorks WR   84
Attleborough, Norfolk   29
Aubigny, Henry de   252
Aubigny, William de, of Belvoir   211, 225
Augmentation Office, London   88
Aumale, William count of   213
Aunby Heath, Lincs   63 n.97
Ayr, Scotland   46
Ayton, Andrew   169, 181
Ayton, Yorks NR   172

Baddesworth, John, rector of Laxton, Notts   29
Bagford, John   10 n.13, 18
Ball, John   13, 252
Ballad Society   96
Balliol, Hugh de   213
   Robert de   213
Banastre, Adam de   157
Banister, Robert   137
Barking, Richard of, Exchequer clerk, chancellor's scribe, writer of the chancellor's roll   247–48
Barlow, Derek   207
Barnes, Patricia   140–41 n.52
Barnsdale, Rutland   121, 122, 133–34
Barnsdale, Yorks WR   9, 17, 21, 23, 26, 28, 29, 33, 35, 36, 58, 75, 90, 91, 92, 111, 112, 116, 117, 129–137, 157, 174, 185, 187, 189, 193, 199, 241

Index

chapel in (fictional) 9–10, 91
lodge in (fictional) 22
Barnsdale Bar, Yorks WR 130, 132, 137, 157, 200 n.60, 250
Barnwell priory, Cambs 177
cartulary of 82
Barry, C. E. A. E. 82, 94
Basdeo, Stephen 78 n.38
Bassingbourn, Robert of, Exchequer clerk, treasurer's scribe, writer of the pipe roll 247–251, 253
rector of Grimsby, Bradley and Scartho, Lincs 249
rector of Mexborough, Yorks WR 249
see also Hugh of 249; Humphrey of 248; Muriel of 253; Warin of 248
Beaufey, Emma de 235
Beaumonde, John 49
Beckwith, William 190
Bedworth, Cheshire 129
Beheading *see* Decapitation
Bel, Hugh le, 236
Bell, Adam 36, 61, 67, 79, 81, 108, 115, 192, 228
Bellamy, John 19, 117–18, 231–32
Belvoir castle, Leics 55, 211
priory, prior of 169, 251
Berefot, Geoffrey, of Wakefield 242
Bessinger, J. B. 20
Beverley, Yorks ER 17, 167
Birchden, Sussex 167
Birrell, Jean 188
Blackbourne hundred, Suffolk 176
Blackhood names 171
Blount, Thomas 68
Bloweberme, Walter 201
Blyth, Notts 22–23, 132–33
Bocking, Sussex 171
Bodleian Library, Oxford 58 n.2, 68, 85
Bodmin, Cornwall 44
Booth, Paul 38 n.16
Boroughbridge, Yorks WR, battle of (1322) 105
Boulogne, count of 192, 204 n.83, 229
Boulton, Roger son of Adam of 215
Bower, Walter, abbot of Inchcolm 8–9, 37, 38, 40, 105, 112, 199
Bradbury, Jim 183–84
Bradford on Avon, Wilts 201
Bradle, Dorset 173
Bradley, Ralph of 249
Bradley, Lincs, church 248–49
Bradwell, Derbys 128
Brampton, Cumberland 129
Brandsby, Yorks NR 46, 52
Branxton, Northumb 166–67
Brathwait, Richard 137
Braunton, Devon 44
Bricchnoth, Martin 177
Bridgnorth, Salop 45
Bridport, Dorset 44, 177
Bristol, Glos, St Nicholas parish 45, 83
British Museum, London 57, 68, 71, 82, 85
Broadhood names 172
Broadsides 57, 59–60
Brodun, Osbert 242
Brome, James 148
Bromsgrove, Worcs 204
Brun, William 242
Bunny, Notts 200, 201 n.64
Burgh, Hubert de 217, 222, 238
Burghwallis, Yorks WR 137
Burgundy, Charles duke of 14
Burnley, Lancs 45
Burton, Thomas, 251 n. 93
Bury St Edmunds, Suffolk, merchants of 139, 158–59
Byron, Sir John 148

Call, John 14
Richard 14
Cambridge, Christ's College 42
Cambridge, Corpus Christi College 63 n.97
Cambridge, King's College 177
Cambridge, Trinity College, archives 30
Cambridge, University Library 10, 13, 18 n.38, 73–74
manuscript of *Robin Hood and the Monk*, 10

manuscript of *Robin Hood and the Potter*, 13–14
Camden, William 143–44
Campsall, Yorks WR, parish church 91, 135, 241
Canteshangre, Thomas, Hampshire coroner, 179
Capehood names 172
Carlecotes, Matilda of 242
Carlisle, Cumb 92, 229
   earl of 138
   justice, sheriff and mayor of 36
Carlton in Lindrick, Notts 239, 241
Carlton Ride, London 88, 257
Carpenter, Kevin 122–23
Carter, Jakke 252
Cashio hundred, Herts 167
Caythorpe, Notts 234
Chagford, Devon 44
Chambers, E. K. 98–99
Chancery, resident at York 113
Chapbooks 60, 207
Charford, Hants 171, 176
Charlton, Lionel 138
Charlton Marshal, Dorset 172
Charnock Richard, Lancs 157
Charter of the Forest (1217 and 1225) 189, 193
Chaucer, Geoffrey 29, 34
Chellington, Beds Map 2
Chenonceux, Touraine, France 234
Chester, honour of 235
Chester, John de Lacy constable of 213, 235
   Roger de Lacy constable of 224
Chester, Ranulf (Randolf) earl of 81, 99, 217, 219 (of Lincoln)
Child, Francis 1, 10, 12, 14, 18, 20, 66, 73, 93–97, 98, 102, 110, 111, 155, 163, 198–99, 251, 257
Chippenham forest, Wilts 189
Chudleigh, Devon 44
Churchwardens' accounts 43–44
Cirencester, Ralph of 168
Cirencester abbey, Glos, abbot of 168
Clawson, W. H. 18–19, 98
Clifton, Notts 150
Clipsham, Rutland 167

Cockfield, Robert of 225, 227 n.78, 238
Coke, Sir Edward 74
Colchester, Essex 171
Cole, Henry 256
Colnaghi, Martin 207
Colt Hoare, Sir Richard 85
Colyton, Devon 44
Combe Keynes, Dorset 172
Common Bench, at Westminster 168, 174, 186, 187, 189, 212–13, 217, 219–22, 248 n.77, 252–53
   sitting at York 187
Constable, Simon le 196
Copland, William 16, 17, 18 n.39, 55
Corbridge, Northumb 169
Cornish, John 54
Cornwall, men of 189
Coroners, outlawed 206
Coroners' rolls, Bedfordshire 163
   Hampshire 179
Coss, Peter 19
County court, plea rolls 246
Court of Star Chamber 49–50, 54
Coventry, Warw 171
Cradeley, John 49
Crecy, France, battle of (1346) 140
Crepin, Ralph 196
Criminal gangs, composition of 202
   clergy in, 202
   women in, 202
Crockford Bridge, Hants 179
Croscombe, Somerset 43
Crowland abbey, Lincs, chronicle of 211, 251
Crowle, Worcs 47
Croydon, Surrey 44 n.31
Cullin, John 139, 158
Cultural studies 120–21
Cundall, Joseph 79

Dale abbey (Stanley Park), Derbys 62
D'Athée, Gerard 168 n.17, 234
D'Aubigny, Henry de 252
D'Aubigny, William de 211, 225
Dayville, John 37
Decapitation, of fleeing criminals 203–04, 224–25, 241–42
Decapitation, in the tales:

of Guy of Gisborne   28–29, 195
  of a monk and a page, 13, 195
  of a knight, 31
  of the sheriff, 25
Deepdale, Derbys   62, 198
Deering, Charles   149
Derby   62, 198, 230, 234
Derbyshire   11–12, 62, 153–54, 186–87, 230
  county court of, 230
  sheriff of see Nottinghamshire
Deyville, Walter de   219
Dighere, John, of Suffolk   179
Dobin, Dobbe son of   252
Dobson, R. B.   10, 12, 19, 70, 97, 103, 111–12, 115, 117, 120, 122–23, 124–25, 127, 130, 137, 139, 155, 181, 199, 231–32. See also Taylor
Dodsworth, Roger   58, 85, 137
Doncaster, Yorks WR   22–23, 130, 132–33, 135–37, 199, 200, 215
  (Donkesley) Sir Roger of   26, 91, 142; alias Red Roger, 27–8
Doveridge, Derbys   191 n.24
Dudley, Staffs   49
Duket, Lawrence   196
Dumfries, Scotland   46
Dundee, Scotland   46
Dunstable priory, Beds,
  chronicle   189, 196, 225
Durham, bishop of   212 n.7, 217
  palatinate of   70
Dyngley, Roger, mayor of Walsall   48

Eagle Barnsdale, Lincs   134
East Coatham, Yorks NR   177
East Stoke, Notts, battle of (1487)   30
Ebberston, Yorks NR   167
Ecclesfield, Yorks WR   92
Edinburgh   10, 14, 46, 48, 52, 74, 78
Edward, Lord   9, 199
Edwinstowe, Notts   78, 129, 150, 153
  Birkland and Bilhaugh hays in   153
Egan, Pierce, the younger   78–79
Elleford, William de   243
Ellerton, Yorks ER, prior of   217
Enborne, Berks   178, 202
Encyclopedia Britannica   99–100
England, 'high justice' of   22

Enstone, Oxon   52
Erewash, river   198
Essendine, Rutland   167
Essex Head, London   70
Essoiners and attorneys   252–53
Eustace the Monk (Busquet)   192, 229
Evans, Rev Joseph   84
Evans, Michael   128
Evans, Thomas   69
Evelyn, John   138
Evesham, Worcs, battle of (1265)   9, 104
Evingar hundred, Hants   176
Exchequer, effective abolition of (1833)   88
  chancellor's rolls   247
  foreign accounts roll   248
  memoranda rolls   236, 244
  pipe rolls   235, 243, 244–48
  receipt and issue rolls   247
  scribes   235–36, 247–48;
    chancellor's, 247–48; treasurer's, 247–48
  summonses   246, 247
  treasurer   248
Exeter, Devon   32, 35, 44, 183
  'riots' in (1510)   32
Exton, Rutland   121

Fairhood names   172
Fareham hundred, Hants   176
Farewell, Staffs, nunnery   11
Fauconberg, Eustace de, bishop of London, treasurer (1217–28)   248
  Henry de, sheriff of Nottinghamshire and Yorkshire   231–2
Feckenham forest, Worcs, Linholt wood in   197
Felton, William de   200
Ferrers, Robert   219
Ferrybridge, Yorks WR   130, 132
Fevre, William son of Robert le   119, 182
Finchampstead, Berks   44 n.31
Finlay, George   83 n.54
Finningley, Notts   157
Firguiling, Albinus   242
Fitz Herbert, Peter de   215

Index

Fitz Neal, Richard 247
Fitz Nicholas, Ralph 236, 238
Fitz Walter, Robert 56
Fletching, Sussex 115, 174, 178
  Hungry Hatch in 115
Flower, Cyril 258
Flynn, Errol 186
Folklore Society 101
Follifoot, Yorks WR 169
Folville family 113
Fordun, John of 37
Forest gaols: Rockingham 169, 193
  York, for Galtres forest 193
Forest poachers 188
Foresters 187–88
  fictional 25
Forests as a refuge 189–90
Forman, John of Snelston 191
Fortescue, Sir John 38
Fowler, D. C. 19
Foxe, Richard 49
Friar Tuck 31, 33, 45, 47–48, 50,
  56–57, 77, 99, 115, 206, 229
Fulk Fitz Warin 81
Furnivall, F. J. 72, 96

Gale, Elizabeth 63
  Roger 62
  Thomas, dean of York 63–65, 75
Galtres, Yorks, forest 193
Gaol, in the tales, 13
Gaol delivery records 202, 225, 246
Gaols
  Ilchester 201
  Norwich 14
  Nottingham 230
  Winchester 199, 201
  York 193, 201, 206–07, 215–16,
  226–27
Gent, Thomas 138
Geoffrey, Thomas son of 236
Giggleswick, Yorks WR 242
Gilbert, Henry 186
Gilling wapentake, Yorks NR 241
Gisborne, Guy of 27–32, 67, 71, 79,
  94, 96, 157, 195, 225, 230
Gisburn, Yorks WR 157
Glasgow, bishop of 134, 199
Glasgow, Scotland, university of 40

Glastonbury, Somerset 43
Gloucester, bishop of *see* Warburton
Goadby Marwood, Leics 61–62
Godalming, Surrey 129
Goes, Hugh 18
Goldington, Beds 164, Map 2
Goldsborough, Yorks WR or NR,
  William of (fictitious) 143
Goldsmith's Company, London 102
  n.13
Gooch, Elizabeth Sarah
  Villa-Real 150–51
Gough, Richard 143
Grafton, Richard 56, 59, 75, 143
Granby, Notts 169
Grantchester, Cambs 177
Grantham, Lincs 62, 63, 207
Gray, Douglas 133
Gray's Inn, London 70, 73
Greenhood names 171
Greenleaf, Reynold, of Holderness (an
  alias of Little John) 23–24, 58
'Green Man', the 101–02
Grimsby, Lincs 17, 248–49
  castle, planned 249
  church 248
Gurdon, Adam 94, 199
Gutch, J. M. 14, 83–84
Guyt, Walter 241

Hacheston, Suffolk 176 n.73, 180 n.92
Haddington, East Lothian,
  Scotland 40
Hahn, Thomas 2
Hale, Simon de 217 n.35, 221, 236
  n.29, 238 n.33
Halle, Adam de la 47
Hampole, Yorks WR 241 n.45
Hanawalt, Barbara 202 and n.73
Hangings 206–07
Hannington, Hants or Wilts 178, 184,
  202
Hardelot castle, Boulogne 204 n.83
  forest, Boulogne 192, 229
Hardy, Thomas Duffus 257
Harehope, Northumb 166, 168
Harris, P. V. 106, 115
Harrison, Robert Poges 180–81
Harsyk, Sir John 196

Index

Harting, Sussex   178
Harvard University, Boston, USA   93
Hathersage, Derbys   61
Havering, Essex, park   248
Hawking   24
Hayward, Mary   85
Hazlewood, Yorks WR, park   227 n.78
Hearne, Thomas   63
Henley, Oxon   44 n.31
Hepworth, David   142 n.59, 143, 173 n.60
Herbert, Peter fitz   215, 216 n.29, 218
Heydon, Cambs   248
Heywood, John   148
Higden, Rannulf de   38–39
Highway robbery   206–07
Hilton, Rodney   106–08
Hipperholme, Yorks WR   170
Hobsbawm, Eric   76
Hod, Robert, fugitive   104, 108, 116, 244–48
Holderness, Yorks ER   23, 58, 232, 251
Hole, John   53–54
Holt, Sir James   8, 19, 37, 74, 103, 108–10, 114–117, 119–20, 123, 132, 136, 153, 156, 173–75, 178, 181–82, 230–32, 246, 252
Honiton, Devon   44
Hood, and variants, as the second part of a composite surname, by location   171–73
   Ayton, Yorks NR (Furhode)   172
   Bocking, Sussex (Redhod)   171
   Bradle, Dorset (Tomehod)   173
   Charford, Hants (Redhod)   171
   Charlton Marshal, Dorset (Capehoud)   172
   Colchester, Essex (Redhod)   171
   Combe Keynes, Dorset (Copehoud)   172
   Coventry, Warks (Pyhod)   171
   Dorset (Bolthod, Bolthoud)   173
   Dorset (Greyhoud, Ridhoud)   171
   Dorset (Rachhoud, Rechoud)   173
   Essex (Redhod)   171
   Kingston upon Thames, Surrey (Colhod)   173
   Lancashire (Pikhod)   173
   Lancashire (Ryvenhod)   172
   Lee, Northumb   171
   London (Redhode)   171
   London, Baynard Castle ward (Fairhod, Feirhod)   172
   Middlesex (Colhod)   173
   Newbiggin, Northumberland (Mundihod)   172
   Northumberland (Blachod)   171
   Nottinghamshire (Whithod)   171
   Prudhoe, Northumb (Ridhoud)   171
   Riccall, Yorks ER (Straythode)   172
   Ringmer, Sussex (Grenhod, Grenhoud)   171
   Steetley, Notts (Whythood)   171
   Wakefield, Yorks WR (Grenehod)   171
   Wallingford, Berks (Withhod)   171
   Warwickshire (Pyhod)   172
   Watford, Herts (Litelhoud)   172
   West Tanfield, Yorks NR (Stepelhode)   172
   Westmorland (Piledhod)   172
   Wimborne, Dorset (Copehoud)   172
   Worth Matravers, Dorset (Brodhoud)   172
   Yorkshire (Pykhod)   173
Hood, and variants, as a surname, by location   163–70
   Abbots Ripton, Hunts   170
   Aiskew, Yorks NR   167
   Alnwick, Northumb   Map 3, 167
   Anstey, Herts   170
   Beverley, Yorks ER   167
   Birchden, Sussex   167
   Branxton, Northumb   Map 3, 167
   Cashio hundred, Herts   167
   Chellington, Beds   Map 2
   Cirencester, Glos   168
   Clipsham, Rutland   167
   Coventry, Warks   177
   Ebberston, Yorks NR   167
   Essendine, Rutland   167
   Goldington, Beds   Map 2, 164
   Granby, Notts   169
   Harehope, Northumb   Map 3, 168
   Hipperholme, Yorks WR   170
   Howden, Yorks ER   169

Index

Keysoe, Beds   Map 2
Langton, Yorks ER   167
London   167
Morborne, Hunts   170
Morpeth, Northumb   Map 3, 167
Newburn, Northumb   Map 3, 167
Norfolk   164
Petworth, Sussex   167
Plungar, Leics   169
Radwell, Herts   167
Ramsey, Essex   167
Rockingham, Northants   169
St Albans, Herts   167
Sawbridgeworth, Herts   167
Shenley, Bucks   167
Southminster, Essex   167
Stotfold, Beds   Map 2
Throckley, Northumb   169
Wakefield, Yorks WR   168
Wareham, Dorset   167
Wark, Northumb   Map 3, 168
Whissendine, Rutland   167
Whitwell, Yorks NR   169
Wyton, Yorks ER   170
Hood, Devon   164
Hood, Yorks NR   164, 213 n.11
Hopwas, Staffs, pass of   192
Hornington, Yorks WR   221, 222 n.53
Houghton, Sussex   179
Howden, Yorks ER   169 n.26, 242
Hoyle, Richard   19, 20, 191 n.25
Hungry Hatch, in Fletching, Sussex   115
Hunnisett, Roy   202–03
Hunter, Rev. Joseph   18, 20, 58, 84–97, 105, 114–116, 129–132, 136, 138, 142, 154–55, 163, 170, 256–58; portrait, Figure 3
Hunting and poaching   187–88; by foresters, 188
Huntingdon, Huntington, earl of, Robin Hood as   33, 56, 61, 63, 64, 75, 83, 126
Hurstbourne Regis (Tarrant), Hants   179, 184
Hutton, Ronald   51

Inglewood, Cumberland   36, 97, 155, 192, 229
Ingram, Sir Robert   231
Irish knife *see* Knives
Irishman   201
Ismay, Joseph, vicar of Mirfield, WR Yorks   143
Ispir, Cristian   251 n.93
Ivanhoe, novel by Sir Walter Scott   48, 77
Ives, Robert son of   219–220

Jackson, Richard   149
Jamieson, Robert   10
Jarvis, Thomas   54
Jesucrist, Robert   175
Johnson, Dr Samuel   26, 68
Jonson, Ben   55
Justices itinerant:
  in eyre   175, 189, 196, 197, 214–18, 224–26, 227, 234, 241–42, 245
  of the forest, 187, 197, 211–12
  of gaol delivery   135, 196, 197, 202, 225, 238, 245
  of trailbaston   190, 197, 200, 231

Kane, Stuart   30
Keats, John   77
Keen, Maurice   103, 109–10, 111, 194
Keirincx, Alexander   239
Kenilworth, Dictum of (1266)   89
Keysoe, Beds   Map 2
Kidderminster, Worcs   204
Kidnap   189–90; of sheriff (fictional), 24
Kilburn, Yorks NR, Hood Grange in   164
Kilham, ER Yorks   239
King, Thomas, of Lymington   179
King Alexander III of Scotland   164 n.2
King Charles I   128, 148
King Charles II, Restoration of (1660)   52
King Edward, 'our comely king', unspecified, in the *Gest*   24–26, 90
King Edward I   90, 110
King Edward II   81, 90, 115, 139, 231 household accounts of   87–88
King Edward III   90, 110, 117–18, 125, 130, 139, 140–41, 245 n.59

Index

King Edward IV   110
King Edward VI   51
King George I, manuscripts left to University of Cambridge   10, 73–74 n.22
King George III   72
King Henry I   245 n.59
King Henry III   9, 197, 210, 212, 217, 227, 234, 235, 249, 258
King Henry VII   30, 43 n.28, 128, 136
King Henry VIII   42, 50, 61, 74, 128, 136
King James IV of Scotland   14, 42
King John   56, 78, 79, 81, 168, 192, 210, 212, 216, 229, 234, 235, 248, 249, 257
King John II of France   191
King Richard I   40–41, 56
King's Bench, court of   113, 212
  itinerant   187
Kingston upon Thames, Surrey   43, 44 n.31, 46–47, 48, 128, 173
Kirk Deighton, Yorks WR   250
Kirkleatham, Yorks NR   177, 227
Kirklees priory, Yorks WR   26–27, 141–44
  prioress of   26–28, 64, 75, 79, 91, 92, 142–44
  Elizabeth de Stainton, prioress of   91, 142–44
Kirk Smeaton, Yorks WR   241 n.45
Knaresbrough, Yorks WR   163 n.2
  forest   155, 190
Knight, Stephen   11, 103, 120–22, 125–26, 133–34, 182–83
Knives
  baselard   179
  Irish knife   29–30, 225
  Irish skeens   29–30
  Welsh knife   30 n.66
Kyme family, Lincs   63

Lacy, Alice de   174
  Edmund de, earl of Lincoln   239
  Henry de   174
  John de, earl of Lincoln   235, 239; constable of Chester, 234
  Roger de, constable of Chester   224
Lal (or Laf), Adam   219

Lamcote, Notts   234
Lancaster, knight of (fictional)   22, 154
Lancaster, Thomas earl of   105, 115, 156, 174
Langland, William   8, 81, 99, 124
Langlands, Yorks NR   242
Langton, Yorks ER   167
Latham, Yorks WR   217
Latimer, Hugh   51
Laverock, John   45
Laxton, Notts   29, 187 n.12, 211
  rector of   29
Le Neve, Peter   archivist, 31
Lee, Sidney   99
Lee, Lancs, Sir Henry of   157
  Sir Henry, of Charnock   157
  Sir John   118
  Nicholas of   156–57
Lee, Northumb   171
Lee, Sir Richard atte (fictional), 20, 24–26, 118, 157
  captured by sheriff, 24
  castle of, besieged by sheriff, 24
  wife of, 24–25
Lees, Jim   63
Leicester   45, 133, 190, 201
  St Leonard, 45
  St Mary at the Newarke, 45
Leicester, earl of, Robert sergeant of   243
Leland, John   56, 132, 134, 138, 143
Lenton priory, Notts   11–12, 144, 145, 237
  lands in Derbyshire   11–12
Lenz, Roger de   252
  Simon de   243
Leveson, Walter   49
Lexden hundred, Essex   176
Lexington, Robert of   187 n.12, 225, 227, 241, 245, 254
Leycester, Nicholas de   189–90
Lichfield, dean and chapter of   12
  diocese of   11
Lincoln   175, 217
  battle of (1217)   99
  justices at   175
Lincoln, cathedral library   35, 152–53, 186; *see also* Figure 6

Lincoln green 26, 203
Lindfield, Sussex 115
Linley, Robert 170
Linton, Scotland 52–53
Lisle, Brian de 211, 214, 231
Little John 9, 12–13, 15–17, 21–29, 33, 36, 37, 40, 43–47, 52, 57, 58, 72, 115, 118, 129, 135, 153, 169, 188, 195, 203, 225, 230, 232
  geographical features named after him 127, 138
  a mariner called, 118
  supposed grave, at Hathersage 61
  surnamed Nailor 75
Little John, activities
  ambushes travellers at the Sayles 21, 29, 129
  decapitates a monk 13, 230
  fights the potter 15
  hunts deer 57–58
  kills gaoler 13
  participates in archery contests 13, 23, 24
  participates in the May Games 43–46
  quarrels with Robin Hood 12, 28
  rescues Robin from Nottingham castle 230
  shoots the sheriff in the heart 29, 72
  with Robin at King Edward's court 26
  with Robin at Kirklees 27–28
  wounded by arrow 24
Little John, earliest name references 169
Little John, roles
  as character in the English and Scottish May games 40, 43–47, 52, 99
  as Reynold Greenleaf, serving the sheriff 23, 58; *see also* 115
  as Robin's bow–bearer 12
  as servant of the poor knight 22
  as yeoman of the crown 13
Little John, mariner 118
Little John's Well, Barnsdale 138
Little Staughton, Beds 204
Llangwm, Monmouthshire 101

Lockesley *see* Loxley
Logan, John, of Leith 78
London, bishop of 248
London, great moot at (fictional) 23
  publications at *passim*
  taxpayers (named) in 167, 175n, 197
London: Baynard Castle ward 172
  Chancery Lane 257
  City of 45
  Essex Head 70
  Fleet Street 17
  Newgate prison 227
  St Mary Arches church 196
  Tower of 140, 257
  Westcheap 196
Longleat, Wilts 57
Louis I, count of Flanders 139, 140, 141
Louis II, count of Flanders 139, 141
Louis XVI of France 76
Lowdham, Notts 232, 234
  church of 232, 233; illustrated, Figure 7
  manor of 235
  park of 234, 241
  parson of 234
Lowdham, Eustace of, clerk 232, 234–36
  house of 234
  lands of, in Notts 239
  lands of, in Yorks 239
  rebel against King John 235
  sheriff's clerk and under–sheriff 234–35
  sheriff of Notts and Derbys 234, 237
  sheriff of Yorks 236
  tenant of the Lacy fee 235
Lowdham, Fulk of 234
Lowdham, John chaplain of 232
Lowdham, Walter of, steward of earl of Lincoln 239
Lower, Mark Antony 92
Loxley, Lockesley, fictitious place, supposedly in Notts 57–58
Loxley, Robin of 57
Loxley, Warks 59
Loxley Chase, Yorks WR 57–58

Ludlow, Salop 45, 80
Luxford, Julian 38
Lyndrick, Derbys 198
Lynn, John of 140
Lynn, Norfolk 139–40

Maddicott, John 19, 112–14, 231
Maid Marian 33, 45, 47–48, 50, 56, 59, 100, 106
Maid Marian, novel by Thomas Love Peacock 77
Mair *see* Major
Maitland, F. W. 204–5, 257
Major, John (Mair) 2, 40–42, 47, 56, 58, 74, 75; portrait, Figure 2
Male, Flanders 139, 141, 158–59
Malot, William 242
Manchester, Lancs 45
Manwood, John 134
Marc, Philip, sheriff of Nottinghamshire and Derbyshire 230–36, 238 n.33
Marewde [*unidentified*], Yorks NR 242
Margaret of York, duchess of Burgundy, marriage of 14
Marham, abbot of (fictitious) 49
Marmiun, Robert 219
Marscall, Thomas 242
Marshall, John 32
  Roger 49
Marske cum Redcar, Yorks NR 177
Matheson, L. M. 10, 11, 15,
Matson, Glos 128
Matthews, John 101–02
Mauclerc, Walter, bishop of Carlisle and treasurer 251
Mawgan, Cornwall 45
May, John 146
May Games 42–54, 56, 100–03, 120
  decline of 52–53
McKisack, May 105
Meaux abbey, Yorks ER 251
Meden, river 153
Meekings C. A. F., 194
Melton Mowbray, Leics 45, 190, 211
Mexborough, Yorks WR 249
  church 249–50
  parson of 250

'Meyne', following, retinue 186, 196, 203
Millard, Stephen 53
Milner, William 49
Monk Bretton priory, Yorks WR 91, 99, 136, 142, 249
Monkton Moor, Yorks WR 242
Montacute, William de 179
Montfort, Simon de 9, 37, 89, 94
Moore, John, bishop of Ely 10, 13, 18, 74 n.22
  Robin Hood manuscripts of 10, 13
Moore, Thomas Cooper 151
Morborne, Hunts 170
More, William, prior of Worcester 44 n.31
Morison, Richard 50
Morley wapentake, Yorks WR 242
Morpeth, Northumb 166, 168
Morris Dance 101 and n.13
Mortimer, Roger de 37
Moulton, Thomas de 113, 188 n.12
Mowbray, William de 211
Much the Miller's son 12–13, 21, 23–24, 33, 58, 75, 115, 129, 188, 195, 203
  carries Little John on his back 24
  competes at archery 24
  decapitates a page 13
  kills a gaoler 13
Munday, Anthony, playwright 55–57, 59, 64
Murray, Margaret 100
Murres, Thomas 49
Muskham, Thomas of 62, 198
Muskham, North and South, Notts 190
Myerscough park, Lancs 155–56

Netherbury, Dorset 44
Neufmarché, Adam de, 241
Neve, Peter le 31
Neville, Geoffrey de 215–16, 217 n.35, 220
Neville, Ralph de 250
Nevison, John, sometimes William 207
New Romney, Kent 45
Newark, Notts 27, 190, 207, 234, 251

Index

Newbiggin, Northumb   172
Newburn, Northumb   166, 169
Newgate, London   169 n.22, 227
Newstead priory, Notts   128
Nickson, Nicholas   142
Nieuport, Flanders   139
Norfolk, duke of   31
Norfolk, sheriff of   14
Norwich   137
   prison   14
Norton, Yorks WR   91
Norys, Richard   146
Nostell priory, Yorks WR   249 n.88
Nottingham   11–13, 15–16, 24–26, 29, 58, 72, 90, 91, 104, 116, 144, 145, 148–51, 154, 157, 193–94, 198, 200, 201, 211, 229, 230, 234
   castle   134 n.27, 144, 193
   castle gaol   13, 230, 194
   Hockley in   101
   mayor and burgesses of   147
   St Anne's Well   146, 151
   St Mary's church   11–12, 144–45, 195
      illustrated, Figure 5
      link with the legend   13
      rebuilding of   12
      visited by Robin Hood   12
   St Mary's parish   235
   town walls and gates   11–13
   University of   134
   University College   104
Nottingham, sheriff of (sheriff of Nottinghamshire and Derbyshire, real or fictional)   11–13, 15–16, 18, 21, 23–25, 29, 31, 33, 112, 113, 117, 124, 144, 154, 192, 194, 228, 230, 231–32, 236, 241, 243, 255
   wife of (fictional), 15–16
Nottinghamshire   29, 45, 55, 78, 153-4, 158, 190, 200–02, 207, 235–36, 238
Nottinghamshire eyre (1280)   175
Nurry, Robert   202

Ockbrook, Derbys   198
Ode, as a surname or patronym   170–71
   Abbots Ripton, Hunts   170
   Anstey, Herts   170
   Hipperholme, Yorks WR   170
   Morborne, Hunts   170
   Wyton, Yorks ER   170
Ohlgren, T. H.   11–12, 14, 16, 18, 30, 123, 125
   dating of Cambridge manuscripts   11, 13–14
Ombersley, Worcs   44 n.31
Osland wood, Notts   200
Oswaldslow, Worcs, hundred   197, 204
Outlawry   204–06, 216, 242
   decline of   205–06
   pardoning of   205
Outlaws Song of Trailbaston   190
Owen, L. V. D.   104–05, 108, 116, 244, 246
Oxenforde, John de, sheriff of Nottinghamshire   113
Oxford   51, 67, 68, 85, 231
Oxford, Ashmolean   68
Oxford, Bodleian Library   68
Oxford, Magdalen College   68
Oxford, Merton College   135
Oxfordshire   35, 43, 52
   sheriff of   225 n.70

Page, Roger le, of Compton, Hants   176
Palgrave, Sir Francis   88
Palmer, Robert   118–19, 258
Papplewick, Notts, witch of   55
Paris, France   40
Paris, Matthew   74, 197, 251
Park, Thomas   73
Parker, Martin   59, 61, 62, 64–65, 144
Parliament   192
Paston family of Norfolk   31, 32
   John, I, II and III   14, 31
   Margery, 14
Paston letters   30–31
Pattishall, Martin of   226, 245, 254
Pavage, early grants of   17
   in *Robin Hood and the Potter*, 15
Peacock, Thomas Love   76–8, 153
Pearsall, Derek   13
Peasants' Revolt (1381)   107, 252
Peck, Francis   61–62, 198

Index

Pelham, Sir William 52
Penshurst, Kent 57
Pepys, Samuel 60
Percy, Elizabeth, duchess of
   Northumberland 67
   Henry de 221
   Richard de 211, 221, 222 n.53
   Robert de 218, 221
   Stephen 79
   Thomas, bishop of
      Dromore 26–27, 67–69, 71–74, 75, 80
   William de 221, 222 n.53
'Percy folio', manuscript 26
Perth, Scotland 42, 46
Petworth, Sussex 167
Pickering, Yorks NR 242
Piers Plowman 34, 81, 94, 99
Pilkington, Gilbert 11–12
Pilling, David 170
Pipe Roll Society 104
Pitt, Humphrey 26, 68
Planché, R. J. 59, 63
Pleasley, Derbys, mill 154
   Robin Hood cross 154
Plompton, Yorks WR 155
Plumpton park, Lancs 25, 58, 75, 154–56, 187–88
Plungar, Leics 169
Pollard, Anthony 16, 20, 125, 186, 195
Pontefract, Yorks WR 132, 135, 137, 199, 224
   castle 239–40; *see* Figure 9
   honour of 174
   manor 130
Poole, Dorset 44 n.31
Poole, A. L. 105
Powicke, Sir Maurice 104, 106
Prester John 175
Prestewod, Thomas de 243
Price, Lawrence 60
Prinne, Robert 53
Prisons *see* Gaols
Prudhoe, Northumb 171
Pubbel, John, of Ringwood, Hants, 179
Public Record Office, Chancery Lane, London 92, 104, 106, 118, 139
Pyle, Howard 80

Queen Henrietta Maria 148
Queen Margaret of Anjou 14
Queen Margaret of Scotland 14

Radwell, Herts 167
Raglan, Lord and Lady 101
Raleigh, William 221, 224, 226
Ramsey, Essex 167
Rannulf (Randolf) earl of Chester 99, 219
Ratcliffe on Soar, Leics 175
Rattery, Devon 164
Reading, Berks 44 n.31, 46, 178, 183
   St Lawrence's church 44 n.31
Record Commission 1831–37 85, 88–89
Redbourne, Lincs 248 n.76
Redhood names 171
Retaining of knights and squires 26
Retford, Notts 211
Rethel, county, France 140
Reynolds, J. H. 77
Riccall, Yorks ER 172
Rice, Thomas 49
Richmond, Colin 19, 119
Richmond, Yorks NR 164, 241
   archdeacon of 196
   castle 211, 218
Richmond park, Surrey 128
Rievaulx abbey, Yorks NR 200
Ringmer, Sussex 171
Ringwood, Hants 179
   hundred court of 179
Ritson, Joseph 10, 14, 70–76, 81–82, 83–85, 138, 149, 155–56
   attacked by Thomas Wright 83
   biography of Robin Hood 74–76
   criticisms of Percy's *Reliques* 71–72
   death 73
   republican sympathies 72
Robe, Robbe, as a Christian name 176–77
Robehod surnames: Alexander 176; Gilbert 176; John 176; Robert 176, 179; William 177, 202
Robehoud, John, of Houghton, Sussex 179
Robehoud, Walter, son of William 179

Index

Robehoud family, of Hurstbourne, Hants (named) 179
Robhod family of Walsham le Willows, Suffolk (named) 179–80
Robin Hood chapbooks, garlands and broadsides 60–61
Robin Hood, roles, characteristics, associations and reputation:
   Anglo–Saxon rebel 78, 82
   aristocrat 56–57
   brutality 31, 12, 195
   builder of a chapel in Barnsdale 9, 26, 91
   death, burial and epitaph 26–27, 64, 142–44
   decapitates sheriff 25, 58
   decapitates Guy of Gisborne 28–29, 195
   forest offender 185–89
   generosity to the poor 26
   hatred of bishops and abbots 9–10, 21
   hatred of the sheriff 9–10, 21
   highway robber 185–86, 192–95
   hunter of deer 25
   love for the king 25
   one of the Disinherited 9, 104–05
   outlaw 9, 13, 26
   participant in the May Games in England and Scotland 43–46
   piety and reverence for the Mass 9, 12
   product of Teutonic mythology 82, 89, 95, 98–103
   respect for lesser clergy 9
   respect for women, and veneration of the Virgin Mary 21
   retains knights and squires 26
   rioter 48–50
   robs the rich to give to the poor 46–47 n.47
   royal household servant 26
   skilled archer 15; 'best archer in England', 26
   social rebel 75–76
   yeoman 13, 15, 23, 77
   yeoman forester 186
Robin Hood tales and plays:
   A Lyttel Gest of Robin Hood 17–26
   date 18–20
   king and commoner theme 21
   structure of 20–21
   Play of Robin Hood and the Sheriff 30–31
   Robin Hood and Guy of Gisborne 28–29, 67
   significance of the Irish knife in 29–30
   Robin Hood and the Monk 10–13
   date of 10–11
   links with C15 Nottingham 11
   provenance of 11
   unknown to Ritson 10, 74
   Robin Hood and the Potter 13–17
   commercial theme of 16–17
   date of 10–11, 14–15
   discovery of 10, 13–17
   linguistic link with Norfolk and Suffolk 15
   play based upon the tale of 16
   role of the sheriff's wife in 16
   yeoman audience of 15
   Robin Hood's Death 26–28
   Scotichronicon, untitled story from 8–10
Robin Hood place–names 127–29, 136–39, 141, 146, 153–54
Robin Hood plays, venues 55–57
   in Exeter (1427) 32
   in London 55–56
   in country houses 57
   opera 78
Robin Hood Society, London 70
Robin Hood's Bay, Yorks NR 60, 138–41, 158–59
Robin Hood's Hills, Notts 154
Robin Hood's Stone, Yorks WR 117, 136
Robin Hood's Well, Yorks WR 137–38
Robin Hood's Well alias St Anne's Well, Sneinton, Notts 146–51
Robynhod, Gilbert, of Hungry Hatch, Fletching, Sussex 115, 177, 178–79
Robynhod, Robert, of Harting, Sussex 178
Robynhod, Robinhod, William, of

Tilbrook, Beds/Hunts, 174–75, and Map 2
Robynhoud, John, of Crockford Bridge, Hants 179
Rochford, Lincs 63
Rockingham, Northants, castle 99
   forest gaol 169, 193
Ros, Robert de 213, 217–18
Rose, William, of Loughborough 201
Rotherham, Yorks WR, church 187 n.12
Royal letters 12
   under great seal 20
   under privy seal 11, 13, 20
   under unspecified seal 25
Rutland, as a place of origin of the legend, 121, 126
Ryedale wapentake, Yorks NR 241, 242
Ryvenhod, Hobbe son of 252

Saham, Robert de Saham 253
St Albans abbey, Herts 197
   abbot of 167
St Albans, Herts 167, 197
St Andrews, bishop of 135, 199
St Andrews, Scotland 36, 40, 46
St Breock, Cornwall 44–45
St Columb Major, Cornwall 45
St Columb Minor, Cornwall 45
St Ives, Cornwall 44–45
St Mary's abbey York *see* York
St Neots, annals of 21
St Samer abbey, France 229
Saladin, Henry 175
Salisbury, bishop of 179
Salisbury, William earl of 179, 219
Salisbury, Wilts 201
Sanctuary in churches, claimed by fleeing suspects 241–42
   claimed by Robin Hood 12
Sandleford priory, Berks 177
Sawbridgeworth, Herts 167
Saville, John 143
Say, Geoffrey de 252
Sayles, the, in Barnsdale, Yorks WR 21, 23, 90, 111, 117, 122, 129–132, 134–35, 154, 199–200
Sayles, Richard son of Adam of 130

Sayles, William de, of Campsall 134
Sayles, William del 135
Scalle, Richard 242
Scarborough, Yorks NR 60, 138, 155
Scartho, Lincs, church 248–49
Scathlock, Scarlock, Scarloke, Will 13, 21, 23–27, 28, 33, 115, 118, 203
   helps to rescue Robin Hood from Nottingham 13
   participates in archery contest 24
   waylays travellers at the Sayles 21, 23
   with Robin at King Edward's court 26
Scocia, Adam de 242
Scone, Scotland, abbot of 140, 199
Scott, Sir Walter 48, 58, 72–73, 77–78, 153
Scropton, Derbys 191
Seagrave, Stephen of 227, 241
Selby, Walford 257
Selby, Yorks WR, abbot of 225
Seldeford, Sir John de 197
Seliok, John and Richard 146
Shakespeare, William 55
Sheffield, Yorks WR 84, 85, 130
Shenley, Bucks 168
Shenstone, William 68
Sherewind, Roger 242
Sherwood, Sherwood Forest, Notts 12–13, 33, 38, 55, 61, 75, 78–79, 90, 92, 112, 114, 134, 147, 150–54, 186, 188, 200, 228–29
Shifnal, Salop 26, 68
Shooter's Hill, Kent 42
Shrewsbury, Salop 45, 197
Simone, W. E. 101
Singman, Jeffrey 19, 36, 56, 182
Skelbrooke, Yorks WR 132, 135–37, 200 n.60, 241 n.45
   Sleephill in 241 n.45
Skell, river, Yorks WR 132
Skellow, Yorks WR 241 n.45
Skiplam, Yorks NR 241
Skirbeck, Lincs, Hobbe of 252
Skyrack wapentake, Yorks WR 173
Slingsby, Yorks NR 241
Sloane, Sir Hans 57

'Sloane Life' of Robin Hood   57–58, 74
Sluys, Flanders   140
Smith, Alexander   61
Snaith, Yorks WR   163 n.2
Sneinton, Notts   146, 149
Snelston, Derbys   191
Society of Antiquaries of London   61, 68, 80, 83, 85, 86
South Acre, Norfolk   196
Southey, Robert   77
Southminster, Essex   167
Southwell Minster, Notts   147
Sowerby, Walter of   21
Spichfat, William, of Caythorpe, Notts, 234
Stafford, Jeffrey   232
Stafford, John, bishop of Bath & Wells   35
Staffordshire   48, 90, 187
Staincliffe wapentake, Yorks WR   242
Staincross wapentake, Yorks WR   242
Stainton, Elizabeth de, prioress of Kirklees   91, 144
Stamford, Lincs   61–62, 245 n.63
Stamford moor, Yorks WR   242
Stanley, Yorks WR   170 n.35, 173
Stanley Park, Derbys *see* Dale abbey
Stapleton, Nicholas de   218
Staveley, William de   200
Steetley, Notts   171
Stenton, Sir Frank and Lady Doris   105, 216
Sterndalle, John   31
Stoclive, Adam de   241
Stonely priory, Hunts   175 n.64
Stotfold, Beds   Map 2
Stourhead   Wilts, 85
Stow, John   47 n.47
Strafforth wapentake, Yorks WR   215
Stratford upon Avon, Warks   52
Stratton, Cornwall   44–45
Stubbes, Philip   42, 52
Studley, Wilts   189
Stukeley, Esther or Hester   63
Stukeley, William   62–63, 65, 75, 138
Stuteville, Nicholas de   211
   Robert de, the elder   217
Sudbury, Derbys   191

Summerson, Henry   118–20, 123–24, 175, 194–95
Sutton Scotney, Hants   176
Swan, George   30
Sydney, Robert   57

Tanfield, West, Yorks NR   172
Taylor, J. A   10, 12, 19, 70, 97, 103, 111–12, 115, 117, 120, 122–23, 127, 130, 137, 139, 155, 199, 231–32. *See also* Dobson
Tennyson, Alfred Lord   79, 80
Tewkesbury bridge, Glos   44 n.31
Thame, Oxon   43
Thierry, Augustin   78
Thirsk, Yorks NR   211
Thomas, Keith   100
Thorney Wood, Notts   147
Thornholme priory, Lincs   175
Thornton, John of   218–20, 223, 226
Thoroton, Robert   149
Thorpe, William de, chaplain of Thorpe by Wysall, Notts   200–01
Throckley, Northumb   169
   Robert of   169
Throsby, John   149
Thynne, Sir John   57
Tickhill, Yorks WR   134, 135, 199, 239
   castle   224
   constable of   213
Tilbrook, Beds/Hunts   Map 2, 174, 177
   Richard son of Walter of   175 n.64
Tintinhull, Somerset   43
Toledo, Spain   229
Tomson, Laurence   52
Trent, William a   28
Trent, river   55
Trubleville, Henry de   219
Truesdale, Mark   21
Tuck, Friar   31, 33, 45, 47, 50, 56–57, 75, 77, 99, 115, 206, 229
Tudor, Margaret   14
Turpin, Dick   201, 206–07
Tutbury, Staffs   60
   castle   191
Tuxford, Notts   207
Tyndal, Richard de   241

Underdown, David 54

Vanbrugh, Sir John 138
Venables, Piers 186, 191, 196, 203
Vertue, George 62
Vesci, Eustace de 210
Vinitor, William 223, 227

Wake, Hereward the 33, 81, 94
Wakefield, Yorks WR 105–06, 109, 115–16, 168, 170–71, 173, 231, 242
   Contrariants Roll 105
   court rolls of the manor of 91, 105–06, 109, 115–16, 168, 170
   Hood family of 116, 171, 173
   manor office 105
   tale of the Pinder of 58, 68, 75
Waldron, F. G. 55
Wales, Gerald of 21
Walker, J. W. 105–06, 113 n.43, 115, 130, 136, 143 n.64
Walker, John 49
Wallingford, Berks, prison 171
Walsall, Staffs 49
Walsham le Willows, Suffolk 176
   Robhood family of 179, 180, 184
Wandale forest, Yorks NR 242
Warburton, William, bishop of Gloucester 63
Wareham, Dorset, Henry Hod of 167
Warenne, earl of 213
Wark, Northumb 166, 168
Warton, Thomas 71
Washington, Henry of 242
Watford, Herts 172
Wath upon Dearne, Yorks WR 189
'Watling Street', road in Yorkshire 21, 129, 130 n.11, 131
Watson, John 143
Wednesbury, Staffs 49
Wells, Somerset 43, 53–54
   dean of 53
   St Cuthbert's parish 53
Wemyss, Sir John 36
Wendover, Roger of, prior of Belvoir, chronicler 251
Wenlock, Worcs, priory 197
Went, river, Yorks WR 130–32

Wentbridge, Yorks WR 15, 129, 130, 132, 135–36, 137, 199, 207, 241 n.45
Westminster abbey, abbot of (fictitious) 13
Weston Zoyland, Somerset 54
Wetherby, Yorks WR 169
Wetherby, Robert of 124, 210, 222–24, 226–27, 232, 238–39, 241–44, 246, 253–55, 258
Wheatley, Yorks WR or Notts, John son of Henry of 135, 200–02
Whissendine, Rutland 167
Whitby, Yorks NR 138–40
   men of 140
White, Robert 105
Whitehood surnames 171
Whitwell, Yorks WR 169
Wiles, David 30, 32, 56
Willenhall, Staffs 48–50, 196
William, Richard son of 242
Willoughby, Sir Richard de 113, 190
Wilson, R. M. 99
Wiltshire, parliamentary election return (1432) 115–16
Wimborne, Dorset 172
Winchester, Hants 191, 197, 201, 222 and n.55
   prison 199
   statute of (1285) 192
Wolfall, Robert 54
Wolverhampton, Staffs 49
Women, as criminal gang members 200, 202
Woodbury, Devon 44
Woode, W., horse–keeper 31
Woodplumpton, Lancs 155–56
Woods, as refuge for criminals 189–92
Woodstock, Oxon 52
Woolmer forest, Hants 199 n.56
Worcester, cathedral priory 198
Worcestershire 243, 252
   eyres 197
Worksop, Notts 103, 239
   priory 132 n.16
Worth Matravers Dorset, 172
Wrangbrook, Yorks WR 136, 241 n.45, 242

Index

Wright, Thomas 14, 80–82, 89, 92, 95, 97, 99, 102–03, 106–07
Wright, William Aldis 31 n.71
Wyly, Robert 146
Wynken de Worde, printer 17
Wyntoun, Andrew of, prior of St Serf's, Loch Leven 35–38, 40
Wyre, river, Lancs 155
Wyresdale, Lancs 22, 156–57
    forest, Lea, Lee in 156 and n.117
Wyton, Yorks ER 170
Wytway, Richard 31

Yard, Mrs 53
Yearby, Yorks NR 177
Yeomanry and yeomen 13, 15, 109–10, 114
Yeovil, Somerset 44, 54
York, archbishop of 212, 239, 245
    dean and chapter of, 245
York 22, 27, 84, 113, 130, 135, 187, 188n, 199, 207, 216, 218, 224–27, 242, 245–46, 250, 254–55
    castle gaol 201, 206, 215–16, 220, 226, 245
York, St Mary's abbey 22, 113, 191
    abbot of 22, 58–59, 107, 113, 154
    high cellarer of 22–23, 193
    prior of 22
York, William of 250

www.ingramcontent.com/pod-product-compliance
Lightning Source LLC
Chambersburg PA
CBHW051601230426
43668CB00013B/1940